Geographical Analysis of Higher Education

About Author

Reena Bala has done her schooling from Kendriya Vidyalaya School, Khairi, Chamba. She obtained her B.A. (Geography) honours from Government Post Graduate College Dharamshala, Kangra. She got her M.A. and Ph.D. in Geography from Panjab University, Chandigarh. She also done B.Ed. from HPU, Shimla. She awarded UGC NET-JRF and SRF. She has presented research papers at national and international conferences. She joined teaching profession as Resource Person in the Department of Geography at Government Post Graduate College, Sector 42, Chandigarh. She is actively engaged in teaching and research work. She is a life member of the Association of Population Geographers of India.

Dr. Reena Bala is currently an Assistant Professor (Guest Faculty) at Government Post Graduate College Dharamshala, Kangra district, Himachal Pradesh.

Geographical Analysis of Higher Education

A Study of Hill State

Reena Bala

CONCEPT PUBLISHING COMPANY PVT. LTD.
NEW DELHI-110059

ISBN-13: 978-93-5439-018-0

First Published 2021

Published and Printed by

Concept
Since 1974

Concept Publishing Company Pvt. Ltd.
A/15-16, Commercial Block, Mohan Garden,
New Delhi-110059 (India)
T: 91 11 41101460, 91 11 25351460, 91 11 25351794
E: publishing@conceptpub.com, *W*: www.conceptpub.com

Cataloging in Publication Data--Courtesy: D.K. Agencies (P) Ltd. <docinfo@dkagencies.com>

Bala, Reena, author.

Geographical analysis of higher education : a study of hill state / Reena Bala.
pages cm
Based on the author's thesis (Ph.D.)--Panjab University.
Includes bibliographical references and index.
ISBN 9789354390180

1. Education, Higher--India--Himachal Pradesh. 2. Higher education and state--India--Himachal Pradesh. I. Title.

LCC LA1153.B35 2021 | DDC 378.5452 23

Preface

There is a lot of work done in the field of higher education in general but higher education in hill state, particularly there is not as much work done especially in geographical perspective. This study unfolds the comprehensive work of higher education in spatial and temporal context. The book is based on Ph.D. Dissertation research work funded by the UGC, New Delhi. Basically, this book divided into two sections, the former deals with the comparison of Himachal Pradesh with major states as well as hill states of India and the latter deals with historical evolution through the changing geography of higher education, structural composition, accessibility and availability and quality of higher education in the state.

This book contains five chapters. First section (Chapter I) deals with overview of higher education in India. It identifies the place of Himachal Pradesh among major and hill states of India. Second section deals the scenario of higher education in Himachal Pradesh. Chapter II outlines the changing geography of higher education in Himachal Pradesh. Third chapter examines the structural composition of higher education in Himachal Pradesh. Chapter fourth analyses the accessibility and availability of higher education. Chapter fifth consolidates the quality of higher education and it consists input and output indicators taking data from All India Survey on Higher Education. Finally, major findings and summary of the research work are combined and lastly recommendations were discussed.

Reena Bala

Acknowledgements

Firstly, I am deeply acknowledging my gratitude to Dr. Surya Kant (Formerly Professor and Head of the Department of Geography, Panjab University, Chandigarh) for supervising the work. His constant inspiration, motivation and guidance were crucial to the accomplishment of this task. I am also deeply gratitude to Professor Emeritus Gopal Krishan for invaluable discussions and help in identification of research theme.

I would like to express my sincere gratitude to all the teaching and non-teaching faculty members of the Geography Department, Panjab University, Chandigarh for their help, support and guidance. I extend my special thanks to Professor H.S. Sharma for their kind support for the publication of the book.

Finally, my parents and family and friends always being my side with their love, warm support, care and encouragement. I would like to express my special thanks to University Grants Commission, New Delhi for providing financial support to carry out this research work.

Last but not the least, I would like to extend my gratitude to the staff of Concept Publishing Co. Pvt. Ltd., New Delhi for their extreme support, especially Mr. Ashok Mittal for presenting my ideas in the finest form. However, I am responsible for all the shortcomings and the mistakes.

Reena Bala

Contents

List of Tables and Figures

LIST OF TABLES

LIST OF FIGURES

Abbreviations

AICTE	All India Council of Technical Education
AISHE	All India Survey on Higher Education
B.A.	Bachelor of Arts
B.Sc.	Bachelor of Science
BCI	Bar Council of India
B.Tech	Bachelor of Technology
CAGR	Compound Annual Growth Rate
CABE	Central Advisory Board of Education
C.V.	Coefficient of Variability
DCI	Dental Council of India
FICCI	Federation of Indian Chamber of Commerce and Industry
GDP	Gross Domestic Product
GER	Gross Enrolment Ratio
Govt.	Government
GOI	Government of India
ICT	Information and Communication Technology
IIT	Indian Institute of Technology
M.Phil	Master of Philosophy
M.Tech	Master of Technology
MCI	Medical Council of India
NER	Net Enrolment Ratio
NAAC	National Assessment and Accreditation Council
NDC	National Development Council
NCERT	National Council of Educational Research and Training
NIEPA	National Institute of Educational Planning and Administration
NIT	National Institute of Technology
NSSO	National Sample Survey Office
NKC	National Knowledge Commission
NITI Aayog	National Institution for Transforming India
NKN	National Knowledge Network
NMIECT	National Mission on Education through Information and Communication Technology
NPE	National Policy on Education
NUEPA	National University of Educational Planning and Administration
Sq. Km.	Square Kilometer

IIM	Indian Institute of Management	PCI	Pharmacy Council of India
IISc	Indian Institute of Science	PG	Postgraduate
INI	Institute of National Importance	Ph.D.	Doctor of Philosophy
MHRD	Ministry of Human Resource Development	PPP	Public-Private Partnership
M.Sc.	Master of Science	UGC	University Grants Commission

Introduction

Statement of the Problem

The British rulers, who introduced the modern education in India, needed persons well versed in English language to run lower level administrative work. The education system introduced by them in India was heavily tilted in favour of general education completely ignoring technical and scientific education. The education scenario remained the same even when the British rulers left India after the Independence in 1947.

Of late, we have been trying to reorient it towards the vocational education with a resolve to make India a knowledge economy. Expansion and strengthening of technical and professional education, accelerating growth of gross and net enrolment ratio, making higher investment and opening of higher education to private investment were some of the measures, undertaken in post-economic reforms period starting with the year 1991. Not only the new Institutes of Technology, Management, Medical Sciences and Basic Sciences were opened but the seats were also increased in such already existing institutes.

During the last two and a half decades, radical changes have taken place in the system of higher education system in India. Gross Enrolment Ratio (GER) increased several fold. GER rose 24.5 per cent in 2015-16 from only 0.7 per cent during 1950-51. The number of universities has gone to 753 (47 Central, 345 State, 235 State Private, 123 Deemed Universities, 03 Institutions established under State Legislation) and 41,435 colleges. During the academic session 2015-2016, the total enrolment in all courses and levels in the regular stream was 28.5 million students (UGC, Annual Report, 2016). Technical education has also grown fast during the recent years. The annual enrolment of scientists, engineers and technicians is now more than 2.0 million (950 thousand engineering graduates, 700 thousand diploma holders, 100 thousand computer scientists with post graduate degrees and 240 thousand management professionals, 30 thousand architects and 50 thousand pharma graduates). Against this, there were only 20 universities and 500 colleges in the country with 2.1 lakhs students in higher education at the time of Independence. It is truly called a paradigm shift in higher education of India.

Undoubtedly, there has been a phenomenal growth and physical expansion of higher education in India in the recent decades. Nonetheless, neither the growth nor the physical expansion has been spatially and socially uniform all over the country. Rather, there has been a further widening of regional, sub-regional and social inequalities in higher education infrastructure (physical and human) and educational attainments. Further, it is commonly believed that the quality and standards of higher education institutions have further gone done in post-expansion phase. With a few exceptions, the Report of the Committee for Evolution of the New Education Policy states, “India still lacks universities and institutions that could be considered to be at par with the best universities in the world” (Government of India, 2016:121-122). The Report termed the privately run colleges and universities ‘teaching shops’—ill-equipped, operating with unqualified staff. Also, the Report hinted at their political connections and corrupt practices. It seems that the haphazard growth of higher education institutions further reinforced the problems of quantity, equity, quality and uneven access.

In fact, the different regions, sub-regions, genders (male and female), areas (urban and rural), social (castes, tribes, OBC and upper castes) and religious groups (Hindus, Muslims, Sikhs, Christians and Buddhists) responded differently to the paradigm shift in higher education of India. Some responded favourably, some gently and some other slowly or even indifferently. This was bound to create inequalities of different types, requiring a thorough research investigation.

For example, Himachal Pradesh a hill state having peripheral location responded well to this paradigm shift in higher education. In Himachal Pradesh, the educational institutions as well as enrolment ratio have registered rapid increase. The number of the universities/central level institutions has registered three-fold increase, from 2 in 1971 to 28 in 2016. The higher education colleges recorded nearly ten-fold increase, from 28 to 279, during the same period. Similarly, the number of students enrolled has also increased three times, increasing from 12,471 in 1973-74 to 1.95 lakhs in 2015-2016. There has been an unprecedented growth of privately managed higher education institutions during 2000-2010 especially those of technical and professional disciplines. The rapid expansion of higher education has led to critical concerns about its profit-making nature, unequal access, and declining quality.

The above statements give birth to a variety of questions relating to availability, accessibility, distribution (rural-urban, inter and intra-regional), caste (Scheduled and non-Scheduled) and gender (male-female), relevance and role in socio-economic development, and privatization of higher education in the state of Himachal Pradesh needing a thorough research investigation. However, a cursory look at the available research literature reveals that higher education in Himachal Pradesh is the least investigated research theme in general and in geographic literature, in particular. This will become evidently clear from the review of literature. So far as the geographic literature in India is concerned, the higher education as a research theme in social sciences, in general and geography, in particular failed to attract the interest of geographic community in India. In this context, Himachal Pradesh make a highly rewarding case of research investigation, as wide regional, urban-rural, gender and caste-based inequalities persisted even at high level of educational attainment.

Review of Literature

Education, a field of research investigation has attracted attention of social scientists both in India and abroad. A brief review in the following has been grouped thematically into accessibility, availability, quality and equity, education and development, funding and privatization of higher education in a sequential order.

Accessibility, Availability, Quality and Equity

Chitnis (1972) examined the enrolment of Scheduled Caste students in higher education in the country with a focus on Maharashtra. Kaul (1972) analysed enrolment in higher education since independence to find a multiplication in number of the institutions of higher education resulting in overcrowding, weakening of teacher-taught relations, and the onset of student unrest. He recommended that the selection of students for higher education should be strictly on merit and noted that the provisions for education have to be guided more by assessments of manpower requirements. In a study, Chanana (1993) found that in a multi-cultural and multi-ethnic society like India, the role of gender, caste, class and region is crucial in determining the access to higher education and concluded that the educational policies and programmes are unable to bridge the gap between policy and practice.

Altbach (1993) noted that the Indian higher education suffers from deteriorating standards, occasional unrest and inadequate financial resources. A UNESCO (1998) study noticed the slow progress in the field of women education but expressed satisfaction over slow but steady increase in their enrolment in courses relating to science and technology. However, the study regretted the presence of a critical mass of women in the decision-making process vastly inadequate. Anand (1999) observed that higher education in India is ridden with problems like broadening of access, ensuring equity, and financial crisis. National Sample Survey Office (2001) analysed data collected on employment and unemployment by survey conducted in 1999-2000 to measure disparity in enrolment in higher education on the basis of age and social groups. It was found that there are wide inter-and intra-group disparities in enrolment. Damme (2001) examined the current policies and practices of inter-nationalisation in higher education, developed without much concern for quality assurance. He stated that inter-nationalisation policies and practices nowadays move into activities such as exporting higher education via branch campuses and institutional co-operation, developing transnational university networks and virtual delivery of higher education.

Rani (2002) noted a lack of access and equity in financing of higher education in India in the post-reform period and suggested that the amount of free-ship and scholarship schemes should be in place for an equal access to higher education. Singh (2002) has thrown light on growth and development of higher education in Manipur in post-Independence period. Teferra and Altbach (2004) discussed various issues related to higher education, including access, funding, privatization, governance and autonomy, management, gender gap, research, scholarly communication, language, and the brain drain with reference to African countries. Weisskope (2004) favoured the reservation policy at all levels of higher education, as reservation contributing to attaining of higher education by SC and ST students, who otherwise will not be able to pursue the higher education.

Sundaram (2006) analysed the NSSO data collected in the 55th round (1999-2000) to conclude that there is a clear hierarchy across social groups, the SCs (in urban India) and the STs (in rural India) remaining at the bottom of the ladder, the OBCs in the middle and the non-SC/ST at the top. Interestingly, the study noted the presence of only a marginal difference between the OBCs and the non-SC/ST students. Similarly, Ghosh (2006) concluded that there is a need to extend reservations to different groups in higher education, not because of being a perfect instrument to rectify long-standing discrimination, but for being the most workable methods under the circumstances.

The University Grants Commission (2007) conducted a study of 111 universities to conclude that 31 per cent of them fall under 'A' grade (High quality), 52 per cent in 'B' grade (Medium quality) and remaining 16 per cent under 'C' grade (Low quality). It is observed that 'A' grade Universities generally perform better in respect of faculty strength/department, quality (Ph.D. degree), and facilities (physical and academic). Balakrishnan (2007) concluded that the higher education in India can hardly be called equitable or excellent, despite the recent efforts to improve the situation. Agarwal (2007) analysed the growth of higher education to conclude that in pre-1980 period it was largely confined to courses in languages and the humanities. However, the 1980s witnessed an unprecedented demand for quality higher education relevant to the needs of business and industry, thereby putting considerable stress on governmental resources.

Anandakrishnan (2007) analyzed the Knowledge Commission Report to draw attention to issues missed out in the report. He identified that regional imbalances, uni-disciplinary universities, resistance to the credit system and proliferation of a substandard distance education system were important issues, which failed to draw attention in the report. A report of the working group on higher education (2011) for the Twelfth Five Year Plan analysed the 62nd round of NSSO data (2007-08) that estimated that one-fifth of the students do not pursue higher education for financial constraints. Upadhyay (2007) attempted a comparative study of higher education in terms of student-waste and expenditure-waste during pre-liberalisation and post-liberalisation periods. The study revealed that post-liberalization phase is marked with higher increase in numbers of educated unemployed and drop-outs.

Mishra *et al.* (2008) stated that the country has a developed educational set up in terms of range of programmes and their acceptability in local industry, but lacking in international quality and standards. Chauhan (2008) made a comparative examination of higher education systems of SAARC countries in terms of structure, access, quality, equity, resources and contribution of private enterprises. He observed low female participation, poor quality, and low expenditure on higher education (two per cent to four per cent of the Gross National Product) in all the SAARC countries. Sinha (2008) examined the spatial patterns of accessibility and availability of educational facilities and identified the areas suffering from supply side. Also, he identified backward districts for the purpose of effective implementation of programmes by the UGC.

A study conducted by the University Grants Commission (2008) found that enrolment was the largest in Arts (43.7%) followed by Commerce and Management courses with 19.14 per cent and Sciences with 18.23 per cent. Mohamedbhai (2009) noted that the tertiary enrolment ratio in Sub-Saharan Africa reached only six per cent in 2007, the lowest among the world regions. Agarwal (2009) raised the issues of access and equity and suggested that the affirmative action should follow the concept of equality and opportunity to all, based on merit and work towards a non-divisive casteless society. He felt the need to address the issue of affordability. Chaturvedi and Gupta (2009) studied the quality of higher education in India. Shetty *et al.* (2010) presented a detailed account of higher education and research in ten state universities of India during 2000-2006. Calcutta University ranked number one in research publication with 664 articles per annum in national and international journals. This was followed by Madras, Panjab, Rajasthan and Mysore universities with 600, 582, 538 and 328 research papers, in order. On the other extreme, Patna University published less than 50 and Sikkim Manipal University only five papers per annum. This speaks of wide gap in research productivity of Indian Universities.

Modi (2010), while examining higher education in Arunachal Pradesh observed that there is an urgent need to pay higher attention and to make huge investment to make it productive and relevant. Parekh (2010) observed that for increasing Gross Enrolment Ratio from current level of about 11 per cent to 30 per cent by 2020, there is a need to increase infrastructure (brick and click), teaching staff, accessibility, funds, technological support and address quality so that quality does not get diluted with expansion. Rezende (2010) while presenting an overview of higher education accountability system in Brazil stated that the system assigns grades to each discipline and colleges on the basis of performance of their students on national level. He further added that grades have positive effects.

The concern for quality in education stems from the concern for improving the efficiency of the educational system. Working Group (2011) on higher education set by the Planning Commission for the 12th Plan (2012-17) stated in its report that both the demand and supply side should be visualized properly. The three main components of accessibility, equity and expansion, quality and excellence require emphasis and focus. It advocated for higher financial support to institutions especially those in rural, remote and hilly regions. In addition, huge investment in private sector would be required. Gupta (2011) examined the current state of higher education to note a substantial increase in the number of educational institutions in recent years but lamented for decline in quality.

Jeelani (2011) highlighted the faculty shortage and its implications in central, state, deemed universities and the affiliated colleges in India. Kataria (2011) noted the rapid expansion of colleges in Rajasthan at the cost of quality education. Das (2012), conducting a study on West Bengal, analyzed the self-financing courses with sampled data. He found that self-financing courses are helping the goals of access, equity and quality. Sharma and Sharma (2012) noted a remarkable socio-economic transformation in post-Independence period due to rapid proliferation of higher education in the country. Panda (2012) highlighted various problems faced by the higher education related to quality especially in the pure and social sciences disciplines. He advocated for liberal financial support to the universities and colleges to strengthen higher education in the country.

Varghese (2015) analysed the trends and challenges posed by the massification in terms of equity, improving quality, mobilising funding, managing and regulating the system. In another study, Ahmed (2016) advocated the massification of higher education in Bangladesh. Basil (2017) emphasized on the needs of making higher education viable, relevant, and meaningful to the society and suggested transformative society of socially inclusive and economically progressive one in which all Indians feel valued and have the opportunity to participate fully in the life and activities of their society and economy.

Evolution and Development

Linking higher education with economic development, the University Education Commission (1948), headed by Dr. S. Radhakrishnan, had emphasized the need to translate political independence into economic independence. For this, Commission recommended reorienting the higher education in the context of the five basic tenets of our Constitution: Democracy, Justice, Liberty, Equality and Fraternity. Kothari Commission (1964-66) identified transformation, quality and expansion as the basic needs of higher education in India. The Commission in its report highlighted the importance of science education, work experience and vocationalization. In 1985, a government document entitled "Challenge of Education: A Policy Perspective" identified the high drop-out and low retention rate as the prime reasons, eroding the benefits of education expansion in the country. Recently, the National Knowledge Commission (2005), chaired by Sam Pitroda, recommended various changes to make higher education relevant to current needs.

In the decades of fifties and sixties (20th century), the focus remained on expansion, higher investment and professionalism in the field of higher education, it shifted to removal of regional, urban-rural and social inequalities in availability/accessibility of higher education during the seventies and the eighties. In post-reform period, the focus shifted to inclusiveness, competitiveness, information technology, human resource development, professionalism, use of space technology and involvement of NGOs, corporate sector and foreign investors in higher education. Table 0.1 briefly summarises all this.

Table 0.1: India: Shifting focus in higher education since independence

Period	*Focus*
1950s and 1960s	Expansion (Sectoral and Spatial), Higher investment, professionalism, emphasis on engineering/technological/ management and commerce under AICTE, Reorganisation of the structure of university education to bringing uniformity in higher education, Improvement of infrastructural and academic facilities, Expansion in the number of universities and colleges deteriorating the standard of teaching, and Concern for gender equity through scholarships.
1970s and 1980s	Equality (regional, rural-urban and social), Quality; and Distance education.
1990s onwards	Professionalism refocused, Inclusiveness (focussing on social, economic and physical disabilities), Involvement of NGOs and corporate sector, Competitiveness (Inviting foreign Universities and Investment), Space Technology (Satellite based distance education. Human resource development (creation of professional, technical and managerial manpower), Information Technology (NKN & NMIECT).

Source: Compiled from various sources.

In 2005, Indian Parliament passed a new education policy, Private and Foreign Universities Bill, 2005, paving the way for the establishment of private and foreign universities in India. This opened a new chapter in the history of higher education in India. The idea is welcomed in some quarters for encouraging competition between public, private and foreign universities, which is seen as a positive development towards improving quality of higher education in the country, but apprehended in some other quarters as a step that will render higher education unaffordable for poor and lower sections of Indian society. This opened a new debate in favour or against the involvement of private and foreign players in higher education.

The *Rashtriya Uchchatar Shiksha Abhiyan* (RUSA), a centrally sponsored scheme launched in 2013, amounts to be the first attempt to expand higher education in India. Establishment of state councils is a prerequisite to get funds under the RUSA framework. The main focus of the mission is to reduce regional imbalances or uneven access to improve quality of physical and human infrastructure, to expand institutions in unserved and underserved areas, to create gender equity, and to minimize social and residential bias in higher educational institutions.

Parikh (1967) observed that the higher education has an important role to play in promoting economic development. Taking Kerala as a case study, Tilak (2001) noted incongruity between education development and economic development in the state. To him, universal elementary education is a worthy goal for development of the societies but it does not provide the necessary resources for economic growth. He was of the opinion that the neglect of higher education was the main cause behind this. Bhushan (2004) stated that the role of higher education is quite crucial in knowledge generation, absorption and in the creation of income and wealth.

In another contribution, Tilak (2005) examined the relationship between post-elementary education and development in the context of poverty and other dimensions of social and human development in India. He stated that it is not only literacy and primary education, but also secondary and higher education that makes significant contribution to the economic growth and development. Tavakol (2007) highlighted the importance of higher education in the development of countries. Citing the example of Iran he told technical vocational centres increased in Iran to overcome the shortage of skilled manpower. He credited the Revolutionary Government in Iran for raising research funds by one-half during a short-span of two years (2001-03). He pointed out that the government, the industry, and the university are important stakeholders in socio-economic upliftment.

Asif & Searcy (2014) evolved a composite index for measuring performance in higher educational institutions. FICCI (2014) explored the vision of making Indian higher education system can be made globally relevant and competitive so as to create globally-reputed institutions, attracting international students, faculty and institutions, becoming a hub for globally-fit talent, and building a culture of research, innovation, and entrepreneurship to enable high economic growth. In another report of FICCI (2016) stated that higher education needs to transform itself to remain relevant to the changing socio-economic landscape and recommended some mid-term and long-term appraisals to drive the Indian higher education system towards a more agile industry-integrated system of learning.

Funding Provisions

Ramachandran (1987) studied growth trends in expenditure incurred on higher education in Kerala to find out that the higher educational institutions faced difficulties in coping up with growing demand for higher education due to the paucity of funds. In another study, Tilak and Varghese (1991) analysed funding pattern of higher education in India and examined the desirability and feasibility of various alternative methods of funding the same. Tilak (1992) while reviewing the implementation of the National Loan Scholarship Scheme focused on strengths, weaknesses and problems of educational loan schemes in India. He concluded that student loans make little contribution to improve either the efficiency or equity of higher education in India in the present times.

Roy *et al.* (2000) analysed expenditure on higher education in fifteen Indian states during 1993-98 to find that the actual expenditure on educational services is quite low in the low income states in face of their basic requirements. Gujarat and Maharashtra emerged as the leaders in case of primary education, while Andhra Pradesh and Punjab in secondary and higher educations. The low income states of Uttar Pradesh and Bihar were trailing far behind on all the three counts (primary, secondary and higher education). Rani (2004) noted that current policy in India often favours the diversion of resources from higher to primary level of education resulting in neglect of higher education.

Chakrabarti and Joglekar (2006) examined the pattern and the change in the allocation of government funds for education, particularly higher education to conclude that the states with higher proportion of scheduled population make significantly low expenditure on education. Prakash (2007) studied the trends in financing higher education in India. Agarwal (2007) commenting on the report submitted by the National Knowledge Commission headed by Sam Pitroda found the document excellent to form the base to formulate and strengthen higher education policy. FICCI (2009) identified that innovative financing, liberalisation of regulation and quality assurance mechanisms, use of information and communication technologies (ICT), integration of research with teaching, and vocational education and training were the key agents of change to bridge gaps and strengthen foundation of the Indian higher education system. Muzammil (2012) analysed funding method of higher education in England done on the basis of three criteria: number and types of students, subjects taught, amount and quality of research conducted. He recommended that India should adopt the funding method prevalent in England to improve university education system.

Privatization

Highlighting the importance of public faith in public owned institutions of higher education, Altbach (1999) brought out an interesting factor about United States, where the well-known institutions of higher education were in private sector yet fourth-fifth (80%) of the students attend public owned institutions of higher learning. In an another study, Altbach (2003) provided an overview of privately funded education in Asia-Pacific region, South Korea, Japan, Philippines and Indonesia to conclude that in these countries over 80 per cent of the students attend private institutions. This was reverse of U.S.A. Schukoske (2004) did a comparative study of profit motive versus non-profit motives of private institutions in higher education in the United States.

Wilkinson and Yussof (2005) conducted a sampled study of public and private colleges in terms of enrolment, cost, facilities and quality. They found that public universities were more efficient in satisfying public demand for quality. In a study, UGC (2006) found that unaided institutions constituted more than two-fifths of the total number of higher education institutions. Agarwal (2006) found that higher education in India expanded rapidly over the past two decades due to private sector driven growth. Ballal (2009) observed that issue of expansion and inclusion can be addressed by promoting public private partnership. According to Rani (2010) private institutions in Tamil Nadu have grown sporadically within a short span; more than 90 per cent of the engineering and management colleges in the state were in the private sector. Dash (2011) recommended public-private partnership model in higher education due to the problems of shortage of funds faced by the government.

Otieno (2007) analysed the changing dynamics of higher education in the country to throw light on the private provision and its changing interface with public higher education, the competition between the public and private institutions forcing both to adopt coping strategies, resulting in blurring of boundaries between public and purely private sectors. Levy (2008) described that the access to education is a major issue in higher education all over the world. He analysed that how the privately managed higher education institutions provide better access.

Tilak (2009) analysed the growth of private institutions in higher education and attempted to put together some evidence helping the dilemma to privatise or not to privatise higher education in India. He concluded that the countries with strong public higher education systems could prosper economically, socially, politically, culturally, or educationally. The reverse, i.e. lack of prosperity in all fields was found true about countries with narrow base of higher education. While examining the private sector surge in the developing countries, Varghese (2013) found that private higher education institutions emerge and expand in countries having less developed markets. Tilak (2014) noted that there had been a high growth of privately managed higher education in India since the beginning of the 1990s. He has drawn attention to the dangers involved in having a higher dependence on the private sector to develop higher education in a country like India. Kumar (2014) conducted a study in Meerut to find that the state government has badly failed to regulate the commercialization of higher education and to protect youth from harassment and payment of exorbitant fees. Ravi (2015) analysed the impact of privatization of education in the Indian society. He conducted a field survey in Kanyakumari district of Tamil Nadu of two hundred randomly selected colleges. He found a positive impact of privatization on the number of educational institutions, generation of employment and income opportunities, regional development, and establishment of private educational institutions. Among the negative effects, he found high cost of education, non-qualified faculty, inadequate infrastructure, lack of quality, and exploitation of employees at the hands of private managements. Tilak (2016) advocated for public-private partnership (PPP) concept to develop higher education in India. To him, PPP would minimise the adverse effects of private movement and strengthen the desirable effects of the role of public sector.

Briefly, the following points emerge strongly from the review of literature in the preceding paragraphs:

1. A majority of studies on higher education have been conducted either in the discipline of sociology or education. There are hardly studies conducted with a spatial perspective on the theme.
2. Majority of the studies on accessibility, availability (rural-urban), quality, gender and caste/class gaps in higher education overlooked or paid little attention to geographic implications of such issues.
3. There is a dearth of studies focusing on the spatial implications of privatization of higher education or locational decisions at sub-regional level.
4. There is hardly any study examining the effect of marginal location of an area on the accessibility, availability and inclusiveness of higher education.

5. One can hardly find any comprehensive research investigation of higher education in Himachal Pradesh from geographic perspective.

Finding the research gap in existing literature, the present doctoral dissertation invested the progress of higher education in Himachal Pradesh with the following objectives:

Objectives

The main objectives of the present study are to—

- place Himachal Pradesh within the group of other major states of India and other hill states in the context of higher education,
- study major landmarks in the evolution and growth of higher education in the state,
- study the structural composition of higher education in the state, and
- identify and analyse gaps/disparities in distribution (rural-urban), accessibility and availability, quality and social equity in higher education in the state.

Research Questions

In the light of the above stated objectives, the following research questions were framed and answered with the help of data analysis:

1. How has the present scenario of higher education in history of Himachal Pradesh, evolved with a focus on post-statehood period, starting from 1971? Where is Himachal Pradesh placed in major states of Indian context, especially among the other hill states?
2. What is the impact of government policies on the evolving geographical pattern of higher education in the state?
3. What is the sub-regional pattern of accessibility, availability and quality of higher education in the state?
4. How far is the development of higher education in the state inclusive in terms of residence (rural-urban), gender (male-female) and caste (Scheduled and non-Scheduled?
5. What is the structural composition (in terms of nature,

management and regulatory framework) of Higher education in the state of Himachal Pradesh?

Hypotheses

In the light of above stated research questions, the study proposed and tested the following hypotheses with the help of data analysis:

1. In view of the physiographic conditions of the state, the private sector would locate the institute of higher education at places having locational advantage. Hence, there will be a tendency among privately managed to concentrate such institutions in the places having relatively higher degree of accessibility.
2. Higher education in the state would find a strong impact of government policies on the courses offered by institutions of higher learning. Hence, a large majority of courses in higher education would focus on course in biotechnology, information technology, forestry, horticulture and pharmaceutical and drug industry.
3. A large majority of higher education institutes in the state would be located on the highway (state or national) for the locational advantage.
4. Due to physiographic constraints availability of land imposes serious limitation in the hill state of Himachal Pradesh. Hence, there would be not only a judicious use of land availability by the institutions of higher studies but also educational institutions requiring large size of land e.g. sports institutions would not be located in the state especially if these are run by the private sector.

Data Sources and Methodology

Various secondary sources of data were used to conduct the present study. Among the secondary sources included the following documents namely *All India Survey on Higher Education*, New Delhi, *Education Statistics, Higher Education*, available from the Directorate of Higher Education, Himachal Pradesh, Shimla, *Annual Reports of UGC*, from the Ministry of Human Resource and Development (for different years), Government of India, New Delhi.

For information, Five Year Plan documents available from the erstwhile *Planning Commission*, New Delhi website and *State Planning*

Board, Government of Himachal Pradesh, Shimla were liberally used. Different Gazetteer, libraries and archives having documents pertaining to historical development of higher education in the state were scanned thoroughly in details, as per the requirement.

Tools and Techniques of Analysis

For compilation, tabulation, mapping and analysis of data various cartographic and statistical tools and techniques were pressed into service. Similarly, for mapping distribution of educational institutions choropleth technique was used. Data obtained from various sources were converted into ratio and percentages for most of the attributes studied. Suitable tables and graphs were incorporated to provide snapshot view of these data. For the calculation of the single age-group, Sprague multiplier method has been used to compute the Net Enrolment Ratio (for the age-group 18-23) at the district level. Further, the availability of higher education institutions in terms of area and population was calculated using index method.

The base maps pertaining to location of educational institutions were prepared using the administrative map of Himachal Pradesh as given by the Census of India, 2011. For the purpose of mapping, processed data were categorised on the basis of state average or wherever possible natural breaks in data were employed for identifying the categories. The data were represented cartographically in the form of Choropleth maps to show the distribution of various attributes. These maps were generated through computer aided cartographic techniques using Arc GIS Version 9.3 software. The discussions were based on the tables, diagrams and maps.

Unit of Study

To trace historical roots of higher education in the state historical records and government documents were scanned. The study was based on district level for the mapping of data/information. In all, there were 12 districts in the state.

Period of Study

For an in-depth study of the evolutionary process of higher education focus was placed on the period beginning with British era and traced up to 2016. In the chapter on structural composition and change, where the nature of higher education institutions was studied by classifying under the general, technical, professional, technical-cum-professional and multi-faculty category, period between 1971 and 2016 was covered, by dividing it into sub-periods. For the chapter on accessibility and availability of higher education, data available from Census of India was taken for three Census decades between 1981 and 2011, and this data of in-depth study at the district level was put to use.

Significance of the Study

Education beyond the education imparted at schools includes the higher or tertiary education, provided at the college and university level. Higher education plays a very important role in economic and social development of any society. In Himachal Pradesh, there has been a remarkable growth of higher education since the state gained full statehood in general and 2000 onwards in particular. The present research work attempted to describe and explain the temporal and spatial distribution of higher education in the state. The analysis available through this study will help the planners and policy-makers in the state to make decisions to correct distortions for the smooth growth in future so as to make higher education inclusive in regional, sub-regional areas in terms of the social development carried out in the state of Himachal Pradesh.

Study Area

The study area situated in the heart of the western Himalayas, Himachal Pradesh extend from 30°22′40″ to 33°12′40″ North latitude and 75°47′55″ to 79°04′20″ East longitude. It covers an area of 55,673 km^2. It is hilly and mountainous tract with altitudes ranging from about 450 m to 6500 m above sea level (Fig. 0.1).

In the state, from west to east and south to north, there is an increase in an altitude. The state located in the north India and surrounded by the western Tibetan plateau on its East, to the Uttarakhand on the South-east, and Jammu & Kashmir on the north, Punjab and Haryana surrounds on the west on the south-west.

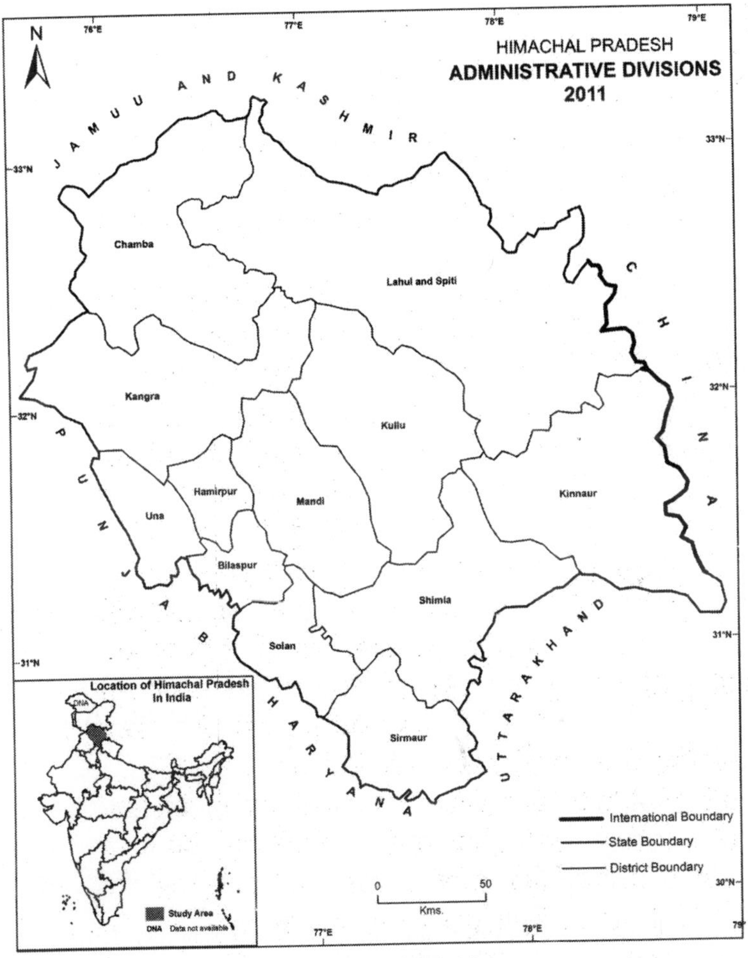

Fig. 0.1: Himachal Pradesh: Administrative Divisions.

Source: Census of India 2011, Administrative Atlas Himachal Pradesh.

Administratively Himachal Pradesh is divided into twelve districts: Chamba, Lahul and Spiti, Kinnaur, Kullu, Mandi, Una, Bilaspur, Hamirpur, Solan, Kangra, Sirmaur and Shimla.

Organization of the Material (Chapter Scheme)

The study was organized into the following five chapters excluding the introduction in the beginning and summary and main findings at the end.

Introduction: It included the conceptual framework of the study by way of presenting statement of the problem, review of existing literature, objectives of the study, research questions, hypotheses, data sources and methodology, unit of study, significance of the study and organization of the material.

I. Himachal Pradesh in National Context: This chapter discussed the existing scenario of higher education in India in general and Himachal Pradesh in particular. A comparison between the major states and Himachal Pradesh, on one hand and other hill states, on the other, remained the main thrust.

II. Changing Geography of Higher Education: The evolution of higher education in the state beginning with pre-Independence era and up to the present times (2016) with a focus on the period from 1971 to 2016. Evolution and growth of higher education was examined in terms of number of higher education institutions including colleges, universities and institutes of national importance with spatial perspective. The role of government policy in evolution, growth and regional distribution remained the focus.

III. Structural Composition and Change: This chapter focused on the composition of higher education in terms of nature, management and regulatory bodies in Himachai Pradesh. The changes taking place in it over the time were also examined.

IV. Accessibility and Avsilability: The regional pattern of accessibility and availability of general and vocational education institutions in the state was separately discussed. Accessibility had been examined in terms of net enrolment ratio, residence (urban-rural), gender (male-female) and social groups (non-Scheduled and Scheduled population) in the state. On the other side, availability was analysed in terms of area and population with higher educational institutions at the district level kept in mind.

V. Quality of Higher Education: It explored the quality of higher education in terms of input and output variables at the college and university level, separately. A number of indicators representing input dimension (human resources and physical infrastructure) and the output dimension (educational attainments) were identified, discussed, mapped and analysed. Finally, an attempt was made to examine the nature of association and spatial correspondence between the input and output dimensions of higher education in the state by making district as a unit of data making and analysis.

Summary and Main Findings: Finally, the main findings of the study arrived at in different chapters were recapitulated and future research agenda outlined.

SECTION A

Higher Education: National Context

I
Himachal Pradesh in National Context

Introduction

This chapter examines higher education scenario of Himachal Pradesh in the national context. The main objective is to compare Himachal Pradesh *vis-a-vis* major states[1] of India in addition to comparing Himachal Pradesh with other hill states.[2] Distribution of higher education institutions, gross enrolment ratio, women enrolment and teacher-pupil ratio has been chosen as the parameters to position Himachal Pradesh among major states of India as well as the other hill states. A geographical approach has been consistently followed to carry out the exercise.

Even a cursory look at the available data on above-said parameters reveals that there is a wide gap between small states and union territories, on one hand, and medium and large sized states, on the other, to make our task difficult.[3] To overcome this, only the states having a population size of more than six million persons have been selected. In this way, population size has been taken as the criterion to differentiate between major and minor states. This has resulted in keeping the eight small sized states and seven Union Territories out of the purview of discussions here. Finally, we are left with 20 states to compare with Himachal Pradesh. However, in the case of hill states, all the ten such states including Himachal Pradesh are the part of our analysis. For making study more realistic, the official age-group (18-23) to attain higher education has been picked up to calculate indices used for data analysis. This age-group has a population of 140.3 million persons making 12.0 per cent of the total population of the country.

For organising the discussions, the chapter has been divided into two sections: (i) examining the spatial distribution of higher educational institutes (colleges and universities, separately), along with gross enrolment ratio, teacher-pupil ratio, and women enrolment, and (ii) comparing Himachal Pradesh with other hill states on the same parameters.

The analysis is based on secondary sources of data, such as reports on higher education, that are available from the University Grants Commission, New Delhi, *All India Survey on Higher Education,* conducted by the Ministry of Human Resource Development, Government of India, New Delhi and *Five Year Plan* documents available from the erstwhile Planning Commission (now, NITI Aayog), New Delhi. The spatial picture of higher education has been arrived at with the help of four indicators namely, universities per ten thousand km^2 and universities per half a million population in the age group of 18-23, number of colleges per thousand km^2, and number of colleges per ten thousand population in the age group of 18-23. At the first level, colleges and universities have been examined separately followed by a combined picture of the two. Weighted index method has been used to arrive at a value for each study unit on each indicator. Finally, a composite index is calculated for each state by diving the summed-up index values of individual indicators with the number of chosen indicators.

Progress of Higher Education

In India, higher education has made a significant progress after the Independence. With 25.9 million students enrolled in higher education, India has the largest higher education system in the world now. It is placed next only to China (FICCI, 2012). The recent data available from the All India Survey on Higher Education (AISHE) reveals that the number of universities has increased twenty-four times (30 to 723) and number of colleges has increased fifty-three times (695 to 36,634) between 1950-51 and 2013-14. There were 30 universities during 1941-51, increased to 55 at the compound annual growth rate (henceforth CAGR) of 6.2 per cent during 1951-61. There has been further expansion during the 1961-71 decade, registering an absolute increase of 48 universities (Table 1.0).

The period from 1951 to 1971 was characterized by rapid growth of higher education institutions. The educational system in India started expanding in the 1950s. Various Commissions and Committees were established to promote higher education in the country. The University Grants Commission (UGC) was also established in this decade. The objective was to finance, regulate and promote higher education through the UGC; the focus remaining on courses in languages and humanities. There were only a few institutions to promote professional education.

Table 1.0: India: Growth of universities, 1951-2014

Years	*Universities (in numbers)*	*Absolute increase*	*CAGR (%)*
1	2	3	4
1951	30	0	0
1961	55	25	6.2
1971	103	48	6.4
1981	133	30	2.5
1991	190	57	3.6
2001	256	66	3.0
2014*	723	467	7.7

Sources: (i) Higher education in India at a Glance, University Grants Commissions, New Delhi, February 2012.
(ii)* All India Survey on Higher Education, 2013-14, GOI MHRD, Department of Higher Education, New Delhi.

Note: CAGR stands for Compound Annual Growth Rate.

For example, Indian Institute of Technology (IITs) and Regional Engineering colleges (now National Institute of Technology) for engineering education, and Indian Institute of Management for management education were only a few and were established with foreign assistance. Growth remaining slow even in the next decade of the 1971-81, the absolute number increased only by 30 universities. The growth rate came down to 2.5 per cent from 6.4 per cent during the 1961-71.

The next two decades registered upward movement in the growth of universities in the country. The decade of 1991-2001 witnessed liberalisation policies even in higher education sector. In 2001, Government of India opened the higher education to the private sector and allowed foreign universities to establish campuses in India. Consequently, there has been a quantum leap in a number of universities in India. While there was not a single private university in India in 1981, their number rose to 467 by 2013-14. The total number of universities increased to 723 by 2013-14 from 256 in 2001, recording an unprecedented increase in a number of universities in India. The number increased during 2001-2014 decade (467 universities) which was nearly thrice of the total number of universities (133) in the country in 1981. This is generally termed as a paradigm shift in higher education in India.

The increase in the number of colleges after the Independence was much more spectacular. There were only 695 colleges in India in 1951. This number went up to 1542 by 1961, giving a decadal increase of 847 colleges and an annual growth rate of 8.3 per cent. By 1971, this number rose to 3604, giving an annual growth rate of 8.9 per cent. As was the case with universities, the growth rate of colleges too slowed down in the next decade (1971-81) coming down to 2.7 per cent. There was momentum witnessed in the growth during the next decade, the number of colleges reaching to 7346 by 1991, registering an annual compound growth rate of 4.5 per cent. The next decade (1991-2001) registered an unprecedented growth, as the number of colleges recorded an increase of 9539, much higher than the total number of colleges in India at 1991. The period 2001-2014 recorded an increase of 19,749 colleges (2013-14), which is largest than the total number of colleges in the country in the year 2001 (Table 1.1).

Table 1.1: India: Growth of colleges, 1951-2011

Years	*Colleges (in numbers)*	*Absolute increase*	*CAGR (%)*
1	2	3	4
1951	695	0	0
1961	1542	847	8.3
1971	3604	2062	8.9
1981	4722	1118	2.7
1991	7346	2624	4.5
2001	16885	9539	8.7
2014*	36634	19749	5.7

Source: As Table 1.0.

The then prime Minister, Dr Manmohan Singh, termed the Eleventh Plan (2007-12) as the "Education Plan". The Plan focussed on the expansion of existing 200 state engineering colleges/institutions and upgradation of the seven technical institutions, establishment of 16 central and 14 World Class Universities, 370 colleges, eight IITs and IIMs, ten NITs, three IISERs, twenty IIITs, two SPAs and 50 centres for strengthening training and research in the country. These were to be established through government funding as well as under Public-Private Partnership [University Grants Commission (UGC), 2011].

The number of universities/institutes/centres in Himachal Pradesh reached 23, the number of colleges was 296 in 2013-14. According to information available from the UGC (first survey of higher education done by Ministry of Education and Social Welfare in 1973-74), this number was one and 32, respectively. It has increased nine and 23 times between 1973-74 and 2013-2014 in the case of colleges and universities, respectively, between 1973-74 and 2013-2014. In 2013-2014, there were four state universities, one central university, two institutes of national importance, and sixteen private universities in Himachal Pradesh. There has been a slow but steady growth of universities in the state between 1971 and 2001. However, during the latest period of 13 years (2001-2014), there has been an unprecedented growth of universities in the state. The number of universities went up to 23, registering an increase of 19 universities in a period of 13 years. What explains this recent unprecedented growth of universities in Himachal Pradesh?

I. Regional Distribution of Universities and Colleges in India

Universities

The overall regional pattern reveals that the states in south India have an edge over their counterparts in other regions of the country. Their combined share of 23.2 per cent in total universities of the country was higher than that of states in western India (21.0%). Both regions, in the combine, shared 44.2 per cent of total universities in India. Against this, their combined share in the total population in the country was 40.8 per cent.

For example, the share of western region in total universities (21.02%) was slightly higher than its population share (20.56%). Unlike, the western region, the respective shares of the north-central region had been 20.2 per cent and 26.0 per cent. One can infer from this that students seeking admission in the university system migrate to states in southern and western India from the regions where the share of universities is lower than their respective shares in India's population. One such region is eastern region, which shares only 13.7 per cent in total universities against 23.7 per cent in the total population of India (Table 1.2).

Evidently, the eastern region had the shortage of universities in comparison to its population share. In such a situation, inter-regional migration of students from university-deficient to university-surplus regions is found out to be the way by admission seekers to higher education institutions in India. However, when there is a vast inter-regional diversity of languages, customs, traditions and employment opportunities in different parts of India, inter-state migration for higher education and jobs leads at times to clashes loaded with ethnic overtones. Obviously, such a scenario has geographic angle. Further, the north-western region, where Himachal Pradesh is also located, had, in combine, 12.03 per cent universities against 6.3 per cent population. The small states and union territories enjoy an upper edge advantage in this regard (Table 1.2).

Table 1.2: India: Distribution of universities by regions, 2013-14

S. No.	*Name of Region*	*No. of Universities*	*Share in total universities (%)*	*Share to total Population* (%)*	*Ratio b/w col. 3 & 4*
	1	2	3	4	5
1.	Southern	168	23.24	20.21	1.15
2.	Western	152	21.02	20.56	1.02
3.	North Central	146	20.19	26.01	0.78
4.	Eastern	99	13.69	23.75	0.58
5.	North Western	87	12.03	6.28	1.92
	Major States	652	90.18	96.81	0.93
	All India	723	100.00	100.00	1.00
	Small States	38	5.26	1.38	3.81
	Union Territories	33	4.56	1.81	2.52

Source: All India Survey on Higher Education (2013-14), GOI, MHRD, Department of Higher Education, New Delhi, 2015.

Note: *Population includes relevant age-group (18-23) of higher education. North western: Jammu & Kashmir, Haryana, Himachal Pradesh, and Punjab; Western: Gujarat, Rajasthan, and Maharashtra, North-Central: Madhya Pradesh, Chhattisgarh, Uttar Pradesh and Uttarakhand; Eastern: Bihar, Jharkhand, Odisha, West Bengal, Assam; Southern: Andhra Pradesh, Kerala, Karnataka, Tamil Nadu and Telangana.

Colleges

Regional imbalance in the distribution of colleges is higher than that of universities. The southern region shares 32.1 per cent colleges against its population share of 20.2 per cent. Similarly, the western region shares 25.2 per cent colleges against 20.6 per cent of country's population. Both regions, in combine, share 57.3 per cent or majority colleges imparting higher education in India. Against this, they have share of only 40.8 per cent in the total population of the country. On the other hand, the eastern region shares only less than one-tenth or 9.8 per cent colleges against nearly one-fourth or 23.7 per cent population of the country (Table 1.3).

This indicates a huge gap between availability of higher education institutions and the population at the regional level in India. To overcome the huge gap between the two, the interested students migrate from deficient states to relatively surplus states especially for professional and technical education courses. The eastern states represent the former and the southern states the latter.

Table 1.3: India: Distribution of colleges by regions, 2013-14

S. No.	Name of Region	No. of colleges	Share in total colleges (%)	Share to total Population (%)	Ratio b/w col. 3 & 4
	1	2	3	4	5
1.	Southern	11769	32.13	20.21	1.59
2.	Western	9216	25.16	20.56	1.22
3.	North-Central	8662	23.64	26.01	0.93
4.	Eastern	3576	9.76	23.75	0.41
5.	North-western	2718	7.42	6.28	0.97
	Major States Average	35941	98.11	96.81	1.01
	All India	36634	100.00	100.00	1.00
	Small States	375	1.02	1.38	0.74
	Union Territories	318	0.87	1.81	0.48

Source: As Table 1.2.
Note: As Table 1.2.

Such a situation is, however, full of geographical, social and economic implications. What happened to the students from north-eastern states in Bengaluru city a few years ago is a glaring example of ethno-regional clashes causing not only serious law and order problem but also economic loss to the nation and individual households.

The north-central region comprising of Madhya Pradesh, Chhattisgarh, Uttar Pradesh, and Uttarakhand shares 23.6 per cent colleges against 26.0 per cent of India's population. In short, there were wide inter-regional differentials in distribution of universities and colleges in India. Southern region is most favourable, while the opposite is true of the eastern region. The northern-western region, where Himachal Pradesh is also located, has almost a balanced situation between its two shares. This is really satisfying to note. Nevertheless, there are significant inter-state differentials in all the regions including the northern region. This is being examined in the following paragraphs.

Universities: Himachal Pradesh among Major States

According to All India Survey on Higher Education, published in 2015, 21 major states including Himachal Pradesh, in combine, had 652 or 90.2 per cent of total 723 universities in the country. Against this, their combined population was 96.8 per cent. This indicates to a mismatch between the universities and population there. On the other hand, small states and union territories had an edge over the major states. Their combined share in total universities was 9.8 per cent against their share of less than 3.2 per cent in country's population (Table 1.4).

Table 1.4: India: Distribution of universities by major states, 2013-14

S. No.	Major States	No. of Universities	Share in total Universities (%)	Share in total Population (%)	Ratio b/w cols. 3 & 4
	1	2	3	4	5
1.	Himachal Pradesh	23	3.18	0.56	5.68
2.	Uttarakhand	24	3.32	0.89	3.73
3.	Haryana	31	4.29	2.27	1.89
4.	Jammu & Kashmir	11	1.52	1.02	1.49
5.	Rajasthan	63	8.71	5.89	1.48
6.	Tamil Nadu	58	8.02	5.53	1.45
7.	Chhattisgarh	21	2.9	2.14	1.36
8.	Punjab	22	3.04	2.44	1.25
9.	Gujarat	44	6.09	5.07	1.2
10.	Karnataka	45	6.22	5.27	1.18
11.	Kerala	18	2.49	2.26	1.1
12.	Assam	18	2.49	2.59	0.96
13.	Telangana	20	2.77	3	0.92
14.	Andhra Pradesh	27	3.73	4.14	0.9
15.	Madhya Pradesh	39	5.39	6.09	0.89
16.	Odisha	21	2.9	3.36	0.86
17.	Maharashtra	45	6.22	9.6	0.65
18.	Jharkhand	12	1.66	2.56	0.65
19.	Uttar Pradesh	62	8.58	16.9	0.51
20.	West Bengal	27	3.73	7.82	0.48
21.	Bihar	21	2.9	7.43	0.39
	Major States	652	90.18	96.81	0.93
	India	723	100	100	1
	Small States	38	5.26	1.38	4.04
	Union Territories	33	4.56	1.81	2.75

Source: As Table 1.2.

Obviously, small sized states and union territories especially the latter attract students from the neighbouring states for studying in universities located there. In the following paragraphs an attempt will be made to examine inter-state disparities within major states.

Among the major states, the share of universities overall ranged from a high of 8.7 per cent in Rajasthan to a low of 1.5 per cent in Jammu &

Kashmir, both located in the northern region. In other words, Rajasthan has a maximum of 63 universities and Jammu & Kashmir, a minimum of 11 universities. Seven states namely, Rajasthan, Uttar Pradesh, Tamil Nadu, Karnataka, Maharashtra, Gujarat and Madhya Pradesh each having more than five per cent, had, in combine, nearly a half (49.2%) of total universities of the country. Their combined population was 54.3 per cent of total population of India. On the other side of the scale, the eight states including Jammu & Kashmir, Jharkhand, Assam, Kerala, Telangana, Chhattisgarh, Odisha, and Bihar, each having below 3.0 per cent share in total universities of the country, had, in combine, only about one-fifth or 19.6 per cent of them. Against this, their combined population share was nearly 24.3 per cent of the total population of India.

In the remaining six states, individual share ranged between three and five per cent, had, in combine, more than one-fifth or 21.3 per cent of the total number of universities against their population share of 18.1 per cent. Obviously, this group of states including Himachal Pradesh, Uttarakhand, Haryana, Punjab, Andhra Pradesh and West Bengal has relative advantage by having higher share in the universities than their percentage in India's population.

Let us now examine the association between universities and population at the level of individual states. As many as eleven of the total 21 major states had higher share of universities than their population share. In another two states (Assam and Telangana) both shares were almost the same. Against this, Bihar's share in universities was only one-third of its share in the total population of India, indicating an acute shortage of universities *vis-a-vis* population in the state. In West Bengal, Uttar Pradesh, Jharkhand, and Maharashtra, these ratios ranged from one-half to two-thirds. It means that their respective share in total universities was much lower than the share in the total population of India. It means either the enrolment and achievements in higher education are low or students were migrating to other states for higher education.

Within the group of eleven states, whose shares in total universities were higher than their respective share in total population of India, there are wide inter-state variations. For example, Himachal Pradesh with 23 universities but relative low share of population recorded the highest ratio of 5.7:1 between universities and population. In other words, the share of Himachal Pradesh in total universities was nearly six times more than its share in the total population of the country. Next to Himachal Pradesh is placed Uttarakhand, another hill state, where the university-population ratio is 3.73:1. The number of universities in Uttarakhand is

24, one more than the number of universities in Himachal Pradesh. In their desire to bring higher education to the door-steps of their residents, the policy-makers in these two hill states opened the floodgates of higher education to private investors following the enactment of the law to this effect by Indian Parliament in the year 2001 and later on the ratification by respective states assemblies. A combination of factors including dust free peaceful ambience and the reasonable/affordable land attracted the private investors to invest in higher education in hill states. It was, however, done with an eye on profit rather than with a sense of altruism as could have been expected in the context of Indian ethos.

Interestingly, the overwhelming majority of universities were located in the districts of these two states that are well connected with their adjoining states as well as the other parts of India. For example, Solan in Himachal Pradesh and Dehradun in Uttarakhand benefitted the most by their close proximity and easy accessibility to plains down below the foothills.

Haryana, distantly ranked at third position after Himachal Pradesh and Uttarakhand, is located very close to the national capital of Delhi. 31 universities located in the state, give a ratio of 1.89:1 between its share of universities and that of its share of population in India. In other words, Haryana accounts for the share of universities in India which is nearly double of its share in the total population of the country. Close proximity to the national capital, having huge demand for higher education combined with relatively affordable land available in Haryana in comparison to Delhi attracted the private investors to open new universities in the state. Gurgaon and Sonipat districts of the state falling in close proximity of the national capital benefitted the most from this situation. Thirteen of the total 31 universities in the state are located in Gurgaon and Sonipat districts. The former has eight and the latter has five universities.

Locational advantage benefitted Solan and Dehradun in the maximum the hill states of Himachal Pradesh and Uttarakhand and Gurgaon (now Gurugram) and Sonipat districts of Haryana. The universities in these districts generally cater to the demand for higher education emanating from outside the state. This has been responsible for creating wide intra-state disparities in the distribution of the institutions of higher learning in such states. In fact, some locations have a distinctive advantage over the other. This is, however, a dynamic process rather than being a static one. Secondly, these states are moving in the direction of capitalist development where investment decisions are taken by the investors or capitalists to fulfil their interest of capital accumulation rather than taking care of public welfare.

Rajasthan, which ranked fourth among major states, had the highest number (63) of universities. Its university-population ratio comes to 1.5:1; meaning that the share of state in the number of universities of the country was one half more than its share in the population of the country. Locationally, a large number of universities under the privatization policy have come up in and around Jaipur city, the state capital headquarters. Jammu & Kashmir, another state, where the number of total universities is though the lowest among the major states, yet university-population ratio was tilting in its favour.

In another six states namely, Tamil Nadu, Chhattisgarh, Punjab, Gujarat, Karnataka and Kerala where the ratio between the shares in universities and population were tilting in favour of universities, a number of the new universities have come up in the post-privatization phase of higher education in India. A majority of such universities were located in and around metropolitan cities especially the state capital headquarters to have locational advantage. A number of new private universities came up on agricultural land in the close proximity to state capitals to run professional and technical courses under self-finance scheme. This kind of development has reactivated centripetal forces, to accentuate disparities in the development of higher education.

On the other side of the scale, the three states, namely Uttar Pradesh, West Bengal and Bihar, where the proportional share of universities is one-half of their shares in the total population of the country, are large both in area and size of population. Due to a mis-match between demand and supply, students aspiring to attain higher and quality education migrate to the other states like Maharashtra, Karnataka, NCT Delhi and Chandigarh (U.T.). This results not only in a significant loss of human capital to the states of their origin but also creates several new problems linked with inter-state migration in India.

Briefly, there are wide inter-state variations in the distribution of universities in India. Inequality in the distribution of universities among states gets further pronounced when their respective shares in total universities and total population of India are compared. About a half (49.2%) of the universities were located in just seven states making it only one-fifth of the total states/union territories of the country. On the other side of the scale, eight states, in combine, had less, i.e. one-fifth (19.6%) of the total universities in India.

Himachal Pradesh stands out at the top among major states of India in terms of university-population ratio. The state had 3.2 per cent of total universities against less than one per cent (0.6%) of India's population. Himachal Pradesh along with Uttarakhand, Haryana, Rajasthan and Jammu & Kashmir have usurped more than one-fifth (21.0%) of total universities against their combined population of about one-tenth (10.6%) of the total population of India. Following the entry of private sector in education sector in 2001, several states including hill states of Himachal Pradesh and Uttarakhand attracted huge private investment in higher education. However, the private capitalism and commercialization of higher education led to regional and sub-regional inequalities in the distribution of higher education institutions. Also, it has resulted in making higher education more expensive and highly differentiated in quality. On the positive side, higher education has made inroads in backward and peripheral areas as well.

Colleges: Himachal Pradesh among Major States

In 2013-14, there were 35,941 colleges in twenty-one major states of India, making it 98.1 per cent of the total colleges (35,941 colleges) of India. The five major states of southern India, in combine, had the largest number (11,769), making nearly one-third or 32.1 per cent of the total colleges of the major states. Against this, their combined share in total population of the country was only about one-fifth (20.21%). The western region closely followed the southern region with 25.16 or one-fourth colleges of all the major states. These two regions shared, in combine, more than one-half or 57.3 per cent colleges located in twenty-one major states of India (Table 1.5).

Against this, their combined population was slightly more than two-fifths (40.8%) of the total population of the country. Evidently, college segment of higher education has relatively higher concentration in southern and western regions of India. Against this, eastern region, which contains nearly one-fourth or 23.7 per cent of the total population of major states, has less than one-tenth or 9.8 per cent of the total number of colleges.

It is followed by the north-central region, having high concentration of population especially in Uttar Pradesh, with less than one-fourth or 23.6 per cent colleges against more than the one-fourth or 26.01 per cent of total population of 21 major states of India. North-west region, which has the smaller percentage share of colleges (7.4%) in the total number of colleges in the major states, has only 6.3 per cent of total population, hence favourably placed in college-population ratio.

Table 1.5: India: Distribution of colleges by major states, 2013-14

S. No.	Major States	No. of Colleges	Share to total colleges	Share to total Population	Ratio b/w col. 3 & 4
	1	2	3	4	5
1.	Telangana	2280	6.22	3.00	2.07
2.	Karnataka	3310	9.04	5.27	1.71
3.	Andhra Pradesh	2568	7.01	4.14	1.69
4.	Himachal Pradesh	296	0.81	0.56	1.45
5.	Kerala	1151	3.14	2.26	1.39
6.	Haryana	1098	3.00	2.27	1.32
7.	Rajasthan	2774	7.57	5.89	1.29
8.	Maharashtra	4498	12.28	9.60	1.28
9.	Uttarakhand	410	1.12	0.89	1.26
10.	Tamil Nadu	2460	6.72	5.53	1.21
11.	Punjab	997	2.72	2.44	1.12
12.	Gujarat	1944	5.31	5.07	1.05
13.	Madhya Pradesh	2136	5.83	6.09	0.96
14.	Uttar Pradesh	5445	14.86	16.90	0.88
15.	Jammu & Kashmir	327	0.89	1.02	0.88
16.	Odisha	1067	2.91	3.36	0.87
17.	Chhattisgarh	671	1.83	2.14	0.86
18.	Assam	536	1.46	2.59	0.57
19.	West Bengal	985	2.69	7.82	0.34
20.	Jharkhand	284	0.78	2.56	0.30
21.	Bihar	704	1.92	7.43	0.26
	Major States	35941	98.11	97.04	1.01
	India	36634	100	100	1.00
	Small States	375	1.02	1.3	0.79
	Union Territories	318	0.87	1.66	0.52

Source: As Table 1.2.

Briefly, among the five major regions of the country, southern, western and north-western regions were advantageously placed in term of college-population ratio. However, the reverse was true of the eastern and north-central regions of India. The deplorable situation was observed in the case of eastern region, having only less than one-tenth of total number of colleges against nearly one-fourth of the total population of the major states of India.

At the level of individual states, Telangana with 6.2 per cent colleges against the 3.0 per cent population of 21 major states was at the top in college-population ratio. It was followed by Karnataka, Andhra Pradesh,

Himachal Pradesh, Kerala, Haryana and Rajasthan. On the whole, eleven or more than one-half of the 21 major states have a ratio of more than one between their respective share of colleges and population. In other words, one half of the major states were better placed in terms of college-population ratio. On the other side of the scale, Bihar was placed at the bottom among all the 21 major states in this context. Bihar shared only 1.92 per cent of colleges against 7.4 per cent population of 21 major states. Bihar was closely followed by Jharkhand and West Bengal (Table 1.5).

The college plays a valuable role in the spread of higher education in India. That is why the number of colleges is nearly 51 times more than the number of total universities in India.

A more realistic picture will emerge after we compare respective shares of major states in the number of colleges with their strength in population. The ratio between the two shares ranged from a high of 1:2.07 in Telangana to a low of only 1:0.26 in Bihar. In other words, Telangana share of colleges was twice of its share in India's population. Against this, Bihar's share in colleges was about one-fourth of its population share of India. Evidently, there is huge disparity in the two shares across various states of India.

In thirteen or more than one-half of 21 major states, the proportional share of colleges was higher than their respective shares of total population. All the major states of southern and western India fall in this category. Himachal Pradesh in north-west India ranks fourth, from the top, in the list of the major states. Here, the ratio of colleges was nearly one and a half times more than its share in India's population.

Against this, nine states, where population shares were higher than their respective shares in the number of colleges in India, were mainly located in eastern, north-eastern and north-central parts of India. In fact, Jammu & Kashmir, from north-western India is the only state that falls in this group of states. In this group, West Bengal, Jharkhand, and Bihar are the three states where respective shares in colleges were even less than one half of their respective shares in India's population. The situation was slightly better in case of Assam.

On the whole, the four states of Assam, West Bengal, Jharkhand and Bihar, all located either in eastern or north-eastern India had the widest gaps between their respective share in the number of colleges and in the population of India. Another five states, where respective shares of colleges were lower than their share in the strength of population included Madhya Pradesh, Uttar Pradesh and Chhattisgarh from the north and central India, Jammu & Kashmir from north-western and Odisha from eastern India. Uttar Pradesh and Madhya Pradesh though have, in combine, 7581 colleges, making more than one-fifth of the total colleges of India, but for huge sizes of population, the balance tilt adversely against the population shares.

Briefly, there are wide inter-state variations in the distribution of colleges among major states of India. Five top ranking states have, in combine, more than one-half of the total number of colleges of India. On the whole, major states, located in southern and western India were favourably placed in this context. Against this, major states located in eastern and north-eastern India are lagging behind all the other states. Himachal Pradesh is placed fourth from the top amongst 21 major states, and within north-western states, it is next only to Haryana.

All such findings have geographical implications. From the states, where the ratio of population is more than the ratio of colleges, students migrate for higher education to states where the ratio of colleges is more than their respective share in population. Not only the financial resources get transferred in the process but the states that suffer out-migration lose human resources. In addition, there are social and cultural implications of such inter-state migrations. However, on the positive side, it leads to national integration.

Availability and Accessibility: Himachal Pradesh among Major States

In the following section, inter-state availability and accessibility of higher education has been discussed. Availability has been examined in terms of area and population, whereas accessibility in relation to gross enrolment ratio, women enrolment and teacher-pupil ratio.

Universities by Area

Calculated per ten thousand square kilometers area of states, there were, on average, two universities per 10,000 km^2 in India during 2013-14. Among major states, the ratio varied from a high of seven universities in Haryana to low of only one in four states (Jammu & Kashmir, Madhya Pradesh, Maharashtra, and Odisha). For Union territories, on the whole, this ratio comes to 30 universities/10,000 km^2. However, in reality, none of the seven union territories has that much of area.

In eight states, namely Haryana, Himachal Pradesh, Kerala, Punjab, Tamil Nadu, West Bengal, Uttar Pradesh and Uttarakhand, there were three or more universities after 10,000 km^2. These states were above the national average of two universities per 10,000 km^2. Notably, four of these eight states are located in the north, two in the south of India and remaining one each in Eastern and North-central India, respectively. There was no state in this category either from the west or east of India (Table 1.6).

Table 1.6: Major States: Area and population served by universities in India, 2013-14

S. No.	Major States	Universities per	
		Ten thousand km²	Half million persons
1	2	3	4
1.	Andhra Pradesh	2	2
2.	Assam	2	2
3.	Bihar	2	1
4.	Chhattisgarh	2	4
5.	Gujarat	2	3
6.	Haryana	7	5
7.	Himachal Pradesh	4	15
8.	Jammu & Kashmir	1	4
9.	Jharkhand	2	2
10.	Karnataka	2	3
11.	Kerala	5	3
12.	Madhya Pradesh	1	2
13.	Maharashtra	1	2
14.	Odisha	1	2
15.	Punjab	4	3
16.	Rajasthan	2	4
17.	Tamil Nadu	4	4
18.	Uttar Pradesh	3	1
19.	Uttarakhand	4	10
20.	West Bengal	3	1
21.	Telangana	2	2
	Major States	2	2
	India	2	3
	Small States	2	10
	Union Territories	30	6

Source: As Table 1.2.

Note: The figures of universities per 10,000 km² area and five lakh population have been around up to nearest number.

A majority (13 of 21) of major states had this average ranging between < 2.0 to < 4.0. These states were located in all parts of India except the north-west. The remaining four states (Madhya Pradesh, Maharashtra, Odisha and Jammu & Kashmir) had the lowest ratio of one university per 10,000 km². On the whole, in 13 of 21 major states, the number of universities per 10,000 km² area was either equivalent to or less than the national average (Fig 1.0). In fact, the states, attracting the private investment in higher education in post-privatization phase, had the higher

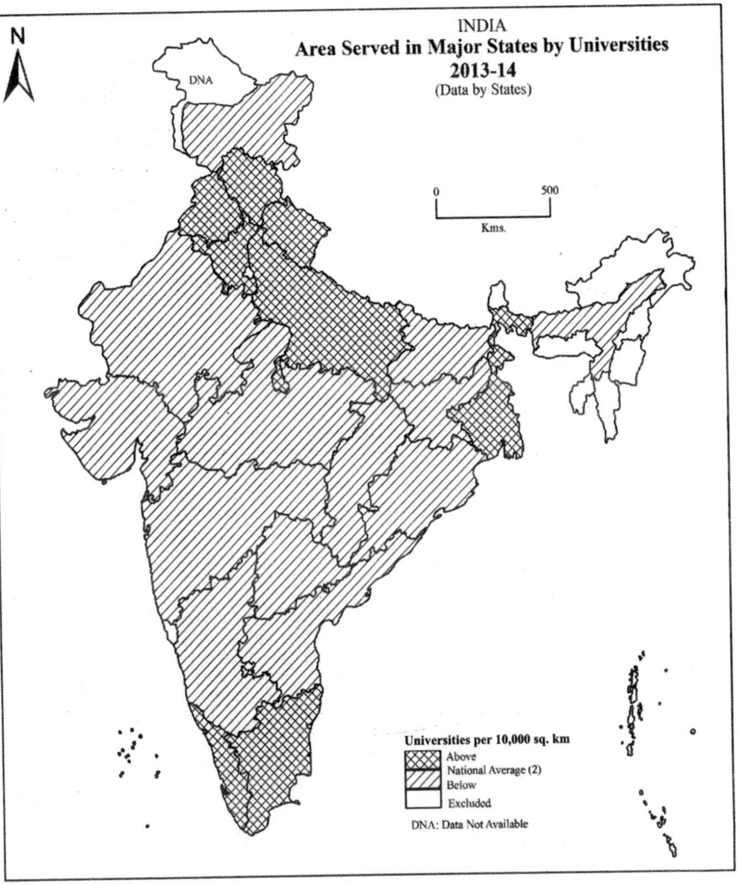

Fig 1.0: India: Area served in Major States by Universities.
Source: All India Survey on Higher Education (2013-14), GOI, MHRD, Department of Higher Education, New Delhi, 2015.

number of universities in area terms. Such states included Haryana, Himachal Pradesh, Uttarakhand, Kerala, and Punjab.

Universities by Population

Inter-state disparities in the distribution of universities get accentuated further when seen in terms of population size. The number of universities per half a million population ranged from a high of 15 in Himachal Pradesh to a low of one university in three states of Uttar Pradesh, West Bengal, and Bihar.

The national average being the three universities per half a million or five lakh population, only the seven major states had this ratio higher than the national average.

On the whole, small states followed by union territories were far better placed than major states in this context (Table 1.6). In the case of small states, this ratio was as high as ten, against this average being only two for major states. However, within major states, there were wide differentials. Three states of Haryana, Himachal Pradesh and Uttarakhand had the average of more than six. In case of Himachal Pradesh, this average was as high as 15 universities per half a million population (Fig. 1.1).

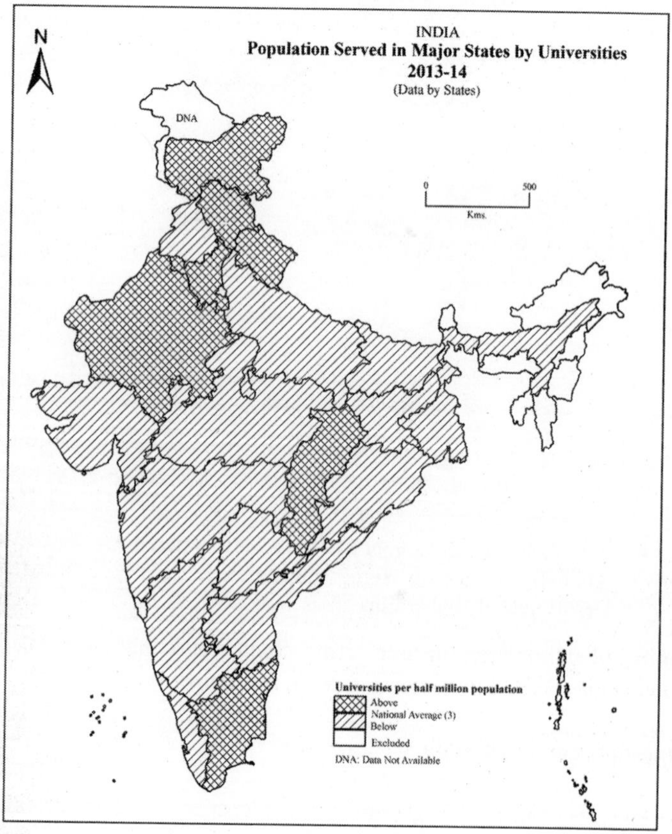

Fig 1.1: India: Population served in Major States by Universities.
Source: As Figure 1.0.

Notably, all these states were located in north India. The dominant majority (15 of 21) of major states had this average between 2.0 and 4.0, and were distributed in all parts of the country. The three states of Bihar, Uttar Pradesh, and West Bengal had the ratio of one university. On the whole, in 10 of 21 major states, the number of universities per half a million population was either equivalent to or less than the average for major states.

Briefly, inter-state inequality in the distribution of universities is quite high especially in term of university-population ratio. Small states and Union territories are placed far better as compared to the major states. Within major states, states with large population size such as Bihar, Uttar Pradesh, and West Bengal fared poorly in this context. Against this, hill states of Himachal Pradesh and Uttarakhand along with Haryana were placed in the leading positions in this group of states (Table 1.8).

Colleges by Area

College-area ratio speaks of spatial justice. The national average being eleven colleges per 1000 km^2, among major states, it ranged from a high of thirty in Kerala to low of only one in Jammu & Kashmir. For Union territories, on the whole, this average was of 29 colleges and for small states it was just two colleges (Table 1.7).

In ten states, namely Kerala, Haryana, Uttar Pradesh, Punjab, Telangana, Tamil Nadu, Karnataka, Andhra Pradesh, Maharashtra and West Bengal, this ratio was higher than or equal to the national average (Fig.1.2). Locationally, five of them were located in the south, three in the north of the country and one each in western and eastern India (Table 1.7).

The average for major states being 12 college per ten thousand persons, there were only nine major states which had higher number than this. Interestingly, Uttar Pradesh ranked third after Kerala and Haryana from the top. Five major states including Kerala, Haryana, Uttar Pradesh, Punjab and Telangana had this ratio of 20 or more colleges per thousand km^2 area. In other words, in these five states there is one college available within the radius of less than four kilometres.

Interestingly, West Bengal, Madhya Pradesh and Bihar, fared very poorly in the case of universities-area ratio, we find them better positioned within the group of states having a college-area ratio less than that of major states average.

Further, it is to be noted here that the hill states of Himachal Pradesh and Uttarakhand, having top positions in case of university-area and

Table 1.7: Major States: Area and population served by colleges in India, 2013-14

S. No.	Major States	Number of Colleges per	
		Thousand km^2	Ten thousand persons
1	2	3	4
1.	Andhra Pradesh	16	4
2.	Assam	7	1
3.	Bihar	7	1
4.	Chhattisgarh	5	2
5.	Gujarat	10	3
6.	Haryana	25	3
7.	Himachal Pradesh	5	4
8.	Jammu & Kashmir	1	2
9.	Jharkhand	4	1
10.	Karnataka	17	4
11.	Kerala	30	4
12	Madhya Pradesh	7	2
13.	Maharashtra	15	3
14.	Odisha	7	2
15.	Punjab	20	3
16.	Rajasthan	8	3
17.	Tamil Nadu	19	3
18.	Uttar Pradesh	23	2
19.	Uttarakhand	8	3
20.	West Bengal	11	1
21.	Telangana	20	5
	Major States	12	3
	India	11	3
	Small States	2	2
	Union Territories	29	1

Source: As Table 1.2.

university-population ratios fared poorly in the case of colleges. Against this, Uttar Pradesh ranked at the third place after Kerala and Haryana in college-area ratio but ranked seventh in university-area ratio among major states. On the whole, all the five major states from south India along with Haryana, and Punjab from north-west fared very well in college-area ratio. Against this, quite the opposite was true of Jammu & Kashmir, Jharkhand, Himachal Pradesh, and Chhattisgarh.

Colleges by Population

On an average, there were three colleges per ten thousand persons in

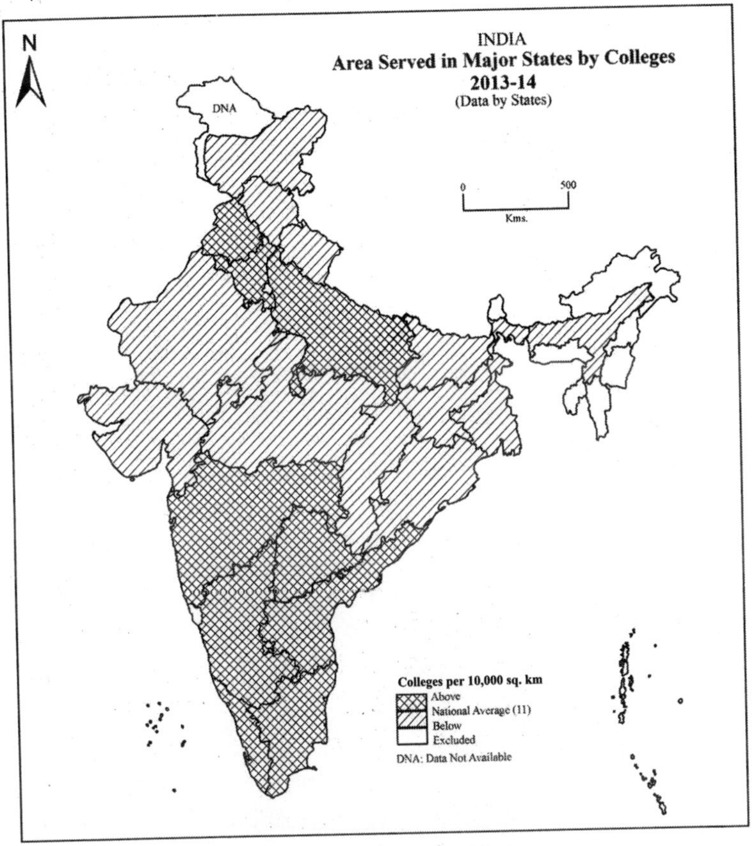

Fig. 1.2: India: Area served in Major States by Colleges.

Source: As Figure 1.0.

India. The ratio ranged from a high of five colleges in Telangana to low of only one in as many as four states of Assam, Bihar, Jharkhand and West Bengal. For Union territories, as a whole, this ratio was one college per 10,000 person. For small states, this ratio was the same in the case of major states (Table 1.7).

In five major states of Andhra Pradesh, Himachal Pradesh, Karnataka, Kerala and Telangana, this ratio was of four or more. On the other side of the scale, in four states of Himachal Pradesh, Jharkhand, Chhattisgarh and Jammu & Kashmir, this ratio was one-half of the average for the major states. In case of Jammu & Kashmir, it is quite surprising to state that there was only one college per 1000 km^2 area. It means that in the state there was only one college available within a radius of about 18 km. It is really a seriously deplorable situation, needing immediate action to rectify the situation.

Except Himachal Pradesh all other states in this group were from south of India. (Fig. 1.3)

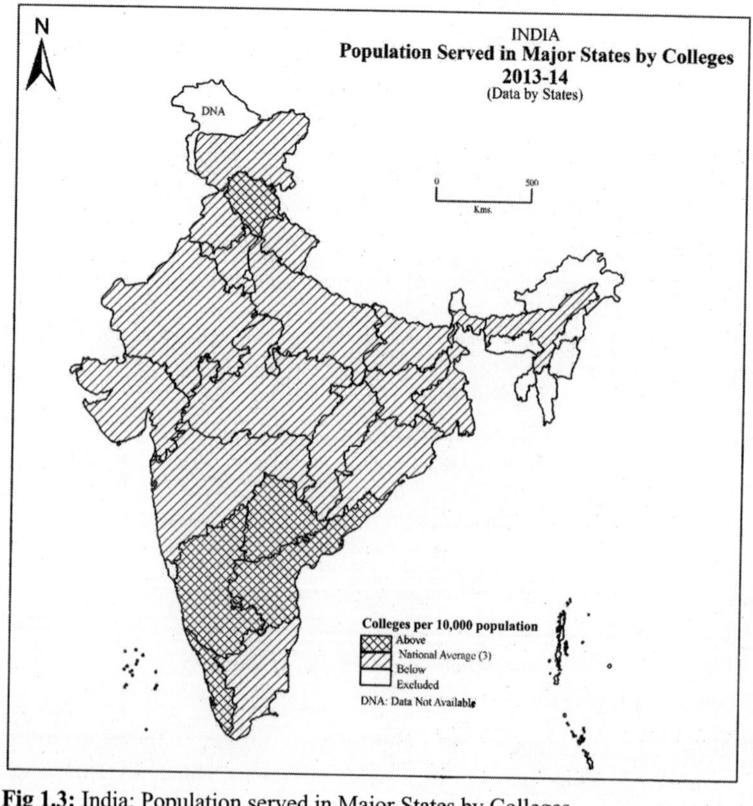

Fig 1.3: India: Population served in Major States by Colleges.

Source: As Figure 1.0.

On the other side of the scale, in four states of Assam, Bihar, Jharkhand, and West Bengal this ratio was of one college per 10,000 population, indicating a very high deficiency of colleges in terms of population. In other words, availability of colleges in terms of population was gravely scarce in these states. People living in the remote areas and densely populated areas of these states must be facing hardship to have access to higher education institutions (Table 1.8).

Table 1.8: Higher Education: Himachal Pradesh among major and hill states of India, 2013-14

S. No.		*Characterization*
1.	●	Since independence India has made a significant progress in higher education. India was next only to China in the world. Still, distribution of universities and colleges in country displayed wide regional and inter-state inequalities. Southern India had an edge over all the regions followed by western-India, the two together had more than two-fifth share of total number of universities, against their two-fifth share of population.
	●	Himachal Pradesh was in the most comfortable position as it enjoyed the ratio of two shares of universities and population. North-central and eastern region were highly deficient in the same. Unevenness in university-population ratio pushes the students from deficient regions to surplus regions.
	●	In regard to colleges-population ratio, southern region held a superior position followed again by the western region. Again the eastern region was followed by north-central region and both were highly deficient regions. North-western region has almost balanced situation.
	●	Himachal Pradesh ranked top in university-population ratio. It has more than three times higher availability of universities than the population. In addition to it, Uttarakhand, Haryana, Rajasthan and Jammu & Kashmir had received huge private investment in higher education. In regard to colleges, Himachal Pradesh was placed at fourth position among 21 major states in India and within north-western India it was next only to Haryana.
	●	The national average was three universities after each ten thousand km^2 area, it ranged from a high of seven universities in Haryana to a low of only one university in four states of Jammu & Kashmir, Madhya Pradesh, Maharashtra and Odisha. Inter-state differentials among the major states were much varied in university-population ratio than university-area ratio. The average for major states being two universities after half a million population, it ranged from a high of 15 universities in Himachal Pradesh to only one university in three states of Bihar, Uttar Pradesh and West Bengal. On the whole, three major states of Haryana, Himachal Pradesh and Uttarakhand had this average of more than six universities.
	●	The national average was 11 colleges per thousand km^2 area, interestingly, Uttar Pradesh ranked third after Kerala and Haryana in the category of major states. In five major states, namely, Kerala, Haryana, Uttar Pradesh, Punjab and Telangana, this ratio was 20 or more colleges or one college available within a radius of less than four kilometres of area. Against this, in four states of Himachal Pradesh, Jharkhand, Chhattisgarh and Jammu & Kashmir this average was of even less than one-half of the average for the major states.

	•	As per the composite index of area and population ratio with universities and colleges in the major states, Haryana ranked at top and Jharkhand at the bottom, indicating Haryana has the highest availability of universities and colleges. Himachal Pradesh falls in the category of high availability states along with Kerala, Tamil Nadu, Telangana, Haryana and Uttarakhand. All these states benefitted from the private investments in higher education after the phase of privatization.
	•	GER of higher education at the state level reveals that Tamil Nadu was at top and Chhattisgarh at the bottom. Himachal Pradesh was placed fifth among 21 major states of India. It was only in the case of five states of Jammu & Kashmir, Kerala, Punjab, Tamil Nadu and Uttarakhand, the female GER was higher than that of males. In Himachal Pradesh male GER was only marginally higher than that of females.
	•	In teacher-student ratio, Karnataka and Tamil Nadu were at the top with one teacher after 14 students, four states of Uttar Pradesh, Bihar, Rajasthan and Jharkhand fared at the bottom with one teacher after 50 students. Himachal Pradesh ranked third along with Maharashtra and Chhattisgarh.
	•	As per a composite index of accessibility prepared on three indices of GER, women enrolment, teacher-pupil ratio it emerged that Tamil Nadu ranked at the top and Bihar at the bottom. Himachal Pradesh ranked sixth. Except Punjab, all the other states having higher rank, except Himachal Pradesh, belonged to the south of India.
2.	•	A comparison of Himachal Pradesh with other Indian hill states is highly revealing where in university-population ratio Himachal Pradesh ranked third after Sikkim and Arunachal Pradesh, in college-population ratio, college-area served ratio and college-population served ratio it fared at the top among all the hill states. As per composite index of area and population served by universities and colleges in hill states, Himachal Pradesh was at the third position after Sikkim and Uttarakhand.
	•	On other parameters such as GER, women enrolment ratio, and teacher-pupil ratio, Himachal Pradesh ranked third, second, second, respectively among the hill category of states. The composite index of accessibility of higher education in Himachal Pradesh enjoyed third position among 10 hill states. It was followed by the Manipur and Sikkim. Arunachal Pradesh was at the bottom, with wide margin. Manipur in GER and Sikkim in teacher-pupil ratio did exceedingly well among the hill states.

Regional Inequality in Levels of Higher Education

A composite picture arrived at, with the help of area and population indicators separately for universities and colleges, has been discussed in the following. A weighted index, prepared with the help of these four indicators, has been calculated for all the 21 major states. The highest score value on different indicators has been assigned a value of 100 and the other values were give proportionate to 100. The scores on different indicators for individual states were summed up and divided by the total number of indicators, four, in this case, to arrive at composite index.

Levels of Higher Education

There are wide inter-state differentials in the distribution of colleges and universities among major states of India. The index value ranged from a maximum of 70.1 for Haryana to a minimum of only 14.9 for Jharkhand, giving a range difference of 55.3 (Table 1.9). The index value of the state at the top is nearly five times higher that of the state at the bottom.

Table 1.9: Major States: Indices of Area and population served by colleges and universities, 2013-14

S. No.	*Major States*	*Universities*		*Colleges*		*Total*	*Composite*
		Area	*Pop.*	*Area*	*Pop.*		*Index*
1	2	3	4	5	6	7	8
1.	Haryana	100.0	33.07	83.82	63.74	280.66	70.16
2.	Kerala	66.09	19.29	100.0	67.14	252.50	63.13
3.	Himachal Pradesh	58.93	100.0	17.94	70.03	246.90	61.73
4.	Uttarakhand	64.01	65.33	25.87	60.74	215.96	53.99
5.	Tamil Nadu	63.62	25.37	63.84	58.55	211.37	52.84
6.	Telangana	24.84	16.13	67.01	100.0	207.98	51.99
7.	Punjab	62.32	21.84	66.81	53.85	204.82	51.21
8.	Karnataka	33.47	20.65	58.25	82.66	195.03	48.76
9.	Andhra Pradesh	24.04	15.77	54.10	81.62	175.53	43.88
10.	Uttar Pradesh	36.71	8.88	76.27	42.43	164.30	41.07
11.	Maharashtra	20.86	11.35	49.33	61.72	143.26	35.81
12.	Rajasthan	26.26	25.88	27.36	62.02	141.52	35.38
13.	Gujarat	31.98	21.01	33.43	50.50	136.93	34.23
14.	West Bengal	43.40	8.36	37.46	16.59	105.81	26.45
15.	Chhattisgarh	22.16	23.80	16.75	41.38	104.09	26.02
16.	Madhya Pradesh	18.05	15.50	23.39	46.19	103.12	25.78
17.	Assam	32.74	16.84	23.06	27.30	99.94	24.98
18.	Odisha	19.24	15.13	23.13	41.83	99.33	24.83
19.	Jammu & Kashmir	15.48	26.15	10.89	42.30	94.81	23.70
20.	Bihar	31.81	6.84	25.23	12.48	76.37	19.09
21.	Jharkhand	21.47	11.34	12.02	14.60	59.44	14.86

Source: Calculated from the Table 1.6 and 1.7

Six major states, having an index value of 52.0 and above have been assigned high level of higher education availability. Six states falling in this group include Kerala, Tamil Nadu, Telangana, Haryana, Himachal Pradesh and Uttarakhand. The former three are from the south and the latter three from the north India.

A variety of factors including privatization of higher education, slow growth of population and historical reasons are responsible for high level of higher education availability in this category of states. The locational advantage in the case of Haryana, Himachal Pradesh, and Uttarakhand has attracted the private investors to invest in higher education by opening new technical and professional colleges and universities in these states after Indian parliament passed a policy opening the gates of higher education to private investors.

This Act was subsequently passed by different state assemblies to pave the way for the private sector. In southern states of Kerala, Tamil Nadu and Telangana, historical factors combined with early privatization of higher education especially the college education were responsible (Fig.1.4).

In Kerala Christian missionaries opened schools quite earlier, providing boost to development of higher education there. Moreover, the princely ruler of Travancore state during pre-Independence period promoted education for the benefit of his subjects. On the other side, Government of Tamil Nadu opened several new government colleges in backward and remote pockets of the state.

In newly born state of Telangana supply-side has become so strong after privatization that several technical and professional colleges were forced to close in face of dwindling demand. A newspaper reported that in wake of poor employability conditions, the two states of Tamil Nadu and Telangana are shutting professional and technical courses, including those in management education (see Livemint e-paper, September, 2015). The AICTE has allowed the discontinuation of 757 such courses. The technical and professional courses/departments that have been allowed to shut, the overwhelming majority (556) was of engineering courses followed by pharmacy (89), computer applications (57) and management (54) courses. Likewise, Maharashtra B-schools applied for closing of nearly 32 departments. In another state of Rajasthan, there were 14 such applications.

Seven states where composite index value ranged between 34.0 and 52.0 come under the moderate category. These included Punjab, Karnataka, Andhra Pradesh, Uttar Pradesh, Maharashtra, Rajasthan, and Gujarat. It is interesting to note that rapid growth of higher education institutions

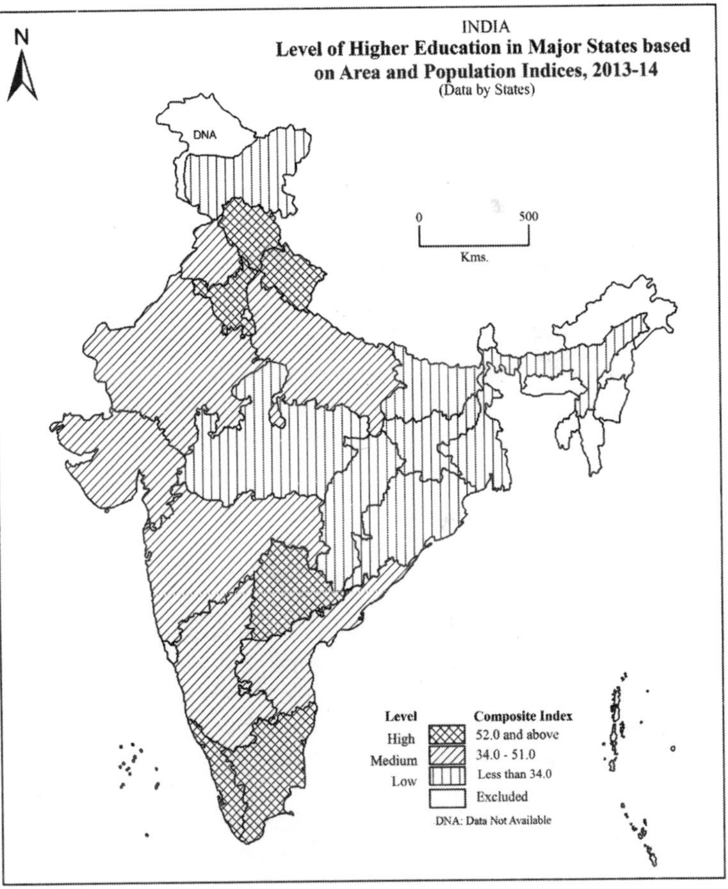

Fig. 1.4: India: Level of Higher Education in Major States based on area and population indices, 2013-14.

Source: As Figure 1.0.

under privatization wave places the states of Uttar Pradesh and Rajasthan in moderate category of higher education institutions.

The remaining eight states, where composite index value ranged less than 34.0, fell in low level of higher education institutions. Except Jammu & Kashmir, all these states were located in eastern or north eastern India. These states have relatively large share of scheduled population (castes and tribes), and Muslim minority along with high incidence of poverty. Private investment in higher education is also low in these states.

Gross Enrolment Ratio

Gross enrolment ratio (GER), computed here as a ratio between persons enrolled in higher education divided by total population in 18-23 age-group and multiplied by hundred, has been used in studies as a popular ratio to measure educational development in a country or region. However, it is a static concept as drop-outs at different stages of higher education are not taken into consideration.

According to All India Survey on Higher Education, published in 2015, GER for India as a whole was only about 21.0 per cent in the year 2013-2014. With this GER ratio, India was lagging far behind some select countries such as United States (95), Russia (77), United Kingdom (61), France (57), Malaysia (36) and China (24) (UNESCO, 2011). The average GER of India was not only low but also there were wide regional disparities.

Within the group of major states, GER ratio ranged from a high of 35.5 per cent in Tamil Nadu to a low of only 12.4 per cent in Chhattisgarh, giving a difference of three times between the high and low of the states (Table 1.10). On the whole, nearly three-fifths or 57.0 per cent of the major states have GER ratio higher than the national average (20.8%). The three states of Tamil Nadu, Telangana, and Uttarakhand, where GER ratio ranged between 30.0 and 36.0 per cent were in the top group, categorized as high GER ratio states. A variety of factors including high enrolment ratio in school education, in-migration of students from neighbouring states for higher education in privately managed professional and technical colleges and universities and relatively higher enrolment of the female population in 18-23 age-group are responsible for this.

Another nine major states, where GER ratio ranged between 20-29 per cent, are categorized into the moderate category. These include Andhra Pradesh, Himachal Pradesh, Haryana, Jammu & Kashmir, Maharashtra, Karnataka, Kerala, Uttar Pradesh and Punjab. None of them belonged to east or north-east India. The remaining nine states, where GER ranged between 12-20 per cent, fall in the low GER category. Including in this group are Rajasthan, Gujarat, Madhya Pradesh, West Bengal, Assam, Odisha, Bihar, Jharkhand, and Chhattisgarh. Most of them are located in a western, eastern and central part of India. Large and rapidly growing population coupled with low per capita income are the characteristics of majority of states in the category. Gujarat, otherwise a developed state needs further explanation for low GER ratio. Its GER ratio of 16.7 per cent places it at 14th rank from the top among 21 major states. Higher

Table 1.10: Major States: Gross enrolment ratio (in%) in higher education, 2013-14

S. No.	*Major States*	*Male*	*Female*	*Total*
1	2	3	4	5
1.	Tamil Nadu	34.47	36.61	35.54
2.	Telangana	36.06	30.26	33.18
3.	Uttarakhand	29.02	33.19	31.06
4.	Andhra Pradesh	31.96	24.65	28.32
5.	Himachal Pradesh	25.94	26.09	26.01
6.	Haryana	24.74	24.54	24.65
7.	Jammu & Kashmir	22.83	25.35	24.05
8.	Maharashtra	24.02	21.57	22.87
9.	Karnataka	22.41	22.66	22.53
10.	Kerala	18.77	25.88	22.34
11.	Uttar Pradesh	19.51	22.88	21.06
12.	Punjab	17.95	24.69	21.05
13.	Rajasthan	19.93	17.91	18.98
14.	Gujarat	17.61	15.69	16.71
15.	Madhya Pradesh	18.25	14.91	16.69
16.	West Bengal	16.79	14.15	15.48
17.	Assam	15.23	14.36	14.79
18.	Odisha	14.97	13.76	14.36
19.	Bihar	14.34	11.95	13.24
20.	Jharkhand	13.56	12.66	13.12
21.	Chhattisgarh	12.76	11.96	12.36
	India	21.00	21.19	20.78
	Major states	20.62	20.84	20.37
	Small States	21.25	21.51	20.98
	Union Territories	41.09	38.83	43.88

Source: As Table 1.2.

education in the Gujarat has concentrated in few districts and particularly new colleges of pharmacy and engineering. State education authorities have also admitted that Gujarat is traditionally lagging behind in terms of higher education (Shukla, S., 2009).

Male-female differentials in GER ratio are quite narrow within states as well as at the national level. Female GER ratio of 21.2 per cent at the national level was marginally higher than male GER ratio (21.0%). Tamil Nadu, Uttarakhand, Himachal Pradesh, Jammu & Kashmir, Kerala, Uttar Pradesh and Punjab make the case of high female GER ratio as compared to their male counterparts. The opposite is true of Telangana, Andhra Pradesh, Maharashtra, Madhya Pradesh, and Bihar. The remaining states of Haryana, Karnataka, Rajasthan, Gujarat, West Bengal, Assam, Odisha, Jharkhand, and Chhattisgarh have marginal differences in male-female GER.

Nevertheless, inter-state differentials in female GER ratio are quite wide. These ranged from a high of 36.6 per cent in Tamil Nadu to a low of 11.95 in Bihar. Nine of 21 major states have lower female GER ratio than the national average of 21.2 per cent. In fact, the average GER for major states (20.8%) was lower than the national average. The union territories, which had the combined female GER ratio of 38.83 per cent, boosted the national average. On the whole, there is a high positive association between female and male GER at the state level. Generally, higher the male GER in the state, higher the female GER and *vice versa*. On the whole, Himachal Pradesh performed well on GER ratio among the major states of India. It is ranked fifth among the major states. The highest position was held by Tamil Nadu to be followed by Telangana, Uttarakhand, and Andhra Pradesh. The bottom five states were Assam, Odisha, Bihar, Chhattisgarh, and Jharkhand. GER and availability of higher education institutions found a strong positive association with each other, the rank correlation value being r = 0.76.

Women Enrolment in Higher Education

Women enrolment for the country as a whole was about 47.2 per cent in 2013-14. It is same for major states as a group (47.2%). For Union territories, as a whole, it was slightly high (47.9%). On the whole, small states (49.3%) were far better placed as compared to major states and union territories (Table 1.11).

Among the major states, as many as 16 states recorded the majority of males who were enrolled for higher education. Against this, there are only five states where women enrolment was higher than that of males. These included Jammu & Kashmir, Kerala, Punjab, Tamil Nadu, and Uttarakhand. In Himachal Pradesh, male enrolment was marginally higher than that of the females.

Teacher-Student Ratio

On an average, there was one teacher after 25 students in the field of higher education in India during the year 2013-14. The teacher-student ratio varied from roughly one teacher after 14 students in Karnataka and Tamil Nadu states to only one after 50 in each of the four states of Uttar Pradesh, Rajasthan, Bihar and Jharkhand. Calculated separately for union

Table 1.11: Major States: Women enrolment (in%) in higher education in India, 2013-14

S. No.	*Major States*	*Male*	*Female*
1	2	3	4
1.	Andhra Pradesh	56.68	43.32
2.	Assam	50.61	49.39
3.	Bihar	58.15	41.85
4.	Chhattisgarh	51.81	48.19
5.	Gujarat	56.01	43.99
6.	Haryana	54.54	45.46
7.	Himachal Pradesh	50.94	49.06
8.	Jammu & Kashmir	49.06	50.94
9.	Jharkhand	53.16	46.84
10.	Karnataka	51.25	48.75
11.	Kerala	41.79	58.21
12.	Madhya Pradesh	58.31	41.69
13.	Maharashtra	55.83	44.17
14.	Odisha	51.84	48.16
15.	Punjab	46.11	53.89
16.	Rajasthan	55.39	44.61
17.	Tamil Nadu	48.47	51.53
18.	Uttar Pradesh	50.14	49.86
19.	Uttarakhand	47.78	52.22
20.	West Bengal	54.78	45.22
21.	Telangana	54.69	45.31
	India	52.75	47.25
	Major states	52.78	47.22
	Small States	50.68	49.32
	Union Territories	52.10	47.90

Source: As Table 1.2.

territories, this ratio was one teacher after 33 students. In this way, Union territories, as a group, were poorly placed as compared to the states, as a whole, in this count (Table 1.12). In five states of Karnataka, Tamil Nadu, Punjab, Kerala and Odisha there was one teacher for each 17 students. Notably, three of them were located in south India.

In another nine or more than two-fifth of major states, there was one teacher for 20 to 25 students. These states included Maharashtra, Himachal Pradesh, Chhattisgarh, Telangana, Gujarat, Haryana, Andhra Pradesh, Madhya Pradesh, Maharashtra, and Assam. As per geographical distribution, they were spread over in almost all the parts of India. Chhattisgarh, Madhya Pradesh and Assam in this group are the states which lagged far behind in the distribution of the institutions of higher

Table 1.12: Major States: Teacher-pupil ratio in higher education, 2013-14

S. No.	*Major States*	*Teachers per 100 Students*
1	2	3
1.	Karnataka	7
2.	Tamil Nadu	7
3.	Punjab	6
4.	Kerala	6
5.	Odisha	6
6.	Maharashtra	5
7.	Himachal Pradesh	5
8.	Chhattisgarh	5
9.	Telangana	4
10.	Gujarat	4
11.	Haryana	4
12.	Andhra Pradesh	4
13.	Madhya Pradesh	4
14.	Assam	4
15.	West Bengal	3
16.	Uttarakhand	3
17.	Jammu & Kashmir	3
18.	Rajasthan	3
19.	Uttar Pradesh	2
20.	Bihar	2
21.	Jharkhand	2
	India	4
	Major states	4
	Small States	4
	Union Territories	3

Source: As Table 1.2

education. Himachal Pradesh was better placed state than the other states in this regard.

In Himachal Pradesh along with Maharashtra and Chhattisgarh, there were five teachers after each 100 students or one after 20 students. In remaining nine states, there was one teacher after 33 to 50 students. These states include West Bengal, Uttarakhand, Jammu & Kashmir, Rajasthan, Uttar Pradesh, Bihar, and Jharkhand, geographically distributed in the north-west and eastern India.

A composite picture arrived at, with the help of three different parameters of accessibility such as GER, Women enrolment ratio and teacher-pupil ratio has been discussed in the following. A weighted index, prepared with the help of three indicators, has been calculated for all the major states. The highest score has been assigned a value of 100 and the other values were obtained proportionate to 100. The scores on different indicators for individual states were summed up and divided by the total number of indicators, three, to arrive at the composite index.

The index value ranged from a maximum of 94.8 in Tamil Nadu and Bihar at the bottom with index value of only 44.6 (Table 1.13). The index value of the state at the top is nearly two times higher than that of the state at the bottom.

Table 1.13: Major States: Composite index of various parameters of accessibility in higher education, 2013-14

S. No.	Major States	GER	Women Enrolment	Teacher-Pupil ratio	Total	Composite Index
1	2	3	4	5	6	7
1.	Tamil Nadu	98.53	88.52	97.39	284.4	94.8
2.	Karnataka	62.48	83.75	100.01	246.2	82.1
3.	Kerala	61.87	100	83.42	245.3	81.8
4.	Punjab	58.82	92.58	86.39	237.8	79.3
5.	Telangana	92.00	77.84	62.78	232.6	77.5
6.	Himachal Pradesh	72.13	84.28	68.10	224.5	75.0
7.	Uttarakhand	86.18	89.71	39.60	215.5	71.8
8.	Andhra Pradesh	78.55	74.42	61.07	214	71.3
9.	Maharashtra	63.29	75.88	70.22	209.4	69.8
10.	Haryana	68.33	78.10	62.07	208.5	69.5
11.	Odisha	39.83	82.73	82.78	205.3	68.4
12.	Jammu & Kashmir	66.74	87.51	38.12	192.4	64.1
13.	Gujarat	46.24	75.57	62.29	184.1	61.4
14.	Chhattisgarh	34.28	82.79	65.11	182.2	60.7
15.	Assam	41.02	84.85	51.53	177.4	59.1
16.	Madhya Pradesh	46.10	71.62	59.39	177.1	59.0
17.	Uttar Pradesh	58.62	85.66	27.37	171.7	57.2
18.	Rajasthan	52.53	76.64	37.39	166.6	55.5
19.	West Bengal	42.92	77.68	39.91	160.5	53.5
20.	Jharkhand	36.37	80.47	24.19	141.0	47.0
21.	Bihar	36.55	71.89	25.42	133.9	44.6

Source: Ranking is based on the basis of Table 1.8, 1.9, 1.10 and 1.11.

6 of 21 major states having index value of 75.0 and above fall in high category states. These were distributed in south and north-west India. These included Tamil Nadu, Karnataka, Kerala, Telangana, Punjab and Himachal Pradesh (Fig 1.5). Himachal Pradesh ranked sixth among high category states. The early privatization of higher education in the states of Tamil

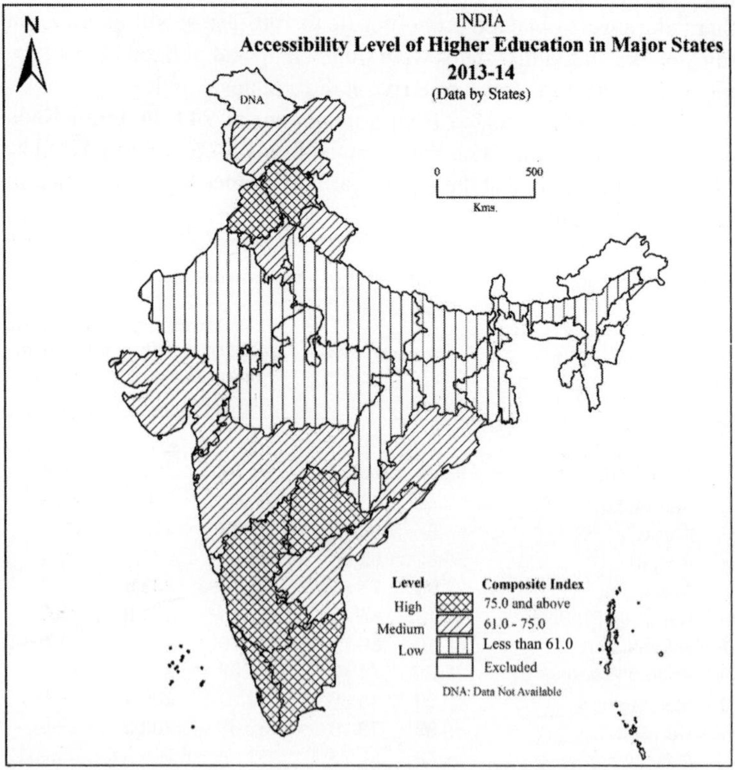

Fig. 1.5: India: Accessibility Level of Higher Education in Major States, 2013-14
Source: As Figure 1.0.

Nadu, Karnataka and Kerala were responsible for the higher accessibility in these states. Himachal Pradesh, socially developed state has higher enrolment ratio and women enrolment were responsible for higher and economically sound Punjab state for the higher women enrolment and teacher-pupil ratio have contributed to fall the same states in the high category.

On the other side of the scale, index value ranging between 61.0 and 75.0 fall in moderate category states. These include Uttarakhand, Andhra Pradesh, Maharashtra, Haryana, Odisha, Jammu & Kashmir and Gujarat. The states of Uttarakhand, Andhra Pradesh, Maharashtra and Haryana have higher number of private educational institutions. Two of them located in north and the other two in south India, no doubt these states attracted the students from the deficient area of educational institutions. The GER of Gujarat and Odisha have recorded very low, than the teacher-pupil ratio and women enrolment, attributed to these states in the moderate category. Andhra Pradesh, Uttarakhand and Jammu & Kashmir have low teacher-pupil ratio than the other two indicators.

Index value below 61.0 falls in low category of states. These included Chhattisgarh, Assam, Madhya Pradesh, Uttar Pradesh, Rajasthan, West Bengal, Jharkhand, and Bihar. Due to the high incidence of poverty, low per capita income, higher share of scheduled population and low private investment were responsible for fall in these states in the low category.

II. Himachal Pradesh among the Hill States

Distribution of Universities and Colleges

Hill states[4] include Jammu & Kashmir, Himachal Pradesh, Uttarakhand, in western Himalaya, and Arunachal Pradesh, Manipur, Meghalaya, Mizoram, Nagaland, Sikkim, and Tripura, in eastern Himalaya. These states differ in their development level and socio-cultural customs and traditions. States in western Himalayas have a patriarchal society, whereas matriarchal society predominates in eastern Himalayan states. Jammu & Kashmir is Muslim-dominated state, Himachal Pradesh, and Uttarakhand are dominated by the Hindus and states in eastern Himalaya by the Christian population. Christian missionaries were quite active in the spread of education among tribals of the eastern Himalayan states during the British rule in India. All these factors are bound to have their impact on the development of education in these states.

In the north-eastern region, the percentage of the tribal population is high in Arunachal Pradesh, Nagaland, Mizoram and Meghalaya, proportional share is more than fifty per cent. This region has seen many inter-ethnic conflicts and disturbances since the independence of the country in 1947.

Notwithstanding the unfavourable climatic conditions, hilly terrain and ethnic conflicts faced by this region, the literacy rate is more than the national average except in Arunachal Pradesh. Jammu & Kashmir in north-west India also has literacy level that is lower than the national average.

Universities: Himachal Pradesh among the Hill States

Uttarakhand and Himachal Pradesh get one-half of the total 94 universities situated in Indian hill states. It means the remaining one-half are distributed in the remaining eight hill states (Table.1.14).

Table 1.14: Distribution of universities: Himachal Pradesh and other hill states, 2013-14

S. No.	Hill States	Universities (in numbers)	% share in total universities	Population (%) 2011	Ratio b/w col. 4 & 5
1	2	3	4	5	6
1.	Sikkim	6	6.38	1.54	4.14
2.	Arunachal Pradesh	7	7.45	3.17	2.35
3.	Himachal Pradesh	23	24.47	14.92	1.64
4.	Meghalaya	10	10.64	6.74	1.58
5.	Mizoram	3	3.19	2.56	1.25
6.	Uttarakhand	24	25.53	23.82	1.07
7.	Nagaland	4	4.26	4.85	0.88
8.	Manipur	3	3.19	6.54	0.49
9.	Jammu & Kashmir	11	11.70	27.28	0.43
10.	Tripura	3	3.19	8.59	0.37
	All Hill States	94	100.00	100.00	1.00

Source: As Table 1.2.

In fact, universities find quite an uneven distribution among the hill states. Uttarakhand with 24 universities was at the top and three states of Mizoram, Nagaland and Tripura, each one having three universities were at the bottom. Bottom level four states of Tripura, Manipur, Nagaland and Mizoram, in combine, have less than one-seventh of the total number of universities in the hill states.

However, some of the hill states have only the small and sparsely distributed population sizes. For example, Sikkim shares 6.4 per cent of total number of universities in the hill states against 1.54 per cent of their total population. In contrast, Manipur having 3.2 per cent of the total number of universities contained 6.54 per cent population of the hill states.

Jammu & Kashmir makes another case where 11.70 per cent of the total number of universities is located against 27.28 per cent of the total population. On the whole, Tripura, Jammu & Kashmir and Manipur present a case of high mismatch between their population and the share of universities among hill states. The reverse is true of Sikkim, Arunachal Pradesh and Himachal Pradesh.

Colleges: Himachal Pradesh among the Hill States

Among the hill states of India, like the rest of the country colleges are the main pillars to spread higher education. In 2013-14, they numbered 1353, making fourteen times more than the universities of the hill states. There are, however, wide inter-state differentials in the distribution of colleges in the hill states. It ranged from a maximum of 410 colleges in Uttarakhand to a minimum of only 13 colleges in Sikkim (Table 1.15).

Three top ranking states namely Uttarakhand, Jammu & Kashmir and Himachal Pradesh, have more than 1000 colleges, these states together, had more than one-fourth share (76.4%) of the total colleges in the hill states. On the other side, Manipur, Nagaland and Meghalaya have, together, only 205 or 15.1 per cent of the total number of colleges of the hill states.

However, an examination of association between proportional shares of different hill states in the total population and the total number of colleges of hill states, presents a different picture.

Table 1.15: Distribution of colleges: Himachal Pradesh and other hill states, 2013-14

S. No.	*Hill States*	*Colleges (in numbers)*	*% share in total colleges*	*Population (%) 2011*	*Ratio b/w col. 4 & 5*
1	2	3	4	5	6
1.	Himachal Pradesh	**296**	**21.88**	**14.92**	1.47
2.	Uttarakhand	410	30.30	23.82	1.27
3.	Manipur	83	6.13	6.54	0.94
4.	Nagaland	60	4.43	4.85	0.91
5.	Jammu & Kashmir	327	24.17	27.28	0.89
6.	Mizoram	29	2.14	2.56	0.84
7.	Meghalaya	62	4.58	6.74	0.68
8.	Sikkim	13	0.96	1.54	0.62
9.	Arunachal Pradesh	26	1.92	3.17	0.61
10.	Tripura	47	3.47	8.59	0.40
	All Hill States	1353	100.00	100.00	1.00

Source: As Table 1.2.

The college-population ratio between the two shares ranged from a high of 1.5:1 in Himachal Pradesh to a low of only 0.40:1 in Tripura. In other words, the share of number of colleges that belonged to Himachal Pradesh was nearly twice of its share in the total population of Indian hill states. Against this, Tripura's share in colleges was about less than one-half of its share of population. Himachal Pradesh ranks first amongst all the hill states. Here, the ratio of colleges was nearly one and a half times more of its share in the total population of all the hill states.

On the other hand, five hill states, whose share in population was more than their respective shares in the number of colleges, were all, except Jammu & Kashmir, located in the eastern region. Jammu & Kashmir, a western Himalayan state, and Mizoram, a eastern Himalayan state are the two states where shares in the total number of colleges were four-fifths of their respective shares in total population of the hill states. On the other side, Meghalaya, Sikkim, and Arunachal Pradesh though have, all together, 101 colleges, making about eight per cent of the total colleges in hill states. Their combined share in the total population of hill states comes to about 12 per cent. The biggest mismatch between the two shares has been found in case of Tripura, Arunachal Pradesh and Sikkim. While, the opposite is true of Himachal Pradesh and Uttarakhand.

Briefly, there are wide inter-state variations in the distribution of colleges among the hill states of India. On the whole, hill states, located in the western Himalayas particularly Himachal Pradesh and Uttarakhand were favourably placed in the distribution of colleges. Himachal Pradesh, in fact, stands at the top among all the hill states both in colleges and universities. Majority of hill states suffer from the mismatch between their respective shares in colleges/universities and population. From these states students migrate to states in the western and southern India along with NCR Delhi and Chandigarh (U.T.) for higher education. Political stability and poor law and order condition created due to militancy and insurgency has also contributed to this. Parents want to send their kids for education to safer and peaceful places.

Availability and Accessibility of Higher Education

An examination of the availability of higher education in terms of area and population will be followed by accessibility in terms of gross enrolment, women enrolment, and teacher-pupil ratio.

Universities by Area and Population

Calculated per ten thousand square kilometres areas of states, there were, on average, two universities at the national level during 2013-14. This ratio was the same for the hill states during the same period. Among hill states, the number of universities per ten thousand km^2 area varied from a high of eight in Sikkim to low of one in the four states of Jammu & Kashmir, Arunachal Pradesh, Manipur, and Mizoram (Table 1.16).

In four states of Sikkim, Uttarakhand, Himachal Pradesh and Meghalaya, there were four or more universities after 10,000 km^2. In majority of (6 of 10) the hill states this average ranged between <3.0 and <1.0. All but one is located in the eastern Himalaya.

At the national level, there was only one university after one lakh persons, i.e. lower than the hill state average of two universities after lakh persons in 2013-14. The number of universities per lakh persons ranged from a high of seven in Sikkim to low of one in three states of Jammu & Kashmir, Manipur and Tripura. In four states of Arunachal Pradesh, Meghalaya, Sikkim and Himachal Pradesh, there were three or more universities after one lakh persons. In majority of (8 of 10) the hill states this average ranged between <3.0 and <1.0.

Table 1.16: Area and Population served by universities: Himachal Pradesh and other hill states, 2013-14

S. No.	*Hill States*	*Universities per*	
		Ten thousand km^2	*Lakh persons*
1	2	3	4
1.	Jammu & Kashmir	1	1
2.	Arunachal Pradesh	1	4
3.	Manipur	1	1
4.	Meghalaya	4	3
5.	Mizoram	1	2
6.	Nagaland	2	2
7.	Sikkim*	8	7
8.	Tripura	3	1
9.	Uttarakhand	4	2
10.	Himachal Pradesh	4	3
	All Hill States	2	2
	All India	2	1

Source: As Table 1.2.

Notes: *Anomaly in data calculation of university-area ratio could not be controlled since area of Sikkim is so small. Actual number of universities in Sikkim is only six.

On the other side of the scale, majority of hill states from north-east India fared poorly on both the indicators of availability, area and population. From these states students migrate to other parts of India for higher education.

Colleges by Area and Population

There were three colleges per 1000 km^2 area in hill states. Against this, the national average was 11 colleges per 1000 km^2 area. Evidently, hill states do suffer a lot on this count, especially in the context of their physiographic conditions. Within hill states, there were wide inter-state variations. It ranged from a high of eight colleges in Uttarakhand to a low of 0.31 per thousand km^2 in Arunachal Pradesh (Table 1.17). Himachal Pradesh has this ratio of five colleges.

Table 1.17: Area and Population served by colleges: Himachal Pradesh and other hill states, 2013-14

S. No.	*Hill States*	*Colleges per*	
		Thousand km^2	*Ten thousand persons*
1	2	3	4
1.	Jammu & Kashmir	3	2
2.	Arunachal Pradesh	0*	2
3.	Manipur	4	2
4.	Meghalaya	3	2
5.	Mizoram	1	2
6.	Nagaland	4	2
7.	Sikkim	2	2
8.	Tripura	4	1
9.	Uttarakhand	8	3
10.	Himachal Pradesh	5	4
	All Hill States	3	3
	All India	11	3

Source: As Table 1.2.

Notes: *Figure less than 0.50 are ignored and above it rounded up to the nearest number, Arunachal Pradesh recorded 0.31.

In the two states of Uttarakhand and Himachal Pradesh, there were five or more universities per thousand kilometres. Notably, these were located in Western Himalaya.

The remaining eight states have this average ranging between <4.0 and <1.0. These states were located in the north-east India with the exception of Jammu & Kashmir. On the whole, the majority of the states have relatively low colleges ratio per thousand km^2 than the state of Himachal Pradesh.

When it comes to college-population ratio, situation was entirely different. The national average and the average for hill states happen to be the same, that is, three colleges per ten thousand persons in the age group of 18-23. Within the group of hill states, there was a wide variation in this context. It ranged from a high of four colleges in Himachal Pradesh to a low of only one college per ten thousand persons in Tripura.

On the whole, there is a huge similarity on this count amongst the vast majority of hill states. Seven of ten hill states have this average of two colleges after ten thousand persons. Six of these were from north-east India and the seventh one was Jammu & Kashmir from north-west region.

A composite index of availability of higher education based on area and population is quite revealing. Sikkim obtained the highest rank and Arunachal Pradesh, the lowest rank among the hill states (Table 1.18).

Table 1.18: Hill States: Availability of higher education in terms of area and population served, 2013-14

S. No.	*Hill States*	*Universities*		*Colleges*		*Total*	*Composite Score*
		Area	*Pop.*	*Area*	*Pop.*		
1	2	3	4	5	6	7	8
1.	Sikkim	100	100	24	43	266.3	66.6
2.	Uttarakhand	53	26	100	87	265.5	66.4
3.	Himachal Pradesh	49	40	69	100	257.7	64.4
4.	Meghalaya	53	38	36	46	173.1	43.3
5.	Nagaland	29	21	47	62	159.2	39.8
6.	Manipur	16	12	48	64	140.1	35.0
7.	Tripura	34	9	58	28	128.8	32.2
8.	Jammu & Kashmir	13	10	42	60	125.6	31.4
9.	Mizoram	17	30	18	57	122.0	30.5
10.	Arunachal Pradesh	10	57	4	41	111.8	28.0

Source: Ranking is based on the basis of Table 1.16 and 1.17.

On the whole, three states of Sikkim, Uttarakhand and Himachal Pradesh fall in higher level of availability of higher education among all the hill states (Fig. 1.6). The same states have the higher number of educational institutes.

In contrast, Tripura, Jammu & Kashmir, Mizoram, and Arunachal Pradesh are placed at lower level in this context. Meghalaya, Nagaland and Manipur are placed in the moderate category.

Gross Enrolment Ratio of Higher Education

The average GER for hill states (25%) was higher than the national average (20.8%). Within the group of hill states, GER ranged from a 36.0 per cent in Manipur to a low of only 16.4 per cent in Arunachal Pradesh, giving a difference of two times between the high and low states (Table 1.19). On the whole, nearly one-half of the states have GER higher than the national average. Three states were above the average of the hill states. Manipur,

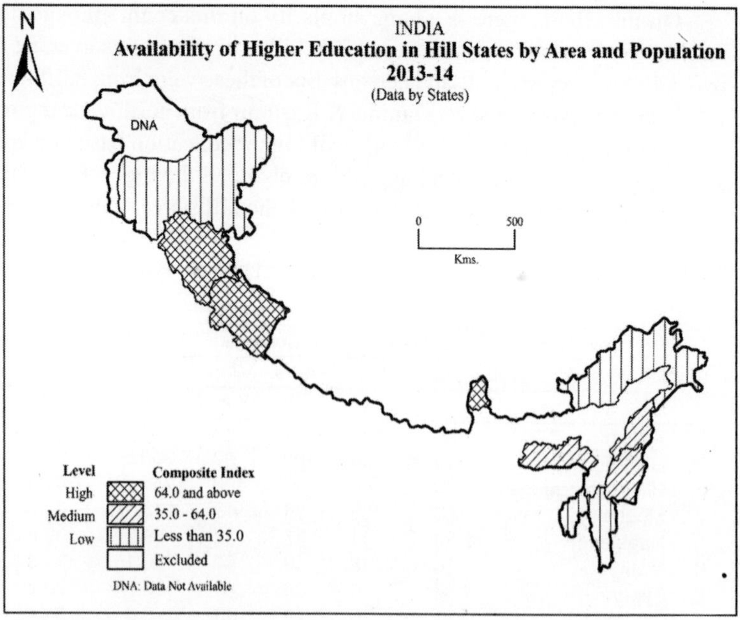

Fig. 1.6: India: Availability of Higher Education in Hill States by area and population, 2013-14.

Source: As Fig. 1.0.

Uttarakhand and Himachal Pradesh having GER between 26.0 and 36.0 per cent are placed in the higher category of GER.

Another three states, where GER ranged between 20.8 to 24.8 per cent, are categorized into the moderate category. These include Sikkim, Jammu & Kashmir and Mizoram.

The remaining four states, where GER ranged between 14.5 to 18.5 per cent, fall in the low category of states. Included in this, these are Meghalaya, Arunachal Pradesh, Nagaland and Tripura. Particularly these states are located in the eastern Himalayas. Notably the female GER of western Himalayan states was far higher than those of the eastern Himalayan states.

In addition, Sikkim and Manipur are also observed with the higher female GER than the GER of males. The rest of the states, i.e. Arunachal Pradesh, Mizoram, Meghalaya, Nagaland, and Tripura recorded higher enrolment ratio for males than enrolment ratio of females. The western Himalayan states have the higher female GER than the eastern states of India.

Table 1.19: Hill States: Gross enrolment ratio in higher education, 2013-14

S. No.	*Hill States*	*Male*	*Female*	*Total*
1	2	3	4	5
1.	Manipur	35.96	36.08	36.02
2.	Uttarakhand	29.02	33.19	31.06
3.	Himachal Pradesh	25.94	26.09	26.01
4.	Sikkim	23.18	26.46	24.77
5.	Jammu & Kashmir	22.83	25.35	24.05
6.	Mizoram	21.66	19.95	20.80
7.	Meghalaya	19.04	17.96	18.50
8.	Arunachal Pradesh	18.52	14.31	16.43
9.	Nagaland	16.17	13.41	14.82
10.	Tripura	16.94	12.11	14.48
	All Hill States	24.43	25.54	24.97
	All India	21.00	21.19	20.79

Source: As Table 1.2.

At the national and the hill state average the male-female differential in GER was almost equal to each other. Five of the 10 hill states recorded higher female GER than their male counterparts. These included Manipur, Uttarakhand, Himachal Pradesh, Sikkim and Jammu & Kashmir. Remaining five states had lower female GER (Mizoram, Meghalaya, Arunachal Pradesh, Nagaland and Tripura).

On the whole, Himachal Pradesh among the hill states performed well as it ranked third from the top position. The highest rank was attained by Manipur, and it was followed by Uttarakhand. These two states are ahead of Himachal Pradesh. The bottom three states are Meghalaya, Nagaland, and Tripura.

Women Enrolment in Hill States of India

In the year 2013-14, women share in the hill states (50.32%) was higher than the same at the national level (47.25%). Five of the hill states recorded that majority of males had enrolled in higher education. These states were Himachal Pradesh, Meghalaya, Mizoram, Nagaland and Tripura. Against this, one-half of the hill states had higher female enrolment in higher education, including Arunachal Pradesh, Jammu & Kashmir, Manipur and Sikkim (Table 1.20).

Table 1.20: Hill States: Women enrolment in higher education, 2013-14

S. No.	*Hill States*	*Male*	*Female*
1	2	3	4
1.	Arunachal Pradesh	47.69	52.31
2.	Himachal Pradesh	50.94	49.06
3.	Jammu & Kashmir	49.06	50.94
4.	Manipur	49.13	50.87
5.	Meghalaya	50.74	49.26
6.	Mizoram	51.80	48.20
7.	Nagaland	55.61	44.39
8.	Sikkim	48.42	51.58
9.	Tripura	57.38	42.62
10.	Uttarakhand	47.78	52.22
	All Hill States	**49.68**	**50.32**
	All India	**52.75**	**47.25**

Source: As Table 1.2.

Western Himalayan states have better share of female enrolment than the eastern states. Sikkim and Manipur have the higher share of female enrolment than their counterpart males. Several reasons have been identified for low female enrolment such as financial constraints, lack of infrastructure, to look after younger siblings and participate in the domestic activities, lack of educational environment at home. The parents think their daughters as the liabilities and it would be very difficult and costly to find out their comparable grooms if the daughters are given higher education.

Teacher-Student Ratio

On an average, there was one teacher after 25 higher education students in India during 2013-14. The average for hill states was also the same. Against this, teacher-student ratio varied from roughly one teacher after 17 students in Sikkim and Mizoram states to only one after 50 students in Arunachal Pradesh (Table 1.21). In two states of Sikkim and Mizoram, there was one teacher for 17 students. Both the states are located in the eastern Himalayas.

In another three states, there was one teacher after 20 students. These states included Nagaland, Himachal Pradesh and Manipur. In Tripura and Meghalaya, there was one teacher after 20 students and in Uttarakhand and Jammu & Kashmir; there was one teacher after 33 students. In most of the north-eastern states higher education institutions are still dependent on the teachers from outside the region as there are many reserved posts which remain

Table 1.21: Hill States: Teacher-pupil ratio, 2013-14

S. No.	*Hill States*	*Teachers per 100 Students*
1	2	3
1.	Sikkim	6
2.	Mizoram	6
3.	Nagaland	5
4.	Himachal Pradesh	5
5.	Manipur	5
6.	Tripura	4
7.	Meghalaya	4
8.	Uttarakhand	3
9.	Jammu & Kashmir	3
10.	Arunachal Pradesh	2
	All Hill States	4
	All India	4

Source: As Table 1.2.

vacant due to lack of availability of qualified candidates from those areas. On the other side, faculty come from the outside have always a tendency to quit the area and take up a job outside the region, if it is available. This is due to the limited scope for improvement, communication problems and to some extent the security reason (De, U.K. 2004: 12). The implication of the low teachers per students leads to dismal performance in these states. Due to the absence of the teachers, the classes are mostly held by the part-time teachers, who cannot take much interest as it does not guarantee their job.

A composite picture arrived at after the summation of values of each state on three different parameters of GER, Women enrolment and teacher-pupil ratio and divided by the number of parameters that is three, reveals that Manipur is at top with index value of 89.4 and Arunachal Pradesh at the bottom with only 58.5 index value. The range difference is 30.9 (Table 1.22).

In other words, the state at the top has a composite index value of two times higher than that of the state at the bottom. The states are categorized into three levels: high, moderate and low

Manipur recorded the highest rank among the hill states of India. Manipur is followed by Sikkim and Himachal Pradesh. There were wide variations in the levels of higher education among the hill states of India (Fig 1.7). Four of the ten hill states having index value between 89.0 and 79.0 are categorised as high. These are Manipur, Sikkim, Himachal Pradesh, and Mizoram. On all the parameters of higher education, they perform well. Interestingly, these four states have higher share of women

Table 1.22: Hill States: Composite index of various parameters of Accessibility in higher education, 2013-14

S. No.	Hill States	GER	Women Enrolment	Teachers per 100 Students	Total	Composite Index
1	2	3	4	5	6	7
1.	Manipur	100.0	97.2	71.0	268.2	89.4
2.	Sikkim	68.9	98.6	100.0	267.5	89.2
3.	Himachal Pradesh	72.2	93.8	77.0	243.0	81.0
4.	Mizoram	57.8	92.1	91.0	240.9	80.3
5.	Uttarakhand	86.3	99.8	45.0	231.1	77.0
6.	Jammu & Kashmir	66.8	97.4	43.0	207.2	69.1
7.	Nagaland	41.1	84.9	77.0	203.0	67.7
8.	Meghalaya	51.4	94.2	57.0	202.6	67.5
9.	Tripura	40.3	81.5	58.0	179.8	59.9
10.	Arunachal Pradesh	45.6	100.0	30.0	175.6	58.5

Source: Ranking is based on the basis of Table 1.19, 1.20 and 1.21.

enrolment than the other parameters and it contributed towards attaining the top four positions. Himachal Pradesh ranked at third place after Sikkim and Manipur (Fig. 1.7).

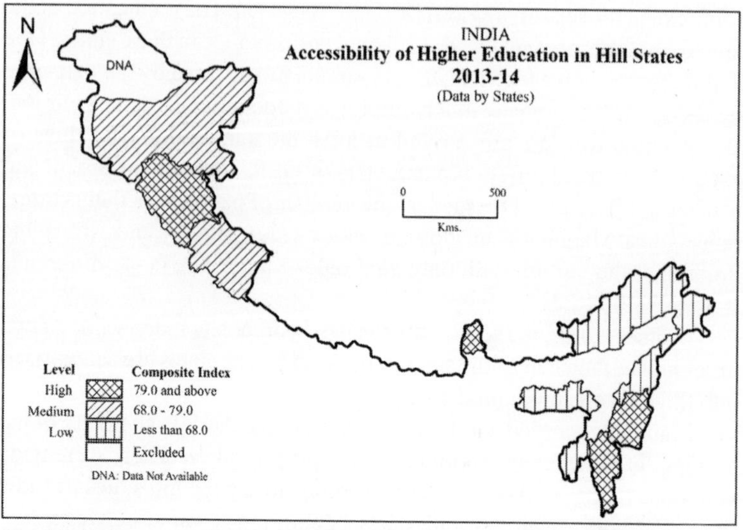

Fig. 1.7: India: Accessibility of Higher Education in Hill States, 2013-14.

Source: As Fig. 1.0.

States having the index value between 79.0 and 68.0 fall in moderate category. There were only two states in this category (Uttarakhand and Jammu & Kashmir). Here the teacher-pupil ratio recorded low than the women enrolment and GER.

Remaining four states having index value less than 68.0 fall in the low category of higher education accessibility. It included Nagaland, Meghalaya, Tripura and Arunachal Pradesh.

On the whole, the top three positions were held by Manipur, Sikkim and Himachal Pradesh, as per the criterion of higher education Himachal Pradesh holds third rank in the Hill states of India. On the other side, bottom three states are Meghalaya, Tripura and Arunachal Pradesh.

Main Highlights

- Ever since the Independence of the country in 1947, India has made a significant progress in higher education. With 25.9 million students enrolled for higher education, India was placed next only to China in the world. Since independence, the number of universities increased 24 times and that of the colleges by 53 times. However, maximum increase took place in the last about two and a half decades beginning with economic reforms of 1991 at the national level.
- 1981 and 2001 are the two critical breaks in numerical growth of higher education institutions in India. As many as 467 new universities were opened between 2001 and 2014 in India, recording an unprecedented annual growth of 7.7 per cent; and this number was nearly thrice of the total universities in India in the year 1981. The increase in the number of colleges was still spectacular, since the total number of new colleges coming between 2001 and 2014 was much higher than the total number of colleges in India in the year 2001.
- The robust growth of universities and colleges in India was, however, marked by wide regional and inter-state inequalities in their distribution. South India had an edge over all the regions of India and in combine with west India had 44.2 per cent of the number of total universities in India against their share of 40.8 per cent in the total population of the country. Against this, eastern and north-central regions were highly deficient in terms of ratios between their shares in total universities and total population of India. North-western India, where Himachal Pradesh is also located, was in the most comfortable position so far as the ratio

between the two shares of universities and population in the entire country are concerned.

- Such imbalances in university-population ratio push the students from deficient to surplus regions to migrate for higher education especially for technical and professional streams which is, certainly healthy from the angle of national integration, but at times leads to clashes tinged with ethnicity.
- In distribution of colleges, southern region holds superior position followed again by the western region. Against this, eastern region followed north-central region and both were highly deficient regions. North-western region had almost balancing situation between its ratio, of colleges and population. Southern region for its lead in technical and professional higher education streams attracts students from all parts of India especially highly deficient eastern region for higher education.
- Among major states, Himachal Pradesh ranked top in university-population ratio. The state had 3.2 per cent of total universities against less than one per cent (0.6%) of India's population; and the state in combination with Uttarakhand, Haryana, Rajasthan and Jammu & Kashmir procured more than one-fifth (21.0%) of the total number of universities against about its one-tenth (10.6%) share in total population of India. The former four states received huge private investment in higher education in post-liberalization period especially after 2001; private capitation and commercialization of higher education has induced sharp regional inequalities in the distribution of higher education institutions and has been instrumental making higher education costlier. Nevertheless, higher education has made inroads in backward and peripheral areas of the country.
- Five top ranking states, in combine, had more than one-half of the total number of colleges in India. The major states located in southern and western region of India were favourably placed against eastern and north-eastern regions. Himachal Pradesh was placed at fourth position amongst 21 major states of India and within north-western India it was next only to Haryana.
- Availability of higher education in terms of area and population terms varied widely among major states. Against the national average of three universities after each ten thousand km^2 area, it ranged from a high of seven in Haryana to a low of only one university in four states of Jammu & Kashmir, Madhya Pradesh

and Maharashtra and Odisha. Eight of 21 major states were placed above the national average and remaining 13 states below the same average. Majority of states had this average between <2.0 to <4.0 universities. States attracting higher private investment in higher education after privatization of higher education recorded higher number of universities in terms of area. Inter-state differentials among the major states were wider in university-population ratio than university-area ratio. The average for major states being two universities after half a million population, it ranged from a high of 15 universities in Himachal Pradesh to only one university in the three states of Bihar, Uttar Pradesh and West Bengal. On the whole, three major states of Haryana, Himachal Pradesh and Uttarakhand had this average of more than six universities. Himachal Pradesh having exceptionally high ratio of fifteen universities per half of a million population.

- Inter-state differentials in college-area and college-population ratio were much more revealing than that of the university-area and university-population ratio. Against the national average of 11 colleges per thousand km^2 area, the average for major states was of 12 colleges, for smaller states of only two colleges and for union territories it was as high as 29 colleges. Nine major states had this average higher than the average for the major states. Interestingly, Uttar Pradesh ranked third after Kerala and Haryana in the category of major states. In five major states, namely, Kerala, Haryana, Uttar Pradesh, Punjab and Telangana, this ratio was 20 or more colleges after 10,000 km^2 or one college available within a radius of less than four kilometres of area. Against this, in four states of Himachal Pradesh, Jharkhand, Chhattisgarh and Jammu & Kashmir this average was even less than one half of the average for major states. In case of Jammu & Kashmir, one college was available within a radius of 18 kms; which was in fact a real deplorable situation needing immediate action to rectify the situation.
- Inter-state differentials were still wide in college-population ratio. While in four major states of Andhra Pradesh, Himachal Pradesh, Karnataka, Kerala and Telangana, college-population ratio was of four or more colleges after ten thousand population. Against this, the ratio was of only one college in four states of Assam, Bihar, Jharkhand and West Bengal. On the whole, a state in the southern region fared well on this count, while quite the opposite

was true of states in north-east and eastern India. Among major states Himachal Pradesh shared second rank with Telangana along with Haryana, Karnataka and Kerala.

- Based on composite index of area and population ratio with universities and colleges in the major states, Haryana ranked number one, with index value of 70.1, and Jharkhand was at the bottom, with index value of 14.9, indicating Haryana has the highest availability of universities and colleges in terms of area and population, while the opposite was true of Jharkhand. Himachal Pradesh fell in the category of high availability states along with Kerala, Tamil Nadu, Telangana, Haryana and Uttarakhand. All these states benefitted from the private investment in the field of higher education after privatization phase of higher education in India.
- Gross Enrolment Ratio (GER) popularly used indicators to measure the health of higher education at the state level, which revealed that Tamil Nadu was at top position with GER value of 35.5 per cent and Chhattisgarh at the bottom, with GER value of only 12.4 per cent. Himachal Pradesh was placed fifth with GER value of 26.0 per cent among the 21 major states of India.
- GER ratio differed widely between females and males among major states of India. While, on the whole, small states and Union territories were better placed as compared to the major states in India, the major states differed widely from each other on this count. In dominant majority of major states, male GER was higher than female GER, it was only in case of five states of Jammu & Kashmir, Kerala, Punjab, Tamil Nadu and Uttarakhand, the female GER was higher than that of the males. In the Himachal Pradesh, male GER was only marginally higher than that of the females.
- In teacher-student ratio, which was one teacher after 25 students at the national level, major states varied widely from each other. While Karnataka and Tamil Nadu were at the top position with one teacher after 14 students, four states of Uttar Pradesh, Bihar, Rajasthan and Jharkhand were placed at the bottom with one teacher after 50 students. Himachal ranked third along with Maharashtra and Chhattisgarh within the group of major states.
- A composite index prepared on the basis of the three indices of GER, women enrolment, teacher-pupil ratio is highly enlightening. Among major states, Tamil Nadu ranked at the

top with index value of 94.8 and Bihar at the bottom with index value of only 44.6. Himachal Pradesh ranked sixth among 21 major states, with index value of 74.8. All those states that had higher rank than Himachal Pradesh were from the southern belt of the country, with the exception of Punjab.

- A comparison of Himachal Pradesh with other Indian hill states was an eye-opener and was very interesting. While in university-population ratio Himachal Pradesh ranked third after Sikkim and Arunachal Pradesh, in college-population ratio, college-area served ratio and college-population served ratio it fared at the top among all the hilly states. However, in composite index, prepared on the basis of area and population served by universities and colleges in respective states, Himachal Pradesh was at the third position after Sikkim and Uttarakhand.
- On other parameters such as GER, women enrolment ratio, and teacher-pupil ratio, Himachal Pradesh ranked at third, second, second position, respectively among hill category of hill states. Its rank on composite index prepared on the basis of GER, women enrolment and teacher-pupil ratio was third among 10 hill states. Manipur was placed at the top and Arunachal Pradesh at the bottom, with huge difference in their index values among all the hill states. Manipur in GER and Sikkim in teacher-pupil ratio did exceedingly well among the hill states.

NOTES

1. Major states are Haryana, Kerala, Tamil Nadu, Uttarakhand, Punjab, West Bengal, Himachal Pradesh, Uttar Pradesh, Bihar, Karnataka, Gujarat, Andhra Pradesh, Telangana, Jharkhand, Maharashtra, Rajasthan, Odisha, Assam, Chhattisgarh, Madhya Pradesh, and Jammu & Kashmir.
2. Area which are co-extensive with the boundaries of the state or Union Territory, i.e. Hill States namely Jammu & Kashmir, Himachal Pradesh, Arunachal Pradesh, Manipur, Meghalaya, Mizoram, Nagaland, Sikkim, Uttarakhand and Tripura.(Eighth Five Year Plan, Volume: 2)
3. There is no university in Andaman & Nicobar Islands, Dadra & Nagar Haveli, Daman & Diu and Lakshadweep.
4. It is notable here that the hill states are those which are totally in hilly character. As per the India State Forest Report 2011 observed states namely, Jammu & Kashmir, Himachal Pradesh, Uttarakhand, Arunachal Pradesh, Manipur, Meghalaya, Mizoram, Nagaland, Sikkim, and Tripura are entirely (100%) under the hilly terrain. Assam is not included in this study because of their lower hill cover (only 24%) (Planning Commission, 2013).

SECTION B

Higher Education: Himachal Context

II
Changing Geography of Higher Education Institutions

Introduction

After a comparative analysis of higher education scenario in Himachal Pradesh with that of the major Indian states and the other Indian Hill states separately, the present chapter examines the changing geography of higher education institutions in the state.

Higher education picked up late in Himachal Pradesh. Before independence, it was almost non-existent. Even the school education was confined to a few hill stations, capital towns of princely states and British-ruled territories, transferred to Himachal Pradesh from Punjab after latter's linguistic reorganisation in 1966. Difficult terrain, low population density, dispersed settlement pattern, poor road and rail network and subsistent agricultural economy in the state proved real barriers in the path of educational development.

Gradually, the situation improved with the physical consolidation of state in 1966 after the transfer of '*Pahari*' Hindi speaking areas after linguistic reorganisation of the region in 1966 followed by the grant of full statehood to Himachal Pradesh in January 1971. New schools, colleges and universities, both in general and technical education were opened in the different parts of the state with funds from the public exchequer. Concomitantly, the road network also increased to improve physical accessibility in the state. In the 1970s and 1980s, centrally sponsored programmes such as rural, hill and backward area development also contributed to the spread of education in rural and backward areas of the state. During this period, several new colleges were opened up in rural and peripheral areas.

Following the initiation of new economic policy by the Government of India in 1991 especially after the private sector was allowed to invest in higher education by Indian Parliament Act of 2001, there has been a radical change in the geography of higher education in Himachal Pradesh. This is termed as a paradigm shift in higher education scenario of the country.

More than four of each five institutions of higher education in the state were established after 1991. Twenty-three of the total twenty-eight institutes/universities imparting higher education in the state came after 1991. Secondly, overwhelming majority of higher education institutions were established in rural areas under private management. Moreover, there has been a huge shift towards technical and professional education from general education category. This brought in radical changes not only in the management and structural composition but also in the geography of higher education in the state.

Though in a way, the modern education system was introduced in the state during the British rule yet the physical expansion and development of higher education is more or less a post-statehood phenomenon. As we know, Himachal Pradesh got full-statehood in 1971. Between 1971 and 2016, the number of universities in the state rose to 28 from just two in 1971. Similarly, the number of colleges went to 279 from just 28 during the same period. The gross enrolment ratio increased from less than one per cent (0.77%) in 1981 to 34.7 per cent in 2011, and, the net enrolment ratio (in the age group 18-23) went up to 16.7 per cent from only 0.49 per cent during the same period.

In pre-Independence period, there were very few institutions (eight only) of higher education in the state. Moving at a very slow pace after the independence in 1947, higher education gained momentum after Himachal Pradesh got full statehood in 1971. At that time, most of the higher education institutions in the state were in the public sector, located in the urban areas. With the change in economic policy in 1991, the private sector started investing in higher education sector. In Himachal Pradesh, the impact of privatization boom became conspicuously clear after 2000.

During the Eleventh (2007-2012) and Twelfth (2012-2017) Five-Year Plans, many colleges and universities have been established in Himachal Pradesh. Interestingly, the 11th Plan was highly predominated by new colleges and universities imparting technical higher education against the 12th Plan period which was predominated by general education institutions. Similarly, private investment dominated during the former, while the public investment registered the same trend during the latter plan period. By 2016, there were as many as 307 colleges and universities in the state. Of these 161 or more than half of the total number of colleges and universities imparted general education including six multi-faculty colleges, another 122 or about two-fifth imparting technical education and remaining 24 or less than one-tenth providing professional education (Table 2.0).

Evolution and Distribution

In their geographical distribution, more than nine of every set of ten colleges and universities in the state were distributed in less than one-

Table 2.0: Himachal Pradesh: Phase-wise growth and distribution of higher education institutions during 1947-2016

Phases	*General Education*	*Technical*	*Technical cum Professional*	*Professional*	*Multi-Faculty*	*Total*
1	2	3	4	5	6	7
I (At 1947)	6	0	0	0	2	8
II (1947-1970)	17	2	0	1	2	22
III (1971-1990)	25	0	3	1	1	30
IV (1991-2016)	107	104	13	22	1	247
1991-1995	21	1	0	2	0	24
1996-2000	7	5	1	3	1	17
2001-2005	12	22	7	1	0	42
2006-2010	24	68	3	11	0	106
2011-2016	43	7	2	6	0	58
Total	**155**	**106**	**16**	**24**	**6**	**307**

Sources: (i) Statistics of Higher and Technical Education available from the Directorate of Higher Education, Lalpani Shimla, Government of Himachal Pradesh.
(ii) Annual reports of various years from Himachal Pradesh University, Shimla.

third of the state area having elevation below 1500 metres. At the district level, 191 or more than three-fifth were concentrated in four districts of Kangra, Shimla, Mandi, and Solan. Against this, only 42 or one-seventh of the total number of universities/colleges/institutes were located in the five districts of Kinnaur, Lahul and Spiti, Kullu, Chamba and Bilaspur (Table 2.1). In their urban-rural distribution, 246 or eighty per cent were located in the rural areas and remaining twenty per cent in the urban areas. Only about, one-tenth of the state population resides in urban areas (Table 2.1).

Table 2.1: Himachal Pradesh: Urban-rural distribution of higher education institutions by districts, 2016

S. No.	*District Name*	*Urban*	*(%)*	*Rural*	*(%)*	*Total*	*(%)*
1	2	3	4	5	6	7	8
1.	Bilaspur	3	4.9	11	4.5	14	4.6
2.	Chamba	2	3.3	10	4.1	12	3.9
3.	Hamirpur	6	9.8	22	8.9	28	9.1
4.	Kangra	5	8.2	58	23.6	63	20.5
5.	Kinnaur	0	0.0	2	0.8	2	0.7
6.	Kullu	2	3.3	11	4.5	13	4.2
7.	Lahul and Spiti	0	0.0	1	0.4	1	0.3
8.	Mandi	6	9.8	36	14.6	42	13.7
9.	Shimla	17	27.9	31	12.6	48	15.6
10.	Solan	10	16.4	31	12.6	41	13.4
11.	Sirmaur	6	9.8	16	6.5	22	7.2
12.	Una	4	6.6	17	6.9	21	6.8
	Himachal Pradesh	**61**	**100.0**	**246**	**100.0**	**307**	**100.0**

Source: As Table 2.0.

In terms of their management, 53.4 per cent or majority were privately managed (Table 2.2).

Table 2.2: Himachal Pradesh: Management of higher education institutions by districts, 2016

S. No.	*District Name*	*Management types*			
		Govt.	*Govt. Aided*	*Private*	*Total*
1	2	3	4	5	6
1.	Bilaspur	5	0	9	14
2.	Chamba	8	0	4	12
3.	Hamirpur	8	0	20	28
4.	Kangra	33	2	28	63
5.	Kinnaur	1	0	1	2
6.	Kullu	8	0	5	13
7.	Lahul and Spiti	1	0	0	1
8.	Mandi	17	1	24	42
9.	Shimla	26	3	19	48
10.	Solan	13	0	28	41
11.	Sirmaur	9	0	13	22
12.	Una	7	1	13	21
	Himachal Pradesh	**136**	**7**	**164**	**307**

Source: As Table 2.0.

In the following, an attempt has been made to study the changing geography of higher education institutions in Himachal Pradesh.

For the purpose, period between 1947 and 2016 has been divided into four phases. There are well-marked variations in the distributional pattern of higher education institutions at different points of time. Independence in 1947 followed by territorial consolidation in 1966, full statehood in 1971 and change in economic policies in 1991 have shown their remarkable impact on the growth and the distributional pattern of colleges and universities in the state. Accordingly, discussion on the spatial evolution of higher education has been divided into the following four phases:

I. Pre-Independence (before 1947)
II. Post-Independence to Pre-Statehood (1947-1970)
III. Post-Statehood to Pre-Reforms (1971-1990), and
IV. Post-Reforms (1991 onwards)

Table 2.3: (a) Himachal Pradesh: Phases and their characterization in changing geography of higher education, 1947-2016

Phases	*Phase characteristics*
At 1947	Limited modern and Higher Education.
1947-1970	Slow growth and confined to a few locations of some districts. Limited role of Non-governmental organizations, mainly demand oriented and mostly confined to urban areas, wide inter-district disparity in the distribution.
1971-1990	Got momentum but under government control and management, registered physical expansion in rural and backward areas. Dominated by general education in its nature.
1991-1995	Slow growth but covered the entire state including Kinnaur and Lahul and Spiti districts that remained neglected during the entire earlier period.
1996-2000	Still slow pace but entered diversification phase towards technical and professional education. Private investment started making visible impact.
2001-2005	Entered in fast growth mode, private investment increased, technical and professional component increased, started spreading in rural and peripheral areas and number of universities grew fast. A phase of paradigm shift.
2006-2010	Rapid growth, private investment intensified, technical and professional component grew fast, fast expansion towards rural areas. Truly as phase of privatization, ruralization and diversification of higher education. Sharp decline in inter-district distribution of higher education institutions.
2011-2016	Reversal of investment trend from private to public investment, central and state funded colleges and universities emerged in big way, spatially intensified but entered into popularistic phase, quality registered decline with increase in quantity.

I. Pre-Independence Phase

The British rulers for climatic reasons developed several hill stations in different parts of India including Himachal Pradesh. Gradually, such hill stations emerged as centres of development, administrative activities and education. Shimla was developed as the summer capital of British India, Dalhousie as the summer capital of Punjab, Kasauli as a cantonment town and Dharamshala as the headquarters of Kangra district and so on. Hill stations connected through rail and road transport with the plains brought life to the dormant and remotely located hill areas. Famous military schools at Sanawar, Chail and Dalhousie along with St. Bede School at Shimla were established during the British period.

Table 2.3: (b) Himachal Pradesh: Phases in distributional pattern of higher education institutions

Phases	*Distributional pattern*
First Phase (1947-1970)	Randomized distribution
Second Phase (1970-1990)	Tendency towards clustering
Third Phase (1991-2010)	Clustered distribution
Fourth Phase (2011-2016)	Dispersal tendency in distribution

Source: Based on examination data/information and maps prepared for the study of distribution of higher education institutions in the state.

Though entry to such schools was highly restricted yet these schools opened the gates of modern education to hill areas (see Table 2.3a). Gradually, some more schools were established in the town of Shimla, exclusively for the European and Eurasian children. All such schools were administratively placed under the charge of the Inspector of Schools, Delhi Circle. Besides, there were three Convent schools attached to the Convent of Jesus and Mary at Agra. These were Boarding schools for girls. St. Francis was a military orphanage and St. Bede's, a technical college to train female school teachers. In those days matriculation was also a part of the college education.

The early years of the 20th century opened a new chapter in the education system of Himachal Pradesh. In 1904, St. Bede's, a college exclusively for women education, was established in Shimla town. Classes up to senior secondary level were held in this college. Soon thereafter, in 1905, a Research Institute, known as Pasteur Institute of India, was established by the Imperial government at Kasauli (Solan district) for treatment of dog bite. Renamed now as Central Research Institute, it works in collaboration with World Health Organization (WHO) and Immune Biological Laboratory to manufacture vaccines for polios and measles. In 1959, this institute started research degree programme and then undergraduate teaching course in Microbiology in 1961, followed by M.Phil. course in Microbiology in 1979. For the award of degrees, this institute is affiliated to Himachal Pradesh University, Shimla. A college teaching up to matric was founded at Dharamshala (Kangra district) in May 1912. Its foundation was laid by Sir Louis Dane, the then Lt. Governor of Punjab, the college was upgraded to intermediate level in 1926.

Table 2.4: Himachal Pradesh: Change in urban-rural distribution of college/ universities during 1947-2016

S. No.	*District Name*	*Pre-1947*		*1947-1970*		*1971-90*		*1991-2016*	
		U	*R*	*U*	*R*	*U*	*R*	*U*	*R*
1	2	3	4	5	6	7	8	9	10
1.	Bilaspur	1	0	1	0	0	2	1	9
2.	Chamba	0	0	1	0	1	1	1	8
3.	Hamirpur	0	0	1	0	1	3	4	19
4.	Kangra	1	0	1	2	2	5	2	50
5.	Kinnaur	0	0	0	0	0	0	0	2
6.	Kullu	0	0	1	0	0	1	1	10
7.	Lahul and Spiti	0	0	0	0	0	0	0	1
8.	Mandi	1	0	1	0	1	1	3	35
9.	Shimla	1	0	4	3	2	5	10	20
10.	Solan	2	0	2	0	1	2	4	30
11.	Sirmaur	0	0	2	0	0	0	4	18
12.	Una	1	1	1	2	1	1	1	14
Himachal Pradesh		**7**	**1**	**15**	**7**	**9**	**21**	**31**	**216**

Source: As Table 2.0.

Five colleges imparting education in the Sanskrit language were opened during 1923-1931; two in Una and remaining one each in Mandi, Solan and Bilaspur. In all, there were eight colleges/institutes of higher education in the state (Table 2.4 and Fig 2.0).

Briefly, modern and higher education in Himachal Pradesh was highly limited in Pre-Independence era. It was mainly confined to areas under direct control of British rulers and accessible to Indian elite class and the wards of British administrative and army officers. In rest of the territories, ruled by the native rulers, the indigenous *Gurukul* and *Pathshala* system were in operation.

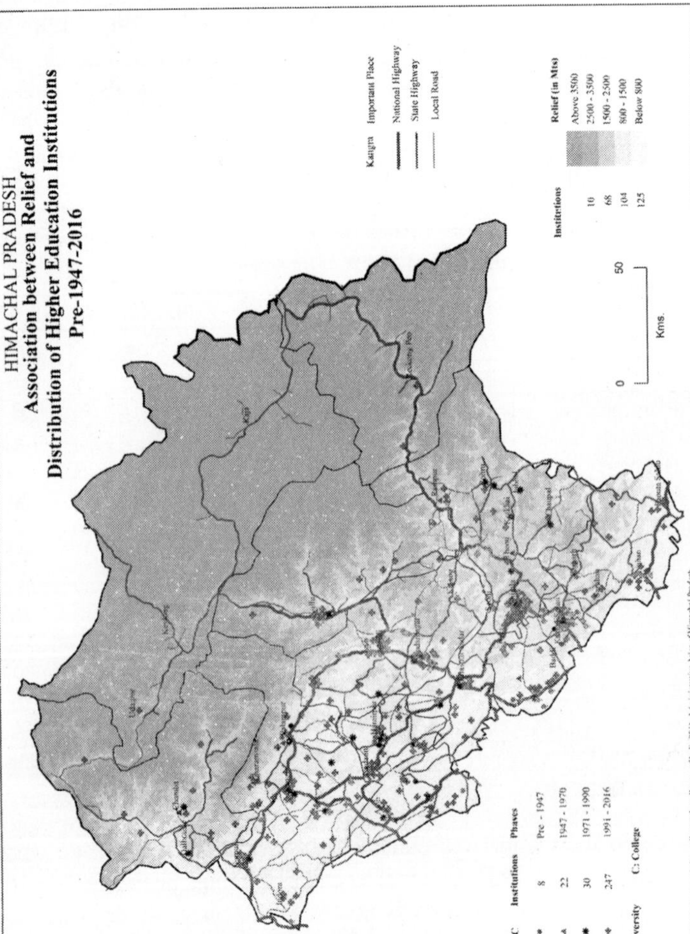

Fig. 2.0: Himachal Pradesh: Association between Relief and Distribution of Higher Education Institutions.

II. Post-Independence to Pre-Statehood Phase (1947-1970)

Soon after the independence of the country, the Government of India focussed on the expansion of education in the country. New schools and colleges were opened in different Indian states. Himachal Pradesh government, of course, accorded its first priority to the school education. Higher education in the state moved at snail's pace. In the year 1947, up-gradation of Government College, Dharamshala to undergraduate level from intermediate college marked the beginning of higher education in Himachal Pradesh, as we understand it today.

The twenty-two new colleges/institutes of higher education including seventeen of general education, two of multi-faculty, one professional and two of technical education were established during this phase (Table 2.0). As per their distribution, seven were located in Shimla, three each in Kangra and Una, and two each in Solan and Sirmaur districts. Of the remaining five, one each was distributed in Mandi, Kullu, Hamirpur, Bilaspur and Chamba districts. There was no college in Lahul and Spiti and Kinnaur districts of the state. Of the 22 colleges, fifteen were located in the urban areas and the remaining in the rural areas. Evidently, demand took precedence over need in locating colleges/institutes of higher education (Table 2.4).

In 1948, a new college imparting general education came at Mandi town of the same district. This was followed by yet another Government college at Bilaspur town in 1952. With the passage of time, several new courses were introduced in the above-said colleges to push them to multi-faculty category colleges/institutions. After a gap of two years, a new 'college of school education' (renamed as State Institute of Education in 1970 and restructured as SCERT in 1984) was opened at Solan in the year 1954. The main objective behind opening such an institute was to improve the quality of education in the state by way of imparting training to in-service teachers. Another teachers' training college (B.Ed.) was established at Dharamshala town (Kangra district) in 1956. During this period, the focus remained only on general education. Thereafter, thirteen new colleges were set up at different places in the state between 1958 and 1969. Thereafter, four more colleges came into existence at Amb (Una district), Nurpur (Kangra district), and at Bhatoli (Kangra district) and Chopal (Shimla district). The former two were managed by the state government. Of the latter two, one was privately managed but government aided college and another was entirely a private college.

During this phase, with the exception of KLB DAV College (1969) at Palampur (Kangra district) and Sanskrit college of Chopal (1970) (Shimla district) all colleges were started by the state government.

The landmark event of this period was the establishment of Himachal Pradesh University at Shimla town in 1970. Prior to this, it was functioning as the Shimla Regional Centre of Panjab University, Chandigarh for post-graduate studies. Another landmark was the establishment of Indira Gandhi Medical College at Shimla town itself. Technical and professional education was sadly lacking in the state, but a need was felt for promoting higher education in technical and professional education field. The same was reflected in the creation of an independent department of technical education at the state level during the financial year 1968-69.

Briefly, higher education sector of the state gained momentum during 1947-1970. As many as, twenty-two new colleges/universities were established in ten districts of the state. Establishment of Himachal Pradesh University and Indira Gandhi Medical College, both in Shimla city, were the landmark achievements of this period. Secondly, starting of post-graduate classes in the select subjects at Government College, Dharamshala and upgradation of school Education College to State Institute of Education along with start of the doctoral research programme at Central Research Institute, Kasauli amounts to another significant development of this period. Dependence on public investment and heavy inclination towards general education were other characteristic features of higher education in the state during this period.

Geographically speaking, higher education in the state was mainly confined to the five districts of Shimla, Kangra, Una, Solan and Sirmaur. Except for Shimla, all other were closely adjacent to Punjab or Haryana states. It was highly oriented to demand, as these were mainly concentrated in urban areas.

III. Post-Statehood to Pre-Economic Reforms Phase (1971-1990)

This phase is remarkable in a variety of ways. The higher education experienced a rapid change not only in the increased number of colleges and universities but also in physical expansion and structural changes.

As many as 26 new colleges (including one multi-faculty college), two universities, one national institute of engineering and technology and a medical college were established during this phase. A shift in government policy in favour of rural and backward areas benefitted such areas as most of the new colleges were located in such areas (Table 2.0).

The 25 new general education colleges established during this period were highly concentrated in a few districts. The three districts of Shimla, Kangra, and Hamirpur, in combine, had 14 or nearly three-fifth of these colleges/institutions. The remaining 11 colleges were distributed in the following manner: two each in Una, Solan, Mandi, Bilaspur and Chamba, and remaining one in Kullu district. A new multi-faculty college, which also came up during this period, was located in Shimla district, raising the number of the new educational institution to seven in a single district. Against this, in two districts of Kinnaur and Lahul and Spiti, any institution of higher education was yet to come up. In Sirmaur district no new institution of higher education was set up during this period. Of the 26 colleges, 19 or nearly three-fourth were located in the rural areas and remaining seven or one-third in the urban areas. Evidently, there has been a locational shift in higher education institutions in favour of rural areas.

Interestingly, as many as eight of the total 25 new general education colleges established during this period were to impart education in Sanskrit language. Locationally, these were distributed in the following manner. Two each were located in Shimla and Kangra districts and one each in Kullu, Hamirpur, Bilaspur and Chamba districts. Established during 1971-1989, six out of the eight colleges were located in rural areas.

Remaining 17 new colleges of general education came in the eight districts of the state. Nearly one-half or eight colleges came up in the two districts of Shimla and Kangra. Another two each came in Solan, Una, Mandi, and Hamirpur districts, and remaining one college came into existence in Chamba district.

In addition to 25 new colleges established during this period to impart higher education in general courses, one more college was started in Shimla city of Shimla district and it was a multi-faculty college. With this, the number of new colleges established during this period in a single district of Shimla went up to seven. Shimla was followed by Kangra district with another six colleges; both, in combine, receiving 13 or one-half of the total new colleges established during this period. Against this, their combined population made only 35 per cent (in 18-23 age group) of the total population of Himachal Pradesh in 1991.

Of the two new Agricultural Universities which came during this period in the state, one was established at Palampur (Kangra district) and another at Nauni (Solan district). The former, now known as Chaudhary Sarwan Kumar Himachal Pradesh Krishi Vishvavidyalaya, was established in 1978 and the latter, renamed now as Dr. Y.S. Parmar Agriculture University, came in 1985. In 1962, the latter was initially established as an agricultural college at Solan, affiliated then to Panjab University, Chandigarh. In 1978, it was accorded the status of the second campus of Himachal Pradesh University, Palampur. It is located 13 kms away from

Solan town on Solan-Rajgarh road.

Under a scheme of the Government of India, Regional Engineering Colleges (RECs) were established in different Indian states. One such REC was established at village Anu (Hamirpur district) in 1986. Later on, it was upgraded to the National Institute of Technology (NIT), again under the scheme initiated by the Government of India. Of late, it has been accorded the status of Institute of national importance.

Establishment of a medical college in the state is yet another landmark of this phase. An Ayurvedic (medicine) college (renamed now as Rajiv Gandhi Government Post Graduate College) was established at Paprola village, (Kangra district) in 1972. Himachal Pradesh government took over its management in March 1978; renaming is the outcome of change in its managerial status.

In their urban-rural distribution, 30 new higher education institutions coming during this phase were located in the following manner. Twenty-one were in rural areas and remaining nine in urban areas. Evidently, there has been a locational shift in favour of the rural areas of the state (Table 2.4 and Fig. 2.0).

IV. Post-Reforms Phase (1991 Onwards)

The new economic policy initiated by the Government of India in 1991 signalled a paradigm shift. The new policy focused on liberalisation, privatisation and globalisation of Indian economy, giving free hand to the state governments to attract private investment (Indian and foreign) in different sectors of the economy including the education. Several new colleges and universities were established in Himachal Pradesh under private management. Moreover, there has been a shift in focus from general to professional and technical education during this period. As many as two hundred twenty-four (224) colleges and twenty-three (23) universities/institutes were established during this phase.

As many as 107 general or more than two-fifth of these were imparting general education, another 104 or two-fifth technical education and remaining 36 or one-fifth imparting the professional or technical-cum-professional education (Table 2.0).

At the district level, 247 new colleges/universities established during this period in the state were distributed in the following manner. Fifty-two in Kangra, 38 in Mandi, 34 in Solan, 30 in Shimla, 23 in Hamirpur, 22 in Sirmaur, 15 in Una, 11 in Kullu, 10 in Bilaspur, nine in Chamba, two in Kinnaur and remaining one in Lahul and Spiti district.

Separately, 24 universities which came during this period were located in the following manner at the district level. The maximum number of eleven universities came in Solan district, followed by Kangra district with five universities, two universities each in the three districts of Hamirpur, Mandi and Shimla and remaining one each in the districts of Sirmaur and Una.

Out of the 247 new higher education institutions coming during 1991-2016, 117 or 47.4 per cent were imparting technical education, another 108 or 43.7 per cent general education and remaining 22 imparting the professional educational courses. So far as their urban-rural distribution is concerned, 216 or 87.4 per cent were located in the rural areas and remaining 31 or 12.6 per cent in the urban areas (Table 2.4 and Fig. 2.0). This amounts to a remarkable shift in locational pattern of higher education in the state. It seems that not only the land prices were high in urban areas but also acquiring large piece of land which was needed to establish higher education institution was a challenging task now. The phase from 1991-2016 has recorded significant variations in the emergence of new colleges/universities in its different sub-phases. Disaggregation of this phase into sub-phases makes a highly revealing story, especially from the point of spatial distribution.

The most remarkable one was that majority of higher education institutions imparted technical and/or professional education. Technical education in the state registered an increase by more than 50 times and professional education by more than 20 times.

Of the 247 colleges/universities established during this phase, only 24 or less than one-tenth came during 1991-1995 (Table 2.0). However, the most interestingly was the establishment of higher education institution in Kinnaur and Lahul and Spiti districts, which had remained neglected since the independence of the country in 1947. Himachal Pradesh government opened higher education colleges in these two districts, which were to provide general education courses. In fact, the overwhelming majority of new colleges opened during 1991-1995 imparted general education courses.

The next sub-phase, 1996 to 2000, saw a slow progress of higher education in the state. In all, 17 new colleges were established during this period against 24 during the preceding phase. Of these, eight were providing general, six in technical, two in professional and remaining one in technical-cum-professional education. Coming up of a new dental college in rural area of Solan district and start of new courses in tourism and hotel management were the salient features of this sub-phase. Establishment of the Directorate of Medical Education and Research in

1997 was another remarkable achievement of this period.

The next sub-phase, 2001 to 2005, has been remarkable in the sense that technical education grew fast during this period. As many as 22 new institutions including one university, Jay Pee University of Information Technology at Waknaghat (Solan district), were established during this period. This is known as World Class University in the field of information and technology (Govt. of India, 2005: 145).

In addition, 12 colleges of general education, seven of technical-cum-professional and one of professional education were also established during this period, impressive majority established under the private management in the rural areas. For example, 17 of 22 colleges/universities of technical education established during this period were located in the rural areas. With exception of one, all came in the private sector, thus it may rightly be called a phase of ruralization, privatization and technicalization of higher education in the state (Table 2.3).

The next sub-phase, 2006-2010, boosted further the technical and professional education in the state. As many as 98 new colleges and eight universities were established during a short span of five years, these were mostly in technical and professional fields. Of these, 60 colleges and eight universities were oriented to technical education, another 11 colleges to professional courses and remaining 24 colleges to general education.

Among the districts, Mandi was at the top with 17 colleges/institutions followed by Kangra with 12 and by Solan with 11; three districts, in combine, subsuming nearly three-fifth of the total 68 colleges and universities imparting technical education. Another three districts of Hamirpur, Shimla and Una having, in combine, additional more than one-fourth of them. Interestingly, 60 of 68 colleges and universities of technical and professional of this phase came in rural areas and 65 of these were privately managed.

Of the remaining 38 colleges and universities of this sub-phase, 24 were of general education and remaining 14 of professional or technical-cum-professional education.

In inter-district distribution, 19 colleges and 5 universities were concentrated in the four districts of Kangra, Shimla, Chamba and Mandi districts, having, in combine, 16 or two-third of those colleges established in this sub-phase. Remaining eight colleges were distributed in as many as six districts of the state.

In the distribution of 11 professional colleges, established during this sub-phase, Kangra and Shimla districts had upper hand again, the two in combine grabbing six or more than a half of such colleges. On the basis of nature, ten were nursing colleges and remaining one was Ayurvedic College. This sub-phase consolidated further ruralization, privatization, professionalization and technicalization of higher education in the state. The districts benefitting the most in this phase were Kangra, Shimla and Mandi. In fact, Mandi district moved to the third position which was earlier held by Solan district.

Briefly, 2001-2010 phase, registered an addition of 15 universities/institutes and 133 colleges, the share of the private institutes, was characterized by privatization and technicalization of higher education in the state (Fig. 2.1).

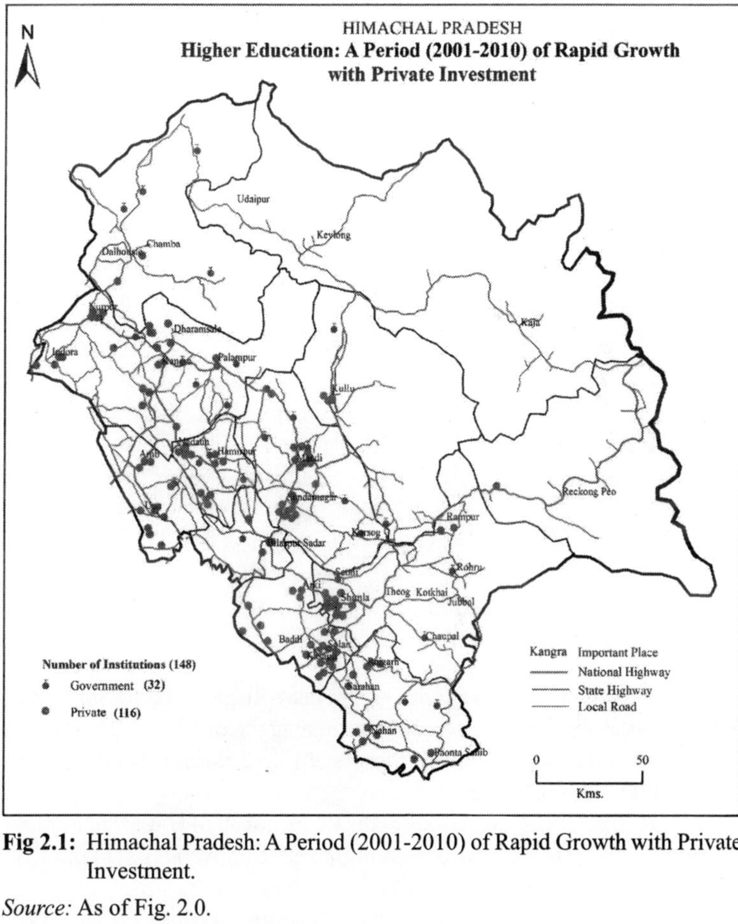

Fig 2.1: Himachal Pradesh: A Period (2001-2010) of Rapid Growth with Private Investment.

Source: As of Fig. 2.0.

The next and the final sub-phase, 2011 to 2016, brought in a record number of colleges and universities in the state. 54 colleges and four universities newly established during this sub-phase make it almost equal to total colleges and universities existing in the state before 1991. The number of colleges and universities in Himachal Pradesh before 1991 was 60 (Table 2.5).

This sub-phase is interesting in more than one ways. This sub-phase recorded a reversal of the trend set earlier during 2001 to 2005 and 2005 to 2010 phases. The higher education moved again from professional and technology education towards general education. As many as 39 or nearly three-fourth of the total 54 new colleges established in the state during this sub-phase were oriented to general education.

Table 2.5: Himachal Pradesh: Urban-rural distribution of higher education: A comparison

S. No.	*District Name*	*Pre-1991*			*Post-1991*		
		Rural	*Urban*	*Total*	*Urban*	*Rural*	*Total*
1	2	3	4	5	6	7	8
1.	Bilaspur	2	2	4	1	9	10
2.	Chamba	2	1	3	1	8	9
3.	Hamirpur	3	2	5	4	19	23
4.	Kangra	7	4	11	2	50	52
5.	Kinnaur	0	0	0	0	2	2
6.	Kullu	1	1	2	1	10	11
7.	Lahul and Spiti	0	0	0	0	1	1
8.	Mandi	1	3	4	3	35	38
9.	Shimla	8	7	15	10	20	30
10.	Solan	2	5	7	4	30	34
11.	Sirmaur	0	2	2	4	18	22
12.	Una	4	3	7	1	14	15
	Himachal Pradesh	**30**	**30**	**60**	**31**	**216**	**247**

Source: As Table 2.0.

Secondly, with a few exceptions, all the colleges established during this sub-phase were under government management (Fig. 2.2). Thirdly, majority of colleges and universities established during this sub-phase were located in rural and remote areas.

At this stage, let us have a look at the Government of Himachal Pradesh policy with regard to opening of new higher education colleges in the state and compare it with ground realities.

The Government of Himachal Pradesh notified a policy on January 2,

2014 in the context of opening the colleges in the state. This was done as per the directions of the Himachal Pradesh High Court. According to this policy document, the state government will open any new college within a radius of 25 kms of the existing degree colleges only if the existing college is overcrowded and enrolment exceeds 3000 students (Govt. of Himachal Pradesh, 2014).

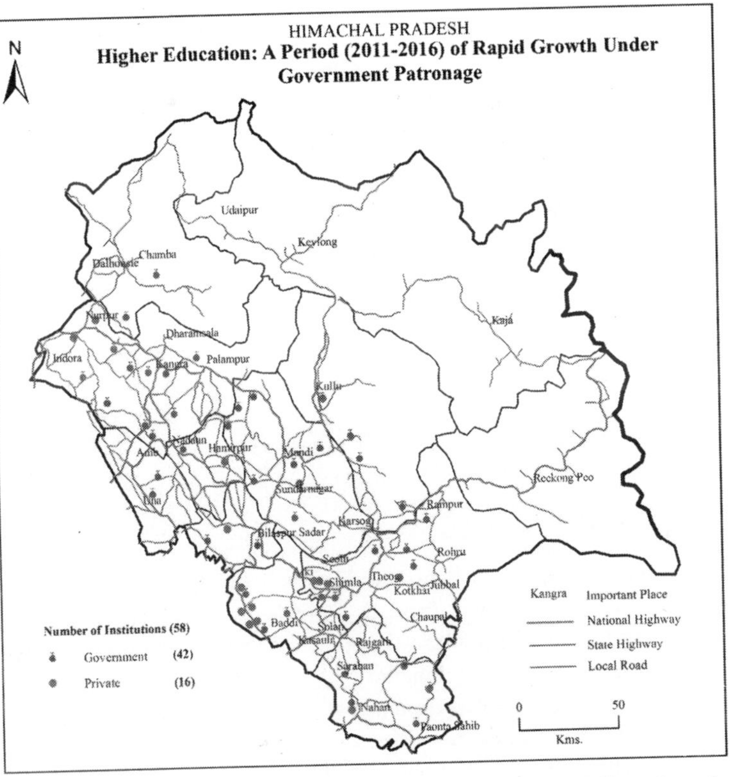

Fig. 2.2: Himachal Pradesh: A Period (2011-2016) of Rapid Growth under Government Patronage.

Source: As Fig. 2.0.

With rare exceptions, newly opened government colleges will run courses in Commerce streams that to after enrolling at least 400 students in Arts stream. Science courses will be opened after ensuring the availability of proper and adequate infrastructure.

As many as 37 new colleges have been established in the state up to 2016 after the enforcement of this policy. Information collected from reliable sources reveal that several of the newly established colleges are yet to get their own buildings. They are operating from the premises of existing 10+2 school and have on their roll two to three faculty members including the college principal. Government degree colleges at Takipur, Ranital (both in Kangra district) and Pangi (Chamba district) face this type of situation. The new college buildings are still under construction.

Further, according to a report filed by Shri Lalit Mohan who is a Correspondent of *The Tribune*, a daily newspaper that is published from Chandigarh (April 4, 2014), he states that the total number of students enrolled at Government College, Kangra Thural was 120, Government College, Nora had 129 students, Government College Nagrota Surian had 99 students, Government College Haripur Guler had 432 students, Government College Khundian had 40 students and Government College Beetan (Una district) about 100 students. The correspondent noted that students from Pangi area prefer to come to colleges in Dharamshala bypassing the newly opened colleges in nearby areas. They feel unsatisfied with the quality of education as well as available infrastructure in the newly opened colleges.

Briefly, the latest phase is characterized by the government investment and management in higher education of the state. Majority of colleges were opened by the Himachal Pradesh Government in remote rural areas with arts and commerce streams, but these were dismally lacking highly in physical as well as human infrastructure.

Distribution at the District Level

There were marked inter-district variations in the distribution of colleges and universities in the state. In all, there were 307 colleges and universities imparting higher education in the state. 28 or less than one-tenth were universities/institutes and remaining more than nine-tenth was colleges. Among districts, it ranged from a low of one college in Lahul and Spiti district to 63 colleges/universities in Kangra district. Four top-most districts namely Kangra, Shimla, Mandi and Solan, in combine, had 191 or 62.0 per cent of the total number of colleges and universities in the state. Against this, their combined population made about 57.0 per cent of total population in the state at 2011 Census. Against this, four lowest ranking districts of Bilaspur, Chamba, Kinnaur and Lahul and Spiti, in combine, had only 29 or 9.4 per cent of the total number of colleges/universities, their combined being about 15.0 per cent of the total number.

In 1947, where there were seven colleges and one Central Research Institute in the state, there was a highly uneven distribution of higher education institutes in the state. A half of higher education institutions in the state were located in two districts of Una and Solan, and another half in other four districts of Bilaspur, Kangra, Mandi and Shimla. Remaining six or one-half of the districts in the state had no college/university. As revealed in CV index value of 0.39, there were very wide inter-district variations in the distribution of higher education institutions at the time of Independence in the state (Table 2.6 and Fig. 2.3a).

During 1947-1970, twenty-one new colleges and one university came into existence in the state; inter-district variations were though large yet were marginally lower in comparison to the 1947 phase. In 1970, nearly one-third came in to being in the single district of Shimla, having the state headquarters. Another, more than one-fourth came in the two districts of Kangra and Una.

Table 2.6: Himachal Pradesh: Inter-district distribution of higher education, 1947 to 2016

S. No.	*District Name*	*1947*	*1970*	*1990*	*2010*	*2016*
1	2	3	4	5	6	7
1.	Bilaspur	1	2	4	11	14
2.	Chamba	0	1	3	10	12
3.	Hamirpur	0	1	5	26	28
4.	Kangra	1	4	11	51	63
5.	Kinnaur	0	0	0	2	2
6.	Kullu	0	1	2	9	13
7.	Lahul and Spiti	0	0	0	1	1
8.	Mandi	1	2	4	34	42
9.	Shimla	1	8	15	34	45
10.	Solan	2	4	7	33	41
11.	Sirmaur	0	2	2	18	24
12.	Una	2	5	7	20	22
	Himachal Pradesh	**8**	**30**	**60**	**249**	**307**
	Average	1.33	3.00	6.00	20.75	25.58
	C.V Index	0.39	0.75	0.70	0.73	0.74

Source: As Table 2.0.

On the other side of the scale, the four districts of Chamba, Hamirpur, Kullu, and Sirmaur, had no institution of higher education before 1947, new colleges were established during this phase. However, remotely located low population districts of Kinnaur and Lahul and Spiti were still without any institution of higher education (Fig. 2.3b).

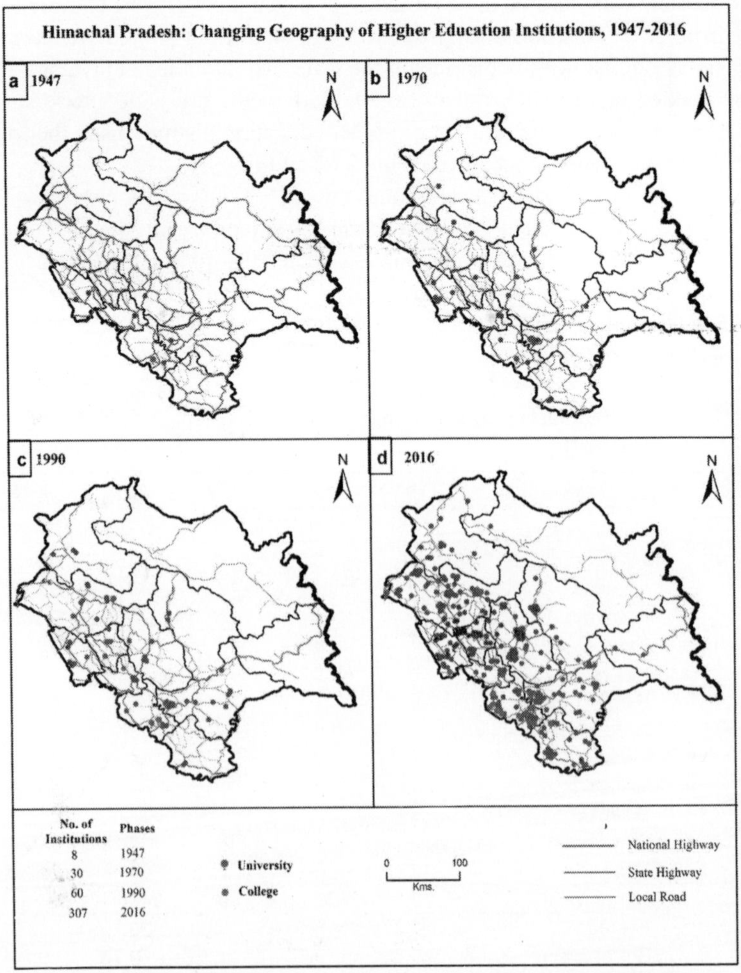

Fig 2.3: Himachal Pradesh: Changing Geography of Higher Education Institutions, 1947-2016.

Source: As Fig 2.0.

The spatial spread of higher education to four more districts of the state, however, districts such as Shimla, Una and Solan had the higher number of education institutes increased the inter-district variations, CV index value increased to 0.75 in 1970 from 0.39 in pre-1947 phase (Fig. 2.4).

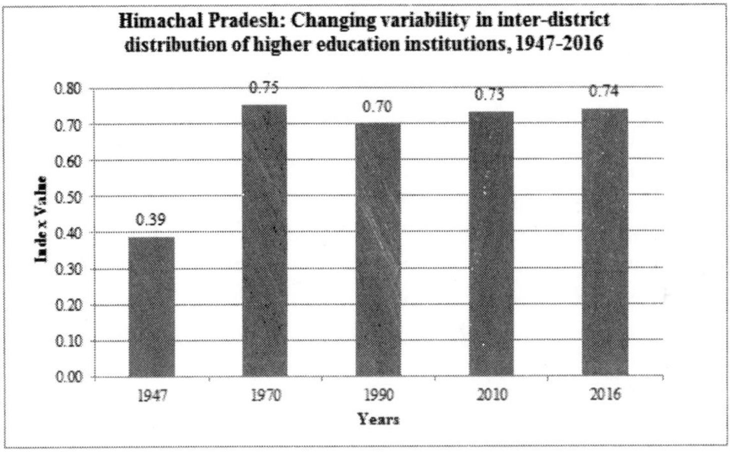

Fig. 2.4: Himachal Pradesh: Changing variability in inter-district distribution of higher education institutions, 1947-2016.

Source: As Table 2.6.

Again during 1971-1990 when 28 new colleges and two universities were established in the state, inter-district variations in the distribution of higher education institution narrowed down further (Table 2.7). The index value of C.V. which was 0.75 in 1970 marginally declined to 0.70 in 1990 (Table 2.6 and Fig. 2.3c). But sadly, Kinnaur and Lahul and Spiti were still without any institution of higher education.

The next phase, from 1991 to 2016, when as many as 223 new colleges and 24 universities were established in the state, inter-district variations in the distribution of higher education institutions got reduced considerably during 1990-2010 to rise again marginally between 2010 and 2016 (Fig. 2.4). During the latter period (2010-2016), there has been a sharp increase in the number of colleges/universities in four districts of Kangra, Shimla, Mandi, and Solan. They benefitted from their locational advantage and political clout. The latter factor played a considerable role in the case of Mandi district, having the privilege of being the parliamentary and assembly constituencies of influential political personalities. However, there is no denying the fact that Mandi district has a long tradition of education.

By 2016, when there are 279 colleges and 28 universities in the state, inter-district variations in the distribution of higher education institutions narrowed down considerably in comparison to pre-statehood phases. In

2016, the share of the top-ranking district (Kangra) in the total number of colleges in the state was about one-fifth or 20.0 per cent, whereas, the top-ranking district (Shimla) before 1971 shared nearly one-third of the total colleges in the state. The combined share of the two top-most districts (Kangra and Shimla) in the total number of colleges was slightly higher than one-third (35.5%), against the two top-most districts sharing one-half of the total in pre-1971 phase. However, universities were disproportionally concentrated in a few districts. Solan district alone had 12 or more than two-fifth of total universities in the state. Another six were concentrated in Kangra district. Both districts, in combine, had more than three-fifth of the total number of universities in the state (Table 2.7 and Fig. 2.3d).

Table 2.7: Himachal Pradesh: Inter-district distribution of colleges/universities, Pre-1947-2016

S. No.	*District Name*	*1947*		*1970*		*1990*		*2016*	
		C	*U*	*C*	*U*	*C*	*U*	*C*	*U*
1	2	3	4	5	6	7	8	9	10
1.	Bilaspur	1	0	1	0	2	0	14	0
2.	Chamba	0	0	1	0	2	0	12	0
3.	Hamirpur	0	0	1	0	3	1	25	3
4.	Kangra	1	0	3	0	6	1	57	6**
5.	Kinnaur	0	0	0	0	0	0	2	0
6.	Kullu	0	0	1	0	1	0	13	0
7.	Lahul and Spiti	0	0	0	0	0	0	1	0
8.	Mandi	1	0	1	0	2	0	40	2$
9.	Shimla	1	0	6	1	7	0	42	3@
10.	Solan	1	1*	2	0	3	0	29	12
11.	Sirmaur	0	0	2	0	0	0	23	1
12.	Una	2	0	3	0	2	0	21	1
	Himachal Pradesh	**7**	**1**	**21**	**1**	**28**	**2**	**279**	**28**

Source: As Table 2.0.

Note: C: College; U: University, (i) * Central Research Institute in Solan, (ii) ** included two Central Government Institutes: Rashtriya Sanskrit Sansthan Garli and NIFT in Kangra, (iii) $ included Indian Institute of Technology, Mandi, and (iv) @ included Central Government Institute of Hotel Management Catering and Nutrition Kufri in Shimla.

Briefly, there were considerable inter-district variations in the distribution of higher education institutions in the state. Four top-most districts namely, Kangra, Shimla, Mandi and Solan had, in combine,

62.0 per cent of the total institutions in the state against their combined population of 57.0 per cent in 2011. Against this, the lowest ranking four districts of Bilaspur, Chamba, Kinnaur and Lahul and Spiti, in combine, had only 29 or less than one-tenth of all institutions in the state against their combined share of about one-seventh in the total population of Himachal Pradesh.

However, inter-district variations in this regard have narrowed down considerably over the period, especially in post-1991 phase. The credit goes to privatization and liberalization policies of the government.

As expected, inter-district variations in the distribution of universities/ institutes were very wide. More than two-fifth of the total 28 universities/ institutes in the state were confined to a single district of Solan. Solan combined with Kangra district had 18 or more than three-fifth of the total number of universities in the state (Table 2.8).

Urban-Rural Distribution

Nine-tenth of the total population living in rural settlement of various sizes, consequently Himachal Pradesh is the most ruralized state in India. As one moves from south to north-east, the number and size of settlements gradually keep on declining. This is mainly due to the prevalence of harsh climatic conditions and rugged and hilly topography. Consequently, population is sparsely distributed and physical accessibility poor. Under the circumstances, issues associated with demand for and supply of higher education along with location of educational institutions become of crucial significance.

In 2016, 245 or 80 per cent of the total number of colleges and universities in the state were located in rural areas. These were widely distributed in rural areas of 12 districts in the state. The number ranged from a high of 57 in Kangra district to a low of only one in Lahul and Spiti district. Kangra district was followed by Mandi with 36, Solan with 32 and by Shimla with 28. These four top ranking districts, in combine, had 62.4 per cent or more than three-fifth of the total number of rural colleges and universities in the state. On the other side of the scale, four lowest ranking districts of Chamba, Bilaspur, Kinnaur and Lahul and Spiti had, in combine, only 23 or less than one-tenth of the total rural colleges/ universities in the state (Table 2.8).

On an average, 20 colleges/universities per district were located in rural Himachal Pradesh. Five districts namely Kangra, Mandi, Solan, Shimla and Hamirpur had this ratio higher than the state average. In other words, the majority of the districts have this average lower than that for rural Himachal Pradesh.

Remaining 62 or 20.0 per cent colleges and universities in urban Himachal Pradesh were located in ten districts of the state. Kinnaur and Lahul and Spiti are still predominantly rural districts. Giving an average of six colleges/universities per district in urban Himachal Pradesh, the number ranged from a high of 17 in Shimla district to a low of only two in Kullu district. The two districts of Shimla and Solan had this figure higher than the state average. Another four districts namely Hamirpur, Kangra, Mandi, Sirmaur had this figure similar to the average for the urban Himachal Pradesh (Table 2.8).

Table 2.8: Himachal Pradesh: Urban-rural distribution of colleges/universities Pre-1947-2016

S. No.	*District Name*	*1947*		*1970*		*1990*		*2010*		*2016*	
		U	*R*	*U*	*R*	*U*	*R*	*U*	*R*	*U*	*R*
1	2	3	4	5	6	7	8	9	10	11	12
1.	Bilaspur	1	0	2	0	2	2	3	8	3	11
2.	Chamba	0	0	1	0	2	1	3	7	3	9
3.	Hamirpur	0	0	1	0	2	3	6	20	6	22
4.	Kangra	1	0	2	2	4	7	6	45	6	57
5.	Kinnaur	0	0	0	0	0	0	0	2	0	2
6.	Kullu	0	0	1	0	1	1	2	7	2	11
7.	Lahul and Spiti	0	0	0	0	0	0	0	1	0	1
8.	Mandi	1	0	2	0	3	1	6	28	6	36
9.	Shimla	1	0	5	3	7	8	15	19	17	28
10.	Solan	2	0	4	0	5	2	9	24	9	32
11.	Sirmaur	0	0	2	0	2	0	6	12	6	18
12.	Una	1	1	2	3	3	4	4	16	4	18
	Himachal Pradesh	**7**	**1**	**22**	**8**	**31**	**29**	**60**	**189**	**62**	**245**

Source: As Table 2.0.

However, urban-rural distribution of colleges and universities has changed significantly since independence of the country in 1947. In 1947, seven of the total eight colleges in the state were located in the urban areas, indicating urban concentration of higher education in the state. There was only one college of higher education in rural area of Una district. By 1970, the situation recorded a marginal improvement. Then, out of 30 colleges/ universities in the state, eight or more than one-fourth were located in rural areas. Of these three each was located in Una and Shimla districts and remaining two were in Kangra district. In rest of the districts, there was no higher education institution. Between 1970 and 1990 situation changed radically. In 1990, rural and urban areas had almost equal number of colleges/universities in the state. There were 29 colleges/universities in rural areas against 31 in urban areas. Interestingly, in some districts such as Hamirpur, Kangra, Shimla, and Una higher education institutions were more in number in rural areas than urban areas. While the reverse was true for Mandi and Solan districts. In case of Bilaspur district, there were an equal number of colleges in urban and rural areas. Sirmaur district was a unique case of not having any college in rural areas. While Kinnaur and Lahul and Spiti districts were still without any higher education institution.

In between 1990 and 2010, private investment started pouring in higher education sector. Not only the number of colleges and universities recorded rapid increase but there was a phenomenal increase in the number of colleges and universities in rural areas as well. While the number of colleges/universities increased only by 29 in the urban areas, it increased by 160 in the rural areas. By 2010, the number of colleges/universities in the urban areas was only 60 against 189 in the rural areas. Of the total 249 colleges in the state, rural areas shared more than three-fourth or 75.9 per cent of the total number. By 2010, all the districts in state had more colleges/universities in the rural areas than their urban counterparts. In some of the districts such as Kangra, Mandi, Solan and Hamirpur, the number of colleges/universities in the rural areas was more than their urban counterparts. In a way, disparities in urban-rural distribution of higher education institutions registered a reversal of trend in favour of rural areas. This is explained by the fact that the land to establish colleges/universities was available at cheaper rates in the rural areas than the urban areas. On the other hand, privatization boom took supply to the demand side.

Between 2010 and 2016, there has been a further increase in a number of colleges/universities in the state. There has been a quantum jump in a number of colleges/universities in the rural areas of the state. The number of colleges/universities in the rural areas rose from 189 in 2010 to 245 in 2016, registering an increase of about 30 per cent in five years. Against this, the number rose from 60 to only 62 in urban areas during the same period, registering an increase of only about 3.0 per cent (Table 2.8).

In all the districts, with the exception of Kinnaur and Lahul and Spiti which are entirely rural, the number of rural colleges/universities was more than that of its urban counterparts. In fact, no new college/university was established in urban areas of any district except Shimla where the two new colleges were established between 2010 and 2016. All other districts recorded high increase in a number of colleges/universities in their rural areas. Kangra district alone registered an increase of 12 colleges/

universities during this period followed by Shimla with nine, Mandi and Solan with eight each and Solan with six.

Four districts of Kangra, Mandi, Shimla and Solan, in combine, had nearly two-third of total 56 rural colleges/universities coming during 2010-2016. In post-1990 phase, Mandi district had been the biggest beneficiary of higher education institutions, since their number in the district jumped from only four in 1990 to 42 by 2016 (Table 2.8).

Briefly, Himachal Pradesh makes an interesting story where the higher education institutions find favour with the residents of rural areas. In 2016, more than four-fifth of colleges/universities in the state were located in rural areas. At the district level, all the districts in the state have a higher number of colleges/universities in rural areas than their urban counterparts. Recently, almost all the new higher education institutions have come up in rural areas.

Of the 58 colleges/universities established during 2011-2016 in the state, 56 came up in the rural areas. In districts including Kangra, Hamirpur, Mandi, Solan, Kullu, Una and Sirmaur, urban-rural distribution of colleges and universities is highly in favour of rural areas. Availability of cheap land in rural areas supported by fast and easy available transport facilities has helped this kind of scenario (Table 2.9).

Table 2.9: Himachal Pradesh: Higher education institutes, 2011-2016

S. No.	District Name	Location			Management			
		Urban	Rural	Total	Govt.	Private	Aided	Total
1	2	3	4	5	6	7	8	9
1.	Bilaspur	0	3	3	1	2	0	3
2.	Chamba	0	2	2	2	0	0	2
3.	Hamirpur	0	2	2	1	1	0	2
4.	Kangra	0	12	12	10	2	0	12
5.	Kinnaur	0	0	0	0	0	0	0
6.	Kullu	0	4	4	3	1	0	4
7.	Lahul and Spiti	0	0	0	0	0	0	0
8.	Mandi	0	8	8	7	1	0	8
9.	Shimla	2	9	11	8	3	0	11
10.	Solan	0	8	8	5	3	0	8
11.	Sirmaur	0	6	6	4	2	0	6
12.	Una	0	2	2	2	0	0	2
	Himachal Pradesh	**2**	**56**	**58**	**43**	**15**	**0**	**58**

Source: As Table 2.0.

This, however, is a post-1990 phenomenon in the state. Earlier, the balance was highly in favour of the urban areas. During 1947-1970, a period termed as statehood phase of Himachal, the overwhelming majority of higher education institutions were located in urban areas, highlighting higher urban bias in higher education. The situation dramatically shifted in favour of rural areas after 1990.

Role of Relief and Transport network in Distribution of Higher Education Institutions

1. Distribution of Colleges/Universities by Altitude

In a hilly and rugged terrain, relief plays a determining role in the location of settlements, economic activities and services. Finding leveled and plain land in adequate quantity remains the biggest challenge not only for the common man but also for the planners and policy-makers. River valleys and margins of the hill, generally known as foothills, provide land for locating settlements, and provision of economic activities and facilities. Finding adequate and suitable land, having accessibility is always a challenge to locate various social facilities including educational facilities. Higher education institutions such as colleges, universities and institutes require a large piece of land with road connectivity to locate these and then to expand them in future.

Himachal Pradesh, where the average variation of height from the mean sea level is between 450 metres to 6500 metres, it can be generally divided into three physiographic divisions: (i). Outer Himalayas or the Shivaliks, (ii) Lesser Himalaya or Central zone, and (iii) the Greater Himalaya and Zaskar or Northern zone (Singh *et al.,* 1971, pp. 395-97). The dominant majority of the population in the state is residing either in river valleys or in the outer Himalayan ranges. In fact, there is a distinct clustering of population and economic activities in these two type of areas. Against this, areas of harsh climate and steep and rugged topography are thinly populated.

Under the situation, colleges and universities imparting higher education in the state are bound to be located in foothill zone and river valleys. In the Outer Himalayas, we have districts of Una, Hamirpur, Kangra, Solan and Sirmaur, having large tracks of foothills, plains and Central zone Kullu and Mandi districts have extensive river valleys in the river Beas Basin and hence are blessed with distinctive advantage. Besides, the hill towns such as Shimla, Dharamshala, Kasauli, Dagshai,

Sanawar and Dalhousie, are known for their initiation advantage due to their patronage by the British rulers, these have evolved as the centres of education and administration. In the following section, we have made an attempt to examine the nature of association between the distribution of higher education institutions and the relief in Himachal Pradesh.

In Himachal Pradesh, 229 or three-fourth of total colleges and universities were located in areas having the height below 1500 metres (see Table 2.10 and Fig. 2.5). Of these 125 making two-fifth of the total number of colleges and universities were located in areas having height below 800 metres. Such areas fall mainly in Kangra, Hamirpur, Una, Bilaspur, Solan and Sirmaur districts. These districts are adjacent to plains of Punjab, Haryana and Uttarakhand states. Close proximity to plains attracts students from neighbouring states of Punjab, Haryana, Uttarakhand, Uttar Pradesh and even NCT of Delhi. In between 800 and 1500 metres height areas were located another 104 or one-third of the total number of colleges and universities in the state: 62 or three-fifths of such colleges and universities were located in the three districts of Mandi, Kangra and Solan.

Table 2.10: Himachal Pradesh: Distribution of higher education institutions by relief, 2016

S. No.	District Name	Relief (in metres)				
		Below 800	1500	2500	3500	Total
1	2	3	4	5	6	7
1.	Chamba	0	4	7	1	12
2.	Kangra	41	16	6	0	63
3.	Lahul and Spiti	0	0	0	1	1
4.	Kullu	0	8	3	2	13
5.	Mandi	4	31	6	1	42
6.	Hamirpur	22	6	0	0	28
7.	Una	20	2	0	0	22
8.	Bilaspur	10	4	0	0	14
9.	Solan	14	15	12	0	41
10.	Sirmaur	14	7	3	0	24
11.	Shimla	0	11	31	3	45
12.	Kinnaur	0	0	0	2	2
	Himachal Pradesh	125	104	68	10	307

Source: (i) As Table 2.0, (ii) Transport network data collected: (a) Census of India 2011, Administrative Atlas Himachal Pradesh, (iii) website (http://hppwd.gov.in) of Himachal Pradesh Public Work Department, and (iv) Digital elevation model (DEM): USGS (United State Geological Survey).

Remaining 68 or one-fifth of the colleges and universities in the state were located in areas having a height of more than 1500 metres. Of these only ten colleges were located between the height of 2500 and 3500 metres height in the districts of Chamba, Lahaul and Spiti, Kullu, Mandi, Shimla and Kinnaur districts. All these districts fall either completely or largely in central and greater Himalayan zone of the harsh climate and rugged topography. Evidently, relief plays a great controlling factor in the distribution of population as well as higher educational institutions in the state of Himachal Pradesh. In brief, 800 and 1500 metres height form the two critical breaks in distribution of higher education institutions in Himachal Pradesh. Two-fifth of the total number of higher education institutions in the state were located in places having height of less than 800 metres and another one-third institutions were between the height of 800 and 1500 metres. Against this, only about one-fifth institutions were located in areas having a height of above 1500 metres.

2. Transport Network and Location of Higher Education Institutions

As discussed in the preceding paragraphs, giving the topographic constraints imposed by the hilly terrain of Himachal Pradesh, accessibility rather than availability is more important a factor in the location of colleges and universities in the state. As a result, it is expected that overwhelming majority of colleges and universities in the state will be located either along or in close proximity to state or national highways (Table 2.11).

On the whole, as many as 144 or nearly one-half (46.9%) of the colleges and universities in the state are located either on or in close proximity to the national highways (henceforth, NH) passing through the state. Another 67 or more than one-fifth (21.8%) of total colleges and universities in the state are located along the state highways. Remaining about one-third (31.3%) of them were located along the district and local roads (Fig. 2.5).

The national highways number 20, 21, 22, 70, 72 and 88 pass through Kangra, Mandi, Solan, Shimla, Hamirpur and Sirmaur districts of the state. Overwhelming majority of colleges and universities in these districts are located along with or in close proximity to these highways. For example, 33 of total 63 higher education institutions in Kangra district are located either on NH 20 and NH 88 (Table 2.11). Similarly, 28 of total 42 higher education institutions in Mandi district are located either on NH 20 or NH 21. Almost the same is true for Shimla district, where more than a half of the total 45 institutions fall on national highways.

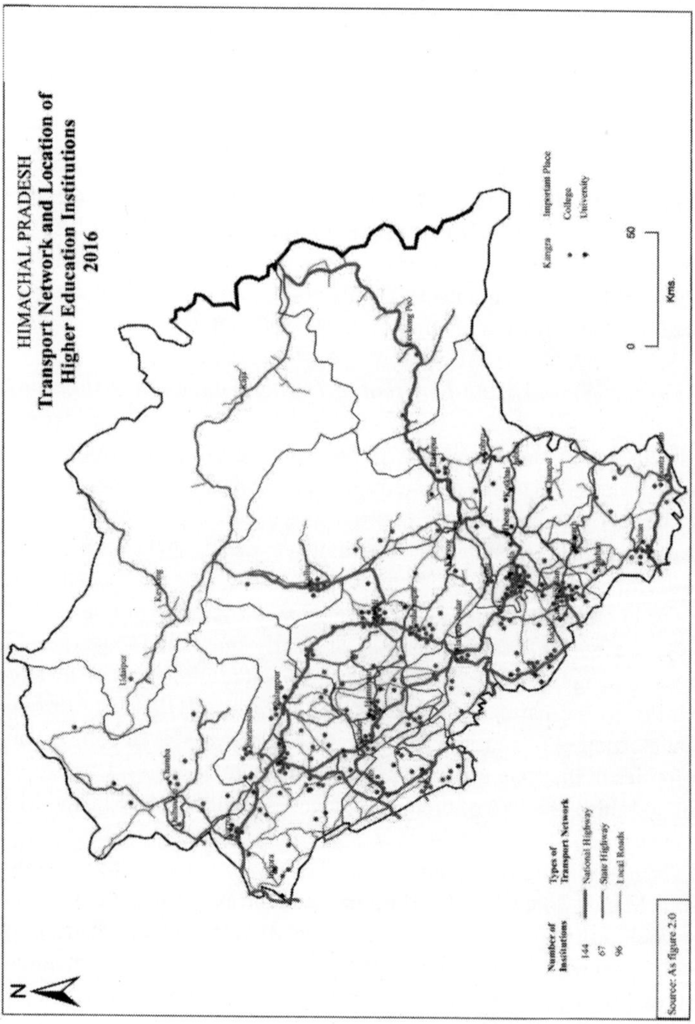

Fig. 2.5: Himachal Pradesh: Transport Network and Location of Higher Education Institutions, 2016.

Table 2.11: Himachal Pradesh: Distribution of higher education institutions along the highways, 2016

S. No.	*District Name*	*National Highways*	*State Highways*	*Local Roads*	*Total Roads*
1	*2*	*3*	*4*	*5*	*6*
1.	Chamba	0	5	7	12
2.	Kangra	33	7	23	63
3.	Lahul and Spiti	0	0	1	1
4.	Kullu	7	2	4	13
5.	Mandi	28	4	10	42
6.	Hamirpur	10	13	5	28
7.	Una	6	6	10	22
8.	Bilaspur	9	1	4	14
9.	Solan	19	11	11	41
10.	Sirmaur	7	9	8	24
11.	Shimla	23	9	13	45
12.	Kinnaur	2	0	0	2
	Himachal Pradesh	**144**	**67**	**96**	**307**

Source: As Table 2.10.

State highways number 1, 2, 8, 9, 10, 16, 23, 32 and 39 are among the most important ones. Overwhelmingly majority of 67 higher education institutions located on state highways (SH) are located along these highways. For example, 13 of total 28 higher education institutions in Hamirpur district are located on SH 32 and SH 39. Solan, Sirmaur and Shimla are other districts where large number of institutions of higher education is located along the state highways.

In Kangra, Shimla, Solan, Hamirpur and Mandi districts a substantial share of total higher education institutions is located along local or district roads.

An independent examination of location of universities reveals that 16 or 57.0 per cent of the total 28 universities are located either on national highways or state highways. Seven of the twelve universities in Solan district are located on NH 22 and NH 21. Universities provide shuttle bus services between university campuses and highways or bus stands and even railway stations.

Briefly, two-fifth of all higher education institutions and nearly three-fifths of universities in the state are located on either national or state highways. This is found out to be a solution to increase accessibility under the conditions of challenge thrown by rugged and hilly topography of the state. This finding empirically validates our hypothesis that in the hill state of Himachal Pradesh higher education institution will have a tendency to be located on the main roads along the national or the state highways.

Main Highlights

- At the dawn of independence in 1947, higher education was almost non-existent in Himachal Pradesh. Even the modern school education was confined to a few hill stations patronized by the Britishers during the colonial rule. In rest of the areas traditional system of *Gurukul* and *Pathshalas* was prevalent.
- Territorial consolidation in 1966 and grant of full statehood in 1971 induced fresh blood and enthusiasm not only among the masses but also among the bureaucrats and politicians for higher attainments in socio-economic development of the state. School education remaining top priority of the government in the beginning, higher education picked up soon to grow at a slow pace and higher education institutions were distributed randomly.
- Growing at a slow pace in the next two decades between 1970 and 1990, higher education in Himachal Pradesh entered fast growth phase under the influence of change in economic policies at the national level. During 1991-2001, there has been a spurt in growth of higher education institutions to reach its peak during the next decade of 2001-2011. Privatization, ruralization and technicalization were the marked features of higher education in the state during post-2001 phase.
- Generally termed as a paradigm shift in the field of higher education, as many as 23 of 28 universities and 125 of total 279 colleges in the state were established in one decade between 2001-2011. Overwhelming majority came in private sector, rural areas and in the field of technical education.
- The latest phase between 2011-2016 is marked with reversal of trend in favour of government investment and general education courses. Though benefitting the peripheral and neglected areas of the state, higher education in the state entered the popularistic phase. Colleges were established without taking proper care of physical and human infrastructure. Several new colleges were established during this phase by the government but these were without their own building and adequate teaching staff. Quality suffered badly in the whole process.
- When in the early phase during 1970s and 1980s, the higher

education in the state was demand-driven; there were wide inter-district and urban-rural disparities in distribution of higher education institutions. However, when it became supply-driven after the entry of the private sector in higher education sector, inter-district and urban-rural disparities in distribution of higher education institutions declined considerably. In Himachal Pradesh, more than four-fifth of the total number of higher education institutions are located in the rural areas. Availability of extensive and cheap land, required for establishing higher education institutions especially universities, in the rural areas attracted the private investors to local higher education institutions in local areas.

- Locational advantage especially in case of Kangra, Solan and Sirmaur districts has played an important role to locate technical and professional colleges and universities in areas bordering Haryana, Uttarakhand, Uttar Pradesh, Panjab and Chandigarh union territory to attract students as well as faculty from these states.
- Location of 28 universities and majority of institutions running technical and professional courses speaks of a happy and healthy situation in case of the hill state of Himachal Pradesh. But most of these are established in private sector, where profit motive is the top-most objective behind entering the field of higher education; it is difficult to say with confidence that Himachalis are the major beneficiaries of technical and professional higher education. Dust free peaceful environment of Himachal Pradesh surely attracts parents as well as wards to get admitted to such institutions in the state. It is however also true that size of middle class is expanding recently in Himachal Pradesh and the middle class households always try to grab white collared jobs especially in the public sector. Hence, the benefit of the rapid expansion of technical and professional higher education in Himachal Pradesh is accruing to Himachalis as well.
- In the hill state of Himachal Pradesh, relief and transport network play an important role in geographical location of higher education institutions. The analysis reveals that 800 metres and 1500 metres height are the two critical breaks in location of higher education institutions in the state. 125 or two-fifth of the total number of higher education institutions in the state were located below 800 metres contours height and another 104 or one-third

were situated between 800 and 1500 metres contour height. In all, three-fourth of the total number of higher educational institutions was located below 1500 metres height in the Outer and Central Himalayas. Secondly, accessibility of higher education institutions in rugged and hilly terrain conditions forced the interested groups to locate colleges and universities in the state on the major transport routes. Nearly, one-half (47.0%) of the colleges and universities in the state were located on national highways passing through the state and another more than one-fifth were located in close proximity to the state highways. Briefly three factors namely, government policies, may it be privatization of higher education or aggressive role of the state government for popularistic reasons, physiographic conditions especially relief and transport network have played crucial role in making and remaking of geography of higher education institutions in the state of Himachal Pradesh.

III
Structural Composition and Change

Introduction

Structure of higher education can be examined in a number of ways. In the available literature it has been generally examined in terms of its nature, management type and regulatory bodies. The present study examines the structure of higher education in Himachal Pradesh in terms of all the above mentioned.

In terms of the nature, higher education can be categorised into (a) general, (b) professional, and (c) technical education. From the angle of management, it can be (i) public, (ii) private, (iii) joint (public and private), and (iv) non-governmental run by NGOs. From the regulatory angle, in the case of India, University Grants Commission (UGC) is the main governing body that provides grants, coordinates activities and maintains standard of higher education in the entire country. However, several autonomous regulatory and statutory bodies have come up to play an important role to regulate institutions of higher education. Such bodies include (i) All India Council for Technical Education (AICTE), (ii) Medical Council of India (MCI), (iii) Indian Council of Agriculture Research (ICAR), (iv) National Council of Teachers Education (NCTE), (v) Dental Council of India (DCI), (vi) Pharmacy Council of India (PCI), (vii) Indian Nursing Council (INC), (viii) Bar Council of India (BCI), (ix) Veterinary Council of India (VCI), (x) Central Council of Indian Medicine (CCIM), (xi) Distance Education Council (DEC), (xii) Council of Architecture (COA), (xiii) Indian Council of Agricultural Research (ICAR), and (xiv) State Councils of Higher Education (SCHE). All such councils are responsible for the recognition of the courses, promotion of professional institutions, regulation of syllabus, provision of grants and maintaining of standards (Fig. 3.0). For example, All India Council of Technical Education (AICTE) is involved in affiliation/de-affiliation of institutions. The structure

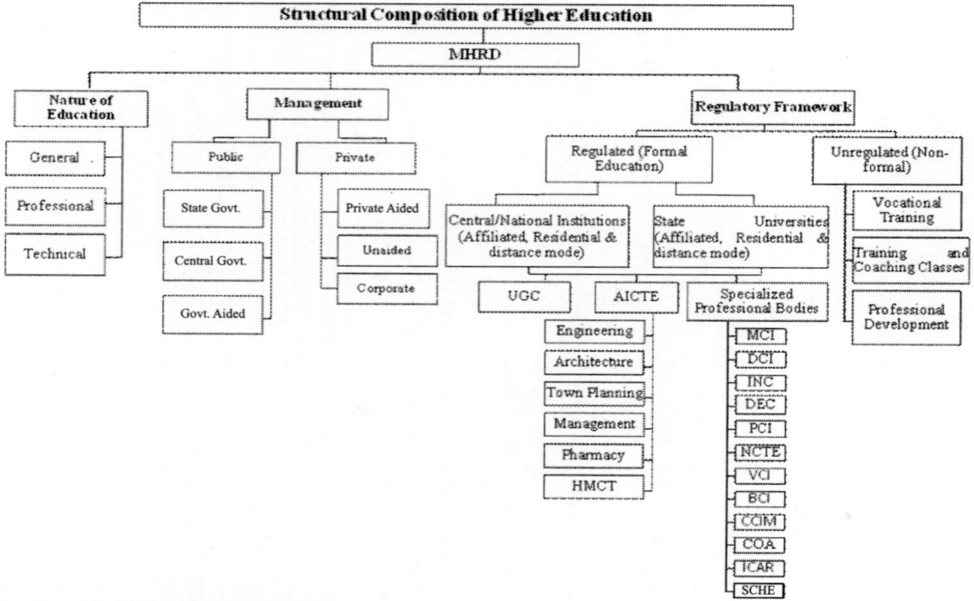

Fig. 3.0: Structural Composition of Higher Education.

Source: Compiled from: (i) Rand Corporation (2013) Report on *Building the Links between Funding and Quality in Higher Education, India's Challenge* and Deloitte (2012), Report on *Indian Higher Education Sector: Opportunities Aplenty, Growth Unlimited* (p. 6).

of higher education in Himachal Pradesh is almost technical education, which involves formulation of teaching courses and regularization as well as promotion of technical education.

In the following, an attempt will be made to examine all these in the same way as was examined at the national level. The union Ministry of Human Resource Development (Henceforth, MHRD) is the central level ministry to govern the higher education in India. Its various regulatory arms are responsible for laying down the quality standards that all the higher education institutions are expected to follow (Daugherty *et al.*, 2013). The MHRD is responsible for education at all levels. Its wing known as the Department of School and Literacy is responsible for the development of school education whereas another wing, the Department of Higher Education takes care of higher education.

While attempting an examination of the structure of higher education in Himachal Pradesh on the basis of its nature, management and regulatory framework, due to the lack of time series data on enrolment by management, forced us to drop the idea. Hence, our discussions here will focus only on nature and regulatory framework of higher education. Secondly, discussions on colleges and universities in the state are organised separately, in order.

I. Nature of Education

A. Colleges

As stated earlier, by its nature, the higher education can be classified into general, professional, and technical education. However, in practice, a single institution of higher education may impart two or more types of education, posing a serious difficulty in classifying the higher education institutions, especially the colleges.

It has been observed that there are colleges in the state where disciplines/subjects relating to arts, humanities, sciences, engineering/ technology or even management are taught on the same campus in the same precincts. In fact, they act as mini-universities. The *Annual Status Report of Higher Education, 2013* classifies higher education into (i) Graduate, (ii) Masters (Post Graduate), (iii) Pre-doctoral/Doctoral degrees in general, technical and professional categories (Government of India, 2012:7) (Also see Fig. 3.1 for details). Another report divides higher education into four broad categories: formal, technical and professional, skill development and vocational training (Deloitte, 2012:6). By the nature, higher education can also be classified as general, vocational, professional or technical (Government of India, 2012:1). In light of all this, the present study adopts

<table>
<tr><th>Completed Years of Age/ Age-groups</th><th colspan="7"></th><th>Years of Education</th></tr>
<tr><td>26</td><td colspan="7" rowspan="2">Ph.D. (5)</td><td>22</td></tr>
<tr><td>25</td><td>21</td></tr>
<tr><td>24</td><td rowspan="2">MS/MD (2)</td><td rowspan="2">MDS (2)</td><td rowspan="2">LL.M. (2)</td><td rowspan="2">Pre-Ph.D</td><td rowspan="3">M.Ed (2)</td><td rowspan="3">ME. M. Phar MBA (2), MSc. Nurs. (2) MCA (3)</td><td rowspan="3">M.Sc. (Agri., Forest, Hort.)</td><td>20</td></tr>
<tr><td>23</td><td>19</td></tr>
<tr><td>22</td><td rowspan="6">MBBS/BAMS (5)</td><td rowspan="6">BDS (5)</td><td rowspan="3">LLB (3)</td><td>MPhil. (2)</td><td>18</td></tr>
<tr><td>21</td><td rowspan="2">M.Sc. M.A. M.Com. (2)</td><td rowspan="2">B.Ed* (2)</td><td rowspan="5">BE, B.Tech. B.Phar., Nurs. (4)</td><td rowspan="5">B.Sc. Agr. For. Hort. (4)</td><td>17</td></tr>
<tr><td>20</td><td>16</td></tr>
<tr><td>19</td><td colspan="3" rowspan="3">B.A., B.Sc., B.Com, BBA, BCA (3)</td><td>15</td></tr>
<tr><td>18</td><td>14</td></tr>
<tr><td>17</td><td>13</td></tr>
<tr><td>3-16</td><td colspan="7">School Education</td><td>1-12</td></tr>
</table>

Fig. 3.1: Higher Education: Hierarchical Structure of Various Programmes.

Source: Modified from the Manju Lohumi (Development of Tertiary Education in Himachal Pradesh, 1996, p. 3).

Note: Agr. = Agriculture, For. = Forestry, Hort. = Horticulture, B. Phar./M. Phar. = Bachelor and Masters of Pharmacy, B.E, M.E = Bachelor and Masters of Engineering, MBBS = Bachelor of Medicine and Surgery, Nurs. = Nursing, LLB = Bachelor and Masters of Law, BAMS = Bachelor of Ayurvedic Medicine and Surgery, BDS/MDS = Bachelor and Masters of Dental Surgery, MS/MD = Masters of Surgery/Doctor of Medicine. (ii) *One year course of B.Ed upgraded into two years from 2015-17. (iii) The figures given in parenthesis shows the duration of the course in years.

its own classification, dividing all the 279 colleges in the state into five categories: General, Technical, Professional, Technical-cum-Professional and Multi-disciplinary (Fig 3.2).

Colleges and Universities, engaged in the pursuit of knowledge beyond 10+2 level, come under higher education, but with a difference. The Universities award their own degrees, whereas the colleges award degrees through the universities of their affiliation. They have to follow entry, operation and exit requirements, as defined by the respective

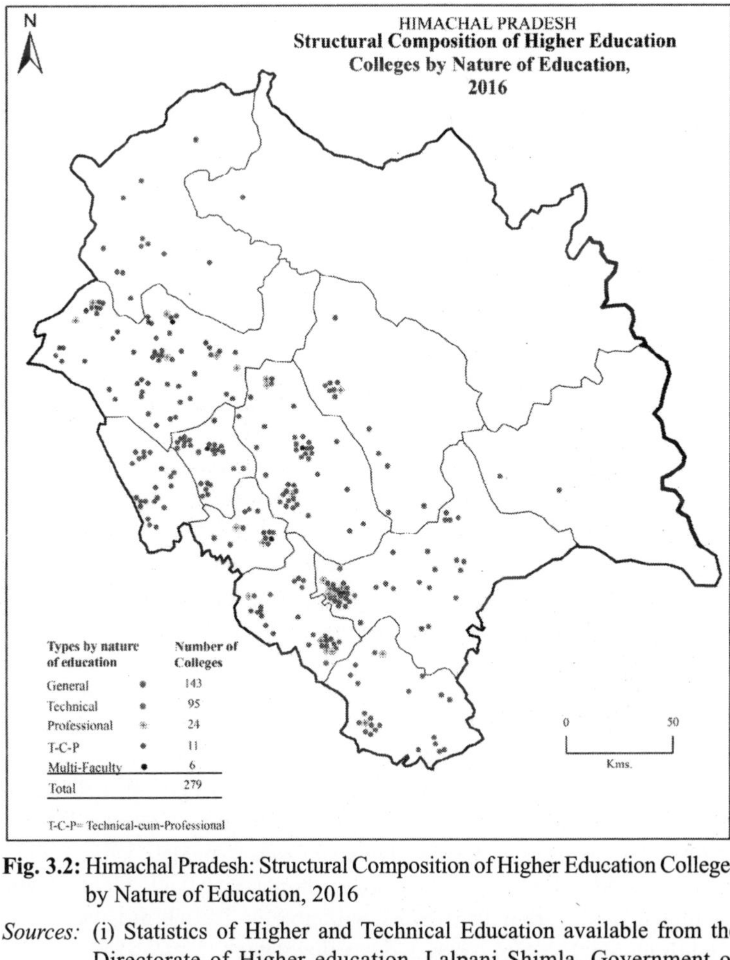

Fig. 3.2: Himachal Pradesh: Structural Composition of Higher Education Colleges by Nature of Education, 2016

Sources: (i) Statistics of Higher and Technical Education available from the Directorate of Higher education, Lalpani Shimla, Government of Himachal Pradesh. (ii) Annual reports of various years from Himachal Pradesh University, Shimla.

Universities. Generally, the colleges are affiliated either to the central or the state universities. Private colleges are usually affiliated to the state universities. In Himachal Pradesh, all colleges running undergraduate courses except the technical ones are affiliated to Himachal Pradesh University (H.P.U.), Shimla. The colleges/institutes imparting technical education are affiliated to Himachal Pradesh Technical University (HPTU) located at Hamirpur town.

A separate university to affiliate either medical or agricultural colleges is yet to be established in Himachal Pradesh. In the neighbouring Punjab, however, there is a separate university of Medical Sciences to affiliate all the medical colleges in the state. In nutshell, the colleges offering degree level courses are required to be affiliated with the universities. In this way, they come under the purview of the same government regulations, covering the universities (Hill, S. and Chalaux, T., 2011:25).

In 2016, general education colleges made more than one-half or 51.3 per cent of the total 279 colleges of the state. Another more than one-third or 34.3 per cent belonged to technical education, distantly followed by professional education colleges with 8.6 per cent, technical-cum-professional with 4.0 per cent and multi-faculty colleges with only 2.2 per cent (Table 3.0).

Evidently, general education dominates the higher education scenario in the state. However, there are significant departures at the district level. Against the state average of 51.3 per cent, the share of general education colleges in total colleges of respective districts ranged from a high of cent per cent in Lahul and Spiti district to a low of 34.5 per cent in Solan district. In other words, higher education is least diversified in case of Lahul and Spiti, against the most diversified one in Solan district. On the whole, higher education is minimally diversified in four districts of Lahul and Spiti, Chamba, Kullu and Kinnaur (Fig 3.5). Against this, it is highly diversified in four districts of Solan, Shimla, Mandi and Sirmaur. The same is statistically supported in Gibbs-Martin index of diversification, calculated to know the degree of diversification in higher education at the district level in Himachal Pradesh (Table 3.1).

Fig 3.3 reveals that four districts of Lahul and Spiti, Chamba, Kullu and Kinnaur, with index value of 0.50, are categorized as low diversification districts. Against this, four districts, namely Solan, Shimla, Mandi and Sirmaur, where index value is higher than 0.60, fall in category of high diversification districts. Remaining four districts of Una, Kangra, Hamirpur and Bilaspur where index value ranged from 0.51 to 0.60 falls in moderate category of diversification.

In highly diversified category, Solan and Sirmaur districts have the advantage of relatively plain topography and their proximity to plains in Punjab, Haryana, Uttarakhand, Uttar Pradesh and even the National Capital Territory of Delhi. Their proximity to plains and better transport links help in attracting students as well as good teaching faculty from the neighbouring states in the plains. In a way, these two districts have locational advantage. On the other hand, Shimla district has benefitted

Table 3.0: Himachal Pradesh: Structural composition of higher education by nature, 2016

a.	**General Education**	**No. of Colleges**
1.	General education courses (Arts, Science, and Commerce and Oriental)	104
2.	General cum technical courses (Arts, Science and Commerce with technical education)	21
3.	Arts/Science/Commerce/Postgraduate/ Technical education (BBA/ BCA/B.Ed)	18
		143 **(51.3)**
b.	**Technical Education**	
1.	B.Ed/M.Ed	55
2.	Pharmacy/Engineering, MBA/MCA/BBA/BCA	22
3.	B.Ed/ M.Ed/BBA/BCA	18
		95 **(34.3)**
c.	**Professional Education**	
1.	Medical Courses	8
2.	Paramedical Professionals	16
		24 **(8.6)**
d.	**Technical cum Professional Education**	
1.	BBA/BCA/Engineering/MBA/Pharmacy/Bio Sciences	1
2.	B.Ed/M.Ed/Professional education (LLB/Bio-Sciences)/Technical (Engineering/Pharmacy/BBA/BCA)	3
3.	Dental/Professional (Bio-Sciences)/Technical (Pharmacy/Engineering)	2
4.	LLB/Technical/Professional	4
5.	Applied cum Life Sciences/Technical	1
		11 **(4.0)**
e.	**Multi-Disciplinary Education**	
1.	Arts/Commerce/Technical (BBA/BCA)/Professional education (Bio technology)	1
2.	Arts/Science/Commerce/Postgraduate/Technical education (BBA/ BCA/B.Ed), Professional education	5
		6 **(2.2)**
All Colleges		**279**

Sources: (i) Statistics of Higher and Technical Education available from the Directorate of Higher education, Lalpani Shimla, Government of Himachal Pradesh. (ii) Annual reports of various years from Himachal Pradesh University, Shimla. (Annexure-I-V)

Table 3.1: Himachal Pradesh: District-wise percentage share of higher education colleges by nature, 2016

S. No.	*District Name*	*General*	*Tech-nical*	*Profes-sional*	*Techni-cal cum profess-sional*	*Multi-faculty*	*Gibbs-Martin Index*
1	2	3	4	5	6	7	8
1.	Bilaspur	57.1	21.4	14.3	0.0	7.1	0.60
2.	Chamba	83.3	16.7	0.0	0.0	0.0	0.28
3.	Hamirpur	44.0	48.0	0.0	4.0	4.0	0.57
4.	Kangra	56.1	31.6	10.5	0.0	1.8	0.57
5.	Kinnaur	50.0	50.0	0.0	0.0	0.0	0.50
6.	Kullu	69.2	23.1	7.7	0.0	0.0	0.46
7.	Lahul and Spiti	100.0	0.0	0.0	0.0	0.0	0.00
8.	Mandi	40.0	47.5	7.5	2.5	2.5	0.61
9.	Shimla	47.6	31.0	14.3	2.4	4.8	0.65
10.	Sirmaur	56.5	21.7	8.7	13.0	0.0	0.61
11.	Solan	34.5	41.4	13.8	10.3	0.0	0.68
12.	Una	57.1	33.3	0.0	9.5	0.0	0.55
	Himachal Pradesh	**51.3**	**34.1**	**8.6**	**3.9**	**2.2**	**0.61**

Source: As of Table 3.0.

from the initial advantage, functioning as a hill town and then the summer capital of British India for its good climate and scenic beauty. Since independence, it has been the state capital of Himachal Pradesh. On the other hand, Mandi district has benefitted from its political clout in recent decades. The district has the privilege of being parliamentary and assembly constituencies of important political personalities in the state including Shri V.B. Singh, the present Chief Minister and his wife, Shri Sukh Ram, former central cabinet minister in Shri Narsimharao government during 1991-1996 and Shri Kaul Singh, important cabinet minister in the present state government headed by Shri V.B. Singh as the Chief Minister. Moreover Mandi, among the erstwhile native states of Himachal Pradesh, has a long tradition of education.

In contrast, four districts having lower diversification of higher education suffers from their peripheral locations, rugged topography and harsh climate, leading to sparse distribution of settlements and low population density. Among these districts, Lahul and Spiti have only one college and that fulfils the requirement of general education. There is a substantial share of tribal population in these four districts. The

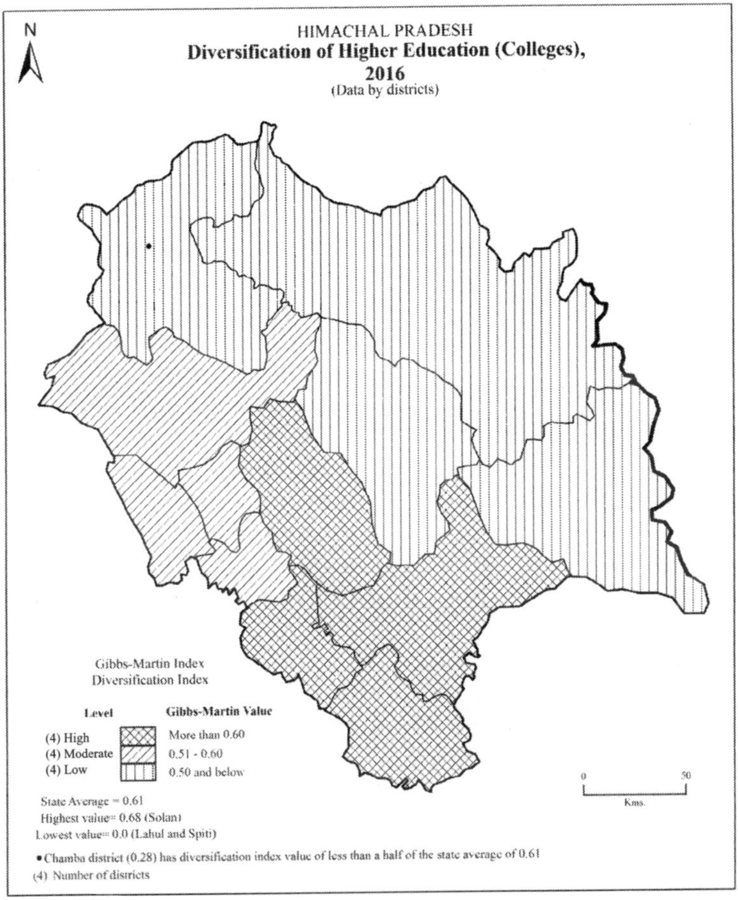

Fig. 3.3: Himachal Pradesh: Diversification of Higher Education (Colleges), 2016

Source: As of Table 3.0.

Government of India provides various concessions to tribals for their socio-economic upliftment. Reservation of seats in educational institutions and provision of scholarships to students belonging to tribal population are a few of such welfare measures. For this and some other reasons, tribals residing in these districts send their children for higher education to cities like Chandigarh, Delhi and Amritsar. In addition, the well to do households of these districts also send their wards to cities in plain areas of the adjoining states namely Punjab, Haryana, National Capital Territory, Delhi and Chandigarh (U.T.). Moreover, these areas are well linked with plains of Punjab, Haryana, Chandigarh and Delhi and have close socio-economic links, which were developed earlier during British rule in India when these areas were part of colonial Punjab.

The remaining four districts having index value between 0.51 and 0.60 and falling in moderate diversification category of districts include Una, Bilaspur, Hamirpur and Kangra. Hamirpur district has the highest share (48.0%) of technical education colleges in its total higher education colleges in the entire state. Yet the district of Hamirpur has no such college that imparts professional education. Similarly, Kangra district where technical colleges make about 32.0 per cent of total colleges, general education colleges still dominate with 56.1 per cent share. In Una, where the share of technical colleges is one-third of the total colleges of the district, surprisingly there is no college imparting a professional education. Again general education colleges dominate the scenario. Locationally, all these districts have close proximity to Punjab, and with exception of Bilaspur district all were a part of the Punjab before its linguistic reorganization in 1966. Hence, a large number of households carry on the tradition of sending their wards to the colleges and universities located in Punjab especially for technical and professional courses. In fact, relatives of several households are domiciles of Punjab.

b. General Education Colleges

In the following section, we discuss briefly general education colleges, by dividing these further in three different sub-categories: those offering (i) general courses only, (ii) general-cum-technical courses, and (iii) undergraduate and postgraduate courses with technical education (Table 3.0). In 2016, 143, or 51.3 per cent of the total 279 colleges in the state were offering courses related to general education.

However, the scenario of higher education has changed considerably over the period of time. In pre-statehood period before 1971, the higher education in the state was greatly dominated by general education. Then, 21 or 75.0 per cent of the total 28 colleges in the state imparted higher education in general courses. Amongst these 21 colleges, nearly one-half or ten were offering purely arts courses. Another ten were running a few technical courses along with general courses at graduate and post-graduate level. The remaining one college was providing general-cum-technical courses (Table 3.2). Colleges imparting technical and professional education were highly limited in number.

Table 3.2: Himachal Pradesh: Distribution of colleges by nature, 1971-2016

Years	*GE**	*%*	*TE**	*%*	*Prof**	*%*	*TCP**	*%*	*MF**	*%*	*Total*
1971	21	75.0	2	7.1	1	3.6	0	0.0	4	14.3	**28**
1981	33	80.5	2	4.9	2	4.9	0	0.0	4	9.8	**41**
1991	46	83.6	2	3.6	2	3.6	0	0.0	5	9.1	**55**
2001	73	77.7	8	8.5	6	6.4	1	1.1	6	6.4	**94**
2011	104	46.0	88	38.9	17	7.5	11	4.9	6	2.7	**226**
2016	143	51.3	95	34.1	24	8.6	11	3.9	6	2.2	**279**

Source: As of Table 3.0.

Note:*GE: General education; TE: Technical education; Prof.: Professional education; TCP: Technical-cum-professional education; MF: Multi-Faculty

In 1981, where the number of the colleges in the state went to 41, 33 or more than 80.0 per cent of them were imparting general education. There had been no change in number of technical/professional/technical-cum-professional education colleges during 1971-1981. The general education courses continued to dominate the higher education scenario in the state.

In the year 1991, when total number of colleges went up to 55, 46 or about 84.0 per cent imparted general education courses. This indicates the growing dominance of general education courses in the field of higher education in the state. It is interesting to note that the number of general education colleges increased by 13, from 33 in 1981 to 46 in 1991. Against this all the other category of colleges registered increase of one college only. The national scenario was also not very different from that of Himachal Pradesh.

After 1991, when there came a notable change in the situation following the change in economic policies at the national level, the demand for technical and professional education increased to make Indian education globally competitive and job oriented. As a result, focus shifted to technical and professional courses. Some scholars have termed it as a paradigm shift in higher education in India. By 2001, where there were 94 colleges in the state to impart higher education, 73 or only 77.7 per cent were imparting general education courses. Evidently, the share of colleges imparting general education courses declined by 6.0 per cent during 1991-2001. Against this, the share of technical education colleges more than doubled: from 3.6 per cent in 1991 to 8.5 per cent in 2001. Similarly, the share of professional colleges rose from 3.6 per cent to 6.4 per cent during this period.

Then after a gap of ten years in 2011, the share of colleges imparting general education courses sharply declined to 46.0 per cent or less than a half of the total number of colleges. Against this, share of technical colleges jumped from 8.5 per cent in 2001 to 38.9 per cent in 2011. Evidently, technical and professional education courses were accorded higher priority over general courses during this period. This was a period when private investment in the sector of higher education got a big push in the state of Himachal Pradesh. Majority of the colleges and universities coming during this period were established in the private sector (Table 3.3).

However, the Government of Himachal Pradesh became active again to promote the higher education in the state. Several new colleges were opened by the state government in the backward and peripheral areas so that a college is available within a radius of 25 kms in all the parts of the state [Government of Himachal Pradesh (GOI), 2014]. In most of such colleges general education courses were introduced. As a result, by 2016, the share of general education colleges rose to 51.2 per cent from 46.0 per cent in 2011. **Evidently, government policy, whether it is about focus on privatization or on public investment in higher education, matters a lot in changing the structural composition of higher education in a state in general and a country as a whole (in particular).**

Inter-District Differentials

In the following segment, we attempt to examine the inter-district differentials in distribution of colleges imparting general education courses. It consists of undergraduate degree courses in the faculties of Arts,

Table 3.3: Himachal Pradesh: Shifting paradigm and reversal of the trend in the structural composition of higher education, 1971-2016

Time-period	Features
1971-1991	• Overdominance of general education courses. Highest in Lahul and Spiti to lowest in Solan district. • Least diversified districts were Chamba, Lahul and Spiti, Kinnaur and Kullu due to their hill terrain, peripheral location and harsh climate playing a negative role. • Maximum diversified districts such as Solan, Shimla, Mandi and Sirmaur due to their locational advantage and historical factors.
1991-2001	• Since 1991 policy, shift towards opening of the new technical education courses. • Paradigm shift in higher education in India. • UGC, AICTE and specialized professional bodies regulated the general, technical and professional education in the state.

2001-2011	• Unprecedented growth of technical education institutes specially teachers' training courses. • Consequently priority given to the technical/professional education courses. • Share of general education colleges decreased during 2001-2011. • Phase of privatization led to the opening of several colleges of technical education. • Fast expansion of the private institutes and need to ensure the quality education G.O.H.P established the Himachal Pradesh Private Educational Regulatory Commission.
2011-2016	• Again public investment in general education colleges started during this period by the present government to gain the sympathy of the people living in the areas without any government college of higher education. • Professional education is in incipient stage and five districts have no professional education colleges such as Chamba, Kinnaur, Lahul and Spiti, Una and Hamirpur. • Nursing colleges have the higher share in the total number of colleges providing professional education. • Slow growth of colleges/institutes/universities imparting technical education. • Three-fifth of the universities oriented towards the technical/professional education. More than half of the universities located in Solan district only due to its location bordering Punjab, Haryana and Chandigarh. • Lack of universities/central level institute in Bilaspur, Kullu, Chamba, Kinnaur and Lahul and Spiti districts. • The state adopted RUSA in Himachal Pradesh University, Shimla and its affiliated colleges to improve the access, equity and quality of higher education.

Science, Commerce and Oriental education, covering courses in the Sanskrit language. In the beginning, all such colleges started with general education courses. However, with the passage of time technical education courses, such as Bachelor of Computer Applications and Bachelor of Business Administration were added on. Of the 143 colleges/institutions imparting general education, 104 or 73.8 per cent were running courses in arts, science and commerce, of course termed as the traditional courses.

The maximum number (63) of such colleges was in Kangra and minimum number (1) was in Lahul and Spiti. Nearly 58.7 per cent of such colleges were located in four districts of Kangra, Shimla, Sirmaur and Mandi. Against this, their combined population (of 18-23 age-group) makes 55.6 per cent of the total population of the state. Moreover, more than one-third or about 37.0 per cent colleges were located in the four districts of Bilaspur, Chamba, Solan, Kullu and Una. In this way, more than nine-tenths or 95.2 per cent of such colleges were distributed in nine districts, having, in combine, 92.4 per cent population of the state. Obviously, there is not much mis-match between the population share (age-group identified as higher education age-group) of districts and their respective shares in total colleges of general education courses in the state. The rest of the five per cent colleges were located in the two districts of Hamirpur and Lahul and Spiti. In Kinnaur district, there is no college that runs courses providing exclusively general.

The share of general education colleges in the total colleges of respective districts makes an interesting story. In Lahul and Spiti district, there was only one college and that too running general education courses. In other words, higher education in Lahul and Spiti was oriented entirely to the general education. In this thinly populated district, development of higher education was lopsided. Next to it was Chamba district, where more than four-fifth or 83.3 per cent of higher education was confined to the teaching of general courses. Bilaspur, Kullu, Sirmaur, Kangra and Una were other districts where the majority of colleges were teaching general courses. Kinnaur is another district in the state where half of the colleges imparted general education as it has only two colleges, one imparting general-cum-technical and another one the technical education. On the other side of the scale, Solan is the only district in the state where colleges of general education make only one-third or 34.5 per cent of the total number of colleges.

Next to Solan was Mandi district having two-fifth or 40.0 per cent share of such colleges. On the whole, Kinnaur, Solan, Mandi, Shimla and Hamirpur are the five districts where the share of colleges running general courses is less than the state average (51.3%). If we exclude Kinnaur district, which is a typical case, then seven of the remaining eleven districts have pre-dominance to dominance of general education courses in the sphere of higher education. **However, it has to be noted that there has been a remarkable change in nature of higher education in the state, from overdominance of general education to just dominance in the last forty-five years between 1971 and 2016.**

Briefly, colleges imparting traditional courses under general education category and making 104 or three-fourth (72.7%) of the total general education colleges in the state dominate in more than half of the districts in Himachal Pradesh. Numerically, more than two-third of such colleges are concentrated in one-third of the districts in the state. Interestingly, Mandi, where such colleges are found in relatively large number, has their share of less than 40.0 per cent of the total colleges in the district.

Twenty-one colleges falling under general category also started technical courses on their campuses. This was done to meet the growing demand for such courses and the encouragement and incentives provided by the state as well as the central governments. For example, the University Grants Commission (UGC), New Delhi provides financial grant for building physical and human infrastructure in the next five years to colleges willing to start vocational courses. Such incentives encouraged the colleges running traditional courses to start vocational courses. In their distribution, 14 out of 21 such colleges were located in the three districts namely Shimla, Hamirpur, and Kangra. Remaining five such colleges were distributed, one each, in Solan, Mandi, Kinnaur, Chamba and Bilaspur districts. Two colleges were in Sirmaur district [See Annexure-I (a) and I (b)].

Remaining about one-sixth or 18 colleges in this category provide under-graduate and post-graduate modern courses such as business administration, tourism management, computer applications, physical education and teachers' training course (B.Ed) along with traditional courses. The largest number, i.e. four of such colleges was in Una district followed by three in Kangra and by two each in Hamirpur, Mandi, Shimla, and Solan districts. Of the remaining four such colleges, one each was located in Bilaspur, Kullu and Sirmaur districts [See Annexure-I (c)].

Another characteristic feature of their distributional pattern was that more than seven of each ten such colleges were located in rural areas. Himachal Pradesh is a least urbanised state where less than one of each ten persons resides in urban areas of the state. From that angle, the share of urban areas, having nearly three in each ten such colleges, was indicative of the higher concentration of such colleges in urban areas. In other words, **general education courses made a dominant character of colleges located in rural areas of the state.**

Briefly, the largest share (or 51.3%) of colleges in the state was still confined to the teaching of traditional courses under general education segment. In four districts of Lahul and Spiti, Chamba, Bilaspur and Kullu, higher education was mainly oriented to general or traditional education. In addition to these four districts another four districts have the share of one-half or 50 per cent or more than one-half of the total number of colleges imparting general education, these districts are Kangra, Kinnaur, Sirmaur and Una (Fig 3.4a). However, of late, more than one-fourth or 27.3 per cent of such colleges have started offering vocational and technical courses along with traditional courses. Growing demand coupled with the offer of financial support from the University Grants Commission, New Delhi for opening vocational and technical courses have been responsible for such a change in structural composition of higher education in the state. Such colleges were highly concentrated in a few districts of the state. Four districts of Kangra, Shimla, Sirmaur, and Mandi accounted for more than 50 per cent or to be precise 56.6 per cent of such colleges. Moreover, these colleges showed a tendency to be concentrated in urban areas, since 20.9 per cent of them were located in urban centres, against urban population making only about 10.0 per cent of the total population of the state.

b. Technical Education

In 2016, 95 or 34.1 per cent of total 279 colleges in Himachal Pradesh were imparting technical education courses, placing technical education next to general education in the state. However, strengthening of technical education in the state is a recent phenomenon. Before statehood in 1971, technical education had only two or just 7.1 per cent of the total number of 28 colleges in the state. These two colleges were associated with the teachers' training courses in the state (Table 3.2).

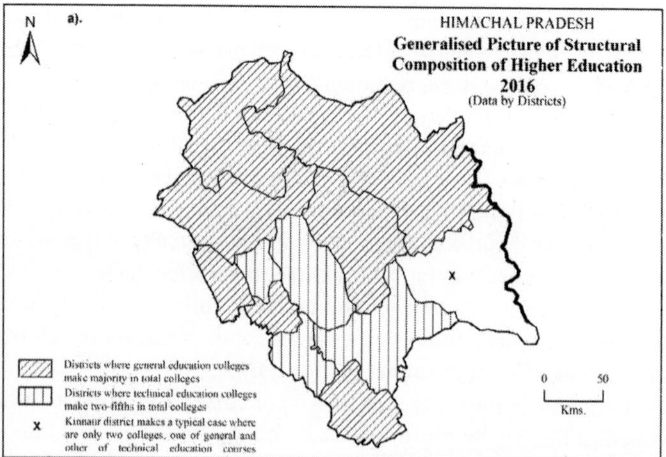

Fig. 3.4: Himachal Pradesh: Generalized Picture of Structural Composition of Higher Education, 2016.

Source: As of Table 3.0.

There has been no change in the number of technical education colleges between 1971 and 1991. After that, this number went up with the coming of six more technical education institutions in the state between 1991 and 2001. In other words, on an average, less than one such college/institution per annum was added during the decade of 1991-2000. In this way, by 2001 when total number of colleges imparting higher education in the state had gone up to 94, the share of such colleges made only 8.5 per cent of the total number of colleges. Evidently, there has been a slow progress in the area of technical education in the state till 2001. The new six such colleges added during 1991-2001 had the following composition of courses. Three of them were of teachers' training, two of pharmacy and remaining one management college.

The next decade of 2001-2011 recorded a spurt in technical education in the state. As many as 80 new colleges of technical education were added to make the total number of such colleges 88 or 39.0 per cent of total number of higher education colleges in the state.

The credit, in fact, goes to privatization wave, in the state, since most of colleges running a variety of technical courses were opened in private sector. Of the total 80 technical colleges established during the decade of 2001-2011 decade in the state, 78 were in the private sector.

After attaining its peak growth during the decade 2001-2011, technical higher education recorded a sluggish growth in the state. Between the year 2011 and 2016, when the total number of higher education colleges in the state went up to 279 from 226 in the year 2011, the number of technical higher education increased by only seven: from 88 to 95. In the year 2016, these made 34.1 per cent of the total number of colleges, against 39.0 per cent in 2011. Evidently, slow growth of technical higher education colleges during 2011-2016 resulted in decline of their share by about 4.0 per cent during this period. Of the new technical colleges, three were running teachers' training courses and the remaining four were providing pharmacy/engineering and management courses.

A majority of technical colleges in the state were providing Bachelor's and Master's Degree courses in the field of teachers' training. This is mainly because of a high demand for trained teachers to teach at the school level as well as to train the teachers further. A further inquiry reveal that overwhelming majority of such colleges, to begin with started B.Ed classes and later on diversified to other technical courses including computer science applications, business administration, engineering and pharmaceutical sciences. 55 such colleges or 58.0 per cent of total technical higher education colleges in the state run B.Ed. and M.Ed. courses. Earlier, the aspirants for such courses used to go to colleges located in the neighbouring states of Jammu & Kashmir, Uttar Pradesh, Punjab and Haryana.

Inter-district distribution of technical higher education colleges is highly revealing. Two-fifths of such colleges are spread in five districts of Mandi, Kinnaur, Solan, Shimla and Hamirpur (Fig 3.4a). In Mandi district, which has the largest number of such colleges in the state, one-half of the total number of colleges in the district was imparting technical courses. On the other side of the scale, four districts of Bilaspur, Chamba, Kinnaur and Kullu, in combine, had only nine of total number of such colleges. Lahul and Spiti district has no such college (Annexure-IIa).

Mandi and Hamirpur were the only districts in the state where more than two-fifth of the total number of colleges were running technical education courses. Kinnaur is an exceptional case, where one of the two colleges is running technical education courses. On the whole, in four districts namely Mandi, Kinnaur, Hamirpur, and Solan the share of such colleges in the total number of colleges of respective districts was higher than the state average of 34.1 (Table 3.1).

Another 22 colleges of this category run engineering/pharmacy/management/computer courses. Considered as job oriented, such courses attract aspirants not only from within the state but also from neighbouring states. Again, the highest number of such colleges was in Mandi, Hamirpur and Shimla districts (Annexure-IIb).

Remaining 18 colleges of this category run business administration and computer application courses along with B.Ed. courses. One-half of such colleges were located in two districts of Solan and Kangra. The rest were spread over Una, Mandi, Hamirpur, Shimla and Kullu districts. It means as many as five districts of Bilaspur, Sirmaur, Kinnaur, Lahul and Spiti and Chamba in the state are without of colleges running such courses (Annexure-IIc).

A large number of such colleges in the state were in the private sector, coming after the change in the economic policies in the form of liberalization in the year 1991-1992. The policy was again modified in 2001 to clear the way for opening of new universities or to tie-up with existing ones in the private sector (foreign as well as Indian). Briefly, 95 or less than one-third of the total number of such colleges in the state, imparting technical education, are running B.Ed. and M.Ed. courses. Such courses, high in demand, were concentrated in five districts of Mandi, Kangra, Shimla, Solan, and Hamirpur. In fact, Mandi is the only district in the state where more than half of the colleges are providing higher education in technical field.

40 or two-fifth of the colleges of this category, run courses such as engineering, computer science applications, business management and pharmacy, these are not only recent in origin but also high in demand. Locationally, such colleges are mainly concentrated in five districts of Mandi, Hamirpur, Solan, Shimla and Kangra in the state.

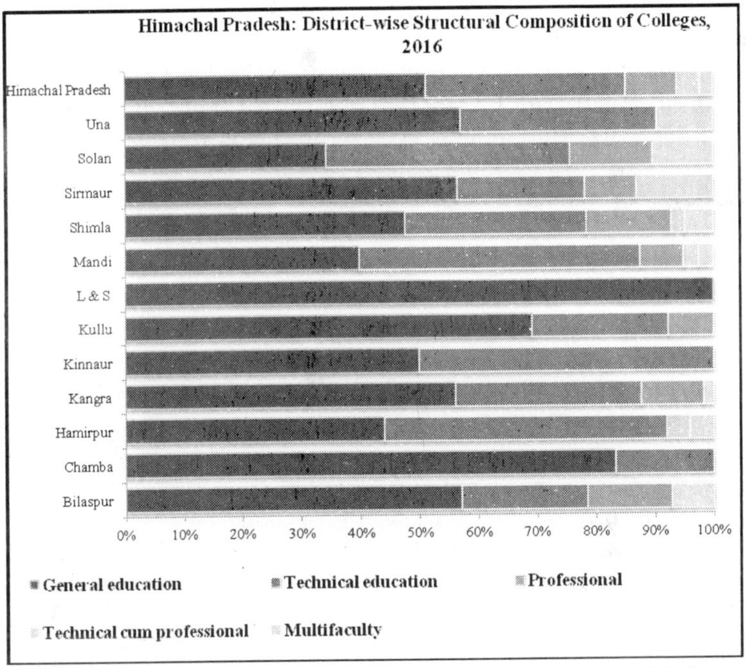

Fig. 3.5: Himachal Pradesh: District-wise Structural Composition of Colleges, 2016.

Source: As of Table 3.0.

c. *Professional Education*

Professional education is in its infancy in Himachal Pradesh. Only 24 or less than one-tenth of the total number of colleges in the state run professional courses. They are running medical and paramedical courses, needing huge financial investment to build infrastructure (Table 3.0). The courses are in Ayurvedic, Dental, Allopathic and Homeopathic system of medical sciences, while the focus of paramedical course is on the training of paramedical staff such as nurses. Medical courses take more than four years, against these paramedical courses which are of four to six years duration. Paramedical staff training courses are more recent in origin out of these two streams.

As in the case of technical higher education colleges, the year 2001 acts as water divide in case of professional colleges as well. The number of such colleges was only six in the year 2001. It rose to 17 in the year 2011 and then to 24 in 2016. Earlier in 1971, when Himachal Pradesh got statehood, there was only one college of this kind. Growing at a snail's pace between 1971 and 1981, it recorded high growth between 1991 and 2001, when number grew by 300 per cent: from two to six. Between 2001 and 2011, the number of professional colleges jumped to almost three times its original number to increase to about 40.0 per cent between 2011 and 2016. Against this, technical education colleges recorded an astounding increase of eleven times during the decade of 2001-2010 (Table 3.2).

In 2016, 24 professional colleges made only about 9.0 per cent of the total 279 colleges in the state. Against this, technical higher education colleges made 34.0 per cent of the total number of colleges. Evidently, professional higher education in the state is not only progressing at a slower pace but also is far behind the technical education (Fig. 3.4b).

The internal composition of 24 professional colleges in the state was as follows. Eight or one-third of the total number of colleges were running courses such as M.B.B.S, M.S. and M.D. In their distribution, they were located in the four districts of Kangra, Mandi, Shimla and Solan. Another, sixteen or two-third such colleges were running paramedical courses such as B.Sc. (nursing), and M.Sc. (nursing). One-half of paramedical colleges were located in the two districts of Kangra and Shimla. Remaining, one-half were widely spread in the five districts of Solan, Bilaspur, Kullu, Mandi and Sirmaur. On the whole, professional higher education colleges in the state were mainly confined to the four districts of Kangra, Shimla, Mandi and Solan, having, in combine, about four-fifth of total such colleges in the state.

Unfortunately, professional higher education colleges are still non-existent in five of twelve districts or 40.0 per cent districts of the state (Fig. 3.4b). These include Chamba, Hamirpur, Kinnaur, Lahul and Spiti and Una districts. **Evidently, in Himachal Pradesh higher education in the field of professional courses is not only in the stage of infancy but also highly confined in locational terms** [Annexure-III (a) and (b)].

d. Technical-cum-Professional Education

Only a small share of 4.0 per cent of the total number of colleges of state offered professional courses along with technical courses (Table 3.0). Professional courses, such as pharmacy, dentistry and law are offered along with engineering, computer science, teachers' training, management and bio-technology courses (Annexure-IV (a)].

Each one of these colleges deals in a variety of courses. These colleges were mainly concentrated in three districts of Sirmaur, Solan and Una where eight of the eleven such colleges were located. Remaining three were located in the three different districts of Hamirpur, Mandi, and Shimla. All of them have a recent origin and are privately managed (Table 3.2). The majority of these colleges were established after 2002. Further, the dominant majority was located in relatively plain areas, well linked with neighbouring states of Punjab, Haryana and Uttarakhand.

e. Multi-Disciplinary Courses

Remaining six or only 2.2 per cent of the total colleges were running multi-faculty courses both at undergraduate and post-graduate levels. Such colleges were not only few in number but also scattered in different parts of the state (Table 3.0). This may be termed as random distribution. Of the six such colleges, the two were located in Shimla and the remaining in the four districts of Hamirpur, Bilaspur, Kangra and Mandi. Interestingly, all such colleges were located in the urban areas. Multi-disciplinary colleges offered courses in Arts, Science, Commerce, Computer Applications, Business Administration, Biotechnology, Microbiology, and Tourism (See Annexure V).

B. Universities

Universities are known for higher education and research, provided at the graduate, post-graduate and doctoral research level. Universities, deemed universities and institutions of national importance are largely autonomous, which empowers them to design, develop and offer programmes relevant to and appropriate for the national needs. The universities/institutes of national importance are located only in seven of 12 districts in the state. These include Kangra, Hamirpur, Sirmaur, Solan, Shimla, Mandi and Una. In other words, there is no university/institute of national importance in Bilaspur, Kullu, Chamba, Kinnaur and Lahul and Spiti districts (Fig. 3.6).

In terms of their management, these are managed by government as well as private sector. Those managed by government can further be classified into state universities and central universities. Private universities can also be classified into those managed by the trusts and those managed by families or industrial houses/enterprises.

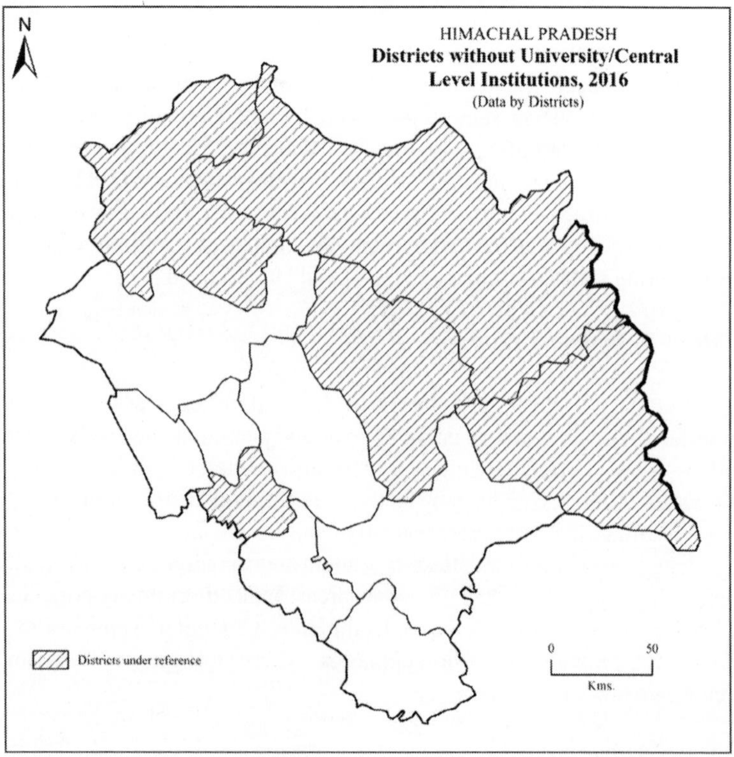

Fig. 3.6: Himachal Pradesh: Districts without University/Central level Institutions, 2016.

Source: As Table 3.0.

Like colleges, universities can also be classified into: (i) integrated/ general, and (ii) professional and technical. In terms of evolution, dominant majority of universities in the state were established during 2008-2014. As many as 19 of the total 28 universities/institutes were established during this period. In the following section, an attempt will be made to discuss universities by their nature.

a. General/Integrated Universities

Of the total 28 universities in the year 2016, working under different management types, 11 or roughly two-fifths were integrated or general by nature. Except for the Himachal Pradesh University, Shimla, the remaining universities are relatively recent in their origin. Till 2002, there were only eight universities in the state. The number increased by 20 during the span of 14 years between 2002 and 2016.

Himachal Pradesh University, situated in Shimla and established in 1970, is the oldest university in the state. All the colleges in the state were affiliated to it till recently. With the establishment of technical university at Hamirpur, all the technical colleges are affiliated now with this university (Table 3.4). In 2016, six of each ten universities in the state were technical/professional by nature.

Table 3.4: Himachal Pradesh: Classification of universities by their nature, 2016

Sl. No.	*Nature*	*Number*	*% of the total*
1	2	3	4
1	Integrated	11 (2)*	39.3
2	Technical/Professional	17 (4)*	60.7
	Total Universities	**28**	**100.00**

Source: As Table 3.0.

Note: * In the parenthesis are the institution established by the Central Government in the state. (see Annexure VI and VII)

b. Technical/Professional Universities

Locationally, 17 technical/professional universities in the state are distributed in the following manner. Nine or more than half of these were located in district of Solan alone. It was distantly followed with three in Kangra district, with two each in Hamirpur and Shimla and with one in Mandi district. Two districts of the state have more than five universities/central level institutes such as Kangra (6) and Solan (12). These two districts accounted for two-third of the total number of universities/central level institutes of the state (Fig. 3.7).

In terms of management, nine technical/professional universities were functioning under the private management. In a way these are self-financed universities where fee structures are quite high in comparison to the government managed universities. Remaining, eight universities are in the government sector. Among the government managed universities, five were managed by the Central Government and three by the state government. Obviously, there is predominance of private sector, which is closely followed by the Central Government. In the field of technical higher education, the role of Himachal Pradesh government was minimal.

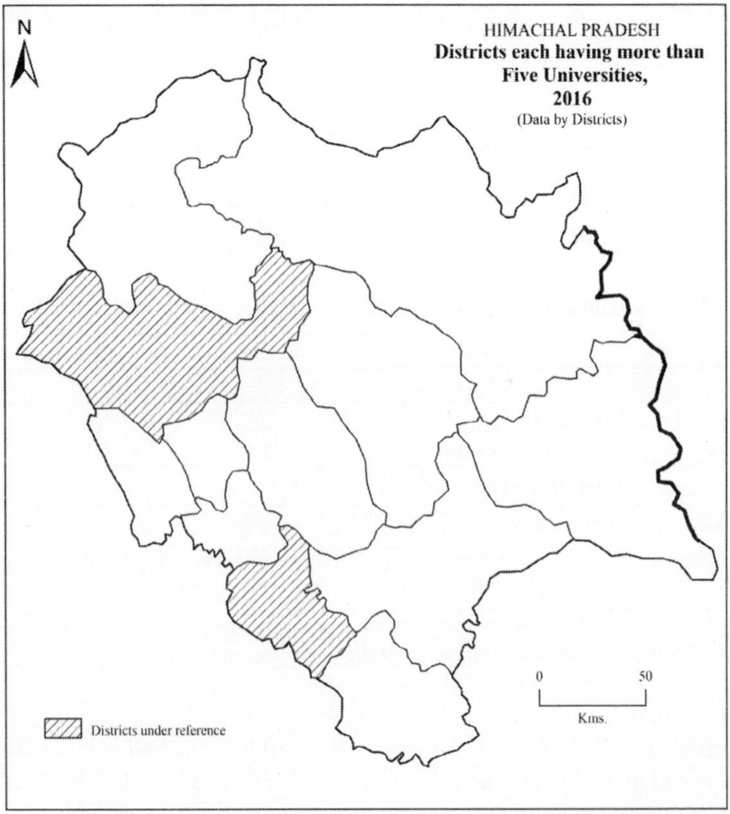

Fig. 3.7: Himachal Pradesh: Districts each having more than Five Universities, 2016.

Source: As Table 3.0.

In 2012, there were sixteen private universities in the state, the former ex-chief minister Shri Prem Kumar Dhumal's government had decided to allow only twenty private universities to function in the state and further preferred to locate these only in the four districts of Bilaspur, Chamba,

Kullu and Mandi as the state had reached a saturation point (Express News Service, Shimla, 6 April, 2012).

The dominant share of technical/professional universities in the total number of universities in the state speaks of a healthy situation. However, it has to be understood in terms of cost of such kind of education, if the universities are managed privately. Secondly, the share of Himachali students in the total number of students enrolled in different courses in such universities is important to know for understanding the benefits accruing to Himachali students. Unfortunately, we could not lay our hands on such kind of data/information; it could be highly revealing. Even in case of Central Government managed universities/institutes, there is a national policy to admit students or employ staff from other states of India. If profit motives are the main consideration behind opening the universities in private sector and dominant majority of students admitted to different technical or professional courses in such universities belongs to other states then location of such universities in the state of Himachal Pradesh is not going to help the Himachali students much. Location of nine of the total 17 technical/professional universities of the state in a single district of Solan is a pointer in this direction. Selection of Solan district and location of these universities at places bordering Haryana, Punjab and Chandigarh (U.T.) speaks a lot. However, one cannot deny the fact that Himachal Pradesh is progressing well in economic terms and the size of middle class has expanded in the last three decades or so. Middle class households are predominantly salaried class in India. Hence, they send their wards for higher education courses preferably to procure grab the government jobs.

II. Regulatory Framework

India is a federal country. There are three different lists of functions and duties:

(i) Central list, (ii) State list, and (iii) Concurrent list.

Higher education is in the concurrent list of functions. Under this, both Central and state governments are involved, having a joint responsibility but with upper hand of the Central Government in case of any dispute or difference of opinion. A regulatory framework is evolved for smooth running of functions, operating at different spatial scales.

The regulatory framework is a multi-layered system at university and college levels, referring to rules or orders issued by an executive authority or regulatory agency of a government and having the force of law (Singh, 2008:4). The regulatory body has the authority to lay down norms and standards, recognise or derecognize courses and institutions. There are different type of universities, such as Central University, State University, Private University, Deemed University and Institute of National Importance. They awarded their own degrees and certificates. On the other side, colleges award degrees through the universities of their affiliation. The regulatory framework has two parts: (i) regulated/formal education, and (ii) unregulated/non-formal education. The former includes the institutes of higher education that impart recognised degrees, diplomas or certificate at university/college level. The latter provides educational or innovative services to formal institutes. For example, language training, tutorials/coaching centres, education services companies, content providers and corporate training centres come under this.

At the central and state level, there are multiple agencies to regulate the formal education system. These include University Grants Commission (UGC), All India Council of Technical Education (AICTE) and specialised professional bodies, regulating the general, technical and professional education, respectively. They issue a number of regulations and rules covering the wide range of academic standards to be fulfilled by all the recognized institutions.

Besides, there are several professional councils/regulatory bodies managing different professional and technical courses (Fig 3.1). The council approves/covers a number of programmes of technical and professional education at under-graduate and post-graduate levels in various fields of engineering and technology, architecture, pharmacy, nursing, hotel management and catering technology, management and computer applications. They are made responsible for the recognition of courses, promotion of professional institutions, regulation of the courses, provision of grants and other awards in various fields of education. Each council has its own set of rules and mandates for the concerned institutions (Table 3.5).

Various committees and commissions set up by the Government of India from time to time have given recommendations in reports submitted to the government. The most prominent includes the report of the National Knowledge Commission in 2006 proposing a super-regulatory body, instead of different type of councils, called as the Independent Regulatory Authority for Higher Education (IRAHE). The Ministry of Human Resource Development (MHRD) appointed another committee headed by Professor Yash Pal, the former Chairman of U.G.C. It

Table 3.5: Higher Education: Regulatory bodies in India

S. No.	*Regulatory Bodies*	*Functions*
1.	University Grants Commission (UGC)	Coordination, determination and maintenance of standards in higher education. It governs: • number of working days, • number of lecture hours per subject, • minimum eligibility for student enrolment and for teachers to teach a course, and • release of grants to individual institutions.
2.	All India Council of Technical Education (AICTE)	Proper planning and co-ordination of development of technical education.
3.	Distance Education Council (DEC)	• Promotion of open university and distance Education systems. • Coordination and determination of standards of teaching, evaluation and research.
4.	Bar Council of India (BCI)	Co-ordination, determination and maintenance of standards in legal education and profession.
5.	National Council for Teacher Education (NCTE)	• Achieving planned and co-ordinated development of the teacher education system. • Regulation and proper maintenance of norms and standards of teacher education.
6.	Medical Council of India (MCI)	• Regulation and maintenance of standards of medical education.
7.	Pharmacy Council of India (PCI)	Prescription, regulation and maintenance of minimum educational standards for the training of pharmacists uniformly in the country.
8.	Indian Nursing Council (INC)	Regulation and maintenance of uniform standards of training for Nurses, Midwives, Auxiliary Nurse-Midwives and Health Visitors.
9.	Dental Council of India (DCI)	Regulation of the Dental Education, Profession, ethics in the country and recommend to the Government of India to accord permission to start a dental College, higher courses and increase seats.
10.	Central Council for Research in Homeopathy (CCRH)	Maintenance of the Central Register of Homoeopathy.
11	Central Council of Indian Medicine (CCIM)	Maintenance of the Central Register of Indian Medicine.

Source: Govt. of India (2005) Report of Central Advisory Board of Education Committee on Autonomy of Higher Education Institutions, Ministry of Human Resource Development, New Delhi.

recommended for an apex body; National Council for Higher Education and Research (NCHER) in 2011 to regulate the higher education sector. The Committee expressed against the commercialization of higher education and discouraged profit making private institutions, while recommending encouraging partnership with non-profit private organizations in higher education. Under pressure from different organizations including the U.G.C. and unions, no decision has yet be taken on dismantling U.G.C. and other apex bodies to constitute a regulatory authority to govern higher education in India.

In India, there are two accrediting agencies: (i) The National Board of Accreditation (NBA), and (ii) National Assessment and Accreditation Council (NAAC). The former was established by the All India Council for Technical Education (AICTE) in 1994 to regulate technical education and accredit programmes in technical education. NBA in its present form came into existence on 7th January, 2010. The latter was established by the University Grants Commission (UGC) in the same year to accredit the universities and the institutions of general higher education (Table 3.6).

Table 3.6: Higher Education: Accreditation agencies

Agencies	*Criteria*
National Assessment and Accreditation Council (NAAC) *Assigns grades: A (very good), B (Good), C (satisfactory), and D (unsatisfactory)*	Evaluation: 1. Curricular aspects; 2. Teaching-learning and evaluation; 3. Research, consultancy and extension; 4. Infrastructure and learning resources; 5. Student support and progression; 6. Organization and management; and 7. Innovation and Best practices.
National Board of Accreditation (NBA) *Assigns three statuses: Accredited, provisionally Accredited and Not Accredited*	Accreditation process starts with *Self-Assessment Report*, filled by the institutions for the programmes that are applying for the accreditation: 1. Vision, mission and programme educational objectives, 2. Programme Outcomes, 3. Programme curriculum, 4. Students' performance, 5. Faculty Contributions, 6. Facilities and Technical support 7. Academic support units and teaching-learning process, 8. Governance, institutional support and financial resources, 9. Continuous improvement.

Source: Compiled from the Report of Regulatory Structure of Higher Education in India, Centre for Civil Society. Retrieved from http://ccs.in/sites/default/files/research/research-regulatory-structure-of-higher-education-in-india.pdf.

The purpose of the accreditation is to create a set of standards for all institutions of higher education and to encourage institutions to be the best. The goal behind accreditation of institution is to inform the interest groups such as students, parents, and employers about the standard of an institution, and to encourage competition among institutions, may it be college or university. Higher education institutions get qualified for accreditation only after they have had two rounds of graduates, or have been in existence for six years. The main purpose of assessment and accreditation is improvement and enhancement of quality, recognizing excellence, accountability, provision of information and benchmarking or it simply acts as a measure of quality assurance.

At the national level, MHRD presents the ranking under National Institutional Framework (Henceforth, NIRF), gives a common overall rank to all major institutions and, in addition, separate rank for the universities and discipline-specific rank in engineering, management and pharmacy. General degree colleges were also ranked for the first time in 2017. NIRF provides for ranking of universities and colleges in the country on five broad parameters. This criterion has the following ranking parameters and weightages in 2017. (i). Teaching, Learning and Resources (TLR) (0.30), (ii) Research and Professional Practice (RP) (0.30), (iii) Graduation Outcomes (GO) (0.20), (iv) Outreach and Inclusivity (OI) (0.10), and (v) Perception (PR) (0.10). All the five parameters are further divided into sub-heads.

As per the UGC regulation 2016, the teaching/faculty at the college and university level should be recruited on the basis of the set criteria. Such as for assistant professor, there should be good academic record at the Master's degree level and National Eligibility Test (NET) conducted by the UGC, CSIR or similar test accredited by the UGC like SLET/SET. The teacher require a minimum score, as stipulated in the Academic Performance Indicator (API) based on Performance Based Appraisal System (PBAS) developed by the UGC in its Regulations, to qualify. This score is different for the post of Assistant Professor, Associate Professor and Professor. The API scores earned on the basis:

Category I: Teaching, Learning and Evaluation Related Activities (Direct teaching, examination duties and innovative teaching).

Category II: Professional Development, Co-Curricular and Extension Activities (Co-curricular, extension and field based activities, administrative responsibility, participation in Board of studies, academic and administrative committees, participation in talks, seminar, conferences, lectures in refresher courses).

Category-III: Research and Academic Contributions (Research paper published in referred journals, Publication of books with ISBN/ ISSN number, chapters in books, published by National and International level publishers with ISBN/ISSN number as approved by the University, Research projects: Major Projects with grants above Rs. 5 lakhs, Major Projects with grants above Rs. 3 lakhs up to Rs. 5 lakhs, Minor Projects with grants above Rs. one lakh up to Rs. 3 lakhs, Research guidance, fellowships/awards/invited lectures).

The work load for the teachers at the college and university level as per the UGC rules is as follows: the direct teaching of 16/14/14 hours (of 60 minutes) per week for Assistant Professor/Associate Professor/ Professor, respectively. The UGC has set up Academic Staff Colleges (renamed as Human Resource Development Centres in 2015) in different universities/institutions in the country. The academic staff colleges conduct specially designed orientation programmes for newly appointed lecturers and refresher courses for in-service teachers to inculcate the quality of self-reliance through awareness of the social, intellectual and moral environment as well as to discover self-potential and confidence. The newly appointed teachers may have to attend the orientation programme/ course up to six years of continuous services.

Briefly, at the national level, the Ministry of Human Resource Development at the national level Central Government provides grants to the UGC and established central universities in the country. On the other hand, state governments are responsible for the establishment of state universities and colleges and provide plan-grants for their development and non-plan grants for their maintenance. The co-ordination and co-operation between the union and the states are brought about in the field of education through the Central Advisory Board of Education (CABE).

Rashtriya Uchchatar Shiksha Abhiyan (henceforth, RUSA), launched in 2013 spread over the two plan periods (Twelfth and Thirteenth) is a centrally sponsored scheme (CSS), aims at providing strategic funding to eligible state higher educational institutions. Its key objectives are to improve access, equity and quality in higher education through planned development at the state level. The funding provided on sharing basis between the Centre and state governments is in the ratio of 90:10 for North-Eastern States, Sikkim, Himachal Pradesh, Uttarakhand and Jammu & Kashmir, and 65:35 for Other States and Union Territories. There is a norm based funding under RUSA and future grants would be outcome dependent. The State Higher Education Council (SHEC), an autonomous body through which RUSA works in the state.

Himachal Pradesh is one of the pioneers to adopt RUSA system. As per the RUSA guidelines, Himachal Pradesh government introduced semester system in Himachal Pradesh University and its affiliated colleges from the academic session 2013-2014. Instead of three annual examinations for graduation, the students from 2013 onwards appeared in six half yearly examinations for getting degrees in Humanities, Science and Commerce courses. The students are offered courses under choice-based credit system (CBCS) and the final examination conducted by Himachal Pradesh University at the end of every semester. Except for compulsory and a core courses, a student is granted freedom to select courses from a wide range of papers/courses of the major subject of her/his choice. After a student cumulates the requisite number of successful credits (passed), i.e. at least 120 credits for an undergraduate degree, the programme is considered to be complete. As per the RUSA guidelines, an academic year comprises 180 working days, divided into two semesters, each having at least 90 working days.

Also, the Government of Himachal Pradesh followed the UGC regulations, regarding the adoption of the API based personal Based Appraisal system for the promotions of teachers and other equivalent cadres of government degree colleges (Sanskrit and librarians) under Career Advancement Scheme (CAS), amended from time to time on the recommendation of the UGC.

Recruitment of the posts of Assistant Professors, College Principals and College Librarians in the government colleges of Himachal Pradesh and Acharyas and Pracharyas in government Sanskrit colleges of Himachal Pradesh on the basis of the merit, advertisement at the national level and selection by the HPPSC as per the recruitment and promotion rules for the concerned posts. The workload of the teachers having full employment has been fixed at 40 hours (of 45 minutes) a week for 30 working weeks (180 teaching days) in an academic year.

As per the NAAC guidelines, the Internal Quality Assurance Cell (henceforth, IQAC) was established in all the government colleges of the state since 2009 to achieve higher and better quality of higher education. The IQAC acts as the documentation and record-keeping cell for the institution. The IQAC has been empowered to introduce, wherever feasible, the student feedback system as per the NAAC guidelines. The prime task of the IQAC is to develop a system for conscious, consistent and catalytic improvement in the performance of institutions. The IQAC is aimed at making a significant and meaningful contribution in the post-accreditation phase of Institutions. However, feedback from the students has been opposed by teaching faculty unions in all parts of the country.

As per UGC Regulations, besides the indexed publications documented by various discipline specific databases, drawn by the H.P. University Shimla-5, through committees of subject experts and ISBN/ ISSN experts: (a) a comprehensive list of National/ Regional level journals of quality in the concerned subjects; and (b) A comprehensive list of Indian language journals/periodicals/official publication volumes of language bodies and upload them on the University website, periodically updated.

In Himachal Pradesh, there are renowned institutes like National Institute of Technology, Hamirpur known for quality education in the field of technical education. Apart from these institutes, Government of India opened the institutes including Indian Institute of Technology (IIT) in different states. In Himachal Pradesh, IIT has been established at Mandi town, the district headquarters of Mandi district and National Institute of Fashion Technology (NIFT) in Kangra district.

Himachal Pradesh has allowed private investment in higher education of the state. The state government has established Himachal Pradesh Private Educational Institutions Regulatory Commission, 2010 which acts as an interface between the state government and central regulatory bodies for ensuring appropriate standards of admission, teaching, examination, research, extension programmes and protection of the interest of the students enrolled in the private educational institutions. In its vision document, the regulatory commission states that it will work to make Himachal Pradesh a preferred choice of students for quality education and would strive to make the state a recognized hub and a preferred choice of students for quality education. It ensures that the admissions in the private institutions are based on national common entrance test or the state common entrance test.

Also, it conducts inspection of private institutions as well as monitors and regulates fees structure in private educational institutions. All the private educational institutions in the state such as degree colleges, management, law, engineering, medical, pharmacy, paramedical institutions and universities etc. come under its purview. It is also empowered to issue notices to private institutions in case of non-compliance with regard to admission norms in different technical and professional degree courses. According to a report published in *Times of India*, a daily news-paper that it issued notice to five private universities for violating admissions rules and norms. These included APG University, Shimla, Shoolini University and Manav Bharti University both in Solan, Baddi University of Emerging Science and Technologies in Baddi and Sri Sai Ram University, Palampur.

Earlier in 2012, the regulatory commission imposed a fine of Rs. one crore on Manav Bharti University for a number of irregularities.

Main Highlights

- In the structural composition of higher education in Himachal Pradesh, colleges offering general education courses dominate. Their share being more than a half (51.3%) of total number of colleges of the state in 2016, general education colleges share ranged from a low of 34.5 per cent in Solan district to a high of cent per cent in Lahul and Spiti district. In other words, higher education is least diversified in latter district and the most diversified in the former one.
- The maximum number (63) of such colleges was in Kangra and minimum (1) in Lahul and Spiti. Nearly 58.7 per cent of such colleges were located in four districts of Kangra, Shimla, Sirmaur and Mandi. Against this, their combined population (of 18-23 age-group) makes 55.6 per cent in total population of the state. Another more than one-third or about 37.0 per cent were located in four districts of Bilaspur, Chamba, Solan, Kullu and Una. In this way, more than nine-tenths or 95.2 per cent of such colleges were distributed in nine districts, having, in combine, 92.4 per cent population of the state. Obviously, there is not much mis-match between the population share (age-group identified as higher education age-group) of districts and their respective shares in total colleges of general education courses in the state. The rest of the five per cent colleges were located in the two districts of Hamirpur and Lahul and Spiti. In Kinnaur district, there is no college running general education courses exclusively.
- The share of general education colleges in total colleges of respective districts makes an interesting story. In Lahul and Spiti district, there was only one college and that too running general education courses. In other words, higher education in Lahul and Spiti was oriented entirely to the general education. In this thinly populated district, development of higher education was lopsided. Next to it was Chamba district, where more than four-fifths or 83.3 per cent of higher education was confined to the teaching of general courses. Bilaspur, Kullu, Sirmaur, Kangra and Una were other districts where the majority of colleges were teaching general courses. Kinnaur is another district in the state

where one-half of the colleges imparted general education as it has only two colleges, one imparting general-cum-technical and another one the technical education. On the other side of the scale, Solan is the only district in the state where colleges of general education make only one-third or 34.5 per cent in total colleges.

- Broadly speaking, higher education is structurally least diversified in four northern districts of Chamba, Lahul and Spiti, Kinnaur and Kullu, while reverse is true of Solan, Shimla, Mandi and Sirmaur districts: Factors like locational advantage, physiographic setting and initial advantage have played a crucial role in diversification of structural composition of higher education at the district level in the state.
- Structure of higher education in Himachal Pradesh has been changing over the period. It was overdominated by the general education colleges, but registered a shift towards technical education colleges after 1991, coinciding with change in economic policy reform, i.e. liberalization at the national level. Surge in demand for technical education courses, following change in economic policies, technical education recorded spurt in opening of new colleges teaching such kind of courses.
- However, it has to be noted that there has been a remarkable change in nature of higher education in the state, from over-dominance of general education to just dominance in the last forty-five years between 1971 and 2016.
- Briefly, colleges imparting traditional courses under general education category and making 104 or three-fourth (72.7%) of the total general education colleges in the state dominate in more than two-fourth of the districts in Himachal Pradesh. Numerically, more than two-third of such colleges are concentrated in one-third of the districts in the state. Interestingly, Mandi, where are found such colleges in relatively large number, has their share of less than or 40.0 per cent in total colleges in the district.
- Another characteristic feature of their distributional pattern was that more than seven of each ten such colleges were located in rural areas. Himachal Pradesh is a least urbanized state where less than one of each ten persons reside in urban areas of the state. From that angle, the share of urban areas, having nearly three in each ten such colleges, was indicative of the higher concentration of such colleges in urban areas. In other words, general education courses made a dominant character of colleges located in rural

areas of the state.

- Briefly, the largest share (or 51.3%) of colleges in the state was still devoted to the teaching of traditional courses under general education segment. In four districts of Lahul and Spiti, Chamba, Bilaspur and Kullu, higher education was highly oriented to general or traditional education. In addition to these four districts another four districts have the share of one-half or more than one-half have the college of general education such as Kangra, Kinnaur, Sirmaur and Una. However, of late, more than one-third or 27.3 per cent of such colleges have started offering vocational and technical courses along with traditional courses. Growing demand coupled with the offer of financial support from the University Grants Commission, New Delhi for opening vocational and technical courses have been responsible for such a change in structural composition of higher education in the state. Such colleges were highly concentrated in a few districts of the state. Four districts of Kangra, Shimla, Sirmaur, and Mandi accounted for more than majority or 56.6 per cent of such colleges. Moreover, these colleges showed a tendency to concentrate in urban areas, since 20.9 per cent of them were located in urban centres, against urban population making only about 10.0 per cent in total population of the state.
- There has been no change in number of technical education colleges between 1971 and 1991. After that, this number went up with the coming of six more technical education institutions in the state between 1991 and 2001. In other words, on an average, less than one such college/institution per annum was added during 1991-2001 decade. In this way, by 2001 when total number of colleges imparting higher education in the state had gone to 94, the share of such colleges made only 8.5 per cent in total colleges. Evidently, there has been a slow progress in technical education in the state till 2001. The new six such colleges added during 1991-2001 had the following composition of courses. Three of them were teachers' training, two pharmacy and remaining one management college.
- The next decade of 2001-2011 recorded a spurt in technical education in the state. As many as 80 new colleges of technical education were added to make the total number of such colleges 88 or 39.0 per cent in total higher education colleges in the state.

- A majority of technical colleges in the state was running Bachelors and Masters Degree courses in teachers' training. This is mainly because of a high demand for trained teachers to teach at the school level as well as to further train the teachers. A further inquiry reveal that overwhelming majority of such colleges to begin with started B.Ed. classes and later on diversified to other technical courses including computer science applications, business administration, engineering and pharmaceutical sciences. 55 or 58 per cent of total technical higher education colleges in the state run B.Ed. and M.Ed. courses. Earlier, the aspirants for such courses use to go to colleges located in neighbouring states of Jammu & Kashmir, Uttar Pradesh, Punjab and Haryana.
- Inter-district distribution of technical higher education colleges is highly revealing. Two-fifth of such colleges is distributed in five districts of Mandi, Kinnaur, Solan, Shimla and Hamirpur. In Mandi district, which has the largest number of such colleges in the state, one-half of total colleges in the district were running technical courses. On the other side of the scale, four districts of Bilaspur, Chamba, Kinnaur and Kullu, in combine, had only nine of total such colleges. Lahul and Spiti district has no such college.
- Another 22 colleges of this category run engineering/pharmacy/management/computer courses. Considered as job oriented, such courses attract aspirants not only from within the state but also from neighbouring states. Again, the highest number of such colleges was in Mandi, Hamirpur and Shimla districts.
- A large number of such colleges in the state were in the private sector, coming after the change in economic policies in mid-1991. The policy was again modified in 2001 to clear the way for opening of new universities or to tie-up with existing ones in the private sector (foreign and India). Briefly, 95 or less than one-third of total colleges in the state, imparting technical education, are running B.Ed. and M.Ed. courses. Such courses, high in demand, were concentrated in five districts of Mandi, Kangra, Shimla, Solan, and Hamirpur. In fact, Mandi is the only district in the state where more than a half of colleges are running technical higher education courses.
- 40 or two-fifth colleges of this category, running courses such as engineering, computer science applications, business

management and pharmacy, are not only recent in origin but also high in demand. Locationally, such colleges were mainly concentrated in five districts of Mandi, Hamirpur, Solan, Shimla and Kangra in the state.

- As in case of technical higher education colleges, the year 2001 acts as water divide in case of professional colleges too. The number of such colleges was only six in 2001. It rose to 17 in 2011 and then to 24 in 2016. Earlier in 1971, when Himachal Pradesh got statehood, there was only one college of this kind. Growing at a snail pace between 1971 and 1981, it recorded high growth between 1991 and 2001, when number grew by 300 per cent: from two to six. Between 2001 and 2011, professional colleges jumped to almost three times to increase to about 40 per cent between 2011 and 2016. Against this, technical education colleges recorded an increase of eleven times during 2001-2011.
- With privatization of higher education in 2001, termed as a paradigm shift in higher education in India, technical education recorded unprecedented increase in number of colleges teaching technical education courses. Number of such colleges rose to 88 by 2011 from only 8 in 2001 and the share of such colleges in total colleges in state went to 38.9 per cent from just 8.5 per cent during the same period. Against this, the share of colleges teaching general courses fell down to 46 per cent from about 78 per cent during this period. However, 2001-2011 decade proved a peak period in the growth of technical higher education in the state, as there has been a sluggish growth of technical colleges between 2011 and 2016. This indicates to melting down of privatization pot within a decade in the hill state of Himachal Pradesh.
- Year 2011 marked the reversal of trend again towards the public investment in higher education in the state. Against the sluggish growth of technical education colleges, there has been spurt in growth of general education colleges in the state. Of the 53 new colleges opened in the state during 2011-2016, 41 were general education colleges with investment made by the Government of Himachal Pradesh. Political populism driven by the desire to win the next state assembly elections, due in December 2017, brought smile on the face of people living in those tehsils or sub-tehsils which were without any government college of higher education till date. Norm of 25 radius to have a new government college was

adjusted and re-adjusted in such a manner as if there was no such norm. If, such a norm there, it was on papers only. This resulted in giving an upper hand again to general education colleges in overall structural composition of higher education in the state. The essence of the story is government policy which is guiding force behind making or remaking of structural composition of higher education in the state of Himachal Pradesh.

- Professional education is still in the infancy stage in Himachal Pradesh. The share of colleges teaching such courses in the total number of colleges was less than one-tenth in 2016. There were only four districts of Bilaspur, Kangra, Shimla and Solan where the share of professional colleges in the total number of colleges of these districts was more than 10 per cent. Professional higher education in the state is highly oriented to nursing course (bachelors or masters degree courses). In 2016, 24 professional colleges made only about 9 per cent in total 279 colleges in the state. Against this, technical higher education colleges made 34 per cent in total. Evidently, professional higher education in the state is not only progressing at a slow pace but also far behind of technical education. On the whole, professional higher education colleges in the state were mainly confined to four districts of Kangra, Shimla, Mandi and Solan, having, in combine, about four-fifths of totals such colleges in the state.
- Thanks to privatization boom, structural composition of higher education at the university in Himachal Pradesh is highly in favour of technical and professional education. Of the 28 universities in the state, 17 or three-fifths are oriented to technical/ professional courses. Nine or more than a half of such universities were located in a single district of Solan, bordering Punjab, Haryana and Chandigarh Union Territory. Majority of technical and professional universities being in private hands, profit motive having the upper hand, it is difficult to say with confidence that Himachalis are the main beneficiaries from the presence of these universities in the state. High concentration of such universities in the two districts of Solan and Kangra, which adjoin neighbouring Punjab, Haryana, Uttarakhand and Uttar Pradesh state, is an indication to benefits going to the neighbouring states. Nevertheless, there is no denying of the fact that size of middle class has grown over the time especially in recent decades in Himachal Pradesh. The middle class households always want to

grab white collared jobs especially those in government sector hence promote their kids to go for technical and professional courses which are currently quite high in demand.

- Different districts have benefitted in different ways to diversify the structure of higher education therein. For example, Solan and Sirmaur districts benefitted from locational advantage, Shimla due to initial advantage combined with its status as the state capital headquarters, Hamirpur from getting the regional engineering college established under the Central Government scheme as early as in 1986 and Mandi district from its growing political clout in the recent decade.
- Even in case of Central Government managed universities/ institutes, there is a national policy to admit students or employ staff from other states of India. If profit motives are the main consideration behind opening the universities in private sector and dominant majority of students admitted to different technical or professional courses in such universities who belong to other states then location of such universities in the state of Himachal Pradesh is not going to help much the Himachalis. Location of nine of total 17 technical/professional universities of the state in a single district of Solan is a pointer in this direction. Selection of Solan district and location of these universities at places bordering Haryana, Punjab and Chandigarh (U.T.) speaks a lot.

IV
Accessibility and Availability

Introduction

This chapter examines accessibility and availability of higher education in the state in terms of residence (urban-rural), gender (male-female) and social groups (non-Scheduled and Scheduled population). The accessibility has been examined with the help of net enrolment ratio (henceforth NER) in the 18-23 age-group. Most of the studies on accessibility of higher education use NER for this purpose. For calculating this, the number of students actually enrolled in higher education in a district has been taken as numerator and the total population of 18-23 age-group, as denominator, the outcome multiplied by 100. NER has been calculated separately for total, rural, urban, male, female and Scheduled (Caste and Tribe) and non-Scheduled population to study residential (rural-urban), gender (male-female), and social (Scheduled and non-Scheduled) differentials in NER at the district level in Himachal Pradesh.

NER indicates the following (i) the demand for higher education in a region or sub-region, and (ii) government policies and programmes to promote higher education; the historical factors playing a role in the background.

For measuring, accessibility in terms of residence, gender, and social groups, the following indicators were pressed into service:

(i) Residence

A. Rural youth in 18-23 age-group, enrolled in higher education as per cent in total rural population of this age-group in a district.

B. Urban youth of 18-23 age-group, enrolled in higher education as per cent to total urban population in this age-group in a district.

(ii) Gender

C. Males in 18-23 age-group, enrolled in higher education as per cent of total male population of this age-group in a district.

D. Females of 18-23 years of age-group enrolled in higher education as per cent of total female population of this age-group in a district.

(iii) Social groups

E. SC/ST youths in 18-23 age-group, enrolled in higher education as per cent to total SC/ST population of this age-group in a district.

F. Non-SC youth in 18-23 age-group, enrolled in higher education as per cent to total Non-SC population of age-group in a district.

A differential index was calculated to examine differentials in higher education accessibility between urban-rural, male-female and Scheduled and non-Scheduled population in the state. Also, differentials were examined for general and vocational education, separately. This is mainly because of the fact that vocational education is considered more job oriented than the general education. Hence, a better position in vocational education provides an advantage over the general education.

There are, of course, some data constraints. During 1981 and 1991 enumerations, Census of India collected data on higher education in accordance with the streams: graduation, post-graduation, engineering, medicine and teaching and published these by categorizing into levels/ streams, such as graduation, post-graduation, engineering, medicine and teaching. However, coming to 2001 census decade, such data were presented under the two main headings, i.e. college education and vocational education. The former included general and university level education and the latter technical and professional education. Since vocational education includes diploma level courses also, it distorts enrolment figures under the vocational education courses.

For dealing with this kind of data comparability problem, a way was found out by excluding the share of diploma/polytechnic holders from the vocational education, computed for individual years between 2001 and 2010. Separate information for diploma/polytechnic holders is available in the publication entitled *Selected Education Statistics,* published by the Ministry of Human Resource Development, Government of India, New Delhi.

NER in Himachal Pradesh

At the national level, Himachal Pradesh is included in the category of well performing states. Nonetheless, the higher education especially the vocational education has remained quite low in the state. Even in 2001, NER of vocational education was as low as 0.68 per cent. NER of vocational education, however, picked up after 2001 to reach up to 5.53 per cent within a decade in 2011. It seems that the year 2001 acted as water mark in the history of NER in Himachal Pradesh for the two main reasons: (i) shift in focus from general to vocational courses, and (ii) opening of higher education to the private sector.

In the following, NER of Himachal Pradesh has been examined at the district level. A weighted index method has been used to calculate NER by residence, gender and social groups (Scheduled and non-Scheduled population) at the district level. For studying the change in NER[1] at the district level, a period of 30 years (1981-2011), has been taken. However, for non-availability of data for earlier decades NER for the social groups, a period of 10 years has only been covered (i.e. 2001-2011).

There still remains a problem with the available data/information on net enrolment in higher education. Data on enrolment were not available for 18-23 age-group or each year of age but at an interval of 5 years such as 15-19, 20-24 and so on. For extracting data for 18-23 age-group, the present study applied Sprague Multiplier[2] technique to compute single year enrolments in higher education.

Further, for obtaining Weighted Score Index (WSI), the following procedure was put in service. The highest NER value in a case of any unit or for a district in the state for selected indicators was assigned a value of 100, the maximum value on the scale of 0-100. All other NER values were calculated proportionally in relation to 100.

These relative weights were summed up to prepare the composite index for different dimensions and finally for the overall level of higher education development for each district. The weighted score method helped us in smoothening high skewness in net enrolment ratio, as in the present case.

In the following, NER of Chamba district has been calculated, as an example:

In Chamba district, total enrolment in general courses are 5,488 persons and in vocational education 1,532 persons and the total population in 18-23 age group is 62,074 persons.

(i) General education - 5488/62074 × 100 = 8.9 per cent
(ii) Vocational[3] - 1532/62074 × 100 = 2.5 per cent

The index value in each case will vary from a high of 100 to a low of 0 (zero). Hundred will indicate to be the top-most position and 0 to be the lowest position of a study unit on a particular indicator. In view of higher importance of vocational education *vis-a-vis* general education, we have calculated two indices separately before combining the two into a composite index.

In the following, the steps involved in the calculation of NER for general education have been demonstrated with example of Hamirpur and Chamba districts. The former has the highest and the latter the lowest NER for general education in the state.

NER for Hamirpur = 23.6 per cent, and Chamba = 8.8 per cent

(i) NER value 23.6 per cent for Hamirpur has been assigned a value of 100
(ii) Then, weighted index value for Chamba district.
Hamirpur index value of 23.6 per cent = **100**
NER for Chamba is = 8.8 per cent
Weighted index value for Chamba = 100/23.6 × 8.8= **37.2**

In this way, weighted index value for Hamirpur is 100 and for Chamba is 37.2. Accordingly, the index values for all the districts were calculated on all the indicators before arriving at the composite index of higher education accessibility in each case.

For measuring availability of higher education at district level, area and population were taken as the two parameters. Colleges per 1000 km^2 of the area and per lakh of the population (in the age-group of 18-23 years) in a district were calculated for individual districts in the state. Both area and population have their own importance, the former is important when the size of areal units is large and the latter when density of population is high. In former case serving all parts of an administrative unit carries utmost significance, whereas in latter case serving population is the most challenging task. District-wise index of area and population has been calculated for colleges, in the following manner, illustrated with example of Solan district. Colleges in Solan per 1000 km^2 area and per hundred thousand persons (in the age-group of 18-23 years) have been calculated as follows:

The number of colleges in Solan district = 29

Population (18-23 age group) = 71,440 persons
Area (in Km^2) = 1936

(i) colleges per 1000 km^2 area in Solan district = 29 × 1000/1936
= 15 colleges/1000 km^2

(ii) colleges per 100 thousand persons = 29 × 1,00,000/71,440
= 40.6 or about 41 colleges/1,00,000 persons

It has to be noted here that since no location-allocation concept applied in case of education in Indian states, especially the higher education, the students aspiring for higher education sought admission in adjoining districts of the same state or of neighbouring states. For example, a student doing his/her Bachelor of Engineering in a college in Solan district may be residing in Sirmaur district and must be commuting daily between his/her college and residence.

This happens more frequently in the case of colleges located in areas of bordering districts. In Himachal Pradesh, students from Bharmour and Pangi Subdivisions of Chamba district move to Dharamshala (Kangra district) Shimla district for higher studies. Nevertheless, available data provides a fairly good idea of supply as well as the demand side of higher education.

In a way, the availability of colleges in an area speaks of supply side and accessibility of demand side. It would be interesting to understand the nature of association between these two dimensions of higher education. In other words, where supply is high/low in relation to high/low demand for higher education.

I. Accessibility

Higher Education Accessibility: An Overview

In 2011, NER in Himachal Pradesh was 16.7 per cent. In other words, only about one-sixth of the total youth in 18-23 age-group was enrolled for higher education in the state. Earlier in 1981, NER was only 0.5 per cent. In other words, only one out of 200 young persons in the age-group of 18-23 was enrolled for higher education. Evidently, enrolment for higher education in Himachal Pradesh was not only very low in the past but also continues to be so even today. Higher education in the state picked up fast in the 1990s to go into double-digits by 2001 (11.4%) and then to 16.7 per cent in 2011 (Table 4.0).

Table 4.0: Himachal Pradesh: District-wise net enrolment ratio (general) higher education, 1981-2011

(Figures in %)

S. No.	District Name	General			
		1981	*1991*	*2001*	*2011*
1	2	3	4	5	6
1.	Chamba	0.09	0.25	5.71	8.84
2.	Kangra	0.32	1.01	11.81	19.14
3.	Lahul and Spiti	0.04	0.09	4.93	22.49
4.	Kullu	0.25	0.9	9.03	13.32
5.	Mandi	0.31	0.84	11.25	15.46
6.	Hamirpur	0.27	0.96	17.07	23.64
7.	Una	0.24	1.1	10.79	16.22
8.	Bilaspur	0.33	1.13	13.93	17.14
9.	Solan	0.65	1.09	8.86	12.7
10.	Sirmaur	0.25	0.5	6.76	12.08
11.	Shimla	1.77	2.56	16.83	23.61
12.	Kinnaur	0.06	0.56	7.16	12.17
	Himachal Pradesh	**0.49**	**1.08**	**11.37**	**16.66**
	C.V Index	1.22	0.68	0.39	0.30

Source: Census of India, Himachal Pradesh Socio and Cultural Tables (C-Series) of 1981, 1991, 2001 and 2011. Office of the Registrar General and Census Commissioner, New Delhi, India.

The scenario related to vocational streams was still poor. In 2011, NER in vocational stream was only 5.5 per cent and negligible 0.03 per cent early in 1981. Interestingly, there are striking inter-district, urban-rural, male-female and social inequalities in higher education enrolment ratio even at low level of higher education development in the state.

In 2011, among districts, NER ranged from a high of 23.6 per cent in Shimla district to a low of only 8.8 per cent in Chamba district, giving a range difference of about 15.0 per cent. Separately for vocational streams, inter-district inequalities were still clearly noticeable. These ranged from a high of 10.3 per cent in Hamirpur district to only 1.4 per cent in Kinnaur district. Urban-rural inequalities in NER were equally marked both in general and vocational education. The NER of higher education for urban areas was nearly twice of that of rural areas. The former was 24.82 per cent in contrast to 15.7 per cent of the latter. In vocational education, it was 10.7 per cent for the urban areas and only 4.9 per cent for the rural areas. Between Scheduled Castes and non-Scheduled population, it was 14.1 per cent for the former and 18.0 per cent for the latter.

Interestingly, inequalities in the field of general education in Himachal Pradesh go in favour of females. NER for the female population was 17.8 per cent against 15.6 per cent for the male population. Even in the rural areas, NER for females was higher than that of males. However, in the case of vocational education, the balance was in favour of males. In 2011, the NER of vocational education for males was 5.4 per cent against 4.1 per cent for the females. Even in the case of Scheduled Castes population, NER for female and male population in general education was almost the same. For the former, it was 14.6 per cent and for latter 14.8 per cent.

In the following, an attempt will be made to examine temporal, spatial (inter-district and urban-rural), gender (male-female) and social class [Scheduled (Tribe and Caste) and non-Scheduled population] differentials in NER.

A. Trends in NER, 1981-2011

During the last three decades between 1981 and 2011, there has been a spectacular increase in NER of Himachal Pradesh. NER has gone to 16.7 per cent in 2011 from merely 0.5 per cent in 1981. The state acquiring full statehood status in early 1971 induced a new enthusiasm and zeal among the leadership and the bureaucracy of the state to achieve a higher level of development; the then chief minister of the state, Shri Y.S. Parmar, placed the highest priority on education and road development.

Besides opening of new schools and colleges, existing ones were strengthened and upgraded, boosting the prospects of both the school and college education. In recent decades especially after 1991, coinciding with the liberalization of economic policies in India to attract private investment in different sectors including education, Himachal Pradesh has benefitted a lot from private investment in higher education since the state has been liberal in opening higher education to private sector. This has resulted in opening of the new colleges and universities both in public and private sectors, registering a quantum leap in NER between 1991 and 2001: from 1.08 per cent to 11.4 per cent. The NER continued to grow further in the next decade between 2001 and 2011, to reach to 16.7 per cent by 2011.

However, different districts in the state responded differently to the privatization policy. Against the state average of 0.5 per cent in 1981, it ranged from a high of 1.8 per cent in Shimla district to negligible (only 0.04%) in Lahul and Spiti district.

In one-half of the twelve districts in the state, namely Lahul and Spiti, Kinnaur, Chamba, Una, Bilaspur, Kullu and Sirmaur, NER ratio was either equivalent to or less than one-half of the state average. It was only in two districts of Solan and Shimla where NER ratio was higher than the state average. In fact, the NER ratio of Shimla district was responsible for keeping state average on the higher side.

The physiographic conditions of the state have remarkable impact on NER in the field of higher education. As one moves from lower Himalayan zone to middle and then to higher and trans-Himalayan zones, NER keeps on declining. Lack of threshold population coupled with the paucity of financial resources, required to open higher education institutions in the state government seem to be the plausible reasons behind all this.

Coming to 1991, when NER state average more than doubled to reach from 0.5 per cent in 1981 to 1.1 per cent, the inter-district disparity was still wide but had considerably narrowed. The coefficient of variability index (henceforth, CV) came down from 1.22 in 1981 to 0.68 in 1991 (see Table 4.0 and Fig. 4.0). NER ranged from a high of 2.6 per cent for Shimla district to low of only 0.1 per cent for Lahul and Spiti district. This time seven of the twelve districts had NER lower than the state average. Such districts included Lahul and Spiti, Chamba, Sirmaur, Kinnaur, Mandi, Kullu and Hamirpur. In three districts of Chamba, Lahul and Spiti and Sirmaur, the ratio was less than one-half of the state average. On the whole, all the districts registered an increase in net enrolment ratio, but six districts of Kangra, Kullu, Hamirpur, Una, Kinnaur and Bilaspur performed

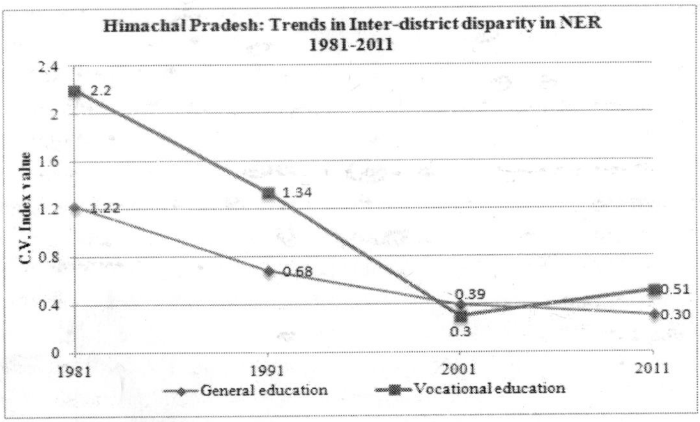

Fig. 4.0: Himachal Pradesh: Trends in Inter-district disparity in NER, 1981-2011.

Source: As Table 4.0.

far better than other districts of the state. In their case, NER increased thrice or more than that. Against this, Solan, Sirmaur, Shimla, Lahul and Spiti recorded an increase and became twice of the earlier number. On the whole, narrowing down of inter-district disparities in NER was the most satisfying achievement of this decade.

There has been a spurt in NER after 1991. The absolute number of students enrolled in higher education went up from about 6.5 thousand in 1991 to 82 thousand in 2001, registering an increase of more than twelve times. In proportional terms, NER jumped up to 11.4 per cent in 2001 from only 1.1 per cent in 1991. Among districts, it ranged from a high of 17.1 per cent in Hamirpur to a low of 4.93 per cent in Lahul and Spiti, registering a range difference of about 12.0 per cent points. In four districts (Hamirpur, Shimla, Bilaspur, and Kangra) this ratio was higher than the state average. Another two districts, Mandi and Una, had this ratio in two digits, which was quite close to the state average. All the districts in the state performed well especially those having low NER in 1991, Lahul and Spiti, Chamba and Hamirpur districts being the case in point. Against this, the lowest gain was registered in Shimla, Solan and Una districts, having relatively better NER in 1991. The inter-district disparity in NER was also reduced; CV index value came down from 0.68 in 1991 to 0.39 in 2001.

During 2001-2011, when NER increased further to 16.7 per cent registering an increase of more than 5.0 percentage points, inter-district inequalities in NER further declined. The CV index value came down from 0.39 in 2001 to 0.30 in 2011 (Fig. 4.0). In 2011, NER ranged from a high of 23.64 per cent in Hamirpur district to a low of 8.8 per cent in Chamba district. Five districts, namely, Hamirpur, Shimla, Lahul and Spiti, Kangra and Bilaspur had NER higher than the state average of 16.7 per cent. On the other side of the scale, Chamba district had single digit NER, which was nearly one-half of the state average.

In relative terms, Lahul and Spiti followed by Kangra, and Shimla districts were high and Chamba, Kullu, Mandi, Bilaspur and Solan were the low gainers. The high increase of NER in Lahul and Spiti district was attributed to opening of a new college in the district. While Kangra and Shimla districts gained due to their political clout along with attracting the private investment in higher education. During 2001-2011, when NER increased further to 16.7 per cent registering an increase of more than 5.0 percentage points, inter-district inequalities in NER declined further.

Thanks to the private investment, NER in vocational courses in the state went from merely 0.03 per cent in 1981 to 5.5 per cent in 2011. There had been a rapid increase in NER between 1991 and 2001, from 0.04 per cent in 1991 to 0.68 per cent in 2001. The NER continued to grow further during the next decade, to reach to 5.5 by 2011 (Table 4.1).

However, the different districts responded differently. Against 0.03 per cent NER for the state as a whole in 1981, it ranged from a high of 0.15 per cent in Shimla district to only 0.01 per cent in the four districts of Kangra, Mandi, Kullu, Bilaspur and Sirmaur.

Table 4.1: Himachal Pradesh: District-wise net enrolment ratio in vocational higher education, 1981-2011

S. No.	*District Name*	*Vocational*			
		1981	*1991*	*2001*	*2011*
1	2	3	4	5	6
1.	Chamba	0.0*	0.01	0.37	2.50
2.	Kangra	0.01	0.01	0.61	6.29
3.	Lahul and Spiti	0.0*	0.0*	0.58	3.23
4.	Kullu	0.01	0.0*	0.50	2.78
5.	Mandi	0.01	0.03	0.64	5.38
6.	Hamirpur	0.00*	0.02	0.70	10.28
7.	Una	0.00*	0.14	1.05	6.79
8.	Bilaspur	0.01	0.03	0.77	8.45
9.	Solan	0.03	0.02	0.83	5.97
10.	Sirmaur	0.01	0.03	0.64	3.46
11.	Shimla	0.15	0.11	0.79	5.14
12.	Kinnaur	0.00*	0.00*	0.35	1.43
	Himachal Pradesh	**0.03**	**0.04**	**0.68**	**5.53**
	C.V. Index	2.20	1.34	0.30	0.51

Source: As Table 4.0.

Note: *NER is negligible.

In five districts of the state (Chamba, Lahul and Spiti, Hamirpur, Una and Kinnaur), NER ratio was almost zero. It was only in two districts of Shimla and Solan where the NER ratio was equivalent to or higher than the state average (Table 4.1).

Coming to 1991, when NER for the state as a whole moved marginally higher from 0.03 per cent in 1981 to 0.04 per cent in 1991, the inter-district disparity was still wide, but considerably reduced. The value of coefficient of variability (CV) index declined from 2.20 to 1.34 between 1981 and 1991 (Fig. 4.0). NER ranged from a high of 0.14 per cent in Una district to a low of only 0.01 per cent in Chamba and Kangra districts. This time only two (Shimla and Una) of twelve districts had NER higher than the state average. In three districts (Lahul and Spiti, Kullu and Kinnaur), the ratio was almost zero. The highest increase was noticed in Una district.

There was a remarkable spurt in NER after 1991. The absolute number of students enrolled in higher education went up from only about 200 in 1991 to five thousand in 2001, increasing by twenty-six times. In proportional terms, NER jumped to 0.68 per cent in 2001 from only 0.04 per cent earlier in 1991. Among districts, it ranged from a high of 1.05 per cent in Una to a low of 0.35 per cent in Kinnaur. Five districts (Hamirpur, Una, Bilaspur, Solan and Shimla) had this ratio higher than the state average and another two districts, Mandi and Sirmaur, fared close to the state average. The inter-district disparity in NER reduced, CV index value being 0.30 in 2001.

In 2011, when NER for the state rose to 5.5 per cent, registering an increase of more than 5.0 percentage points, the trend in inter-district inequalities reversed, CV index increasing from 0.30 in 2001 to 0.51 in 2011 (Fig. 4.0). NER ranged from a high of 10.3 per cent in Hamirpur district to a low of 1.4 per cent in Kinnaur district, registering a range difference of 8.9 per cent. This is attributed to increased private investment in higher vocational education. Private investment was guided by locational advantage. Five districts, namely, Kangra, Hamirpur, Una, Bilaspur, and Solan had NER higher than the state average of 5.5 per cent. The two districts of Mandi and Shimla had almost equivalent to the state average. In relative terms, Hamirpur followed by Bilaspur, and Kangra districts were higher and Chamba, Mandi, Shimla and Solan the low gainers in this regard. High increase in NER of Hamirpur district is attributed to locational advantage attracting private investment in technical higher education. Kangra and Shimla districts gained due to the early start of higher education institutions there.

B. Male-Female Differentials in NER, 2001-11

(a) General/College Education

As evident in differential index value of 0.2 per cent between male-female NER, there was slightly higher male NER in 2001. Among districts, it ranged from a high of 0.6 in Chamba district to a low of 0.2 in five districts (Kangra, Hamirpur, Bilaspur, Sirmaur and Shimla). Male-female differential index, in NER at district level is highly revealing (Table 4.2). Three districts of Chamba, Kullu and Mandi were above the state average (0.2%), revealing higher male-female differential in NER. In Una, Solan and Kinnaur districts, there was gender equality in NER. Lahul and Spiti is the only district in the state where female NER was higher than that of the males. One possible explanation of this may be that males, desirous of higher education move to other districts of state or outside the state and female students generally stay back to get educated within the district. This can be attributed to the mindset of the male-dominated society.

The scenario shifted in favour of females by 2011. In all but three districts (Chamba, Kullu and Mandi), female NER was higher than that of males. In 2011, the NER for males and females was 15.6 and 17.8 per cent, respectively, average differential index being -0.13. On the whole, one-third of the districts recorded index value below the state average, indicating low differentials in male-female NER (Fig. 4.1).

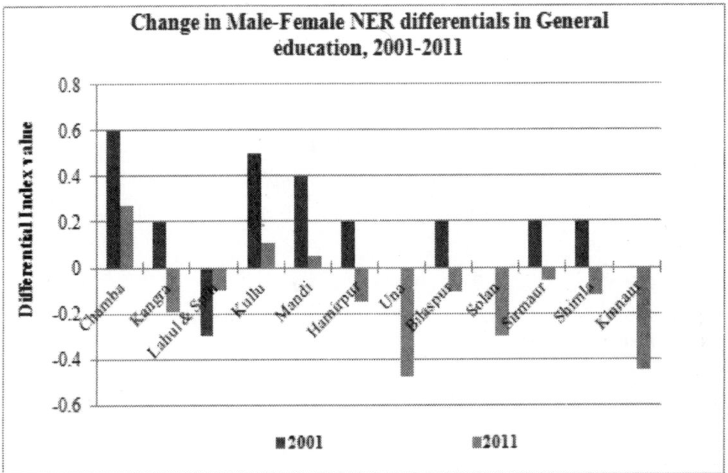

Fig. 4.1: Change in Male-Female NER differentials in General education, 2001-2011.

Source: As Table 4.2.

Changing attitude towards female higher education coupled with increased availability of educational institutions contributed to this. In addition, Government of Himachal Pradesh also encouraged female education by providing fee concessions and scholarships. However, it has to be noted that female NER which is better than that of male is confined to conventional courses only. In case of vocational courses, male NER is clearly higher than that of the females. It means in vocational education male NER is more than that of women, whereas in conventional courses women had an upper edge.

(b) Vocational Education

In 2001, the average differential index value was quiet low (0.5). There were only three districts, where index value was higher than state average. Among districts, it ranged from a high of 0.7 in Hamirpur to a low of 0.2 in Solan and Kinnaur districts. Six of the twelve districts in the state (Chamba, Kangra, Kullu, Una, Bilaspur, and Sirmaur) had this value equivalent to the state average. It was only Lahul and Spiti district which recorded differential in negative (-0.8) indicating high NER for females than the males. It is, however, to be noted that there is no vocational college in the district. It means students enumerated in higher vocational education were studying in the colleges located outside the district, but enumerated during censuses in Lahul and Spiti district (Fig. 4.2).

Table 4.2: Himachal Pradesh: NER differential index of general and vocational education by sex and residence, 2001-11

S. No.	District Name	Male-Female differential Index				Urban-Rural differential Index			
		General		Vocational		General		Vocational	
		2001	2011	2001	2011	2001	2011	2001	2011
1	2	3	4	5	6	7	8	9	10
1.	Chamba	0.6	0.27	0.5	0.7	3.4	1.6	3.8	2.4
2.	Kangra	0.2	-0.19	0.5	0.6	1.0	0.3	0.3	0.4
3.	Lahul and Spiti*	-0.3	-0.10	-0.8	0.1	*	*	*	*
4.	Kullu	0.5	0.11	0.5	0.4	1.8	0.5	2.2	1.9
5.	Mandi	0.4	0.05	0.6	0.6	2.0	0.5	4.0	1.6
6.	Hamirpur	0.2	-0.15	0.7	0.7	0.8	0.0	1.2	0.6
7.	Una	0.0	-0.48	0.5	0.6	0.7	0.2	0.5	0.4
8.	Bilaspur	0.2	-0.11	0.5	0.5	1.1	0.2	2.4	1.0
9.	Solan	0.0	-0.30	0.2	0.2	0.7	0.3	0.7	0.6
10.	Sirmaur	0.2	-0.06	0.5	0.1	3.0	0.9	1.6	2.6
11.	Shimla	0.2	-0.12	0.6	0.1	1.5	0.6	1.9	1.7
12.	Kinnaur*	0.0	-0.45	0.2	-0.2	*	*	*	*
	Himachal Pradesh	**0.2**	**-0.13**	**0.5**	**0.5**	**1.4**	**0.5**	**1.7**	**1.0**

Source: Census of India, Himachal Pradesh Socio and Cultural Tables (C-Series) of 2001 and 2011. Office of the Registrar General and Census Commissioner, India.

Note: *Entirely rural district.

They might, however, be living or not living in the district. Solan and Kinnaur districts had this value below the state average. In 2001, average differential index value being positive, indicates to male students NER higher than that of their female counterparts (Table 4.2).

In 2011, the NER for males and females were 6.7 per cent and 4.1 per cent, respectively; differential index value being 0.5. This indicates to low male-female NER differentials in higher education in the state. Among districts, differential index value ranged from a high of 0.7 in Chamba and Hamirpur districts to a low of 0.1 in three districts of Lahul and Spiti, Sirmaur and Shimla. Five districts of Chamba, Kangra, Mandi, Hamirpur, and Una had this value higher than the state average. As stated earlier, vocational higher education is the first preference of male students, who try their level best to get admitted to such courses. Some of the districts such as Hamirpur, Una, Mandi, and Sirmaur have a good number of vocational higher education institutions located there (Fig. 4.2).

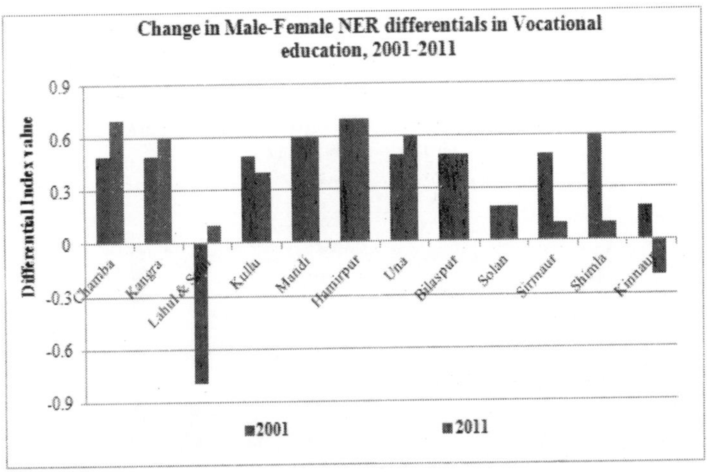

Fig. 4.2: Change in Male-Female NER differentials in Vocational education, 2001-2011.

Source: As Table 4.2.

It is, however, interesting to note that with increase in female and male NER during 2001-2011, male-female differentials on this count increased. The positive thing is that differentials were not very wide across districts.

C. Urban-Rural Differential, 2001-11

(a) General/College Education

Notably, two of the twelve districts in the state do not have any urban centres, so our discussions will remain confining to ten districts only. In 2001, the average urban-rural differential index value was 1.4 against only 0.2 in case of male-female NER differentials. Evidently, urban-rural differentials in NER were wider than male-female in the state. In other words, NER was more unequal in terms of urban-rural than social classes. In 2001, urban NER was 26.0 per cent against only 9.5 per cent for rural areas. In five of the twelve districts, this value was higher than the state average. Such districts were Chamba, Kullu, Mandi, Sirmaur and Solan. It ranged from a high of 3.4 in Chamba to a low of 0.7 in Una and Solan districts. Two districts of Lahul and Spiti and Kinnaur were entirely rural (Table 4.2).

During 2001-2011, differential in urban-rural NER registered a sharp decline to come down from 1.4 per cent in 2001 to 0.5 per cent. It was true of majority districts in the state. However, there has been a steep fall in the four districts of Sirmaur, Hamirpur, Mandi and Kullu. In case of Hamirpur district, differential index value was nil in 2011.

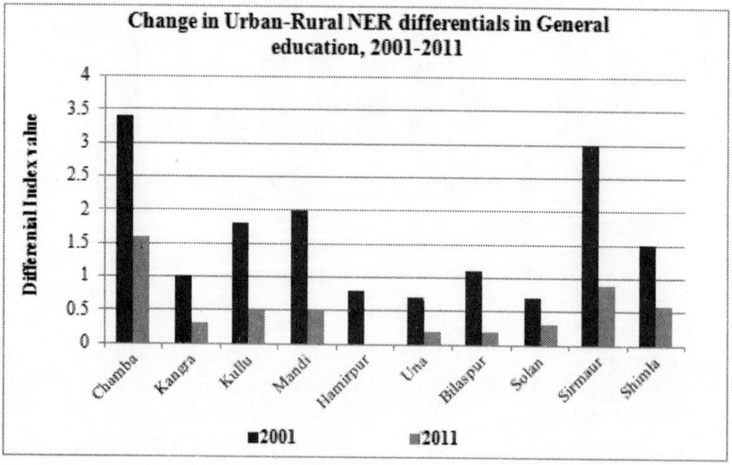

Fig. 4.3: Change in Urban-Rural differentials in General education, 2001-2011.
Source: As Table 4.2.

At district level, it ranged from a high of 1.6 for Chamba district to as low as nil in Hamirpur. Of the ten districts, having both rural and urban areas, three districts of Mandi, Sirmaur and Shimla had differential index value higher than the state average. Another two districts (Kullu and Mandi) had the same as the state average and five districts had below the state average (Fig. 4.3).

In this way, urban-rural differentials in NER declined sharply during 2001-2011. Geographical spread of higher education institution to rural and peripheral areas as a result of privatization policy was largely responsible for this.

(b) Vocational Education

In 2011, urban-rural differential index for vocational education was 1.0. Earlier in 2001, this value was 1.7. Evidently, urban-rural differentials in NER declined during 2001-2011. This is attributed to spatial spread of higher vocational education institutions toward the rural areas coupled with higher attraction of students to vocational courses for their job potentials in comparison to conventional courses.

In majority of districts, there has been a decline in urban-rural disparity, as is evident in differential index value. The maximum decline was recorded in case of Mandi district followed by Chamba district. Against this, Sirmaur district registered sharp increase, differential index value rose from 1.6 in 2001 to 2.6 in 2011. Another district, Kangra, recorded a marginal increase from 0.3 in 2001 to 0.4 in 2011 (Table 4.2). On the whole, five out of the ten districts (excluding Lahul and Spiti and Kinnaur) had differential index value higher than the state average. Vocational higher education in Himachal Pradesh is still at a low level, existence of wide urban-rural differential in vocational education NER does not speak of a healthy trend (Fig. 4.4).

D. Non-Scheduled Versus *Scheduled Differentials in NER*

As expected, NER of non-Scheduled population was higher than that of Scheduled (Castes plus Tribes) population in Himachal Pradesh. It was true of general and vocational education both. In 2011, NER of non-Scheduled and Scheduled population was 18.0 per cent and 14.0 per cent, respectively for general education courses. Earlier in 2001, the respective shares were 13.2 per cent and 6.8 per cent. Evidently, not only did NER for both non-Scheduled and Scheduled population grew fast but the gap between the two NER also declined during 2001-2011.

The growth of NER in case of Scheduled population was faster than that of non-Scheduled population. This helped in narrowing down the gap between NER of non-Scheduled and Scheduled population. This speaks of a healthy trend from the angle of social inclusiveness.

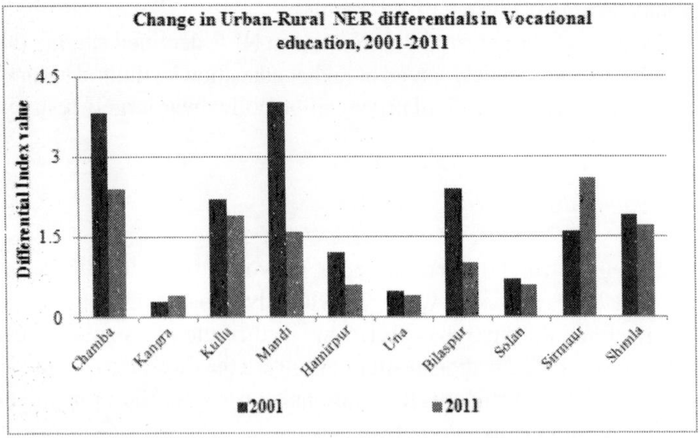

Fig. 4.4: Change in Urban-Rural NER differentials in Vocational education, 2001-2011.

Source: As Table 4.2.

(a) General Education

The average differential index value for general education was 0.24 in 2011. In four districts namely, Chamba, Lahul and Spiti, Hamirpur and Kinnaur differential index was negative, indicating higher NER for Scheduled population in comparison to non-Scheduled population in these districts. It is understandable in case of Chamba, Lahul and Spiti and Kinnaur districts, where tribal population is predominant. In Lahul and Spiti and Kinnaur districts Scheduled Castes and Tribes in combine make more than three-fourths of total population. In Chamba, their combined strength is about 48.0 per cent. Hence, higher NER of Scheduled population than non-Scheduled population makes some sense. But in case of Hamirpur, Scheduled population makes less than one-fourth of the total population, higher NER of Scheduled population than non-Scheduled population is quite surprising and needs further investigation. In case of Hamirpur, NER of Scheduled population was 25.18 per cent against this NER of non-Scheduled population was 23.11 per cent in 2011 (Table 4.3). Earlier in 2001, NER of Scheduled population was lower than that of non-Scheduled population. How it surpassed NER of non-Scheduled population in a single decade (2001-2011) is not only interesting but also worthy of further investigation.

Table 4.3: Himachal Pradesh: Net Enrolment Ratio of non-Scheduled and Scheduled population in general and vocational Education, 2001-2011

S. No.	District Name	General				Vocational			
		Non Scheduled		Scheduled		Non Scheduled		Scheduled	
		2001	2011	2001	2011	2001	2011	2001	2011
1	2	3	4	5	6	7	8	9	10
1.	Chamba	7.69	8.30	3.36	9.41	0.57	2.86	0.55	2.05
2.	Kangra	12.94	19.31	7.54	18.72	0.67	6.89	0.37	4.39
3.	Lahul and Spiti	1.70	8.64	8.23	25.90	0.90	1.24	0.42	3.63
4.	Kullu	10.75	14.12	5.08	11.69	0.60	3.01	0.28	2.17
5.	Mandi	12.94	15.90	7.32	14.53	0.76	5.84	0.35	4.13
6.	Hamirpur	18.51	23.11	12.50	25.18	0.74	10.73	0.54	8.27
7.	Una	11.62	20.28	7.85	10.00	1.10	8.45	0.86	3.96
8.	Bilaspur	15.81	17.34	9.11	16.69	0.87	9.09	0.49	6.47
9.	Solan	10.17	13.27	5.38	11.52	0.85	6.78	0.77	3.93
10.	Sirmaur	8.18	18.68	3.35	5.40	0.75	5.56	0.37	1.19
11.	Shimla	19.92	25.26	7.97	19.54	0.95	5.87	0.32	3.01
12.	Kinnaur	7.26	1.40	7.13	19.21	0.69	0.25	0.25	2.12
Himachal Pradesh		**13.19**	**18.03**	**6.75**	**14.06**	**0.78**	**6.42**	**0.66**	**3.55**

Source: Census of India, Himachal Pradesh Socio and Cultural Tables (C-Series) of 2001 and 2011.

In rest of the districts, NER differential was positive, indicating higher NER of non-Scheduled population. Fortunately, differential index value was not that high. It is relatively high only in case of Sirmaur and Una districts (Table 4.4).

Earlier in 2001, differential index of NER between Scheduled and non-Scheduled population was 0.57. It means there has been a sharp decline in differentials between the two populations during 2001-2011. One can safely assume that higher education quickly spread among Scheduled Castes and Tribes in the state during 2001-2011 decade. It is attributed to government policies oriented to make higher education socially inclusive. During the decade, state government as well as Central Government made sincere efforts to prop up NER in higher education; the way was exerting focus on inclusiveness. That would mean bridging social, regional and residential gaps in higher education accessibility. Secondly, with privatization of higher education private investment in higher education moved to remote areas where cheap land was available. To compensate students, private sector provided the bus services to students to reach colleges/universities from their places of living (Table 4.4 and Fig. 4.5).

Table 4.4: Himachal Pradesh: NER differential index of non-Scheduled and Scheduled population in general and vocational education, 2001-2011

S. No.	District Name	NER differentials index value			
		General		Vocational	
		2001	2011	2001	2011
1	2	3	4	5	6
1.	Chamba	0.76	-0.13	0.05	0.32
2.	Kangra	0.46	0.03	0.49	0.40
3.	Lahul and Spiti	-1.32	-0.77	0.83	-0.74
4.	Kullu	0.63	0.18	0.64	0.30
5.	Mandi	0.50	0.09	0.63	0.32
6.	Hamirpur	0.35	-0.09	0.30	0.24
7.	Una	0.35	0.63	0.23	0.66
8.	Bilaspur	0.48	0.04	0.49	0.31
9.	Solan	0.54	0.14	0.10	0.48
10.	Sirmaur	0.71	1.10	0.58	1.26
11.	Shimla	0.71	0.24	0.80	0.56
12.	Kinnaur	0.02	-1.46	1.26	-1.30
Himachal Pradesh		**0.57**	**0.24**	**0.48**	**0.52**

Source: Census of India, Himachal Pradesh Socio and Cultural Tables (C-Series) of 2001 and 2011.

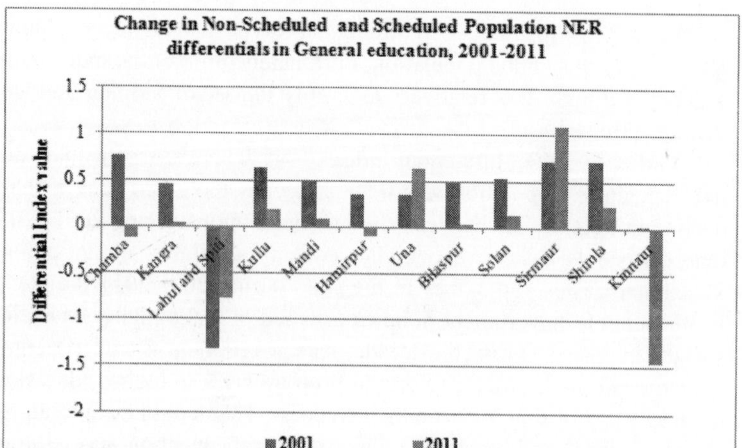

Fig. 4.5: Change in Non-Scheduled and Scheduled Population NER differentials in General education, 2001-2011.

Source: As Table 4.4.

All the districts in the state recorded decline in NER value except Una and Sirmaur. The highest decline was registered in Kinnaur district followed by Chamba, Shimla and Bilaspur. The reverse was true of Solan and Kangra districts.

(b) Vocational Education

The vocational higher education recorded higher differential index than general education between NER of Scheduled and non-Scheduled population in the state of Himachal Pradesh. Its differential index value in 2011 was more than twice that of general education in the same year. The index value of the former was 0.52 and that of the latter one was 0.24.

This denotes that there were wide differentials in NER of vocational than that of general higher education in the state. Getting admitted in vocational courses is not only tougher but also fee structure is higher than general education courses. These are mostly in the private sector, so vocational courses are generally self-financed, making it difficult for traditionally deprived sections of Himachali society to enrol their wards in such courses. In three districts (Shimla, Una and Sirmaur) differential index value was higher than the state average; it was negative in case of tribal majority districts of Kinnaur and Lahul and Spiti. For obvious reasons, differential index was in favour of Scheduled population in these two districts.

Quite disappointingly, there has been an increase in differential index value for vocational education during the period of 2001-2011, rising to 0.52 in 2011 from 0.40 in 2001. However, there was a mixed trend at the district level. Four districts (Chamba, Una, Solan and Sirmaur) recorded an increase in differentials index value and the rest registered a decline (Fig. 4.6).

Briefly, the social differentials in NER of general courses declined during 2001-2011. The reverse was true for vocational courses. Vocational courses are considered more oriented towards jobs than general courses and these involve higher competition to get admitted even after paying hefty fee than the general courses, a large segment of Scheduled population in the state finds it beyond their financial resources to admit their wards in such courses. When higher education gets highly commercialised, as is the case with vocational education, purchasing power comes in operation where socio-economically weak sections of society, generally having low purchasing power, go in the background and higher purchasing power comes to replace them. This leads to widening the gap in NER of two sections of the society.

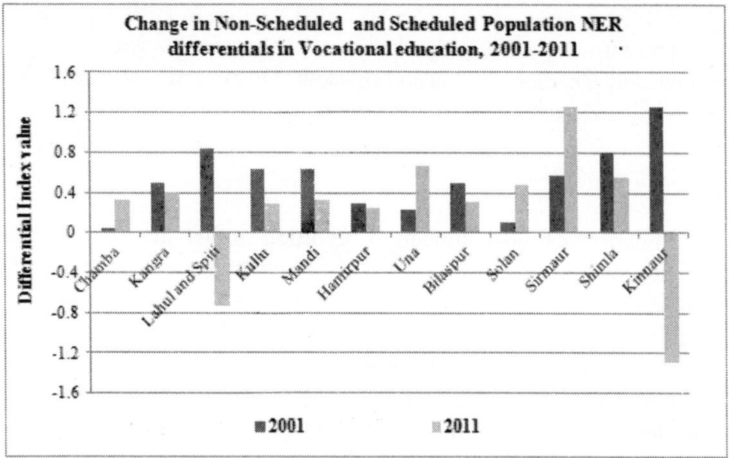

Fig. 4.6: Change in Non-Scheduled and Scheduled Population NER differentials in Vocational education, 2001-2011.

Source: As Table 4.4.

Accessibility: A Composite Picture

In the preceding discussions, we examined accessibility to higher education in Himachal Pradesh in terms of gender, residence and social factors for general and vocational education, separately. In the following, an attempt has been made to present a combined picture of higher education accessibility by one composite index derived by combining NER values in male, female, rural, urban, Scheduled population and non-Scheduled population of individual districts. Weighted index method has been used to calculate male, female, rural, urban, Scheduled and non-Scheduled NER values for individual districts followed by summing up of all these values to be divided by total number of NER, the number being six in the present case. The composite indices have been prepared and discussed for general and vocational education, separately.

The composite indices of general and vocational higher education have been discussed in the following section in order. Highest value of any district of NER has been assigned the value of 100; other districts have been given index values proportionately. Both the indices calculated, separately for 2001-2011.

(a) General Education Courses Index

In 2011, the general education weighted index value ranged from a high of 93.1 for Hamirpur to a low of only 40.8 in Chamba district. The state average index value being 67.8 for Himachal Pradesh, five districts had this value higher than the state average (Table 4.5 and Fig. 4.7A). Five districts having composite index value higher than the state average are categorized as high in terms of higher education accessibility for general education.

Table 4.5: Himachal Pradesh: Index values of NER of general education in higher education, 2011

S. No.	*District Name*	*General NER, 2011*						*Composite Index*
		Male	*Female*	*Rural*	*Urban*	*N-Sch**	*Sch**	
1	2	3	4	5	6	7	8	9
1.	Chamba	45	30	34	66	33	36	40.8
2.	Kangra	78	83	80	75	76	72	77.2
3.	Lahul and Spiti	96	94	95	0	34	100	83.9
4.	Kullu	63	50	54	59	56	45	54.4
5.	Mandi	71	59	63	70	63	56	63.9
6.	Hamirpur	98	100	100	72	91	97	93.1
7.	Una	56	80	68	57	80	39	63.1
8.	Bilaspur	73	71	72	61	69	64	68.3
9.	Solan	49	58	50	48	53	44	50.6
10.	Sirmaur	53	49	47	66	74	21	51.5
11.	Shimla	100	99	84	100	100	75	93.0
12.	Kinnaur	45	61	52	0	6	74	47.3
Himachal Pradesh		**70**	**70**	**66**	**74**	**71**	**54**	**67.8**

Source: As Table 4.0.

Note: *N-Sh: Non-Scheduled population; Sch: Scheduled population.

In 2011, more than one-third of the districts had index value higher than the state average. Based on this, five districts have been categorized as districts of high accessibility in general education and remaining seven falls in the low accessibility category (Table 4.6).

(b) Vocational Education Courses Index

In 2011, the vocational education index value ranged from a high of 100 for Hamirpur to a low of only 14.9 in Kinnaur district. The state average index value being 54.7, six districts had value higher than the state average. It included Kangra, Mandi, Hamirpur, Una, Bilaspur and Solan (Table 4.7

Table 4.6: Himachal Pradesh: Classification of districts according to level in Accessibility of general education, 2011

Accessibility index	*Name of districts*
High (67.8 and above)	Hamirpur (93.1), Shimla (93.0), Lahul and Spiti (83.9), Kangra (77.2), Bilaspur (68.3) **(Total = 5)**
Low (Less than 67.8)	Mandi (63.9), Una (63.1), Kullu (54.4), Sirmaur (51.5), Solan (50.6), Chamba (40.8), Kinnaur (47.3) **(Total = 7)**

and Fig. 4.7 B). The rest of the districts that were below the state average included Chamba, Lahul and Spiti, Kullu, Sirmaur, Shimla and Kinnaur.

Table: 4.7: Himachal Pradesh: Composite index value of NER of vocational education in higher education, 2011

S. No.	*District Name*	*Vocational NER, 2011*						*Composite index*
		Male	*Female*	*Rural*	*Urban*	*N-Sch*	*Sch*	
1		2	3	4	5	6	7	8
1.	Chamba	25	23	22	50	27	25	28.5
2.	Kangra	60	62	62	54	64	53	59.2
3.	Lahul and Spiti	24	44	33	0	12	44	31.3
4.	Kullu	24	31	23	48	28	26	30.2
5.	Mandi	50	55	49	84	54	50	57.2
6.	Hamirpur	100	100	100	100	100	100	100.0
7.	Una	63	68	66	58	79	48	63.7
8.	Bilaspur	77	89	80	100	85	78	84.8
9.	Solan	47	76	54	54	63	48	56.9
10.	Sirmaur	26	48	26	71	52	14	39.5
11.	Shimla	39	70	27	71	55	36	49.6
12.	Kinnaur	10	23	15	0	2	26	14.9
Himachal Pradesh		**49**	**60**	**50**	**66**	**60**	**43**	**54.7**

Source: As Table 4.0.

Note: As Table 4.5.

In this way, in 2011, five districts, where index value was above the state average have been categorized as the high and remaining seven districts of value below than the state average as low on accessibility in vocational higher education (Table 4.8).

Due to their locational advantage, private investors invest to establish educational institutes in these districts of the state. Therefore, the NER of such districts was higher than the state average. The rest of the districts have harsh climatic conditions, low population share and low number of vocational education institutes was attributed to low NER in vocational higher education in these districts.

Table 4.8: Himachal Pradesh: Classification of districts according to level in Accessibility of vocational education, 2011

Accessibility index	*Name of districts*
High (54.7 and above)	Hamirpur (100), Bilaspur (84.8), Una (63.7), Kangra (59.2), Mandi (57.2), Solan (56.9) **(Total = 5)**
Low (Less than 54.7)	Shimla (49.6), Sirmaur (39.5), Lahul and Spiti (31.3), Kullu (30.2), Chamba (28.5), Kinnaur (14.9) **(Total = 7)**

Source: As Table 4.7.

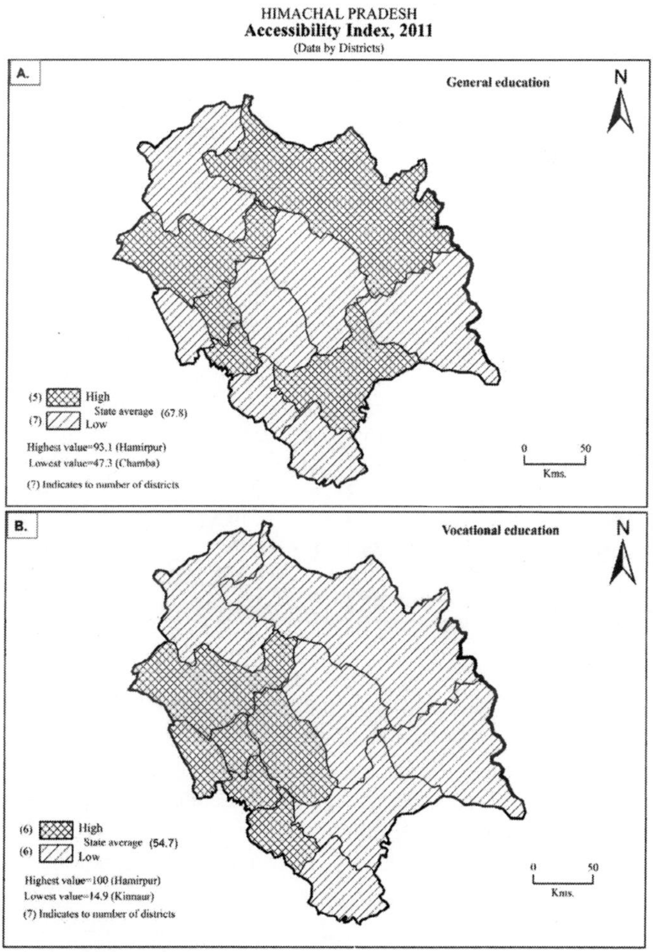

Fig. 4.7: Himachal Pradesh: Accessibility Index, 2011.

Source: As Table 4.6 and 4.8.

Further, a combined index of NER general and vocational education of higher education accessibility has been calculated to find out the overall scenario of accessibility to higher education in the state. It has been calculated for the two decades of 2001 and 2011, separately. Nine of the twelve districts in the state recorded negative change in index values of their composite of higher education accessibility, ranging from a high of 16.0 in Una district to a low 2.2 in Bilaspur district. Three districts registering positive change included Hamirpur, Kangra and Lahul and Spiti. The state average on this count was -4.8 (Table 4.9).

Table 4.9: Himachal Pradesh: Change in composite index of higher education accessibility (college level), 2001-2011

S. No.	*District Name*	*Index value*		*Change*
		2001	*2011*	*2011-2011*
1	2	3	4	5
1.	Chamba	41.8	34.6	-7.2
2.	Kangra	61.7	68.2	6.5
3.	Lahul and Spiti	53.6	57.6	4.0
4.	Kullu	51.3	42.3	-9.0
5.	Mandi	68.6	60.5	-8.1
6.	Hamirpur	81.2	96.5	15.3
7.	Una	79.4	63.4	-16.0
8.	Bilaspur	78.8	76.6	-2.2
9.	Solan	62.2	53.7	-8.5
10.	Sirmaur	51.3	45.5	-5.7
11.	Shimla	78.1	71.3	-6.8
12.	Kinnaur	44.7	31.1	-13.6
Himachal Pradesh		**66.0**	**61.2**	**-4.8**

Source: As Table 4.0.

In 2001, the average composite index value of general and vocational education accessibility for the state was 66. Then more than one-third of the districts recorded this index value above the average composite index value. It included Mandi, Hamirpur, Una, Bilaspur and Shimla districts. Remaining seven districts were below the state average. In 2011, when state average value was 61.2, Kangra district replaced Mandi district, the name of districts above average remained the same (Table 4.10).

Table 4.10: Himachal Pradesh: Classification of districts by higher education accessibility, 2011

Accessibility index	*Name of district*
High (61.2 and above)	Hamirpur (96.5), Bilaspur (76.6), Shimla (71.3), Kangra (68.2), Una (63.4) **(Total = 5)**
Low (less than 61.2)	Mandi (60.5), Lahul and Spiti (57.6), Solan (53.7), Sirmaur (45.5), Kullu (42.3), Chamba (34.6), Kinnaur (31.1) **(Total = 7)**

Source: As Table 4.9.

The index unfolds that in 2011 the demand for higher education was higher in less than half of the districts (Table 4.10). Districts having low demand for higher education included Lahul and Spiti, Solan, Sirmaur, Kullu, Chamba, Kinnaur and Mandi districts. It indicated the following factors:

1. The pent up demand for higher education especially the vocational, which got released in the closing years of the 20th century, reached its climax within a short period by 2011. This is supported by sharp decline registered in index values of Mandi, Solan and Sirmaur districts between 2001 and 2011.
2. Poor quality of higher education combined with physical accessibility problems might have resulted in decrease in the demand for higher education especially in case of Lahul and Spiti, Chamba and Kinnaur districts. From these districts, a substantial number of students got enrolled for higher education in Kullu, Kangra and Shimla districts, respectively.

II. Availability

The availability of higher education has been examined in terms of area and population. Theoretically speaking, availability of higher education institutions, in area and population terms bends towards supply side, it has been examined here at four points of time 1991, 2001, 2011 and 2016 by taking district as unit of study. It will help us to understand, the changing scenario of supply side of higher education in Himachal Pradesh. Area has been computed per 1000 km^2 and population per hundred thousand (or per lakh) population.

For calculating availability of colleges in terms of population, total population in the age-group of 18-23 has been taken instead of the total population, because the study concentrates on this age-group. Since persons of 18-23 age-group remain in higher education, this will make our analysis closer to the ground reality. Further, we have examined here availability of higher education institutions in area and population terms, separately. We begin with an examination of changing share of general and vocational education colleges in total at district level. It will unfold change in the structure composition of higher education at the district level.

There has been a significant change in composition of higher education in Himachal Pradesh during 1991-2016. In 1991, colleges running general/ traditional courses predominated (84.0%), the total number of colleges in the state. If we exclude Kinnaur and Lahul and Spiti districts, where not even a single college existed up to 1991, five of the remaining ten districts in the state had cent per cent general education colleges. Among the remaining districts, it ranged from a high of 80.0 per cent in Solan district to a low of 70.0 per cent in Kangra district. In relative terms, higher education was least diversified in five districts and most diversified in Kangra district. On the whole, higher education in Himachal Pradesh was predominantly traditional by 1991. In the five districts of the state, there was no vocational education college and in another two districts, by 2001, the share of general education colleges came down to about 78.0 per cent from 84.0 per cent in 1991. Still, there was no vocational college in the five districts of the state.

In Solan district, which had the most diversified higher education scenario, 50.0 per cent colleges were running vocational courses. Solan was followed by Hamirpur with 40.0 per cent. Earlier in 1991, the share of vocational higher education was nil in Hamirpur district. On the other side of the scale, the share of vocational colleges in the total number of colleges declined in the three districts of Bilaspur, Kangra and Mandi.

However, the share of vocational colleges registered dramatic increase during the decade of 2001-2011. The government policy which emphasized to focus on vocational education and increased private investment in higher education was largely responsible for this. Already there was pent up demand for vocational education in the state, the private investors tried to encash it by opening colleges entirely focusing on vocational courses.

Consequently, by 2011, the share of colleges running general or traditional courses in the state declined such an the extent that vocational colleges turned into majority. The share of vocational colleges went up to 54.2 per cent in 2011 from 22.3 per cent in 2001. In contrast, the share of general colleges came down to 45.8 per cent from about 78.0 per cent during this period. Thanks to the state government policy under Chief Minister Virbhadra Singh of Indian National Congress to have at least one Government College in each of assembly constituencies in the state. The state government opened several new colleges in backward and peripheral areas. With a few exceptions, all such colleges were to teach general traditional courses. As a result, the share of colleges teaching general courses rose again to get majority mark in 2016 (51.3%). There were, of course, wide inter-district differentials on this count. The share ranged from 100.0 per cent in Lahul and Spiti district to about 35.0 per cent in Solan district (Table 4.11).

Table 4.11: Himachal Pradesh: Changing share of general and vocational higher education colleges in total by districts, 1991-2016

S. No.	District Name	1991		2001		2011		2016	
		G	V	G	V	G	V	G	V
1	2	3	4	5	6	7	8	9	10
1	Bilaspur	75.0	25.0	83.3	16.7	63.6	36.4	57.1	42.9
2	Chamba	100.0	0.0	100.0	0.0	80.0	20.0	83.3	16.7
3	Hamirpur	100.0	0.0	60.0	40.0	41.7	58.3	44.0	56.0
4	Kangra	70.0	30.0	80.0	20.0	51.1	48.9	56.1	43.9
5	Kinnaur	0.0	0.0	100.0	0.0	50.0	50.0	50.0	50.0
6	Kullu	100.0	0.0	100.0	0.0	66.7	33.3	69.2	30.8
7	Lahul and Spiti	0.0	0.0	100.0	0.0	100.0	0.0	100.0	0.0
8	Mandi	75.0	25.0	77.8	22.2	30.3	69.7	40.0	60.0
9	Shimla	78.6	21.4	75.0	25.0	43.8	56.3	47.6	52.4
10	Solan	80.0	20.0	50.0	50.0	25.0	75.0	34.5	65.5
11	Sirmaur	100.0	0.0	80.0	20.0	47.1	52.9	56.5	43.5
12	Una	100.0	0.0	100.0	0.0	52.6	47.4	57.1	42.9
	Himachal Pradesh	**83.9**	**16.1**	**77.7**	**22.3**	**45.8**	**54.2**	**51.3**	**48.7**

Source: Statistics of Higher and Technical Education available from the Directorate of Higher education, Lalpani Shimla, Government of Himachal Pradesh.

Note: G stands for GENERAL and V for VOCATIONAL.

In seven of the twelve districts in the state, general education colleges dominated the total number of colleges. On the other side of the scale, five districts had the dominance of vocational colleges in 2016. In fact, Kinnaur was such a district, where there were only two colleges, one imparting vocational education and another general, whereas there was only one college in Lahul and Spiti, those too teaching general/traditional courses.

Briefly, it is the government policy, may it be privatization of higher education or having at least one government college in all the state assembly constituencies in the state, which has played the most important role in changing the structure of higher education between general and vocational education in the state.

In the following section, we examine availability of higher education at the district level in terms of area and population covered by colleges. The main objective is to capture inter-district differentials in this regard and to compare with norms, if any, set by the government in this context.

(i) Area Served

Between 1991 and 2016, there has been spectacular increase in the availability of higher educational institutes in Himachal Pradesh. In 1991, there was only one college to serve 1000 km^2 area in the state. By 2016, there were nearly five colleges to serve the same area. Happily, there has been progressive increase in the availability of educational institutes in terms of area.

At the district level, more than a half of the districts in 1991 had this ratio higher the state average. These included Bilaspur, Hamirpur, Kangra, Shimla, Solan, Sirmaur and Una. Except Shimla, all other districts in this category are adjacent to the Punjab and Haryana plains. Una district, which recorded the highest ratio (4.5 colleges/1000 km^2), had been a tehsil of Hoshiarpur district of Punjab before its linguistic reorganisation in 1966. The entire district has relatively plain topography and fairly even distribution of population. In pre-Independence period, the present Una district was a part of British ruled territory in Punjab. In contrast, Kullu district had the lowest ratio of 0.4 colleges per 1000 km^2. In other words, there was one college after 2500 km^2 area in the Kullu district. Any higher education college was yet to come in two districts of Lahul and Spiti and Kinnaur which are predominantly dominated by tribals. On the whole, history of education development, terrain and population acted as the controlling factors of the availability of higher education institutions at the district level in the state (Table 4.12).

In 2001, when there were on average about two colleges (actually 1.69 colleges per 1000 km^2 area) in Himachal Pradesh, this ratio ranged from about 9 colleges in Hamirpur district to 0.1 in Lahul and Spiti district. In other words, there was roughly one college to serve 100 km^2 in Hamirpur district and to 10,000 km^2 area in Lahul and Spiti district. Still another way to say the same is that in the former district there was one college within a radius of 3.2 kms and in the latter district it was within a radius of about 32.0 kms. Definitely, there were wide inter-district disparities in the availability of colleges in terms of area.

Table 4.12: Himachal Pradesh: Trend in area served by higher education colleges, 1991-2016

Sl. No.	*District Name*	*Educational colleges per 1000 km²*			
		1991	*2001*	*2011*	*2016*
1	2	3	4	5	6
1.	Bilaspur	3.4	5.1	9.4	12.0
2.	Chamba	0.5	0.6	1.5	1.8
3.	Hamirpur	3.6	8.9	21.5	22.4
4.	Kangra	1.7	3.5	7.8	9.9
5.	Kinnaur	0.0	0.2	0.3	0.3
6.	Kullu	0.4	0.7	1.6	2.4
7.	Lahul and Spiti	0.0	0.1	0.1	0.1
8.	Mandi	1.0	2.3	8.4	10.1
9.	Shimla	2.7	3.1	6.2	8.2
10.	Solan	2.6	5.2	12.4	15.0
11.	Sirmaur	1.1	1.8	6.0	8.1
12.	Una	4.5	5.2	12.3	13.6
	Himachal Pradesh	**1.01**	**1.69**	**4.08**	**5.01**
	C.V Index	0.74	0.88	0.85	0.80

Source: (i) Statistics of Higher and Technical Education available from the Directorate of Higher Education, Lalpani Shimla, Government of Himachal Pradesh. (ii) District-wise area calculated from the report of the Government of Himachal Pradesh. Socio-economic indicators of H.P., 2013, Department of Economics and statistics H.P., Shimla, p. 3.

On the whole, eight districts had this ratio which was higher than the state average. Those districts that had this ratio below the state average included Chamba, Kinnaur, Kullu, and Lahul and Spiti districts. All the four districts fall in higher and Trans-Himalayan zone having higher altitude, difficult terrain, harsh climate and sparse distribution of population. Inter-district disparities in college-area ratio widened between 1991 and 2001, as revealed in increased C.V. index value during this period (0.88 in 2001 from 0.74 in 1991).

Coming to 2011, when the average college-area ratio more than doubled to reach more than four colleges per 1000 km² area, inter-district disparities in this regard marginally declined. The C.V. index value came from 0.88 in 2001 to 0.85 in 2011. Among districts college-area ratio ranged from a high of about 22 colleges after 1000 km² in Hamirpur district to a low of 0.1 in Lahul and Spiti district, where no new college was established during 2001-2011. In other words, on an average, in Hamirpur district a college was serving an area of about 47 km² area, against 1000 km^2 area in Lahul and Spiti district. Among districts, Hamirpur was followed by Solan district with a ratio of 12.4 colleges/1000 km^2 and by Una with 12.3 colleges. Shimla district having state capital headquarters in it was lagging far behind these districts with a ratio of 6.2 colleges/1000 km^2.

Four districts, Hamirpur, Mandi, Solan and Una, recorded the rapid increase in the number of colleges in area terms, since their ratio was more than twice during 2001-2011. Sirmaur, Bilaspur, and Kangra districts also recorded impressive increase in the availability of colleges in terms of area.

During 2001-2011, Himachal Pradesh experienced private investment in higher education. Several new colleges and universities were established by the private sector in the state. These colleges and universities were located in the districts where pent up demand for higher education especially vocational was quite high and also a strong possibility of attracting students from adjoining districts of Punjab, Haryana and Uttar Pradesh. This is explained by demand-supply equation. In other words, higher the demand for higher education, higher would be the supply in the form of new colleges/universities. This was especially true of institutes running vocational courses.

When college-area average ratio in the state moved from 4.1 in 2011 to 5.0 colleges/1000 km^2 in 2016, inter-district disparity on this count were further reduced. This was mainly because of the fact that the process of opening new colleges slowed down. Perhaps, this happened due to the change in demand-supply equilibrium. During 2011-2016, some new colleges were established in different parts of the state, opened mostly in peripheral and backwards areas. These were opened by the state government to teach traditional courses. In 2016, college-area ratio ranged from a high of 22.4 colleges/1000 km^2 area to a low of only 0.1 in Lahul and Spiti district. Five districts of Hamirpur, Solan, Una Bilaspur and Mandi had this ratio more than double of the state average. In all, as many as eight districts had this ratio higher than the state average. Bilaspur, Mandi and Solan districts performed better than other districts on this count during 2011-2016.

However, there was no change in the ranking of the districts on this count between 2011 and 2016. Decline in inter-district inequality in college area ratio is mainly attributed to the decision of the state government to open new colleges in peripheral and backward areas of the state under its policy of having at least one government degree college in all the state assembly constituencies.

Briefly, there has been a spectacular increase in the availability of colleges in terms of area in the state during 1991-2016. The most robust increase was registered between 2001 and 2011 when college-area ratio more than doubled, from less than two colleges/1000 km^2 to more than four colleges/1000 km^2, the private investment in higher education sector of the state playing an important role in this. Private investment, which was based on the concept of demand-supply equation, not only increased the availability of colleges in area terms but also reduced inter-district gap on this count. With the exception of Mandi district, all those districts performing well on this count shared boundaries/borders with neighbouring states of Punjab, Haryana and Uttar Pradesh.

In 2016, when inter-district gap in college-area ratio was further reduced, state government policy of having at least one government degree college in all the state assembly constituencies is credited with reduction in inter-district inequalities in college-area ratio. By 2016, there was one college available within a radius of 4.5 kms in the state. This ratio was of more than 10 kms in the year 1991.

(ii) Population Served

In 1991, there were, on an average, more than nine colleges after one lakh population in Himachal Pradesh. Roughly, there was one degree college after about 11 thousand persons in Himachal Pradesh. There were, however, wide inter-district disparities on this count. The number of colleges per lakh persons ranged from a high of about 19 in Shimla district to a low of less than five in the Mandi district. In two districts of Kinnaur and Lahul and Spiti no degree college existed till 1991. Of the remaining ten districts in the state, one-half districts had this ratio that was lower than the state average. In Mandi district, this ratio was less than one-half of the state average. Among the five districts (Bilaspur, Shimla, Hamirpur, Una, and Solan) which had this ratio of more than ten colleges after one lakh population, Shimla was the only district which has higher altitudes. Rest of them have areas of low altitude of Shiwalik Himalayas and share borders with the neighbouring state of Punjab (Table 4.13).

After a decade in 2001, when college-population ratio from 9.3 in 1991 moved to 13, inter-district disparities on this count declined further. This happened mainly because of the opening of new degree colleges in Kinnaur and Lahul and Spiti districts. These two districts did not have even one higher education institution till 1991. Among districts, college-population ratio ranged from a high of about 24 colleges/one lakh population in Lahul and Spiti to only about 8 in Chamba district.

Table 4.13: Himachal Pradesh: Trend in population served by higher education colleges, 1991-2016

S. No.	District Name	Educational institutions/colleges per lakh population			
		1991	2001	2011	2016
1	2	3	4	5	6
1.	Bilaspur	12.2	15.3	26.2	33.3
2.	Chamba	6.7	7.6	16.1	19.3
3.	Hamirpur	10.1	21.3	51.1	53.2
4.	Kangra	7.4	12.5	27.8	35.2
5.	Kinnaur	0.0	11.3	21.4	21.4
6.	Kullu	5.7	8.9	16.6	23.9
7.	Lahul and Spiti	0.0	23.6	29.1	29.1
8.	Mandi	4.5	8.4	30.1	36.5
9.	Shimla	18.8	18.2	32.9	43.2
10.	Solan	10.1	15.3	33.6	40.6
11.	Sirmaur	7.0	9.4	25.9	35.0
12.	Una	15.8	15.8	33.1	36.5
Himachal Pradesh		**9.3**	**13.0**	**29.1**	**35.7**
C.V Index		0.52	0.37	0.32	0.28

Source: (i) Census of India, Himachal Pradesh single year age returns (C-5 Table) for 1991 and C-8-10 Tables for 2001 and C-13 for 2011, Office of the Registrar General and Census Commissioner of India. (ii) Data on number of colleges were used from the report on Statistics of Higher and Technical Education available from the Directorate of Higher Education, Shimla and Annual reports of various years of HPU, Shimla.

In both the districts, there was a significant presence of tribal population and overall population distribution was also low and dispersed. Lahul and Spiti district did not have any degree college till 1991. In case of Lahul and Spiti district, the small population size is mainly responsible for such a high ratio. Secondly, students in large number migrate to Kullu for higher studies. The district with second highest ratio was Hamirpur, ratio being 21.3 colleges/lakh persons. Earlier in 1991, Hamirpur shared fourth rank with Solan district. It has happened mainly because of its very good performance during 1991-2001. Its college-population ratio jumped from 10.1 in 1991 to 21.3 in 2001. A number of new colleges were opened in private sector to cater to the increased demand for vocational courses. Other districts performing well on this count included Mandi, Bilaspur and Solan. Mandi district even though they had low ratio in 2001, yet its college-population ratio increased almost twice during 1991-2001. On the other side of the scale, Una district registered no change in its ratio and Shimla district recorded a marginal decline during this period.

The next decade (2001-2011) registered a phenomenal increase in college-population ratio in the state. The state average jumped from 13.0 in 2001 to more than 29 colleges/one lakh population (in the age-group of 18-23) in 2011. This was mainly the effect of the privatization policy adopted by the state government. Privatization of higher education in the state resulted in opening of a large number of new colleges especially to cater to the demand of vocational education in different districts of the state. Mandi district recorded the highest jump of more than two times in its college-population ratio followed by Sirmaur district, recording almost the same increase. Other districts in the group included Hamirpur, Kangra, and Solan districts. On the other side of the scale, Lahul and Spiti, Shimla, Bilaspur, Kinnaur and Kullu districts registered low increase in their college-population ratio.

In 2016, when this ratio rose further to reach about 36 colleges/lakh persons, there was a further decline in inter-district disparities on this count. Among districts, this ratio ranged from a high of 53.2 colleges/ lakh persons in Hamirpur district to a low of only 19.3 in Chamba district, differing by about 34 colleges/lakh persons. In other words, Hamirpur district had 34 more colleges for per lakh population in comparison of Chamba district. This is a huge gap, yet low in comparison to 1991.

Interestingly, the biggest gainer during 2011-2016 was Kullu followed by Sirmaur, Shimla, Bilaspur and Kangra districts. The reverse was true of Kinnaur, Lahul and Spiti, Hamirpur, and Una districts, which performed high or moderate during 2001-2011. It seems that a saturation level was reached at a given level of educational development in these districts. Against this, districts performing well during this period benefitted from Himachal Pradesh government policy of having at least one government college in all the state assembly constituencies. Backward and peripheral areas in all such districts benefitted from this policy decision.

Briefly, college-population ratio recorded a phenomenal increase in Himachal Pradesh between 1991 and 2016. A major part of this increase occurred during 2001-2011, when private investment in higher education stepped up rapidly following a change in higher education investment policy at the state level. The inter-district disparities declined concomitantly with increase in college-population ratio. Some of the districts such as Mandi, Sirmaur, Solan, Kangra and Hamirpur which had initially the low or moderate level of college-population ratio, recorded rapid increase in post-2001 period. The reverse was true of districts such as Shimla, Una and Bilaspur, reaching the saturation level.

Availability: A Composite View

In the preceding discussion, we examined availability of higher institutions (colleges) in terms of area and population, separately. In the following paragraphs an attempt is made to present a composite picture of availability based on the combined strength, of these two indicators. For this purpose, index method has been used, in place of ranking method. The objective is to highlight inter-district distance or gap, which hides the ranking method. For examining the change, 2001 and 2011 have been selected for it being a period of remarkable change in the availability in terms of area and population both.

In 2001, when index value ranged from a high of 95 for Hamirpur district to a low of only 20 for Chamba district, for one-half of the districts index value was higher than 50. These included Hamirpur, Bilaspur, Solan, Lahul and Spiti, Shimla and Una districts. Against this, three districts namely, Chamba, Kinnaur and Kullu had this value of one-half or less of 50. Former districts may be termed as 'high' and the latter ones as 'low' on the availability of higher education. The remaining three districts may be termed as 'moderate'.

In 2011, when index value ranged from a high of 100 for Hamirpur district to 19 for Chamba district, disparities in combined index of availability increased. Earlier in 2001, six districts had index value which was higher than 50, now the number of such districts was only four (Table 4.14). However, the number of districts having index value 2.5 or less remained the same as in 2001, majority of districts (six in numbers) fell in between these two categories of districts. This happened mainly because of the fact that some districts recorded the fast growth against the majority of districts growing at a slow pace or at the same pace as the earlier decade of 1991-2001.

Change in index value during 2001-2011 makes an interesting reading. As many as eight of the twelve districts in the state recorded negative change in their weightage index values, indicating downfall in their relative position among districts. The maximum fall of 21 points was recorded in Lahul and Spiti district which saw opening of a new college during 1991-2001 and thereafter no new college was opened in this district. It was followed by Bilaspur district with a negative change of 13 points in its weighted index during 2001-2011. Another district of sharp decline in its weighted index value was Shimla. Rest of the negative change districts recorded only a marginal decline in their index values during this period.

Table 4.14: Himachal Pradesh: Change in Higher education availability by districts, 2001-2011

S. No.	*District Name*	*Index value*		*Change (2001-2011)*
		2001	*2011*	
1	2	3	4	5
1.	Bilaspur	61	48	-13
2.	Chamba	20	19	-1
3.	Hamirpur	95	100	5
4.	Kangra	46	45	-1
5.	Kinnaur	48	42	-3
6.	Kullu	23	20	-3
7.	Lahul and Spiti	100	57	-21
8.	Mandi	31	49	18
9.	Shimla	56	47	-9
10.	Solan	61	62	1
11.	Sirmaur	30	39	9
12.	Una	63	61	2
	Himachal Pradesh	**46.8**	**49.3**	**2.5**

Source: As Table 4.12 and 4.13.

On the other side of the scale, Mandi district recorded the highest increase in its index value, revealing that district recorded rapid increase in the availability of higher education institutions (colleges) in terms of area and population during 2001-2011 (Fig. 4.8). It was followed by Sirmaur and Hamirpur districts. Rest of the districts recorded only marginal positive change in their index values. In this way, three districts of Mandi, Sirmaur and Hamirpur recorded rapid increase in the availability of higher education both in terms of area and population, with Lahul and Spiti, Bilaspur and Shimla districts the tempo in between.

Accessibility and Availability: A Cross-examination

In the preceding discussion, accessibility and availability of higher education in Himachal Pradesh has been examined, separately. Representing two different but inter-connected dimensions of higher education, accessibility and availability are cross-examined in the following segment. The main objective behind such an exercise is to understand the nature of association existing between the two at the district level.

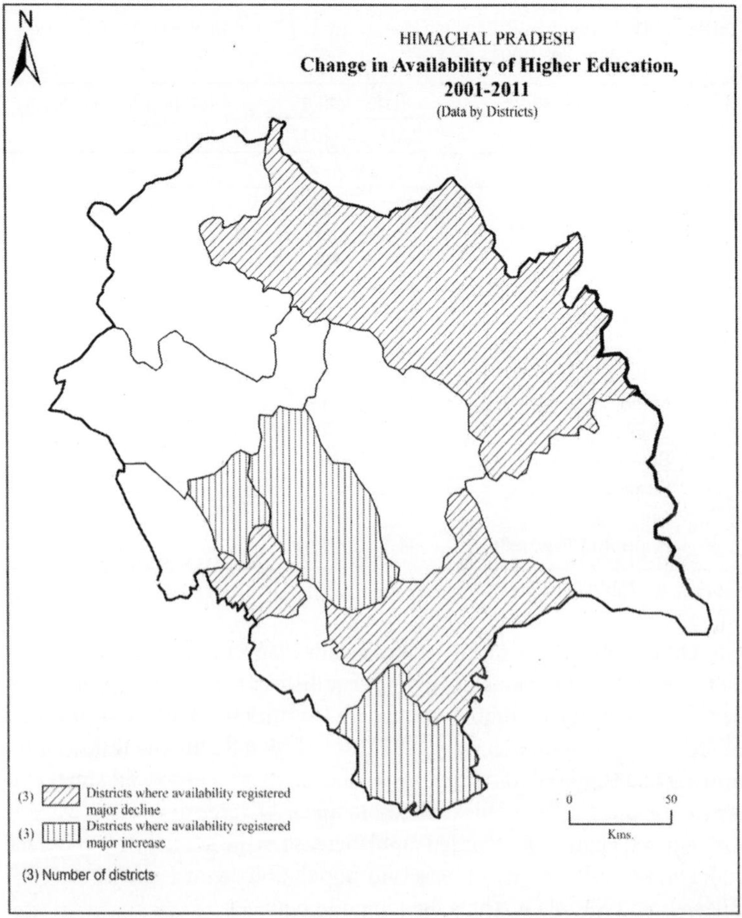

Fig. 4.8: Himachal Pradesh: Change in availability of higher education, 2001-2011.

Source: As Table 4.14.

Accessibility is measured with the help of net enrolment ratio (NER) and availability in terms of area and population in the present dissertation. The former is represented by the six indicators and the latter by the two. To begin with, we prepared composite index of accessibility and availability separately using weighted index method; done only for 2011. Thereafter, the two composite indices are separately discussed and twelve districts in the state have been classified into two categories, high and low, taking state average value as the cut-off point. Then, the two categories are cross-examined and mapped to see conformity/non-conformities between the two. The main objective is to identify districts where the two (accessibility and availability) converge on each other or diverge from each other. Such an exercise will help the planners and policy-makers in the state to rectify the situation by removing an anomaly between these components of higher education in the state.

Table 4.15: Himachal Pradesh: Association between levels of availability and accessibility of higher education at district level, 2011

Level of availability/accessibility	*Name of district*
High/High	Hamirpur, Una
High/Low	Lahul and Spiti, Mandi, Solan
Low/High	Bilaspur, Kangra, Shimla
Low/Low	Chamba, Kinnaur, Kullu, Sirmaur

Source: As Table 4.10 and 4.14.

The results of cross-examination presented in Table 4.15 are quite revealing. In two districts of Hamirpur and Una, availability and accessibility of higher education go hand-in-hand. In other words, both are high in these two districts. On the other side of the scale, in another four districts of Chamba, Kinnaur, Kullu and Sirmaur both are low (Fig. 4.9). In this way, in one-half of the districts in the state availability and accessibility of higher education corresponds with each other. In another three districts of Bilaspur, Kangra, and Shimla, notwithstanding low availability of higher education institutions, accessibility is high. It means these districts could overcome the deficiency in availability of higher education institutions within these districts by way of their external links. Secondly, Kangra and Shimla districts have some of the oldest universities located in them, which have been kept outside the purview of the analysis here. Against this, Lahul and Spiti, Mandi and Solan districts present the case of low accessibility in spite of high availability of higher education institutions. This means that available higher institutions stand underutilized or supply is more than the demand for higher education in these districts. This needs immediate attention of policy-makers for corrective measures, otherwise market forces will come in operation. In other words, those higher education institutions that will fail to compete will be wiped out in due course of time.

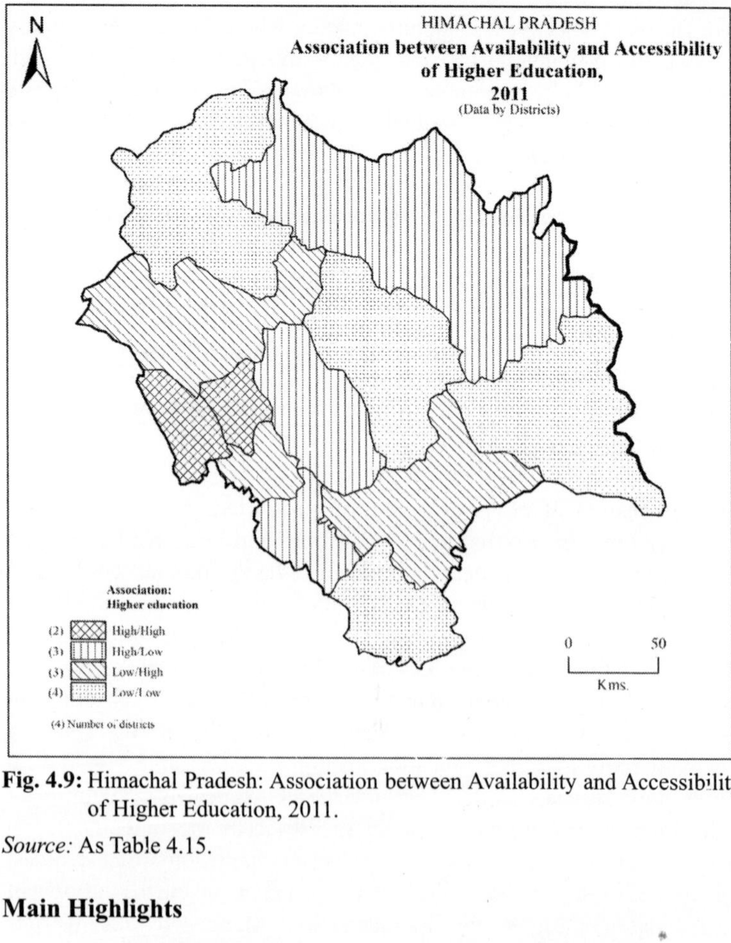

Fig. 4.9: Himachal Pradesh: Association between Availability and Accessibility of Higher Education, 2011.

Source: As Table 4.15.

Main Highlights

- Accessibility and availability of higher education, measured with the help of a number of indicators, was not only low but also differed widely in time and space in the state. In 2011, only about one-sixth of total youths in 18-23 age-group were enrolled in higher education. Earlier in 1981, NER was only 0.5 per cent. In other words, only one out of 200 young persons in the age-group of 18-23 were enrolled for higher education. The vocational education, in particular, remained quite low both in the availability and accessibility till recently. Even in 2001, NER of vocational education was as low as 0.68 per cent, picking up after 2001 to reach up to 5.53 per cent within a decade by 2011. In a way, the year 2001 acted as water mark in the history of NER in Himachal Pradesh for the two main reasons: (i) shift in focus from general to vocational courses, and (ii) opening of higher education to the private sector.

- Himachal Pradesh has benefitted a lot from private investment in higher education since the state has been liberal in opening higher education to private sector, resulting in opening of the new colleges and universities both in public and private sectors, registering a quantum leap in NER between 1991 and 2001: from 1.08 per cent to 11.4 per cent. The NER continued to grow further in the next decade between 2001 and 2011, to reach to 16.7 per cent by 2011.
- However, different districts in the state responded differently to privatization policy. Against the state average of 0.5 per cent in 1981, it ranged from a high of 1.8 per cent in Shimla district to negligible (only 0.04%) in Lahul and Spiti district. In one-half of the twelve districts in the state, namely Lahul and Spiti, Kinnaur, Chamba, Una, Bilaspur, Kullu and Sirmaur, NER ratio was either equivalent to or less than one-half of the state average. It was only in the two districts of Solan and Shimla where NER ratio was higher than the state average. In fact, the NER ratio of Shimla district was responsible for keeping state average on the higher side.
- There are striking inter-district, urban-rural, male-female and social inequalities in higher education enrolment ratio even at the low level of higher education development in the state. In 2011, NER ranged from a high of 23.6 per cent in Shimla district to a low of only 8.8 per cent in Chamba district, giving a range difference of about 15.0 per cent. Separately for vocational streams, inter-district inequalities were still sharp, ranging from a high of 10.3 per cent in Hamirpur district to only 1.4 per cent in Kinnaur district. Urban-rural inequalities in NER were equally marked both in general and vocational education. The NER of higher education for urban areas was nearly twice of the rural areas. The former was 24.8 per cent against only 15.7 per cent in the latter. In vocational education, it was 10.7 per cent for urban areas and only 4.9 per cent for the rural areas. Between Scheduled Castes and non-Scheduled population, it was 14.1 per cent for the former and 18.0 per cent for the latter.

- Interestingly, the general education inequalities in Himachal Pradesh go in favour of females. NER for females was 17.8 per cent against 15.6 per cent for the males. Even in rural areas, NER for females was higher than that of males. However, in the case of vocational education, the balance is in favour of males, the NER of vocational education for males was 5.4 per cent against 4.1 per cent for females in 2011. Even in the case of Scheduled Castes population, NER for female and male population in general education was almost the same. For the former, it was 14.6 per cent and for latter 14.8 per cent.
- The physiographic conditions of the state have remarkable impact on NER in higher education. As one moves from lower Himalayan zone to middle and then to higher and trans-Himalayan zones, NER keeps on declining. Lack of threshold population coupled with the paucity of financial resources, required to open higher education institutions in the state government seem to be the plausible reasons behind all this.
- As is evident from differential index value, urban-rural disparity in NER declined in the majority of districts. The maximum decline was recorded in Mandi district followed by Chamba district. Against this, Sirmaur district registered sharp increase, where differential index value rose to 206 in 2011 from 1.6 in 2001. Another district, Kangra, recorded a marginal increase from 0.3 in 2001 to 0.4 in 2011. On the whole, five of the ten districts (excluding Lahul and Spiti and Kinnaur) had differential index value higher than the state average. Vocational higher education, which is still at low level in Himachal Pradesh, recorded wide urban-rural differential in vocational education NER. It is not a healthy trend.
- As expected, NER of non-Scheduled population was higher than that of the Scheduled (Castes plus Tribes) population in Himachal Pradesh. It was true for both general and vocational education. In 2011, NER of non-Scheduled and Scheduled population were 18.0 per cent and 14.0 per cent, respectively for general education courses. Earlier in 2001, the respective shares were 13.2 per cent and 6.8 per cent. Evidently, not only NER for both non-Scheduled and Scheduled population grew fast but also the gap between the two NER declined during the decade 2001-2011. The growth of NER in case of Scheduled population was faster than that of non-Scheduled population, helping in narrowing down gap between

NER of non-Scheduled and Scheduled population. This makes not only a healthy trend from the angle of social inclusiveness but also speaks of the success of government policies in this context.

- The combined picture of accessibility in general and vocational education in the state reveals that there is a decline in demand for higher education across districts, indicating a saturation stage in demand for higher education especially in districts, where private colleges and universities came up quickly in the last ten to fifteen years.
- Availability of higher education in the state recorded a spectacular increase during the period of 16 years 1991-2016. The most robust increase was registered between 2001 and 2011 when college-area ratio more than doubled, from less than two colleges/1000 km^2 to more than four colleges/1000 km^2, the private investment in higher education sector of the state playing an important role in this. Private investment, which was based on the concept of demand-supply equation, not only increased the availability of colleges in area terms but also reduced inter-district gap on this count. Interestingly, with the exception of Mandi district, all those districts performing well on this count shared borders with neighbouring states of Punjab, Haryana and Uttar Pradesh, indicating response to outside the state demand.
- In 2016, when inter-district gap in college-area ratio was further reduced, state government policy of having at least one government degree college in all the state assembly constituencies is credited with the reduction in inter-district inequalities in college-area ratio. By 2016, there was one college available within a radius of 4.5 kms in the state. This ratio was of more than 10 kms in 1991.
- Among districts, the biggest gainer was Kullu followed by Sirmaur, Shimla, Bilaspur and Kangra districts. The reverse was true of Kinnaur, Lahul and Spiti, Hamirpur, and Una districts, performing high or moderate during 2001-2011. It seems that a saturation level was attained there. Against this, districts performing well during this period benefitted from Himachal Pradesh government policy of having at least one government college in all the state assembly constituencies. Backward and peripheral areas in all such districts benefitted from this policy decision.

- The college-population ratio recorded a phenomenal increase in Himachal Pradesh between 1991 and 2016. Major change occurred during 2001-2011, when private investment in higher education stepped up rapidly following a change in the higher education investment policy at the state level. The inter-district disparities declined concomitantly with increase in college-population ratio. Some of the districts such as Mandi, Sirmaur, Solan, Kangra and Hamirpur which had initially the low or moderate level of college-population ratio, recorded rapid increase in post-2001 period. The reverse was true of districts such as Shimla, Una and Bilaspur, which had reached the saturation level.
- A cross-examination of accessibility and availability of higher education in the state is highly revealing. In six districts of the state (Hamirpur, Una, Chamba, Kinnaur, Kullu and Sirmaur) availability and accessibility goes hand-in-hand. In other words, both are high/low in these districts. In another three districts of Bilaspur, Kangra, and Shimla notwithstanding the low availability, accessibility is high. It means these districts could overcome the deficiency in availability by way of their external links. Secondly, Kangra and Shimla districts have some of the oldest universities located there, kept outside the purview of the analysis here. Against this, Lahul and Spiti, Mandi and Solan districts present the case of low accessibility in spite of high availability of higher education institutions. This means that available higher institutions stand underutilized or supply is more than the demand for higher education in these districts. This needs immediate attention of policy-makers for corrective measures, otherwise market forces will come in operation. In other words, those higher education institutions which fail to compete will be wiped out in due course of time.
- Finally, the analysis in the chapter makes it evidently clear whether it is accessibility or availability of higher education in the state, the two government policies of allowing private investment in higher education and the decision to open at least one government degree college in all the assembly constituencies in the state played a crucial role either in narrowing down or widening the gaps in availability or accessibility of higher education in the state.

NOTES

1. It is the important measure to understand the real picture of enrolment in higher education. High percentage of NER denotes higher enrolment age groups of 18-23 years, recognized officially the relevant age-group to estimate the enrolment ratio in higher education.

$$\text{Net Enrolmement Ratio} = \frac{\text{Pupil enrolled in 18-23 age group}}{\text{Totol population in 18-23 age group}} \times 100$$

2. This method is used due to the unavailability of single year age-group data for attending colleges and vocational education. Data available only at five years age intervals like 15-19, 20-24 etc. Therefore single year age returns has been computed for the age-group of 18-23 during 1981-2011.
3. The vocational figures are free from the values of diploma/polytechnic holders.

V
Quality of Higher Education

Introduction

Today, quality of higher education is the most talked about issue in India. It is generally believed that quality of higher education has deteriorated with its recent expansion. Even the measures taken by the University Grants Commission (UGC) of India to improve the quality of higher education proved to be antithesis of its objectives. For example, it is commonly believed that measures such as National Eligibility Test (NET), introduced for the recruitment of university teachers, orientation and refresher courses for in-service university teachers and research publications and participation in seminars and conferences for career advancement have failed to produce the desired results.

Under such circumstances, understanding of higher education quality and its measurement has become one of the core sub-themes of any research on higher education. In fact, it is now difficult to ignore quality issue by any research work on higher education. In the present chapter, we examine the quality of higher education in Himachal Pradesh at the district level. But before that, it is important to define quality of higher education and review the available indicators used in literature to measure it.

Quality of Higher Education: Definition and Measurement

Quality of education is differently defined by different scholars and organizations. For example, during the colonial rule in India meaning of quality education was confined to replacement of indigenously educated and trained personnel by those favouring the British rule in India (Naik, 1975:43). According to the World Conference on Higher Education quality, a multidimensional concept, embraces various dimensions including teaching and academic programmes, research and scholarships, staffing, students, infrastructure and academic environment (UNESCO, 1998:58). According to Prasad (2006: 67) quality of education is mainly a function of motivated students, committed staff, good infrastructure, and efficient governance systems. In India, the *Rashtriya Uchchatar Shiksha Abhiyan (RUSA)* outlines the quality of higher education in terms of suitable infrastructure, trained faculty, teacher-pupil ratio and effective pedagogy in higher education institutions (RUSA, 2013:2). Evidently, the quality of higher education is differently perceived and defined. Hence, the parameters used to measure its quality also differ widely.

Today, a number of institutions/organizations accord ranking to the universities at the global level. Let us have a brief review of the parameters used by such organizations to rank universities at the global or regional scales.

In 2009, the Shanghai Jiao Tong University ranked 500 top universities in the world on the basis of the following parameters. These included (i) quality of education, (ii) quality of faculty, (iii) research output, and (iv) the size of the institution. The Times Higher Education world's university rankings identify top 50 universities of the world in 2008 on the basis of parameters such as (i) research quality, (ii) graduate employability, (iii) international outlook, and (iv) teaching quality. In 2009, *Financial Times* Magazine ranked top 100 universities in the world on the basis of the following parameters: (i) weighted salary, (ii) per cent of salary increase, (iii) placement/employment and, (iv) research.

In India, National Assessment and Accreditation Council (NAAC), an autonomous body of the University Grants Commission, New Delhi, has adopted seven fold criteria to assess the quality of higher educational institutions in the country. These included (i) curriculum, (ii) teaching (learning and evaluation), (iii) research (consultancy and extension), (iv) infrastructure and learning resources, (v) student support and progression, (vi) governance and leadership, and (vii) innovative practices.

The National Institutional Ranking Framework (henceforth, NIRF), constituted by the Ministry of Human Resource Development, Government of India, New Delhi, for ranking all the colleges and universities in the country, has evolved five-fold criteria for ranking higher education institutions at the national level. This five-fold criterion has been further divided into sub-heads; all assigned appropriate weights. Thirty per cent weightage has been provided to two parameters of (i) teaching, learning and resources, and (ii) research and professional practices; another twenty per cent to graduation outcome and remaining ten per cent to outreach and inclusivity, and (ii) perception. The Colleges and Universities were ranked separately.

The ranking is, in fact, done at different levels. The first level of ranking is done for colleges and universities, separately. At the next level, colleges, universities and institutions teaching general, technical/ engineering, management and pharmaceutical education courses are ranked separately. At the third level, all categories of higher education institutions are added to make one category for national level ranking. One hundred top ranks are assigned in all segments. However, in the case of management and pharmaceutical courses ranking is limited to fifty.

The separate ranking of colleges done for the first time in 2017 revealed an extremely poor picture of colleges in Himachal Pradesh. Of more than 300 colleges in the state, only one college, Swami Vivekanand Government College, Ghumarwin (Bilaspur district) participated in the ranking system to find no berth among the top hundred colleges of the country. However, of 29 universities/central level institutions in the state, the two, Dr. Y.S. Parmar University of Horticulture and Forestry, and Jaypee University of Information Technology (both in Solan district) found place among the top 100 universities of the country, the former ranking 51st and the latter 93rd. In the engineering category, Indian Institute of Technology (IIT) at Mandi was placed 28th, National Institute of Technology (NIT), Hamirpur 59th and Jaypee University of Information Technology, Solan 83rd among the top 100 universities of India. In category of pharmaceutical sciences, Shoolini University of Biotechnology and Management Sciences, Solan got 39th rank among the top fifty such institutes in India. In management category, none of the colleges/institutes located in Himachal Pradesh found berth among top 50 management colleges/institutes in India. Definitely, it was a mixed bag, some good and some bad news for Himachal Pradesh, in national level ranking system done for the higher education institutions in 2017.

Indicators used in Present Study

It can be seen from the above discussions that quality of higher education is differently conceptualized and defined by the different scholars and organizations. Even at different periods of time in history, the higher education was differently perceived and defined. Consequently, the indicators used to measure it also differ.

However, there is a common thread in all exercises undertaken to measure quality of higher education, that is, the indicators used to measure quality of higher education in different exercises belong either to infrastructure (input) or attainment (output) dimensions. Indicators related to infrastructure include, playground per thousand students, library per thousand students, computer centres per thousand students, laboratory per thousand students, teachers per hundred students, or female teachers to the total faculty members, all coming under the inputs of higher education. Input indicators can further be divided into two: (i) human resources, and (ii) physical infrastructure. Similarly, attainment indicators, like percentage of students appearing in All India merit of students passed, percentage of students getting campus placement of the total students appearing in final year examination, percentage of female students appearing in merit list, student of rural background finding their place in the university or all India merit list, students getting admission for further studies in institutions of national/international repute or students getting success in civil services examination, all coming under the category of output indicators of higher education.

Keeping in view discussions on measurement methods and indicators used in different studies on the theme and availability of data/information with us from various sources at the district level, the present study selected the sixteen indicators, four from human resource, nine from physical infrastructure facilities and three from output dimension of higher education, respectively (Table 5.0).

Based on these indicators, three indices were prepared: (i) human resource index, (ii) physical infrastructure index, and (iii) educational attainment index. For calculating the indices, weighted index method, used in earlier chapters of this study too, has been pressed into service. An aggregate or composite index has been prepared by summing up indices arrived at in case of individual indicator and then divided by the total number of indicators belonging to each dimensions. Further, composite index is arrived at by clubbing together index values of all indicators used to calculate input and output indices. These were mapped and discussed separately. The main objective behind this is not to mix up these two different dimensions of higher education i.e. input and output, speaking of different aspects of it. Rather, we have compared the two, input and output, so as to understand the mis-match or grey areas between the two. In other words, which are districts where output or achievements in higher education are better in spite of poor inputs and *vice versa*.

There are wide inter-district variations in different components and indicators of the quality of higher education in Himachal Pradesh, needing a brief discussion on the component and indicators of the quality of higher education in the state.

Table 5.0: Himachal Pradesh: Indicators of quality of higher education

Subset		*S. No.*	*Indicator/component and composite indices*
Component index of human resources			
I	Human Resource	1	Percentage of professors and equivalents to total teaching faculty
		2	Percentage of female teachers to total teachers
		3	Percentage of permanent teachers to total teachers
		4	Teachers per 100 students
Component index of physical infrastructure			
II	Physical Infrastructure	1	Playgrounds per 1000 students
		2	Auditorium, theater and conference hall per 1000 students
		3	Libraries per 1000 students
		4	Laboratories per 1000 students
		5	Health centres/dispensary per 1000 students
		6	Computer centres per 1000 students
		7	Gymnasium/fitness centre and indoor stadium per 1000 students
		8	Separate common rooms and hostels per 1000 female students
		9	Information technology (NKN and NMEICT) per 1000 students
Component index of educational attainment			
III	Educational Attainments*	1	Percentage of graduate+ in total 20+ age-group to total population
		2	Percentage of graduate+ in total 20+ age-group to total rural population
		3	Percentage of graduate+ in total 20+ age-group to total female population

Source: Human and physical indicators have been calculated data available from Government of India (2015). All India Survey on Higher Education, 2012-13, Department of Higher Education, MHRD, New Delhi.

Note: *Data on educational attainments extract from Census, 2011. Office of the Registrar General and Census Commissioner, India.

I. Human Resources

(i) Percentage of Professors and Equivalents to Total Teachers

Only a very small proportion (6.3%) of college teachers is designated as professor or equivalents in Himachal Pradesh. Against state average of 6.3 per cent, the share ranged from a high of 14.5 per cent in Shimla district to nil in at least six districts of the state. There was negligible number of professors in Mandi district. Only Shimla district had this share above the state average (Table 5.1).

Most of the colleges in Shimla city of the same district have PG courses. As per U.G.C. guidelines, a fix proportion of postgraduate teaching faculty is to be promoted as professors, if found eligible. That is the reason of a very high share of professors in the total teaching faculty of Shimla district. Sirmaur and Solan districts are distantlly second and third in ranking.

Table 5.1: Himachal Pradesh: Human resource in colleges by districts, 2012-13

S. No.	*District Name*	*Professors and Equivalents (%)*	*Female Teachers (%)*	*Permanent teachers (%)*	*Teachers/100 students (number)*
1	2	3	4	5	6
1	Bilaspur	0.0	38.6	78.1	3.8
2	Chamba	0.0	32.0	96.9	4.7
3	Hamirpur	0.0	41.7	88.1	4.3
4	Kangra	2.8	40.6	88.2	3.9
5	Kinnaur	0.0	29.0	100.0	8.2
6	Kullu	0.0	43.8	93.1	2.2
7	Lahul and Spiti	0.0	0.0	92.9	17.9
8	Mandi	0.1*	45.3	94.8	4.1
9	Shimla	14.5	49.2	92.3	5.2
10	Sirmaur	4.8	41.0	96.5	7.3
11	Solan	4.3	48.2	96.2	6.2
12	Una	0.7	41.0	90.1	3.7
Himachal Pradesh		**6.3**	**43.9**	**91.7**	**4.5**

Source: Government of India (2015). All India Survey on Higher Education, 2012-13, Department of Higher Education, MHRD, New Delhi.

Note: *Figures less 0.50 are ignored and above it rounded up to the nearest number, Mandi recorded 0.1 per cent of professors/equivalents.

(ii) Percentage of Female Teachers to Total Teachers

Relatively higher share of female teachers in higher education institutions speaks of gender equality in higher education. This also encourages the enrolment of more female students in higher education. The percentage of female teachers in the total number of teachers recorded 43.9 per cent at the state level. The share ranged from a high of 49.2 per cent in Shimla to a low of 29.0 per cent in Kinnaur district. Lahul and Spiti is the only district in the state without any women faculty in higher education. In seven districts, this share was more than two-fifth of the entire teaching faculty in the stream of higher education in the colleges.

Against this, the share of female teachers was less than one-third in Kinnaur and Chamba districts. Both these districts along with Lahul and Spiti have large tribal population and harsh physiographic conditions. The female teachers of government colleges from other districts try their best to avoid transfers to these districts. On the other side of the scale, local female teachers are not only low in number but also make effort to get posted to other districts such as Kullu, Shimla, Mandi and Kangra. This is what came to light during the personal discussions with knowledgeable individuals having good understanding of the local situation.

(iii) Percentage of Permanent Teachers to the Total Teachers

Higher share of permanent faculty in the total teaching faculty symbolizes stability and maturity of faculty members, giving their best possible to the students as well as to the institute they serve. In this context, we found that more than nine faculty members out of each ten higher education faculty members in Himachal Pradesh were permanent teachers. This implies that permanent teachers were more than 90 per cent of the total number of teachers. There are, however, wide inter-district variations. It ranged from 100.0 per cent in Kinnaur to less than 80.0 per cent in Bilaspur district.

Interestingly, the share of permanent teachers increases as one move from lower to middle and higher altitudes in the state. Districts adjoining to Punjab and Haryana plains have low share of permanent teachers in total faculty as compared to districts located on higher altitudes. This can be explained by the two factors: (i) the number of students getting enrolled in colleges of districts located on the lower altitudes keep on changing annually more frequently than those located on the higher altitudes; and (ii) the number of privately managed colleges, where private management appoints more teachers on ad hoc basis, is larger in districts falling in close proximity of the plains of Punjab and Haryana.

(iv) Teachers per 100 Students

Pupil/student-teacher ratio refers to the number of learners enrolled at a given level of education divided by the number of teachers. This ratio is a significant measure of quality education. Where the ratio is high, the students may miss personal attention from the teacher, resulting in poor results. Against this, the low ratio leads to a closer and personal interaction between a teacher and the students in the classroom. A teacher can better identify the areas where the student may need further assistance. Therefore, learners get more value out of their education. It maintains the better standards of education.

In Himachal Pradesh, on an average, there were 4.5 teachers after only every one hundred students. Against this, the number varied from a high of 18 teachers in Lahul and Spiti to a low of only 2.2 teachers in the Kullu district. One-half of the districts recorded this ratio which was higher than the state average. The difference between the top ranking and the lowest ranking district was more than eight times. Interestingly, all three districts where physiographical conditions are harsh, population distribution is sparse and share of tribal population is high, the rank varies from high to very high in this context. The low ratio of students per teacher does not speak of better quality of imparted education. Rather it indicates the poor student enrolment in colleges located there. The investigations reveal that the poor quality of physical and human infrastructure forces them to seek admission in colleges outside the respective districts. Students in large number get admission in colleges situated in other districts, namely those from Lahul and Spiti to Kullu district, those from Chamba district to Kangra district and from Kinnaur to Shimla district. As a result, very high ratio speaks of the same poor situation rather than good and bad situations. This is due to peculiar physiographic and demographic characteristics of Himachal Pradesh.

Composite Index of Human Resource Indicators

The composite index of human resources, prepared by summing the weighted indices arrived at on the basis of four indicators of human resources for the entire district in the state, is highly revealing. The average index value being 62.3, the index ranged from a high of 80.3 in Shimla district to a low of 49.7 in Una district.

Table 5.2: Himachal Pradesh: Composite index of human resources in colleges by districts, 2012-13

S. No.	District Name	Professors and equivalents	Female Teachers	Permanent Faculty	Teachers per 100 students	Composite index of Human resources
1	2	3	4	5	6	7
1.	Bilaspur	0	79	78	21	59.2
2.	Chamba	0	65	97	26	62.7
3.	Hamirpur	0	85	88	24	65.7
4.	Kangra	19	83	88	22	52.9
5.	Kinnaur	0	59	100	46	68.2
6.	Kullu	0	89	93	12	64.7
7.	Lahul and Spiti	0	0	93	100	64.2
8.	Mandi	0	92	95	23	69.9
9.	Shimla	100	100	92	29	80.3
10.	Sirmaur	33	83	97	40	63.3
11.	Solan	30	98	96	35	64.6
12.	Una	5	83	90	20	49.7
Himachal Pradesh		**43**	**89**	**92**	**25**	**62.3**

Source: Calculated on the basis of Table 5.1.

Shimla district fared very high on three of the four indicators, against this Una fared extremely poor on one indicator and below the state average on the other three indicators. Shimla, Mandi, Kinnaur and Hamirpur districts, making a compact group on the map, have index value of higher than 65.0 (Table 5.1 and Fig. 5.0).

Mandi and Hamirpur districts had nil value on indicator of professors/ equivalents among all the faculty members and pretty well in the rest of the indicators. Kinnaur, Lahul and Spiti and Chamba districts fared very high on the indicators of permanent teachers and teacher-student ratio; it had nil index value of professors and equivalents among all the faculty members. Sirmaur and Solan districts had low value of professors/ equivalents and performed well on the indicators of permanent teachers and teacher-student ratio.

Another district, Kullu also fared pretty well, in the context of female and permanent teachers and noted below the state average in teacher-student ratio. Most of the districts ranking low on this count fared poorly in share of professors and female teachers in the total faculty and low than the state average among all the indicators. These included Bilaspur, Kangra and Una districts. Index value of female teachers was high in Solan district than the state average and the reverse was true of Sirmaur district.

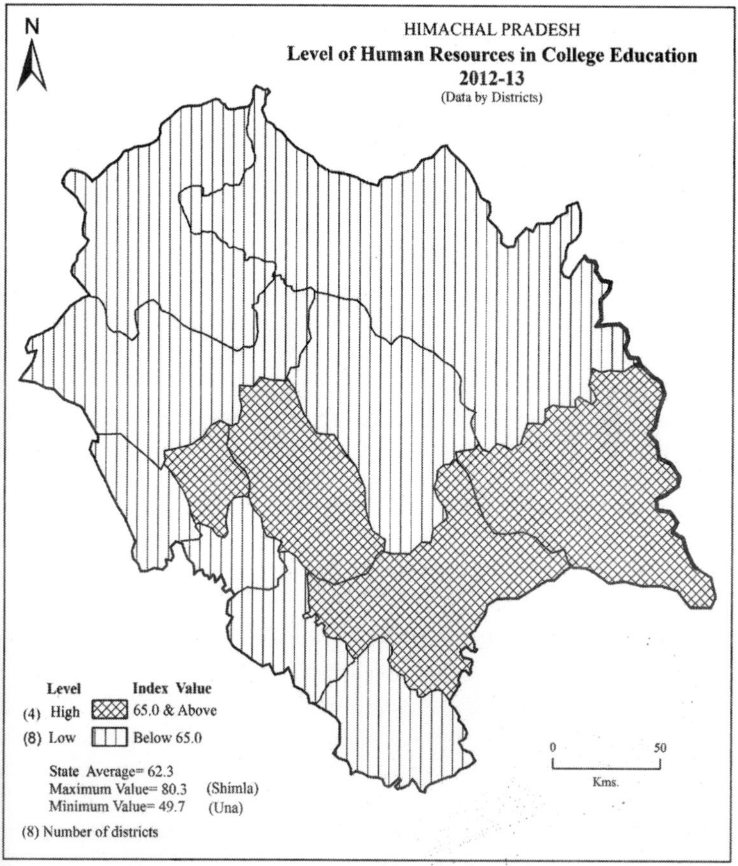

Fig. 5.0: Himachal Pradesh: Level of Human Resource in College Education.
Source: As Table 5.1.

Briefly, human resources in the colleges differed widely at the district level in the state. Four districts of Shimla, Mandi, Kinnaur and Hamirpur unfolded high human resources. The rest of the districts of the state fared low on their performance on different indicators of human resources (Fig. 5.0).

II. Physical Infrastructure

Physical infrastructure such as playgrounds, conference halls, libraries, laboratories, health centres/dispensaries, computer centres, women's hostel and internet connectivity play an important role in enhancing the quality of higher education in a state or district. In the following, a brief discussion has been organized on inter-district variations in their distribution in the state (Table 5.3).

(i) Playground per 1000 Students

This goes without saying that only a healthy body has a healthy mind. To translate this into reality, the colleges and the universities develop playgrounds on their campuses for students. In Himachal Pradesh, there were, on average, roughly two playgrounds after 1000 students during 2012-13 academic sessions. Among districts, there were wide differentials in this context. It ranged from a high of about 13 playgrounds in Lahul and Spiti district to a low of only one per thousand students in Kullu district. In seven districts namely, Lahul and Spiti, Kinnaur, Sirmaur, Solan, Mandi, Chamba and Hamirpur availability of playgrounds in colleges was above the state average. Notably, Lahul and Spiti and Kinnaur districts, where the total number of students in colleges is quite low in comparison to other districts, this ratio is quite high.

Government provides, as a policy, financial assistance to provide at least one playground per college on campuses. In Kinnaur district, there are two colleges and in Lahul and Spiti district only one. The number of students in these two tribal dominated districts is quite low, since the students from other districts hardly migrate to these districts for higher education. In contrast, the well-to-do households from these two districts generally prefer to send their wards either to other districts within the state or to colleges in the neighbouring states of Punjab, Chandigarh (U.T.) and NCT of Delhi. This is the main reason behind very high ratio of playgrounds in these two districts. On the other side of the scale, Sirmaur and Solan, have relatively plain topography, this ratio is relatively low in these districts.

(ii) Libraries per 1000 Students

In words of the most innovative and versatile American musician, "If you want to get paid, go to colleges. If you want an education, go to library". Definitely, the library has a crucial place in spreading as well as enhancing the quality of education especially the higher education. The quality of higher education, which is tinged with multi-dimensional character, finds the functioning of library in the core of all such aspects.

In today's high tech learning environment, the library as a learning resource is gaining increasingly high academic space and time in the life of a learner. In times ahead, this will be even more so. Other than the availability of library and library resources, most important parameter to judge the library facility is the use of library facility by its users. This can be judged by average number of books issued/returned per day, number of reference enquiries made by users per month, number of services delivered per-user per month, average number of users visiting or consulting documents on the monthly basis, number of reputed journals and so on. Unfortunately, we have no such data/information available with us. What we have is the number of libraries in the colleges by districts, calculated in terms of the total students in a district.

In Himachal Pradesh, there were, on average, roughly two libraries after 1000 students per college in 2012-13. Among districts, it ranged from a high of about 13 libraries in Lahul and Spiti district to a low of 1.6 per thousand students in Bilaspur district. In seven districts, namely Lahul and Spiti, Kinnaur, Sirmaur, Solan, Mandi, Chamba and Hamirpur availability of library in colleges was above the state average. Notably, Lahul and Spiti and Kinnaur districts, where the total number of students in colleges is quite low in comparison to other districts, this ratio is quite high. In real sense, such a situation does not speak of better situation, rather indicates to a peculiar situation created by locational factors.

(iii) Laboratories per 1000 Students

It is a room or building equipped for scientific experiments, research or teaching or for the manufacture of drugs or chemicals. In all the experimental sciences, labs are of crucial importance. In labs, students learn methods to sharpen their skills.

In Himachal Pradesh, there were, on an average, four laboratories per thousand college students during 2012-13. Among districts, there were wide differentials in this context. It ranged from a high of about 13 laboratories in Lahul and Spiti district to a low of only 2.4 labs per thousand students in Kullu district. In eight districts namely, Lahul and Spiti, Kinnaur, Sirmaur, Solan, Shimla, Mandi, Chamba, and Hamirpur availability of labs in colleges was above the state average. In remaining four districts of Kangra, Una, Kullu and Bilaspur, it was lower than the state average.

Table 5.3: Himachal Pradesh: Physical infrastructure in colleges by districts, 2012-13

S. No	District Name	Playground	Library	Laboratory	Health Centre	Computer Centre	Auditorium theatre and conference hall	Gymnasium/ fitness centre and Indoor stadium	Separate common room for girls and Girls Hostel	NKN and NMEICT
		Per thousand students								
1	2	3	4	5	6	7	8	9	10	11
1.	Bilaspur	1.62	1.62	3.07	0.65	1.13	2.26	1.13	4.26	0.81
2.	Chamba	1.94	2.90	4.35	0.97	2.42	2.90	2.42	4.53	0.97
3.	Hamirpur	1.88	2.53	5.64	0.74	1.88	2.21	0.57	3.57	0.82
4.	Kangra	1.68	1.79	3.43	0.71	1.72	2.09	0.60	3.74	0.45
5.	Kinnaur	5.29	5.29	5.29	0.00	5.29	7.94	0.00	12.94	2.65
6.	Kullu	1.07	2.44	2.44	*0.15*	0.92	2.14	*0.46*	1.40	0.15
7.	Lahul and Spiti	12.8	12.8	12.8	*0.00*	12.8	*0.00*	*0.00*	46.51	12.8
8.	Mandi	1.95	2.01	4.56	1.03	1.84	2.66	1.08	5.49	0.76
9.	Shimla	1.20	1.67	3.86	0.57	1.51	2.45	1.20	3.93	0.83
10.	Sirmaur	3.09	3.67	6.95	1.54	3.09	6.56	3.67	9.92	0.97
11.	Solan	2.21	2.28	6.62	1.26	2.76	4.02	1.89	7.57	1.10
12.	Una	1.67	1.85	3.26	0.62	1.41	2.03	1.23	3.79	0.62
Himachal Pradesh		**1.77**	**2.1**	**4.32**	**0.84**	**1.82**	**2.68**	**1.21**	**4.57**	**0.77**

Source: As Table 5.1.

Note: *Figures less than 0.50 are ignored and above it rounded up to the nearest number. Kullu recorded ratio of 0.15 and 0.46 in health centre and gymnasium fitness centre, respectively.

Among others, availability of labs is highly associated with the nature of subjects offered to students in a college. If the number of colleges running courses which do not need labs is quite large in a district, the number of labs will also be less. Mostly, it is science and engineering/technology courses that require lab work. Arts and Humanities courses hardly need labs. In Kullu district, where the number of labs is the lowest in the state, the number of students in different courses is relatively high and arts and humanities courses are dominant in college teaching.

(iv) Health Centre per 1000 Students

On college campuses, the availability of medical facilities is a must for taking care of health problems of students, staff and non-teaching staff, especially those residing in the campus. The University Grants Commission, New Delhi believes that a safe, secure and cohesive learning environment is an essential precondition for quality education. It should be the prime concern of educational administrators across the country to ensure that students are safeguarded against attacks, threats and accidents, both man-made and natural. With this in mind, the Commission has formulated guidelines to transform higher education institutions into oasis of safety, security and study.

On an average, there was one health centre after every one thousand college students in Himachal Pradesh during 2012-13. It ranged from a high of 1.26 health centres in Solan to a low of 0.15 in Kullu district. There was a complete absence of any health centre on the college campuses in the two districts of Kinnaur and Lahul and Spiti and negligible number was found in the Kullu district. In one-half of districts in the state, the average ranged from 0.15 to 0.74 health centres after each 1000 students. Included in this category are Bilaspur, Hamirpur, Kangra, Kullu, Shimla and Una districts. Obviously, many of the colleges, not only in these six districts but other districts of the state as well do not have either a dispensary or a health centre on their campus. Further investigation reveals that many colleges do not have even the first-aid material on their campus, making it a more serious issue.

(v) Computer Centre Per 1000 Students

In the digital era, computer technology is a must. In Himachal Pradesh, there were roughly two computers after 1000 students in colleges. Against this, it ranged from a high of about 13 computers in Lahul and Spiti district to a low of about one in the Kullu district. Majority of students from Lahul and Spiti district come to government college Kullu for higher education. The computers arc definitely there in Lahul and Spiti but there are only a few users. While, quite the opposite is true of Kullu district. Again, colleges imparting technical and professional courses especially computer science and/or information technology are bound to have more computers in comparison with those colleges that offer arts and humanities courses.

(vi) Auditorium, Theater and Conference Hall Per 1000 Students

As per the UGC guidelines, there should be infrastructure in the colleges in terms of auditoriums, theaters and conference halls. The colleges are supposed to follow the UGC guidelines during the construction of the main college buildings. Approximately, the three auditoriums/theaters/ conference halls are there after each thousand college students in Himachal

Pradesh. There are, however, wide inter-district disparities in this regard. The number ranged from about eight in Kinnaur district to only two in the Una district. In general, districts having more technical and professional colleges have higher quantity of such infrastructure. In almost all the engineering colleges of different districts such an infrastructure is an essential prerequisite.

(vii) Gymnasium/Fitness Centre and Indoor Stadium Per 1000 Students

Gymnasium/fitness centre and indoor stadium is a means of physical and mental development of the students. University Grants Commission supports financially the development of sports infrastructure in various colleges and universities. During the 12th Plan (2012-2017), government focused on the development of sports infrastructure and equipment in universities and colleges to engage students fruitfully in their leisure hours. The aim of the scheme is to enhance capacity building with an idea to prepare the sports persons so as to represent India in international events in order to boost the nation pride.

In Himachal Pradesh, there was, on an average, one gymnasium/ fitness centre and indoor stadium per thousand students in the colleges. It ranged from a high of 3.67 in Sirmaur to less than one (0.57) in Hamirpur district. There was no facility of gymnasium/fitness centre and indoor stadium or negligible number in Kinnaur and Lahul and Spiti districts and the latter was in Kullu district. In three districts of Hamirpur, Kangra, Mandi, such an infrastructure was below the state average.

(viii) Separate Common Room and Hostels for Girls Per 1000 Students

The National Education Policy (1986) placed a focus on women empowerment and education. Unfortunately, a large number of educational institutions in the country do not have proper infrastructure facilities for women. It is generally believed that the availability of facilities for women would improve their enrolment and participation in higher education. During the XI Plan (2007-12), the U.G.C. introduced the special scheme for the construction of girl's hostels in colleges. Hostel, as a residential unit, can foster community living and provide security, especially for women students. Today, women constituted one-third of the total enrolment in higher education. In Himachal Pradesh, on an average, there were about three (separate) common rooms per 1000 girl students. It ranged from a high of 46.5 in Lahul and Spiti district to a low of only one per thousand female students in Kullu district. In five districts including Kinnaur, Lahul and Spiti, Mandi, Sirmaur and Solan this facility was available and was higher than the state average.

(ix) Information and Communication Technology Per 1000 Students

The National Knowledge Network (NKN) and National Mission on Education through Information and Communication Technology (NMEICT) were envisaged as a centrally sponsored scheme to leverage the potential of ICT to enhance the gross enrolment ratio in higher education during the 11th Plan (2007-2012). NMEICT, which has been instrumental in bringing about a technology based revolution in the sphere of higher education, it rests on the two principles, of connectivity and content-creation of the mission, to ensure easy access of quality education for every student in the country. For sharing resources and research, it also envisages the setting up of a National Knowledge Network (NKN) interconnecting all knowledge institutions in the country with gigabit capabilities. It was expected to increase Gross Enrolment Ratio (GER) in Higher Education by five percentage points during (2007-2012) and ensure access and equity in higher education.

The Mission has two major components *viz*., (a) content generation, and (b) connectivity along with provision of access devices for institutions and learners. It seeks to bridge the digital divide, i.e. the gap in the skills to use computing devices for the purpose of teaching and learning among urban and rural teachers/learners in higher education domain and empowering those, remaining untouched by the digital revolution (First Post e-paper, January 05, 2009).

In Himachal Pradesh, on an average, there is less than one NKN and NMEICT per 1000 students. There are, however, wide inter-district variations in this context. It ranges from a high of 12.8 in Lahul and Spiti to a low of 0.76 in Mandi district. Three-fourths of the districts were above the state average. Such districts included Bilaspur, Chamba, Hamirpur, Kinnaur, Lahul and Spiti, Mandi, Shimla, Sirmaur and Solan. It is one of the facilities provided under the central government scheme to all colleges on the basis of some norms, at least one to each college, irrespective of enrolment in a college. Colleges where enrolment of students in different classes is relative low, ratio *vis-à-vis* students goes high and *vice versa*.

For example, the trans-Himalayan districts such as Lahul and Spiti, Kinnaur and Chamba, where students enrolment in colleges is relatively low since quite of a large number of students from these districts enrol either in neighbouring districts of Kangra, Kullu and Shimla or in the districts outside the state, the ratio of such facilities per 1000 students is quite high. Against this, ratio goes down in the districts where students enrolment is high for two reasons (i) in-migration of students from surrounding areas, and (ii) number of persons getting enrolled in higher education, in a specific age-group, itself being relative high.

Composite Index of Physical Infrastructure Indicators

A composite weighted index calculated on the basis of weighted score arrived at for each indicator of physical infrastructure facilities in colleges at the district level is highly revealing (Table 5.4).

Table 5.4: Himachal Pradesh: Index values of physical infrastructure indicators and composite score index for colleges, 2012-13

S. No.	District Name	Playground	Library	Laboratory	Health Centre	Computer Centre	Auditorium theater and conference hall	Gymnasium/ fitness centre and Indoor stadium	Separate common room for girls and girl hostels	NKN + NMEICT	Composite index
1	2	3	4	5	6	7	8	9	10	11	12
1.	Bilaspur	12.6	12.6	23.9	43.1	8.8	28.6	30.6	9.2	6.3	19.5
2.	Chamba	15.1	22.6	34.0	64.5	18.9	36.7	65.4	9.7	7.6	30.5
3.	Hamirpur	14.7	19.8	44.0	49.0	14.7	27.9	15.5	7.7	6.4	22.2
4.	Kangra	13.1	14.0	26.8	47.3	13.4	26.5	16.1	8.1	0.0	20.7
5.	Kinnaur	41.3	41.3	41.3	0.0	41.3	100.0	0.0	27.8	20.7	44.8
6.	Kullu	8.3	19.0	19.0	0.0	7.1	27.0	0.0	3.0	0.0	13.9
7.	Lahul and Spiti	100.0	100.0	100.0	0.0	100.0	0.0	0.0	100.0	100.0	100.0
8.	Mandi	15.2	15.7	35.5	68.7	14.4	33.6	29.3	11.8	5.9	25.6
9.	Shimla	9.4	13.0	30.1	38.2	11.8	31.0	32.4	8.4	6.5	20.1
10.	Sirmaur	24.1	28.6	54.2	100.0	24.1	83.1	100.0	21.3	7.5	49.2
11.	Solan	17.2	17.8	51.6	84.0	21.5	50.9	51.5	16.3	8.6	35.5
12.	Una	13.0	14.4	25.4	41.1	11.0	25.6	33.3	8.2	4.8	19.6
Himachal Pradesh		**13.8**	**16.2**	**33.7**	**56.1**	**14.2**	**33.9**	**32.7**	**9.8**	**6.0**	**24.0**

Source: Calculated on the basis of Table 5.3.

Based on nine indicators of physical infrastructure discussed above, the average composite index value for the state as a whole comes to 24.0. Against this, composite index value ranged from a high of 100.0 in Lahul and Spiti district to a low of only 13.9 in Kullu district, indicative of sharp inter-district inequalities in higher education physical infrastructure facilities in the colleges. Kullu district fared below the state average on all but one indicator of physical infrastructure facilities. It was placed above state average only in library facility per 1000 students. In contrast, it fared highly poor on indicators such as health centre, information technology, fitness centres and computer centre. On the other side of the scale, Lahul and Spiti district fared at the top in six of the nine indicators of physical infrastructure (Fig. 5.1). As per the rest of the three indicators, its index value was nil.

On the whole, in more than one-half (7) of the districts of the state physical infrastructure index value was less than 30.0. Four of these seven districts namely Bilaspur, Hamirpur, Kangra, and Una were located in close proximity to Punjab plains. The topography was relatively plain, population density high and enrolment in the colleges quite good. Shimla district, having state capital headquarters in it, also happens to be in this category. The district has relatively large number of colleges but also receives students in large numbers from all over the state for studying in colleges especially those located in Shimla town. This leads to a higher burden on available physical infrastructure in the colleges located there. Remaining Mandi and Kullu districts also have less than the index value of 30.0.

On the other side of the scale, two of the five districts namely, Solan and Sirmaur having infrastructure index higher than the index value of 30.0 have larger share of technical and professional colleges in all. In these two districts, the private investment in the field of higher education is also relatively higher. For higher education in the technical and professional fields, physical infrastructure facilities such as laboratories, computer centres, auditorium and internet and information technology etc. are essential requirements. Secondly, privately managed higher education institutions use good physical infrastructure as a weapon to attract students to their institutions.

Briefly, availability of higher level of higher education infrastructure at the college level in the districts of Himachal Pradesh is influenced by the following factors:

1. Low enrolment in colleges of areas having higher altitude and severe climatic conditions. Chamba, Lahul and Spiti and Kinnaur districts fall in this category,
2. Higher share of technical and professional colleges in the total number of colleges, and
3. Better private investment in higher education.

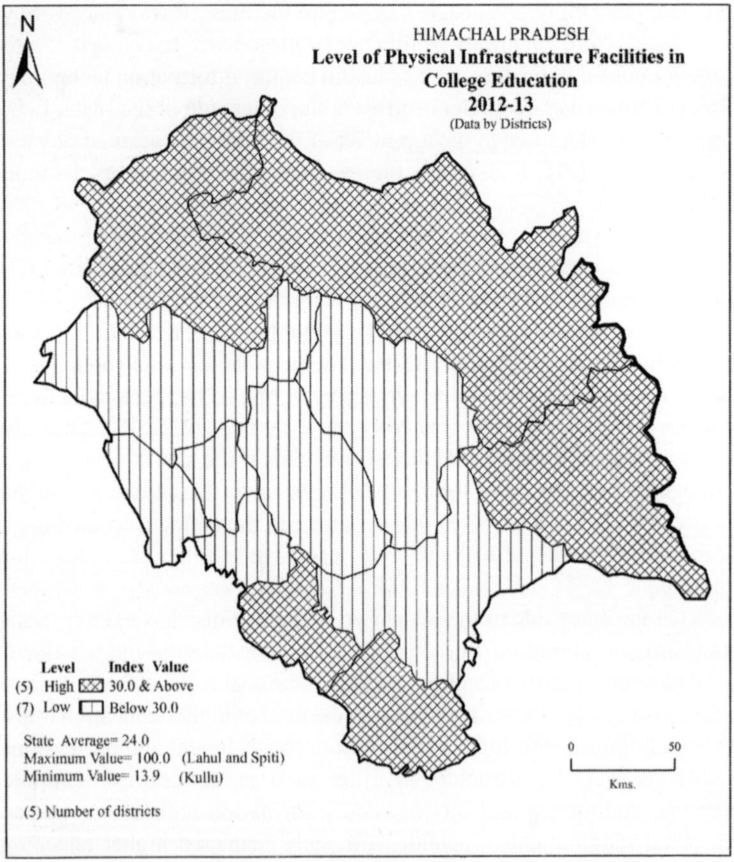

Fig. 5.1: Himachal Pradesh: Level of Physical Infrastructure Facilities in College Education, 2012-13.

Source: As Table 5.1.

Against this, low level of infrastructure is controlled by inter-district migration of students for seeking admission in the institutions imparting higher education.

III. Educational Attainments

Attainment in higher education, an output dimension of higher education, speaks of the quality and standards of higher education in an area.

Three indicators used here for understanding and analyzing the level of educational attainment at district level differ widely among districts in the state. In the following, an attempt has been made to discuss all the three indicators in terms of their inter-district variations, in order.

(i) Graduate Plus in Total Population Aged 20+

In Himachal Pradesh one out of every ten persons in the age-group of 20 and above is a graduate or post-graduate or even more educated than that. There are, however, wide inter-district variations in this regard. The share ranged from about 16.0 per cent in Shimla district to only slightly higher than 5.0 per cent in Chamba district. Obviously, the district at the top has three times higher share than the district at the bottom. However, since this information is available from Census of India 2011, it needs to be interpreted quite carefully. Head of the family or any responsible person, who provides information to the Census enumerator about his/her family/household members, tells after including all those family members living and working/studying in other districts of the state or any other place outside the state.

Secondly, districts having more job opportunities either in industrial or administrative sectors or both attract job seekers and their family members from other districts not only from within the state but also outside the state to come, work and settle down there. In both the cases, ground realities get distorted. We have to see the present information of educational attainment in different districts of Himachal Pradesh in this light.

It is expected that districts having peripheral location, economic backwardness, physiographic conditions and lack of higher administrative states will have lower percentage of graduates plus and *vice versa*. In Himachal Pradesh, four districts namely, Chamba, Kinnaur, Kullu and Lahul and Spiti fall in such category of the districts. With exception of Lahul and Spiti all these districts have this share lower than the state average. The greater presence of people involved in tourism and other government officials dealing with tribal and backward area development programmes might have tilted the balance in favour of Lahul and Spiti district, otherwise it is a peripherally located, sparsely/thinly populated and has undulating terrain district. In all, seven of the 12 districts in the state have this share lower than the state average (Table 5.5). The presence of Kangra and Mandi districts in this category is quite surprising, needing further investigation.

Table 5.5: Himachal Pradesh: Indicators of educational attainment by districts, 2011

S. No.	*District Name*	*Graduate+ in total 20+ age-group population (%)*		
		Total	Rural	Rural female
1	2	3	4	5
1	Chamba	5.3	3.9	2.8
2	Bilaspur	11.0	9.8	8.1
3	Hamirpur	12.2	10.9	9.2
4	Kangra	9.6	8.7	7.7
5	Kinnaur*	8.5	8.5	6.7
6	Kullu	8.5	6.9	4.9
7	Lahul and Spiti*	10.5	10.5	7.0
8	Mandi	8.6	7.1	5.6
9	Shimla	15.5	9.1	7.0
10	Sirmaur	8.1	5.3	4.4
11	Solan	11.2	7.9	6.8
12	Una	9.2	8.2	8.0
Himachal Pradesh		**10.0**	**7.9**	**6.7**

Source: Census of India, Himachal Pradesh Socio and Cultural Tables (C-Series) of 2011. Registrar General Census Commissioner of India.

Note: 1. Share of graduated and above was calculated for age group 20 and above from 2011.
2. *Entirely rural.

Against this, five districts having this share higher than the state average included Shimla, Hamirpur, Solan, Bilaspur and Lahul and Spiti. Concentration of administrative activities coupled with the presence of higher education institutions such as universities and institutes of national importance helped these districts to find place in this category.

(ii) Graduates Plus in Total Rural Population Aged 20+

In rural Himachal Pradesh, on an average, about eight of each 100 persons (in 20 plus age-group) had done graduation and above in the year 2012-13. There were, however, wide inter-district disparities in this context. The share ranged from a high of about 11.0 per cent in rural Hamirpur to a low of only about 4.0 per cent in the rural Chamba (Table 5.5).

On the whole, there is a close correspondence between total and rural share of graduate plus at the district level in the state. These are, however, some interesting exceptions. While Kangra and Una districts fared below the state average in total, both fared above the state average in the rural educational attainments. Two districts, Kinnaur and Lahul and Spiti, are entirely rural in the state. Of the remaining ten districts, four fared below the state average and remaining one district, Solan, fared just equivalent to the state average on this count.

(iii) Graduate Plus in Total Rural Female Population 20+

Female education is considered as an important indicator of women empowerment and development in an area or state or country. Higher female attainments in higher education are of greater significance in every case of rural areas. In rural Himachal Pradesh, on an average, roughly seven out of each 100 females (in 20 plus age-group) were graduate and above.

Among districts, it ranged from a high of 9.2 per cent in Hamirpur to a low of only 2.8 per cent in Bilaspur; difference was more than three times. Hamirpur district is known for its top position in female education in the state. Notably, the districts remaining under princely rule before independence fared much below those under the British rule. Within the category of former princely ruled districts, Mandi fared ahead of all such districts.

Composite Index of Educational Attainments

The composite index value of three indicators of educational attainments ranged from a high of 92.9 in Hamirpur to a low of 33.5 in Chamba district. 70.0 being the state average value, seven of 12 districts in the state were placed higher than this value.

Hamirpur was placed at the top among all the districts and had the highest score value on two of three educational attainment indicators and fared above the state average in the third. In contrast, the lowest ranking district, Chamba, fared poorly in all the three indicators (Table 5.6).

On the whole, with few exceptions, there is a clear cut distinction between the districts which remained under princely states and those under the British rule before independence. However, Lahul and Spiti and Kinnaur, the two tribal dominated districts in the state, have come up well, both positioned well on this count. The reverse, is however, true of Kullu district, falling in the category of poorly placed districts (Fig. 5.2).

Table 5.6: Himachal Pradesh: Composite index of higher education attainment by districts, 2011

S. No.	District Name	Index value			
		Person	Rural	Rural female	Composite
1	2	3	4	5	6
1.	Chamba	34	36	30	33.5
2.	Bilaspur	71	90	88	82.9
3.	Hamirpur	78	100	100	92.9
4.	Kangra	62	80	84	75.1
5.	Kinnaur	55	78	73	69.0
6.	Kullu	55	63	54	57.1
7.	Lahul and Spiti	68	97	76	80.3
8.	Mandi	55	65	61	60.6
9.	Shimla	100	84	76	86.9
10.	Sirmaur	52	49	48	49.8
11.	Solan	72	72	74	72.8
12.	Una	59	75	87	73.6
	Himachal Pradesh	**65**	**73**	**73**	**70.0**

Source: Calculated on the basis of Table 5.5.

Levels of Higher Education Quality

In the preceding pages indicators and dimensions of higher education quality were discussed at the district level. Higher education imparted at the university level has been excluded since higher education at University level does not remain confined to the boundaries of one single district of its location. Hence, it was decided to discuss the quality of higher education at college and university level, separately. For measuring quality of higher education at the university level, we made individual university as a study unit, whereas in case of colleges, the district formed the unit of study.

As stated before, we have taken three components/dimensions of the quality of higher education quality: human resources, physical infrastructure and educational attainment (Table 5.7). On the basis of these three components/dimensions, the composite index score of quality higher education was calculated at the district level.

Of the three components/dimensions, the former two belong to input dimension, while the latter one belongs to output dimension of higher education quality. Theoretically speaking, these two dimensions (input and output) should not be combined together to make the composite index of higher education quality. Rather, these must be examined separately

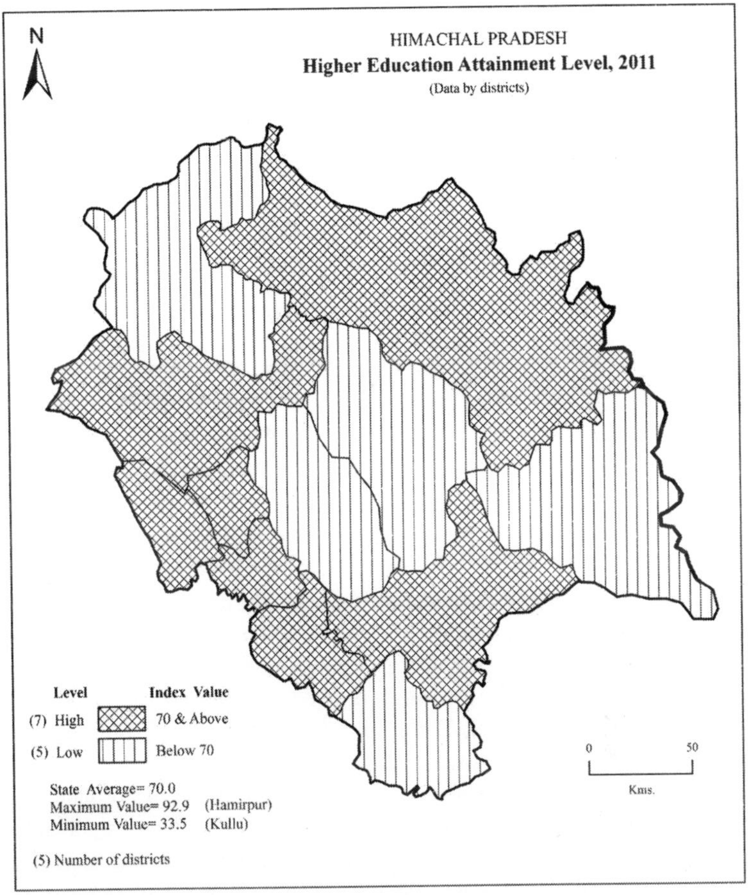

Fig. 5.2: Himachal Pradesh: Higher Education Attainment Level, 2011.

Source: As Table 5.6.

in the light of question: whether input and output dimensions go hand-in-hand or move in different directions? Answer to such questions will help the planners and policy-makers to take corrective measures for the better results (Table 5.7).

However, in most of the studies especially on development, these two dimensions (input and output) are combined together to produce a composite index of development or quality.

In the present study, we attempt the both, in order. To begin with, we shall calculate and map composite index of higher education quality to

Table 5.7: Himachal Pradesh: Index of Quality of higher education by districts

S. No.	District Name	Index			Composite index
		Human Infrastructure	Physical Infrastructure	Attainment	
1	2	3	4	5	6
1.	Bilaspur	59.2	19.5	82.9	53.9
2.	Chamba	62.7	30.5	33.5	42.2
3.	Hamirpur	65.7	22.2	92.9	60.3
4.	Kangra	52.9	20.7	75.1	49.6
5.	Kinnaur	68.2	44.8	69	60.7
6.	Kullu	64.8	13.9	57.1	45.3
7.	Lahul and Spiti	64.2	100	80.3	81.5
8.	Mandi	69.9	25.6	60.6	52
9.	Shimla	80.3	20.1	86.9	62.4
10.	Sirmaur	63.3	49.2	49.8	54.1
11.	Solan	64.6	35.5	72.8	57.6
12.	Una	49.7	19.6	73.6	47.6
	Himachal Pradesh	**62.3**	**24**	**70**	**52.1**

Source: As Table 5.2, 5.4 and 5.6.

identify the level of higher education quality at the district level. This will be followed by an examination of input levels *vis-a-vis* output levels to identify the degree correspondence or collision between the two.

The composite index value differs widely among districts. It ranged from a high of 81.5 in Lahul and Spiti district to a low of only 42.2 in Chamba district. The former district fared very well on the dimensions of physical infrastructure and educational attainment, but its performance on the dimension of human resources was moderate. Against this, Chamba district fared very poorly on educational attainment.

On the whole, six districts, having composite index value more than 55.0, were categorized as high on quality of higher education. These included Hamirpur, Lahul and Spiti, Shimla, Solan, Sirmaur and Kinnaur districts. Lahul and Spiti and Kinnaur, the two tribal majority districts having peripheral location and harsh physiographic conditions, fared very well on the dimension of physical infrastructure availability and human infrastructure.

On the other side, educational attainment was higher in Lahul and Spiti than Kinnaur. Their higher ranking in physical infrastructure availability is explained in low enrolment ratio in comparison to available physical infrastructure facilities, mostly provided by the government on equality basis.

Whereas higher educational attainments are to be understood in terms of stationing of state and central government officials including defence personnel to look after various development projects and guard the international border along the Indo-China border. Their relatively low ranking on human resource availability is explained by negligible share of female teachers and professors or equivalent in the total teaching faculty. Hamirpur, Solan and Sirmaur benefitted from private/government investment in technical and professional educational infrastructure. Shimla has greatly benefitted from its administrative and political hold on the entire state.

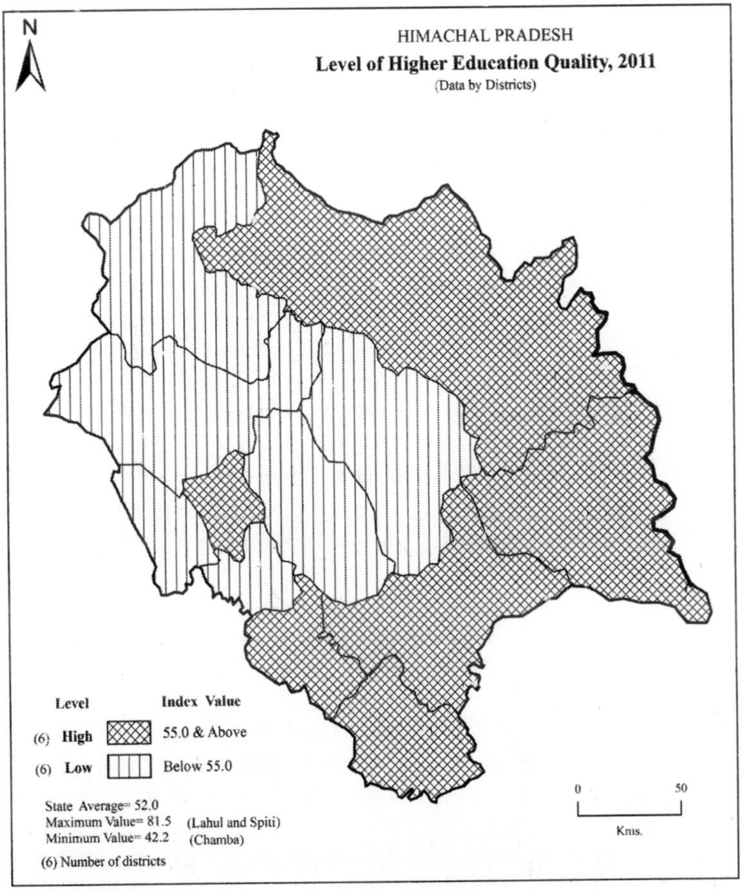

Fig 5.3: Himachal Pradesh: Level of Higher Education Quality, 2011.

Source: As Table 5.7.

The remaining six districts, Chamba, Kangra, Una, Bilaspur, Mandi and Kullu having composite index value of less than 55.0, are categorized in low quality of higher education (Fig 5.3). While, Chamba, Mandi and Kullu remained under princely states, Kangra, Bilaspur and Una stayed under British rule in pre-Independence period. Those remaining under British rule benefitted in terms of educational attainments especially female education but lagged behind in terms of availability of physical infrastructure, since enrolment in higher education are relatively higher in such districts for reasons of higher population concentration.

Briefly, a variety of factors are responsible for disparity in the level of higher education at the district level in Himachal Pradesh. Districts receiving private/public investment in technical and professional higher education registered high level of physical infrastructure, while those remaining under British rule during pre-Independence period recorded high educational attainments. Hamirpur, which tops all the districts in the state on account of quality of higher education, benefitted on both the counts. Tribal population dominated Kinnaur and Lahul and Spiti districts, benefitting from stationing of government officials working in different states and Central Government sponsored programmes and schemes and also defense personnel guarding along the India-China border to claim high level in the field of educational attainments. Also, it registered high level in physical infrastructure for low enrolment in colleges located there.

Input-Output Components: A Cross-examination

A cross-examination of input and output components indices of higher education quality at district level in Himachal Pradesh is highly revealing. The four districts of Hamirpur, Lahul and Spiti, Shimla and Solan find place in high-high combination category of input and output components (Table 5.8 and 5.9). In other words, high degree of human and physical infrastructure availability in these districts has led to high degree of educational attainments. It means both support each other or go hand-in-hand (Fig. 5.4).

In contrast to this, in Chamba, Kinnaur, Mandi and Sirmaur districts high level of human and physical infrastructure failed to produce high level of educational attainments. Either the students coming from other districts benefitted from available infrastructure or available infrastructure could not be utilized to produce desired results in terms of educational attainments. From Chamba district many of the students prefer to enrol in colleges of other districts for better quality education. Mandi district has a higher number of colleges opened by the private investors well equipped in terms of human and physical infrastructure. While Mandi district is getting political patronage now, the political leaders who matter in state as well as national level politics have their electoral stakes in the district. It is a part of parliamentary constituency which was earlier represented by Mrs. Pratibha Singh, wife of the present Chief Minister, Shri Virbhadra Singh, and currently represented by Shri R.S. Sharma of B.J.P. and the Assembly constituency of Thakur Kaul Singh, Health Minister in the present Congress party government of Himachal Pradesh also fall in Mandi district. It is expected that Mandi district will soon come up in the high category of higher education development including quality of education.

Table 5.8: Himachal Pradesh: Input and Output components composite index value by districts

S. No.	*District Name*	*Input (Infrastructure)*	*Output (Educational attainments)*
1	2	3	4
1.	Bilaspur	39.4	82.9
2.	Chamba	46.6	33.5
3.	Hamirpur	44.0	92.9
4.	Kangra	36.8	75.1
5.	Kinnaur	56.5	69.0
6.	Kullu	39.4	57.1
7.	Lahul and Spiti	82.1	80.3
8.	Mandi	47.8	60.6
9.	Shimla	50.2	86.9
10.	Sirmaur	56.3	49.8
11.	Solan	50.1	72.8
12.	Una	34.7	73.6
	Himachal Pradesh	**43.2**	**70.0**

Source: As Table 5.1.

On the other side of the scale, three districts of Bilaspur, Kangra and Una could achieve higher level of educational attainment despite low level of physical and human infrastructure there. All these districts were part of Punjab till reorganization of Punjab in 1966. Their external links with educationally developed districts of Punjab such as Jalandhar, Amritsar and Ludhiana helped people from these districts to benefit in terms of higher education. Hence, education attainment could remain high in spite of poor higher education infrastructure.

Table 5.9: Himachal Pradesh: Association between level of input and output dimensions of higher education

Input/Output	*Name of the district*
High/High	Hamirpur, Lahul and Spiti, Shimla, Solan
High/Low	Chamba, Kinnaur, Mandi, Sirmaur
Low/High	Bilaspur, Kangra, Una
Low/Low	Kullu

Source: Calculated on the basis of Table 5.8.

The remaining one district of Kullu finds conformity between input and output components of higher education. In other words, there is low level of educational attainments owing to low level of human and physical infrastructure. The same district remained under princely rule during the pre-Independence period. Education in general and female education in particular received the least attention of erstwhile princely rulers (Fig. 5.4).

Briefly, in five of the 12 districts in the state input and output component of higher education quality conforms to each other. In other words, high or low level of educational attainments is closely associated with high/low level of physical and human infrastructure availability. In another three districts that could overcome deficiency in higher education infrastructure to achieve high level of educational attainments due to their traditional links with educationally developed districts of neighbouring Punjab, level of educational attainments is high despite low infrastructure. Non-conformity between the two components (input and output) in case of Chamba, Kinnaur, Mandi and Sirmaur districts needs immediate attention of policy-makers and planners in the state. It represents a case of failure to convert opportunity into a boom.

Quality of Higher Education at University Level, 2012-13

In the following, an attempt will be made to measure quality of higher education at the university level using only two components: human resources and physical infrastructure. Due to incomplete information on the third component (educational attainments), we have to drop it.

Secondly, in absence of reliable information of three indicators related to physical infrastructure, we have to drop them. Ultimately, we are left with four indicators from the component of human resources, similar to college level, and six, in place of nine indicators, for measuring physical infrastructure. Lack of reliable information on indicators such

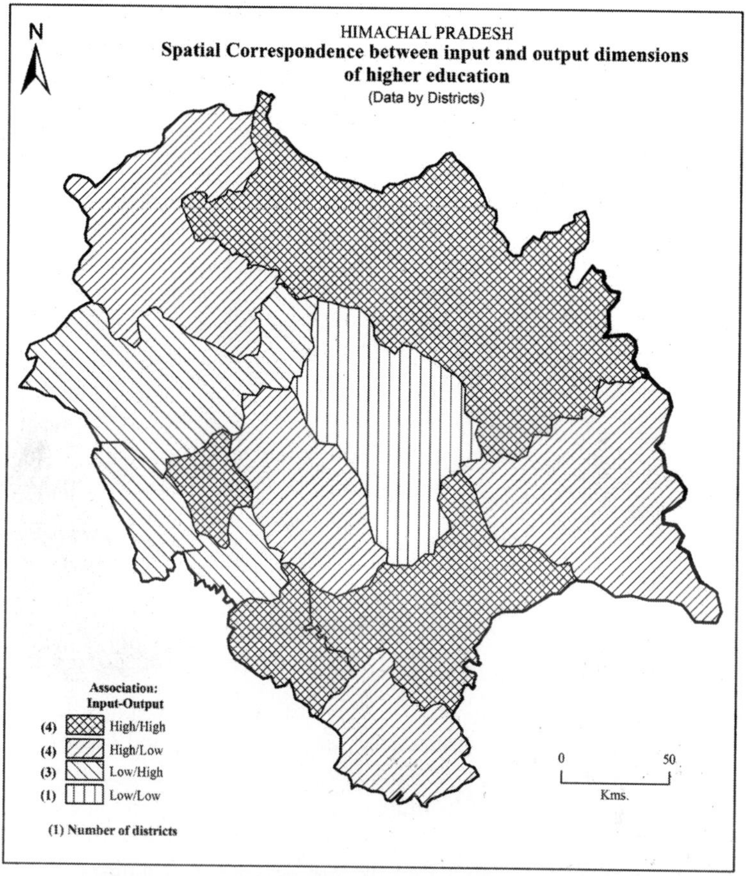

Fig. 5.4: Himachal Pradesh: Spatial Correspondence between input and output dimensions of higher education.

Source: As Table 5.9.

as auditorium, theater and conference hall, gymnasium/fitness centre and indoor stadium and information technology forced us to drop these indicators. Analysis in the following is therefore based on ten indicators, four from human resources and six from physical infrastructure facilities.

Before, having discussions on composite index of higher education quality for university education in Himachal Pradesh, indicators used for the purpose are discussed briefly.

I. Human Resources

(i) Proportion of Professors/Equivalents to Total Number of Teachers

On an average more than one-fifth or 21.4 per cent of total teachers in Himachal Pradesh universities were designated as professor/equivalent in 2012-13. There were, however, wide inter-university disparities in this regard. It ranged from a high of 53.7 per cent in Dr. Y.S. Parmar University of Horticulture and Forestry, Nauni to a low of only 3.0 per cent in India Education Centre University, Baddi, both in the Solan district. Former is a state agricultural university and the latter a private managed university. Secondly, the latter is quite young university in comparison to the former.

Three universities in the state namely, Dr. Y.S. Parmar University of Horticulture and forestry, Nauni, Chaudhary Sarwan Kumar Himachal Pradesh Krishi Vishwavidyalaya, Palampur and Himachal Pradesh University, Shimla are the oldest among universities in the state, all managed by the state government. Each one has more than 30.0 per cent teaching faculty designated professors/equivalents. In fact, the lowest percentage is 38.0 per cent in Himachal Pradesh University, Shimla (Table 5.10). One can infer age of a university and proportional share of teaching faculty designated as professors/equivalent and thus find strong positive association with each other.

Another sixteen universities, where percentage of professor/equivalent in total teachers ranged between 16.4 per cent and 3.0 per cent, were located in Hamirpur, Kangra, Solan, Sirmaur, Shimla and Mandi districts. Except, National Institute of Technology (NIT), Hamirpur and Indian Institute of Technology (IIT), Mandi all were in the private sector and had recent origin. National Institute of Technology, Hamirpur, which is the oldest among them, had the highest share of professors/equivalent in the total number of teaching faculty.

Briefly, the age and management of a university seems to have the strong association with share of professors or equivalents in total teaching faculty at the university level in the state. In other words, older the university in age and managed by the public sector higher would be the share of professors/equivalents in the total teaching faculty.

(ii) Percentage of Female Teachers to the Total Teachers

Symbolizing women's empowerment, higher share of female teaching in the total number of teachers in a university indicates women's role in the

Table 5.10: Himachal Pradesh: Classification of universities according to share of professors and equivalents in total teaching faculty, 2012-13

Professors and equivalents (in%)	*Name of University*
High (More than 30)	Dr. Y.S. Parmar University of Horticulture and Forestry (53.7), Solan, Chaudhary Sarwan Kumar Himachal Pradesh Krishi Vishvavidyalaya (41.6), Kangra and HPU (38.0), Shimla **(Total = 3)**
Low (Less than 30)	NIT (16.4), Hamirpur, Maharishi Markandeshwar University (15.7), Solan, IIT (12.5), Mandi, Shoolini University of Biotechnology and Management Sciences (11.3), Solan, Jaypee University of Information Technology (10.8) Solan, Eternal University (10.2), Sirmaur, Alakh Prakash Goyal (APG) University (9.1), Shimla, Central University of Himachal Pradesh (8.3), Kangra, Career Point University (7.7), Hamirpur, Bahra University (6.9), Solan, Chitkara University (5.1), Solan, Baddi University of Emerging Sciences and Technology (4.7), Solan, Arni University (4.5), Kangra, Manav Bharti University (3.3), Solan, India Education Centre University (3.0) Solan, Sri Sai University (1.2), Kangra **(Total = 16)**
Average = 21.4; National Average = 21.43; C.V. Index = 1.04	

Source: As Table 5.1.

Note: (i) No faculty member was holding professor/equivalent position in Indus International University (Una district).

(ii) Figures in parenthesis indicate to per cent of professor or equivalent in total faculty.

spread of higher education as well as overall development of the region of university's location.

Against the national average of 44.14 per cent, there were 29.0 per cent women teachers in the total university level faculty of Himachal Pradesh (Table 5.11). This means Himachal Pradesh stands low in the national context so far as the share of female teachers in the total university level teachers is concerned.

Among 19 universities under study, the share ranged from a high of 46.0 per cent in Baddi University of Emerging Sciences, Baddi (Solan district) to a low of 15.4 per cent in Career Point University in (Hamirpur district). There were no female teachers on the teaching faculty of Indus International University (Una district).

Table 5.11: Himachal Pradesh: Classification of universities according to share of female teachers in total teaching faculty, 2012-13

Female teachers (in%)	*Name of University*
High (More than 40)	Baddi University of Emerging Sciences and Technology (46.0), Chitkara University (44.7), Solan, Bahra University (43.0), Solan, Eternal University (42.4), Sirmaur **(Total = 4)**
Moderate (20 - 40)	India Education Centre University (34.7), Solan, Manav Bharti University (34.2) Solan, Sri Sai University (32.9), Kangra, Shoolini University of Biotechnology and Management Sciences (30.2) Solan, Maharishi Markandeshwar University (27.5), Solan, Alakh Prakash Goyal (APG) University (27.3) Shimla, HPU (26.5) Shimla, Arni University (24.6), Kangra, Dr. Y.S. Parmar University of Horticulture and Forestry (23.9), Solan, Kangra, Jaypee University of Information Technology (22.3), Solan **(Total = 10)**
Low (Less than 20)	Chaudhary Sarwan Kumar Himachal Pradesh Krishi Vishvavidyalaya (17.6) Kangra, IIT (17.5), Mandi, NIT (16.4), Hamirpur, Central University of Himachal Pradesh (16.7), Kangra, Career Point University (15.4), Hamirpur **(Total=5)**
Average=29.0; National Average=44.14; C.V Index=0.35	

Source: As Table 5.1.

Note: (i) There was no female teacher on teaching faculty in Indus International University (Una district).

(ii) Figures in parenthesis indicate to per cent of female teachers in total faculty.

Interestingly, most of the young and private universities have relatively higher share of female teachers in the total number of teachers in comparison to the old and government managed universities (Table 5.11). This is in contrast to the situation found in the share of professors/ equivalents in total teaching faculty. This may be explained by the following factors:

(i) Young women university teachers can be employed by the private management on mutually negotiated pay-packages. The U.G.C. pay-scales are not strictly followed on the ground of privately managed universities, and

(ii) Higher share of female teachers in the total teaching faculty in private universities help these in getting higher grade at the time of NAAC inspection.

(iii) Percentage of Permanent Teachers to Total Number of Teachers

Symbolizing stability for long term planning and projection of teaching and research at the respective department level as well as in the university as a whole, higher share of permanent teaching faculty among total university teachers is considered as one of the most robust indicators of the quality of higher education.

Table 5.12: Himachal Pradesh: Classification of universities according to share of permanent teachers in total teaching faculty, 2012-13

Permanent teachers (in%)	*Name of University*
High (More than 95)	India Education Centre University (100.0), Solan, Manav Bharti University (100.0), Solan, Baddi University of Emerging Sciences and Technology (100.0), Solan Central University of Himachal Pradesh (100.0), Kangra, Indus International University (100.0), Una, Arni University (100.0), Kangra, Bahra University (100.0), Solan, Alakh Prakash University (100.0), Shimla, Sri Sai University (100.0), Kangra, Career Point University (100.0), Shoolini University of Biotechnology and Management Sciences (99.6), Solan, Hamirpur, Chitkara University (99.5), Solan, Jaypee University of Information Technology (99.3), Solan, Eternal University (98.3), Sirmaur, Maharishi Markandeshwar University (98.0), Solan, IIT (97.5), Mandi **(Total = 16)**
Low (Less than 95)	Chaudhary Sarwan Kumar Himachal Pradesh Krishi Vishvavidyalaya (94.3), Kangra, HPU (90.4), Shimla, Dr. Y.S. Parmar University of Horticulture and Forestry (89.3), Solan, NIT (82.8), Hamirpur **(Total = 4)**
Average = 96.0; National Average = 95.2; C.V. Index = 0.04	

Source: As Table 5.1.

Note: Figures in parenthesis indicate to per cent of permanent teachers in total faculty.

From that angle, Universities in Himachal Pradesh are placed on a higher pedestal in comparison to country as a whole. Since 96.0 per cent university teachers in the state were permanent faculty against national average of 95.2 per cent. In eight of the ten universities in the state, this share was more than 95.0 per cent during 2012-13.

It is, however, interesting to note that all the four universities/institutes where the share of permanent faculty members is less than 95.0 per cent are government managed. These included both the agriculture universities, Himachal Pradesh University, Shimla and National Institute of Technology, Hamirpur. In fact, the latter has the lowest share of permanent teachers in the entire state (Table 5.12). Does this speak of flip-flop on the part of government of India over matters relating to higher education especially in post-reforms period?

Briefly, overwhelming majority of teachers in universities/institutes located in Himachal Pradesh are permanent teachers. Interestingly, private universities have an edge over government managed universities. While, a large number of private universities in the state have cent per cent teachers holding permanent position, this is true only for Central University of Himachal Pradesh, Dharamshala.

(iv) Teacher-pupil Ratio

Lesser the number of students per teacher, higher would be the degree of teacher-pupil interaction, leading to better quality of teaching and research in a university or institution.

In this context, Himachal Pradesh as a whole is placed much better than country as a whole. In Himachal Pradesh, there were six teachers after every 100 students, against the national average of about five after 100 students. There was, however, wide inter-university disparity in this regard. Against the state average of six teachers after each hundred students, it ranged from a high of 31 teachers in India Education Centre University, a privately managed university in Solan district, to a low of less than two in Himachal Pradesh University, a state government managed university in Shimla city of the same district, having a difference of more than twenty times (Table 5.13).

During 2012-13 one-half of the 20 universities in the state had this ratio of less than 10:100. It means that in majority of universities of the state there was not even one teacher after every 10 students. Well known Institute or universities such as Himachal Pradesh University, Shimla, IIT, Mandi, NIT, Hamirpur, all government managed, and Jaypee University of Information Technology (Solan district), privately managed, fall in this category.

On the other side of the scale, of the four universities, each has more than 20 teachers for each 100 students, three were privately managed. Agriculture universities, in general, have relatively high teacher-student ratio. It may be because of the fact that the nature of work in such universities was quite different from other universities. Research on

Table 5.13: Himachal Pradesh: Classification of universities according to teacher-student ratio, 2012-13

Teacher-students ratio (Teacher/100 student)	*Name of University*
High (More than 20)	India Education Centre University (31.0), Solan, Dr. Y.S. Parmar University of Horticulture and Forestry (29.0), Solan, Maharishi Markandeshwar University (25.0), Solan, Manav Bharti University (24.0), Solan **(Total = 4)**
Moderate (10-20)	Chaudhary Sarwan Kumar Himachal Pradesh Krishi Vishvavidyalaya (20.0), Kangra, Alakh Prakash Goyal (APG) University (14.0), Shimla, Sri Sai University (14.0), Kangra, Career Point University (14.0), Hamirpur, Shoolini University of Biotechnology and Management Sciences (12.0), Solan, Central University of Himachal Pradesh (10.0), Kangra **(Total = 6)**
Low (Less than 10)	Arni University (9.0) Solan, IIT (8.0), Mandi, Indus International University (8.0), Una, Eternal University (7.0), Sirmaur, Jaypee University of Information Technology (7.0), Solan, Baddi University of Emerging Sciences and Technology (6.0), Solan, Chitkara University (6.0), Solan, NIT (6.0), Hamirpur, Bahra University (5.0), Solan and HPU (1.5), Shimla **(Total = 10)**
Average = 6; National Average = 2.4; C.V. Index = 0.66	

Source: As Table 5.1.
Note: Figures in parenthesis indicate to the number of teachers per hundred students.

different aspects of agriculture development being the main focus in such universities, teaching acquires the secondary role there. However, it is surprising to find low teacher-student ratio in technological institutes/ universities located in the state, needing further investigation.

Composite Index of Human Resources

A composite index prepared with the help of index method indicates wide inter-university disparity in human resources quality. Index value ranged from a high of 83.4 for Dr. Y.S. Parmar University of Horticulture and Forestry, Nauni (Solan district) to a low of only 41.8 for National Institute of Hamirpur (Hamirpur district). Any University having the top position on all the four indicators should have index value of 100.0 (Table 5.14 and Fig.5.5).

Table 5.14: Himachal Pradesh: Composite index of human resources at university level, 2012-13

Human Resource Index	*Name of University*
High (More than 65.0)	Dr. Y.S. Parmar University of Horticulture and Forestry (83.4), Solan, India Education Centre University (70.2), Solan, Chaudhary Sarwan Kumar Himachal Pradesh Krishi Vishvavidyalaya (68.8), Kangra, Maharishi Markandeshwar University (67.0), Solan **(Total = 4)**
Moderate (50.0 – 65.0)	Manav Bharti University (64.2), Solan, Indus International University (62.6), Una, Eternal University (58.1), Sirmaur, Baddi University of Emerging Sciences and Technology (57.3), Solan, Chitkara University (56.6), Solan, Shoolini University of Biotechnology and Management Sciences (56.1), Solan, HPU (55.9), Shimla, Bahra University (55.7), Solan, Alakh Prakash Goyal (APG) Shimla University (55.1), Sri Sai University (54.5), Kangra **(Total = 10)**
Low (Less than 50.0)	Career Point University (47.9) Hamirpur, Jaypee University of Information Technology (47.8), Solan, Arni University (47.3), Kangra, IIT (46.4), Mandi, Central University of Himachal Pradesh (45.8), NIT (41.8), Hamirpur **(Total = 6)**
Average index value = 54.3; National index value = 60.4; C.V. Index = 0.17	

Source: As Table 5.1.

Dr. Y.S. Parmar University is placed at the top on the first and fourth indicator, in the middle on the second and in the low on the third indicator of quality of human resources. Against this, Indus International University fared high only on third indicator, found no place on the first and the second and in low category on the fourth indicator of quality of human resources. On the whole, four universities were placed in high category. Two of these were managed by the government and other two by the private sector. While the government managed universities were agricultural universities, privately managed universities were engineering-cum-technological universities.

A half of the government managed universities/institutes including IIT Mandi, Central University Dharamshala and NIT Hamirpur fall in the low category of human resource quality. A well known Jaypee University of Information Technology (Solan district), which is a privately managed university, also falls in the low category. Himachal Pradesh University, Shimla, a state government managed university, falls in the moderate category for its high and moderate position on the three indicators and the lowest position on student-teacher ratio.

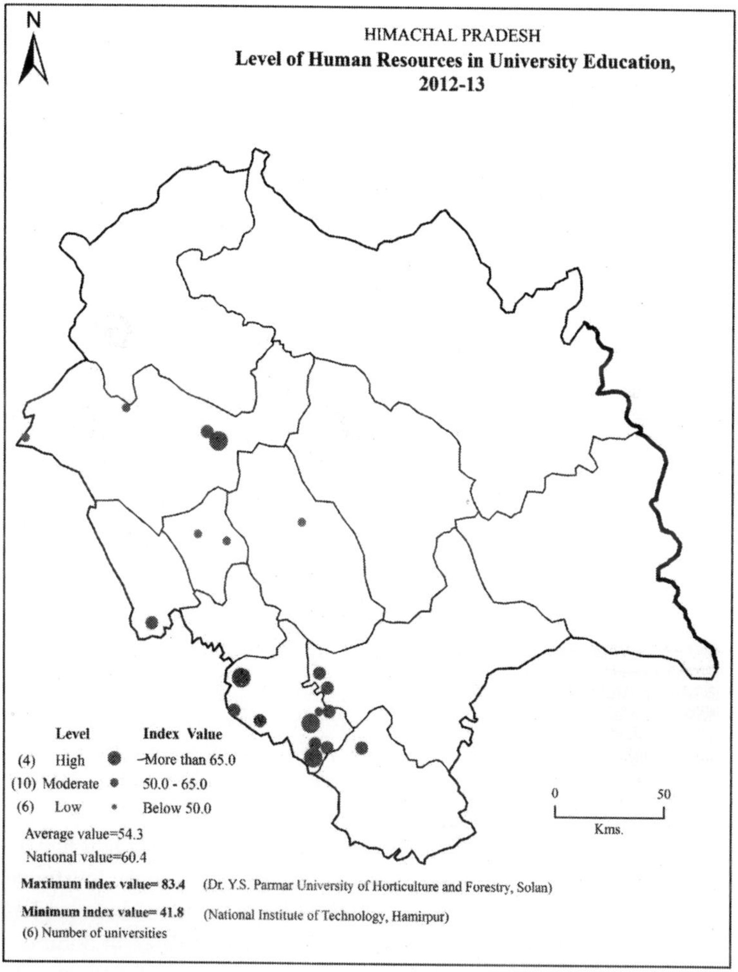

Fig. 5.5: Himachal Pradesh: Level of Human Resource in University Education, 2012-13.

Source: As Table 5.1.

Briefly, there was hardly any clear cut distinction between the old and the new universities or between government and privately managed or between vocational and general education universities on this count. It means different universities fared differently on different indicators, not behaving according to any set pattern.

II. Physical Infrastructure

Physical infrastructure such as library and laboratory plays an important role in the quality of higher education by putting its significant impact on quality of higher education. In all, six indicators selected to examine quality of physical infrastructure at the university level in Himachal Pradesh has been examined in the following segment to understand inter-university disparities.

(i) Playground per Thousand Students

There were 1.7 playgrounds after each 1000 students in the universities of Himachal Pradesh. Himachal Pradesh being a hill state, identifying plain land for sports and games in educational institutions is one of the most challenging tasks. This is the reason that there is no sports institute or university in the entire state. During 2012-13, in six of the 20 universities in the state, there was either no playground or number was negligible per 1000 students. These universities included Central University of Himachal Pradesh, Maharishi Markandeshwar University, Indus International University, Himachal Pradesh University, Shimla, National Institute of Technology and Baddi University. However, national average of only 0.2 playground/1000 students is much more disappointing (Table 5.15).

In another three universities, there was less than one playground after 1000 students. In this way, nearly one-half of the universities in the state had either negligible number of playgrounds per 1000 students or no playground on their campuses.

Of the remaining eleven universities, five or less than a half had 3.0 or more playgrounds after 1000 students (Table 5.15). In short, constraints imposed by hill topography leave little or no room for earmarking land for playgrounds on university campuses in Himachal Pradesh. In dominant majority of universities number of playgrounds per 1000 students was negligible to nominal. There are only five universities in the state where 3.0 or more playgrounds were available per 1000 students. Land availability being the serious constraints, there is no sports university/institute in the entire state. This confirms one of the hypotheses, we proposed in the beginning of our research proposal.

(ii) Library per 1000 Students

There is hardly any need to emphasize on the importance of library

Table 5.15: Himachal Pradesh: Classification of universities according to playground/1000 students, 2012-13

Playground-student ratio (per 1000 students)	*Name of University*
High (More than 2)	Career Point University (10.5), Hamirpur, Alakh Prakash Goyal, Shimla University (4.2), Manav Bharti University (3.9) Solan, Arni University (3.2), Kangra, India Education Centre University (3.1), Solan, Jaypee University of Information Technology (2.1) Solan, IIT (2.1) **(Total=7)**
Low (Less than 2)	Mandi, Chitkara University (1.7) Solan, Sri Sai University (1.7) Kangra, Eternal University (1.2), Sirmaur, Shoolini University of Biotechnology and Management Sciences (1.0) Solan, Dr. Y.S. Parmar University of Horticulture and Forestry (0.8), Solan, Chaudhary Sarwan Kumar Himachal Pradesh Krishi Vishvavidyalaya (0.7) Kangra, Bahra University (0.7) Solan **(Total=7)**
Average = 1.7; National Average = 0.2; C.V Index = 0.97	

Source: As Table 5.1.

Note: (i) No playground in **three** universities included Central University of Himachal Pradesh (Kangra district), Maharishi Markandeshwar University (Solan district) and Indus International University (Una district).

(ii) There was negligible playground to student ratio in **three** universities included Himachal Pradesh University (0.04) Shimla, National Institute of Technology (0.4) (Hamirpur district), and Baddi University (0.4) (Solan district).

for spread of education especially the higher education. Library is an integral part of teaching and research at the level of tertiary education.

On an average, this was more than one library per 1000 students in 15 universities of Himachal Pradesh during 2012-13. The national average being even poorer (0.07 library after each 1000 students) than the state average. Himachal Pradesh as a whole is better placed than country, as a whole. There were, however, wide inter-university disparities on this count. In five universities, there was either no library or the number was negligible in terms of 1000 students. In another five universities, there was less than one library after 1000 students. In contrast, there were only three universities in the state, where five or more libraries existed after 1000 students (Table 5.16).

Table 5.16: Himachal Pradesh: Classification of universities according to Library/1000 students, 2012-13

Library-student ratio (per 1000 students)	*Name of University*
High (More than 2)	India Education Centre University (12.3), Solan, Career Point University (10.5) Hamirpur, Maharishi Markandeshwar University (5.0), Solan, Alakh Prakash Goyal (4.2) Shimla University, IIT (2.1) Mandi **(Total=5)**
Low (Less than 2)	Manav Bharti University (1.9) Solan, Sri Sai University (1.7) Kangra, Central University of Himachal Pradesh (1.4) Kangra, Baddi University of Emerging Sciences and Technology (1.3), Solan, Eternal University (1.2), Sirmaur, Dr. Y.S. Parmar University of Horticulture and Forestry (0.8) Solan, Chaudhary Sarwan Kumar Himachal Pradesh Krishi Vishvavidyalaya (0.7), Kangra, Bahra University (0.7), Solan, Arni University (0.6) Kangra, Jaypee University of Information Technology (0.5) Solan **(Total=10)**
Average= 1.4; National Average=0.07; C.V. Index=1.22	

Source: As of Table 5.1.

Note: (i) There was no library in Indus International University (Una district).

(ii) There was negligible library per student ratio in the four universities included NIT (0.4) Hamirpur, HPU (0.2) Shimla, Chitkara University (0.3) and Shoolini University of Biotechnology and Management Sciences (0.48), both in Solan district.

In the vast majority of universities, this ratio was low. In general, newly established universities/institutes were better placed than older ones on this count. All three universities in the high category on this count were of recent origin and were run privately. In general, well established and old universities fall in low category.

However, one is bound to raise at least two questions in this context: (i) Is it the number of libraries per 1000 students or availability and quality of books per 1000 students in a library, which one is more important? (ii) Secondly, in universities generally there is one main/central library and each department/centre has its own library. In this light, if some other indicators such as number of books/journals per 1000 students in a library and sectional/departmental libraries are incorporated, that would make things more realistic.

Briefly, there are wide inter-university disparities in case of library per

1000 students in universities of Himachal Pradesh. The same is supposed in the high value of C.V. index (1.22). Newly established private sector universities are placed far better than old universities in the state, on this count.

(iii) Laboratories per 1000 Students

Importance of labs cannot be minimized in case of experimental sciences or vocational disciplines. Hence, the nature of discipline is quite important in this regard. Agriculture, engineering, technology and basic sciences are the disciplines, where requirement of labs is an essential prerequisite for teaching and research both.

In this context, available information on universities in Himachal Pradesh provides a complex picture. For example, one of the little known private university, India Education Centre University in Solan district had 247 labs per 1000 students; distantly second to it is another private university, Manav Bharti University again in Solan district had about 39 labs after 1000 students. Both are newly established private universities, where total number of enrolled students was also relatively less.

Agriculture universities in the state, where research is accorded higher focus than teaching, had relatively higher number of laboratories per 1000 students. However, all other government managed universities/ institutes, except agriculture universities, fall in low category on this count (Table 5.17). On the whole, newly established private universities are far better placed than government run universities on this count, agriculture universities being exception to this. Private universities which charge higher tuition fees and have other exorbitant expenses, have lesser number of students per class in comparison to government run universities or colleges. In government run universities or colleges education is highly subsidized in comparison to privately managed colleges and universities. In other words, privatization or commercialization of higher education in India has been, in a way, responsible for encouraging sharp inequalities in available physical infrastructure in universities. Privatization of higher education is more or less responsible for inducing all sorts of inequalities in higher education, starting from rural-urban, male-female, rich-poor to regional and sub-regional.

(iv) Health Centre per 1000 Students

Again, there are wide inter-university disparities on this count in the

Table 5.17: Himachal Pradesh: Classification of universities according to Laboratory/1000 students, 2012-13

Laboratory-student (per 1000 students)	*Name of University*
High (More than 6)	India Education Centre University (246.9) Solan, Manav Bharti University (38.8) Solan, Indus International University (16.8), Una, Sri Sai University (15.2) Kangra, Career Point University (10.5), Hamirpur, Dr. Y.S. Parmar University of Horticulture and Forestry (7.3), Solan, Chaudhary Sarwan Kumar Himachal Pradesh Krishi Vishvavidyalaya (6.2), Kangra **(Total = 7)**
Low (Less than 6)	Maharishi Markandeshwar University (5.0) Solan, Jaypee University of Information Technology (4.7) Solan, Shoolini University of Biotechnology and Management Sciences (4.3) Solan, Alakh Prakash Goyal Shimla University (4.2), Baddi University (3.8) Solan, Central University of Himachal Pradesh (2.7) Kangra, Chitkara University (2.6), Solan, Bahra University (0.7) Solan, Eternal University (1.2), Sirmaur **(Total = 9)**
Average= 9.9; National Average= 0.89; C.V. Index=2.60	

Source: As of Table 5.1.

Note: (i) There is no laboratory in Arni University (Kangra district) and IIT (Mandi district).

(ii) Negligible laboratory per students in two universities of NIT (0.4) Hamirpur, HPU (0.3) Shimla.

state. Nine or nearly 50.0 per cent universities in the state did have either negligible number of health centres per 1000 students or no health centre at all. Another seven universities had less than two health centres per 1000 students (Table 5.18). There is only one university in the state, Maharishi Markandeshwar University, Solan, which has one health centre after 200 students or five after 1000 students. However, in national context, Himachal Pradesh is placed higher than the national average (0.11), on this count.

Among the government managed university/institutes, it is only IIT Mandi, which has two health centres after each 1000 students. Against this, Central University of Himachal Pradesh, Dharamshala does not have any health centre on its campus and Himachal Pradesh University Shimla has one health centre after 20 thousand students.

Table 5.18: Himachal Pradesh: Classification of universities according to health centre/1000 students, 2012-13

Health centre-student ratio (per 1000 students)	*Name of University*
High (More than 2)	Maharishi Markandeshwar University (5.0) Solan, Alakh Prakash Goyal Shimla University (3.0), Indus International University (2.8), Una, IIT (2.1), Mandi **(Total = 4)**
Low (Less than 2)	Sri Sai University (1.7) Kangra, Eternal University (1.2) Sirmaur, Dr. Y.S. Parmar University of Horticulture and Forestry (0.8) Solan, Chaudhary Sarwan Kumar Himachal Pradesh Krishi Vishvavidyalaya (0.7) Kangra, Bahra University (0.7) Solan, Arni University (0.6), Kangra, Jaypee University of Information Technology (0.5), both in Solan district **(Total = 7)**
Average = 1.1; National Average = 0.11; C.V. Index = 0.83	

Source: As of Table 5.1.

Note: (i) There is no health centre in four universities included Career Point University (Hamirpur district), Central University of Himachal Pradesh (Kangra district), India Education Centre University (Solan district), Manav Bharti University (Solan district).

(ii) Negligible ratio existed between health centre and students in National Institute of Technology (0.4) Kangra, Baddi University of Emerging Sciences and Technology (0.4) Solan, Chitkara University (0.3), Shoolini University of Biotechnology and Management Sciences (0.48) Solan and HPU (0.047) (Shimla district).

(v) Computer Centres per 1000 Students

By now computer and information technology is not only an integral part of education at all levels but also that of daily life. For courses relating to engineering and technology, computer technology is a prerequisite.

In Himachal Pradesh, there was, on an average, one computer available to 1000 students studying at the university level. Against this, national average was one computer after more than 5000 students. However, within the state there were wide, inter-university disparities, on this count. It ranged from a high of 21 computer centres per 2000 students in Career Point University to only three per 3000 students in Bahra University, both in the Solan district (Table 5.19).

Table 5.19: Himachal Pradesh: Classification of universities according to computer centre/1000 students, 2012-13

Computer centre-students ratio (per 1000 students)	*Name of University*
High (More than 4.0)	Career Point University (10.5) Hamirpur, Maharishi Markandeshwar University (5.0), Solan, Alakh Prakash Goyal Shimla University (4.2) **(Total = 3)**
Moderate (2 – 4)	Jaypee University of Information Technology (3.7) Solan, Dr. Y.S. Parmar University of Horticulture and Forestry (3.2) Solan, India Education Centre University (3.1) Solan **(Total = 3)**
Low (Less than 2)	Shoolini University of Biotechnology and Management Sciences (2.9) Solan, Indus International University (2.8) Una, Chitkara University (2.6), Solan, Manav Bharti University (1.9) Solan, Sri Sai University (1.7) Kangra, Central University of Himachal Pradesh (1.4) Kangra, Baddi University of Emerging Sciences and Technology (1.3), Solan, Eternal University (1.2) Sirmaur, Chaudhary Sarwan Kumar Krishi Vishvavidyalaya, (0.7) Kangra, Bahra University (0.7), Solan **(Total = 10)**
Average = 2.2; National Average = 0.19; C.V. Index = 0.81	

Source: As of Table 5.1.

Note: (i) There is no computer centre in **two** universities included Arni University in Kangra district and IIT (Mandi district).

(ii) Negligible health centres in **two** universities of NIT (0.4) (Hamirpur district) and HPU (0.04) (Shimla district).

On the whole, four universities had negligible number or no computer per 1000 students, in another ten universities it was less than two computers per 1000 students, in another three between two and four and in remaining three, more than four computer centres after each 1000 students. All but one among the six universities, where the number of the computers/1000 student was two or more, belonged to the private sector, running engineering and technology courses.

Evidently, management type and nature of courses run by universities have a crucial role to play in the inter-university disparities in the availability of computer centres per 1000 students in Himachal Pradesh. In other words, private universities running engineering and technology related courses have more computers per 1000 students and *vice versa* in the state.

(vi) Separate Girls' Common Rooms and Hostels Per 1000 Girl Students

On an average, there were about four hostels per 1000 girls' students in 20 universities of Himachal Pradesh during 2012-13. Against this, national average was only two per 1000 female students. Within Himachal Pradesh, the number varied from a high of more than 143 at India Education Centre University to a low of less than one in Himachal Pradesh University, Shimla (Table 5.20).

Table 5.20: Himachal Pradesh: Classification of universities according to separate common rooms and hostels/1000 female students, 2012-13

Common rooms and girls hostel (per 1000 students)	*Name of University*
High (More than 8)	India Education Centre University (142.9) Solan, Career Point University (76.9) Hamirpur, APG (Alakh Prakash Goyal) Shimla (71.4) University, IIT (69.8), Mandi, Maharishi Markandeshwar University (27.0) Solan, Manav Bharti University (23.3) Solan, Indus International University (20.6) Una, Jaypee University of Information Technology (10.50) Solan, Dr. Y.S. Parmar University of Horticulture and Forestry (9.50) Sirmaur, Chaudhary Sarwan Kumar Krishi Vishvavidyalaya (8.70), Kangra, National Institute of Technology (8.50), Hamirpur **(Total = 11)**
Low (Less than 8)	Sri Sai University (7.60), Kangra, Bahra University (6.50) Solan, Arni University (5.40) Kangra, Chitkara University (4.20), Solan, Eternal University (4.10), Sirmaur, Shoolini University of Biotechnology and Management Sciences (3.90) Solan, Baddi University of Emerging Sciences and Technology (3.70), Solan, Central University of Himachal Pradesh (2.60) Kangra, HPU (2.30) Shimla **(Total = 9)**
Average = 3.7; National Average = 2.2; C.V. Index = 1.44	

Source: As of Table 5.1.

In India Education Centre University, the actual number was not that high but very few numbers of girls students enrolled there. Also, it has come to be seen that in some of the universities especially private universities majority of girls students are day scholars. They come as day scholars to university campus by buses, generally hired by the universities for the purpose and stay at night either in their own homes or as paying guests in nearby towns. This is, in fact, a faster emerging commercial concept in Indian towns, having coaching centres or universities in their surrounding areas or within such towns.

On the whole, in nine (9) of the twenty universities of the state there were less than eight girls' hostels per 1000 female students. In remaining 12 universities it was more than eight hostels per 1000 female students. Among government run universities/institutes two agriculture universities and IIT, Mandi and NIT, Hamirpur falls in the high category of universities (Table 5.20). It is however to be noted here that agriculture universities and IITs, which require large piece of land for their establishment and proper functioning, are located far away from the cities, necessitating that all students stay in hostels.

Composite Index of Physical Infrastructure Indicators

A composite index on the basis of weighted score arrived at for each indicator of physical infrastructure facilities in universities has been calculated. The average composite index value for the universities was arrived at 13.0 against the national average 1.4 only. Evidently, quality of physical infrastructure in universities located in Himachal Pradesh was far superior to the national average. Among universities in the state it ranged from a high of 59.8 for India Education Centre University (Solan district) to a low of only 0.3 for Himachal Pradesh University (Shimla district), registering huge inter-universities inequalities in quality of physical infrastructure facilities (Table 5.21 and Fig 5.6).

India Education Centre University ranks at the top among all the universities in the state, it was placed in high category on second, third and sixth indicators. First and fifth indicator index value recorded higher than the average of all universities. There was no health facility in the same university. It was followed by the Career Point University, ranked second among all the universities in the state. It was placed in high category on first, second, fifth and sixth indicators. Against this, Himachal Pradesh University, Shimla which was placed at the bottom among all the twenty universities in the state, fared in low category almost in all the six indicators. APG University Shimla placed at the third rank, holds higher position than the average of all universities except on the facility of laboratory. On the whole, three universities were placed in high category in terms of quality of physical infrastructure. All these were managed by the private sector. These universities were running engineering-cum-technological courses. More than a half of the universities fell in the low category of physical infrastructure quality.

Table 5.21: Himachal Pradesh: Composite index of physical infrastructure at university level, 2012-13

Physical infrastructure Index	*Name of University*
High (More than 40)	India Education Centre University (59.8), Solan, Career Point University (57.4), Hamirpur, Alakh Prakash Goyal (APG) University (41.4), Shimla **(Total = 3)**
Moderate (10 – 40)	Maharishi Markandeshwar University (34.8), Solan, IIT (21.2), Mandi, Indus International University (17.3) Una, and Manav Bharti University (17.2), Solan Sri Sai University (15.2), Kangra, Solan, Jaypee University of Information Technology (13.2), Solan, Dr. Y.S. Parmar University of Horticulture and Forestry (11.8), Solan, Eternal University (10.3), Sirmaur **(Total = 8)**
Low (Less than 10)	Arni University (8.6), Kangra, Chitkara University (7.6), Solan, Chaudhary Sarwan Kumar Himachal Pradesh Krishi Vishvavidyalaya (6.9), Kangra, Shoolini University of Biotechnology and Management Sciences (6.8), Bahra University (6.4), Solan, NIT (5.9), Hamirpur, Central University of Himachal Pradesh (4.5), Kangra, Baddi University of Emerging Sciences and Technology (4.5), Solan, HPU (0.3), Shimla **(Total = 9)**
Average = 13.0; National Average = 1.4; C.V. Index = 0.98	

Source: As of Table 5.1.

In moderate category, index value ranging 10.0-40.0, there were eight universities, majority of these were managed by the private sector.

Briefly, quality of physical infrastructure differed widely among twenty universities in the state during 2012-13. Overwhelming majority of universities in the state fell in low level category of physical infrastructure. Unfortunately, all the government managed universities/institutes in the state fall in low category of physical infrastructure quality. In contrast, privately managed universities running engineering and technological courses fared better on quality of physical infrastructure. Dominant majority of eleven universities in the state which fall either in high or moderate category of physical infrastructure quality were privately managed, recently established and were running engineering and or technological courses. High fee slabs charged by private sector universities/institutes makes affordability an important issue. Only the students who can afford, the high fees get admitted to private universities. However, it also speaks of the flip-flop on the part of Government in India, which is ignoring the urgent need for investment in higher education in the name of privatization and competition.

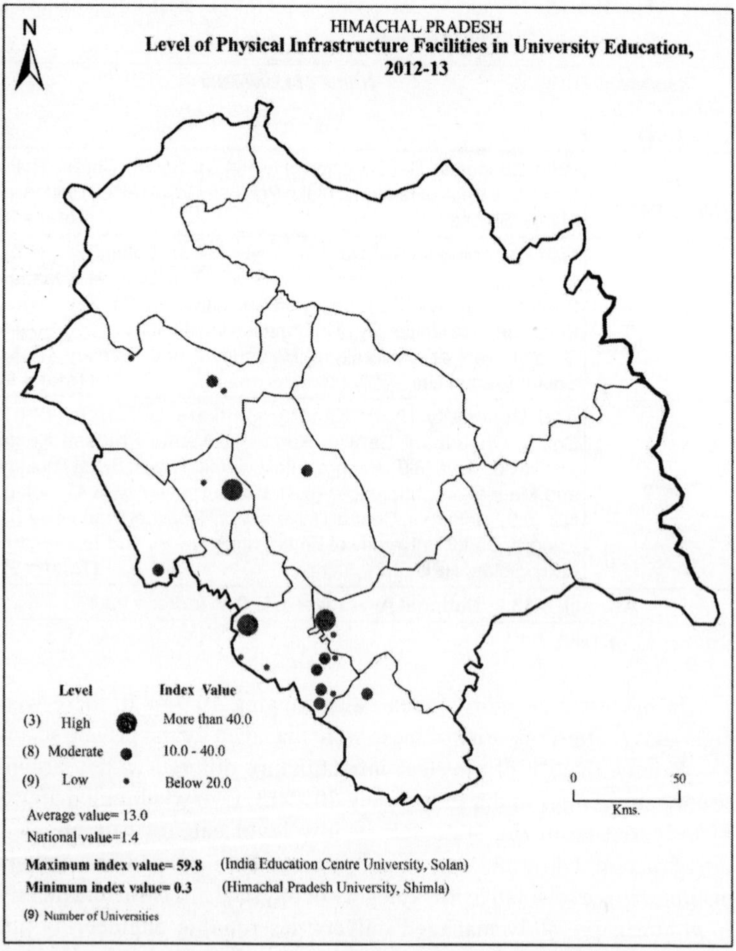

Fig. 5.6: Himachal Pradesh: Level of Physical Infrastructure facilities in University Education, 2012-13.

Source: As Table 5.1.

Level of Quality of Higher Education

In the following section, an attempt has been made to identify levels in the higher education quality at the university level with the help of composite index prepared by summing up of indices of components of human resources and physical infrastructure. These are the components of input indicators. On the basis of these two dimensions, index score of the quality of higher education was calculated at the university level.

These two dimensions are combined together to make the composite index of higher education quality at the university level. Already, there has been a separate discussion on these two components in the preceding pages. Therefore, here an attempt has been made to calculate and map composite index of higher education quality and identify the level of higher education quality at the university level. As already stated that due to paucity of relevant data on output indicators in the context of universities, the study is restricted to the input indicators at the university level. The composite index of higher education quality at university level differs widely. It ranged from a high of 65.0 in India Education Centre University (Solan district) to a low of only 23.9 in NIT (Hamirpur district). The former university placed at the second and first ranking on the criteria of human resources and physical infrastructure, respectively. Against this, NIT (Hamirpur district) fared very poorly on the criterion of human infrastructure and Himachal Pradesh University on the criterion of physical infrastructure (Table 5.22).

On the whole, five universities having composite index value higher than 45.0 have been categorized in high level of higher education quality. Except, Dr. Y.S. Parmar University of Horticulture and Forestry, all were functioning under private management (Table 5.23). Another eleven universities fall or majority of these universities fall under moderate category, index value ranging between 30.0 and 45.0. Except Chaudhary Sarwan Kumar Himachal Pradesh Krishi Vishvavidyalaya and IIT, Mandi, all were privately managed universities, teaching vocational education courses such as engineering, information technology, pharmacy and medical. Locationally, these were located in Solan, Kangra and Sirmaur districts, adjoining Punjab, Haryana and Uttar Pradesh.

The remaining one-fifth of the total number of universities in the state fall in the low category of higher education quality. Three of them were managed by the government. These included oldest university of the state, Himachal Pradesh University, Shimla, NIT, Hamirpur and Central University of Himachal Pradesh (Kangra district). Arni University in Kangra district was the only private university in this group.

Main Highlights

- Three dimensions namely human resources, physical infrastructure and education attainments have been used here to measure the

Table 5.22: Himachal Pradesh: Ranking of universities on weighted indices of components and composite index of quality of higher education, 2012-13

University	*Weighted index value*		
	Human Resources	*Physical Infrastructure*	*Quality of Higher education*
Dr. Y.S. Parmar University of Horticulture and Forestry, Solan	83.3 (1)	11.8 (10)	47.6 (5)
India Education Centre University	70.2 (2)	59.8 (1)	65.0 (1)
Chaudhary Sarwan Kumar Himachal Pradesh Krishi Vishvavidyalaya, Palampur	68.8 (3)	6.9 (14)	37.9 (8)
Maharishi Markandeshwar University, Solan	67.1 (4)	34.8 (4)	50.9 (3)
Manav Bharti University, Sultanpur, Solan	64.2 (5)	17.2 (7)	40.7 (6)
Indus International University, Bathu, Una	62.6 (6)	17.3 (6)	39.9 (7)
Eternal University, Baru Sahib, Sirmaur	58.1 (7)	10.3 (11)	34.2 (10)
Baddi University of Emerging Sciences and Technology, Budha (Makhnumajra), Solan	57.3 (8)	4.5 (19)	30.9 (15)
Chitkara University, Kalu Jhanda (Barotiwala), Solan	56.6 (9)	7.6 (13)	32.1 (12)
Shoolini University of Bio Technology and Management Sciences, Oachghat, Solan	56.1 (10)	6.8 (15)	31.4 (13)
Himachal Pradesh University, Shimla	55.9 (11)	0.3 (20)	28.1 (17)
Bahra University, Solan	55.7 (12)	6.4 (16)	31.0 (14)
Alakh Prakash Goyal (APG) University, Shimla	55.1 (13)	41.4 (3)	48.2 (4)
Sri Sai University, Palampur	54.5 (14)	15.2 (8)	34.9 (9)
Career Point University, Hamirpur	47.9 (15)	57.4 (2)	52.6 (2)
Jaypee University of Information Techno-logy, Waknaghat, Solan	47.8 (16)	13.2 (9)	30.5 (16)
Arni University, Katgarh (Indora), Kangra	47.3 (17)	8.6 (12)	28.0 (18)
Indian Institute of Technology, Mandi	46.4 (18)	21.2 (5)	33.8 (11)
Central University of Himachal Pradesh, Dharamshala, Kangra	45.8 (19)	4.5 (18)	25.1 (19)
National Institute of Technology, Hamirpur	41.8 (20)	5.9 (17)	23.9 (20)
All Universities	**54.3**	**13.0**	**33.7**
National Average	60.4	1.4	30.9
C.V Index	0.17	0.98	0.28

Source: Calculated on the basis of Table 5.14 and 5.21.

Note: Figures in parenthesis indicate to ranks.

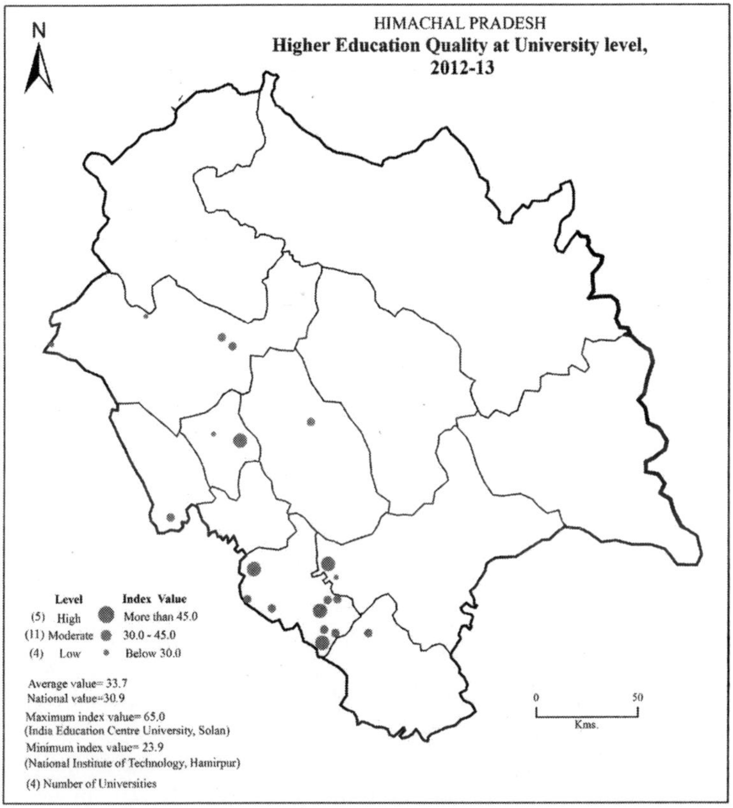

Fig. 5.7: Himachal Pradesh: Higher Education Quality at University level, 2012-13.

Source: As Table 5.1.

quality of higher education in the state, these differed widely among districts as well as universities.

- There were wide inter-district disparities in distribution of human resources for higher education. Only four districts of Shimla, Mandi, Kinnaur and Hamirpur were placed high on this count, the rest of the districts fared low to poor in this regard.
- A variety of factors were responsible for inter-district disparities in physical infrastructure available for higher education in the state. Inter-district movement of students for higher education, share of technical and professional colleges in the total number of colleges in a district and the degree of private investment in

Table 5.23: Himachal Pradesh: Classification of universities according to level of higher education quality, 2012-13

Level	*Name of University*
High (Index value more than 45.0)	India Education Centre University (65.0), Career Point University (52.6) Hamirpur, Maharishi Markandeshwar University (50.9), APG University (48.2), Dr. Y.S. Parmar University of Horticulture and Forestry (47.6) Solan **(Total= 5)**
Moderate (Index value between 30.0-45.0)	Manav Bharti University (40.7), Solan, Indus International University (39.9) Una, Chaudhary Sarwan Kumar Himachal Pradesh Krishi Vishvavidyalaya (37.9) Kangra, Sri Sai University (34.9) Kangra, Eternal University (34.2) Sirmaur, IIT (33.8) Mandi, Chitkara University (32.1) Solan, Shoolini University (31.4), Bahra University (31.0) Solan, Baddi University of Emerging Sciences and Technology (30.9), Jaypee University of Information Technology (30.5) Solan **(Total= 11)**
Low (Less than 30.0)	HPU (28.1) Shimla, Arni University (28.0) Kangra, Central University of Himachal Pradesh (25.1) Kangra, National Institute of Technology (23.9) Hamirpur **(Total= 4)**
All universities average = 33.7, National Average = 30.9; C.V. Index = 0.28	

Source: As Table 5.23.

higher education in a district played an important role among the factors involved in this regard.

- In educational attainments, there was a clear cut distinction between the districts falling in territories that were ruled by the native rulers and the British rule in India during the pre-Independence period. Educational attainments were higher in British ruled areas in comparison to those remaining under princely rulers. However, tribal population dominated districts of Kinnaur and Lahul and Spiti were performing very well in educational attainments.
- The migration of students in large number from three districts having large tribal population namely of Chamba, Kinnaur and Lahul and Spiti to adjoining districts of Kangra, Shimla and Kullu, respectively was largely responsible for creating a paradoxical situation. Such students leave behind huge higher education infrastructure to be used by only a few students but creating additional pressure on the available infrastructure in the colleges of the neighbouring districts. There was more higher education infrastructure available especially in Kinnaur and Lahul and Spiti districts, while quite the opposite was true of Shimla, Kangra and Kullu districts.

- Political patronage helped some districts in the state to attain higher position in educational infrastructure within a short span of one decade. Mandi district is a typical example of this kind. The district is a part of a parliamentary constituency represented till very recently by Mrs. Pratibha Singh, wife of present Chief Minister, Shri Virbhadra Singh; and the assembly constituency of Thakur Kaul Singh, an influential cabinet minister in the present Congress Party Government also falls in the district. In a short span, huge private and public sector investment in higher education has come up in the district.
- In five of the 12 districts in the state, quality of infrastructure and quality of education attainments in higher education correspond to each other. In other words, high or low level of educational attainments is closely associated with high/low level of physical and human infrastructure availability. Another three districts could overcome deficiency in the higher education infrastructure to achieve high level of educational attainments due to their traditional links with educationally developed districts of neighbouring Punjab. Non-conformity between these two dimensions in the case of Chamba, Kinnaur, Mandi and Sirmaur districts needs immediate attention of policy-makers and planners in the state. It represents a case of failure to convert opportunity into a boom.
- The age and management of a university seems to have the strong association with the share of professors or equivalents in the total teaching faculty at the university level in the state. In other words, the older the university is in age and managed by the public sector, the higher would the share of professors/ equivalent in total teaching faculty. However, there was hardly any clear cut distinction between old and new universities on account of the quality of human resources.
- Universities in the state differed widely in the quality of physical infrastructure. The three universities placed in the high category of physical infrastructure quality were managed by the private sector recently established and were running engineering-cum-technological courses. More than a half of the universities fall in the low category of the physical infrastructure quality. Unfortunately, almost all the government managed universities/ institutes fall in the low category of physical infrastructure. High fee slabs charged by private sector universities/institutes makes

affordability an important issue. The students who can afford are admitted to private universities. However, it also speaks of the flip-flop on the part of Government in India, which is ignoring the need for investment in higher education in the name of privatization and competition.

Summary and Main Findings

In consonance with the objectives of presenting a spatio-temporal analysis of the progress of higher education in Himachal Pradesh, the thesis undertook to provide answers to some basic questions: (i) How the present scenario of higher education in the history of Himachal Pradesh has evolved, with a focus on post-statehood which started in 1971?, (ii) Where is Himachal Pradesh placed among major states of India and the other hill states?, (iii) What is the impact of government policies on the evolving geographical pattern of higher education in the state?, (iv) What is the sub-regional pattern of accessibility, availability and quality of the higher education in the state?, (v) How far is the development of Higher education in the state inclusive in terms of residence (rural-urban), gender (male-female) and caste (Scheduled and non-Scheduled?, and (vi) What is the structural composition (in terms of nature, management and regulatory framework) of higher education in the state?

Hypotheses

In the light of the above stated research questions, the study proposed to test the following hypotheses:

- In view of the physiographic conditions of the state, the private sector would locate the institutions of higher education at places having locational advantage. Hence, there will be a tendency among privately managed such institutions to concentrate in the places having relatively higher degree of accessibility.
- Higher education in the state would find a strong impact of government policies on the courses offered by the institutions of higher learning. Hence, a large majority of courses in higher education would focus on courses in biotechnology, information technology, forestry, horticulture and pharmaceutical and drug industry.

- A large majority of higher education institutions in the state would be located on the highways (state or national) for the locational advantage.
- Due to physiographic constraints, the availability of land imposes serious limitations in the hill state of Himachal Pradesh. Hence, there would be not only a judicious use of land availability by the institutions of higher studies but also educational institutions requiring large size of land such as sports institutions would not be located in the state especially by the private sector.

Methodology

Based on the research questions and hypotheses, the research was guided by following methodological steps.

The study was mainly based on various secondary sources of data including the *All India Survey on Higher Education*, New Delhi, *Education Statistics,* and *Higher Education, Annual Reports of UGC.* Different Gazetteers, libraries and archives were scanned through for tracing historical development of higher education in the state.

For compilation, tabulation, mapping and analysis of data various cartographic and statistical tools and techniques were pressed into service. Similarly, for mapping distribution of educational institutions choropleth technique was used. Data suitable tables and graphs were incorporated to provide snapshot view of these data. For the calculation of the single age-group, Sprague multiplier method has been used to compute the Net Enrolment Ratio (for the age-group 18-23) at the district level. Further, the availability of higher education institutions in terms of area and education was calculated using index method.

The study was based on district level for the mapping of data/ information. In all, there are 12 districts in the state.

For an in-depth study of the evolutionary process and progress of higher education in Himachal Pradesh time span from British Period to 2016 was taken into consideration. In the chapter on structural composition, where the nature of higher education institutions was studied by classifying under the general, technical, professional, technical-cum-professional and multi-faculty category, the period between 1971 and 2016 was covered, by dividing it into sub-periods. For the chapter on accessibility and availability of higher education, data available from Census of India for three Census decades between 1981 and 2011 at the district level were extensively used for the purposes of intensive study.

Himachal: The National Context

India made significant progress in the field of higher education after the Independence of the country in 1947. With 25.9 million students enrolled for higher education, India is placed next only to China in the world. Since independence, the number of universities has increased 24 times and that of the colleges 53 times, maximum increase taking place in the last about two and a half decades, beginning with paradigm shift in economic policy-making in the year 1991. 1981 and 2001 were the two critical breaks in numerical growth of higher education institutions in India. As many as 467 new universities were opened in India between 2001 and 2014, recording an unprecedented annual growth of 7.7 per cent; and this number was nearly thrice of the total number of universities in the year 1981. The increase in number of colleges was still spectacular. The total number of new colleges coming up between 2001 and 2014 was higher than that the number of such colleges in 2001.

The robust growth of universities and colleges in India was, however, marked by wide regional and inter-state inequalities in their distribution. South India had an edge over all the regions of India and in combine with Western India it stole 44.2 per cent of total universities in India against their share 40.8 per cent in total population. Against this, eastern and north-central regions were highly deficient in terms of ratios between their shares in total universities and in total population of India. **North-western India, where Himachal Pradesh is located, was in the most comfortable position so far as the ratio between the two shares was concerned.**

Such imbalances in university-population ratio push the students from deficient to surplus regions for higher education especially in technical and professional streams, which is, certainly healthy from the angle of national integration, but at times leads to various clashes tinged with ethnicity.

In distribution of colleges, southern region was holding the superior position followed by the western region. Against this, eastern and north-central regions were highly deficient on this count. North-western region had almost balancing situation between the two shares (colleges and population). Southern region for its lead in technical and professional higher education streams attracts students from all parts of India especially from highly deficient eastern region.

Among major states, Himachal Pradesh ranked top in the university-population ratio. The state had 3.2 per cent of total universities against less than one per cent (0.6%) of India's population; and the state in combination with Uttarakhand, Haryana, Rajasthan and Jammu & Kashmir stole more than one-fifth (21.0%) of total universities against about one-tenth (10.6%) share in the total population of India. The former four states received huge private investment in higher education in post-liberalization period especially after 2001; privatization and commercialization of higher education has induced sharp regional inequalities in the distribution of higher education institutions and has made it costlier. Nevertheless, higher education has made inroads in backward and peripheral areas of the country. Five top ranking states, in combine, had more than one-half of the total number of colleges in India. The major states located in southern and western region were favourably placed against eastern and north-eastern regions. **Himachal Pradesh was placed fourth among 21 major states and fared next only to Haryana within north-western India.**

Availability of higher education in area and population terms varied widely among the major states. Against the national average of three universities after each ten thousand km^2 area, it ranged from a high of seven in Haryana to a low of only one university in four states of Jammu & Kashmir, Madhya Pradesh, Maharashtra and Odisha. Eight of 21 major states were placed above the average and remaining 13 states below it. Majority of states had this average between <2.0 to <4.0 universities. States attracting higher private investment in post-privatization phase recorded higher number of universities in terms of area. Inter-state differentials among the major states were wider in university-population ratio than university-area ratio. The average for major states being two universities after half a million persons, it ranged from a high of 15 universities in Himachal Pradesh to only one university in three states (Bihar, Uttar Pradesh and West Bengal). On the whole, three states of Haryana, Himachal Pradesh and Uttarakhand had this average of more than six universities. **Himachal Pradesh had the exceptionally high ratio of fifteen universities per half of a million persons.**

Inter-state differentials in college-area and college-population ratios were much more revealing than that of university-area and university-population ratios. Against the national average of 11 colleges per thousand km^2 area, the average for major states was of 12 colleges, for smaller states only two colleges and for Union territories it was as high as 29 colleges. Nine major states had this average higher than the average for the major states. Interestingly, Uttar Pradesh ranked third after Kerala and Haryana in the category of major states. In five major states (Kerala, Haryana, Uttar Pradesh, Punjab and Telangana), this ratio was 20 or more colleges after 10,000 km^2 or one college available within a radius of less than four kilometres of area. Against this, Himachal Pradesh along with Jharkhand,

Chhattisgarh and Jammu & Kashmir had this ratio less than one-half of the average for the major states. In Jammu & Kashmir only one college was available within a radius of 18 km; this was indeed really a deplorable situation, needing immediate action to rectify the situation.

Inter-state differentials were still wide in college-population ratio. While in four major states of Andhra Pradesh, Himachal Pradesh, Karnataka, Kerala and Telangana, college-population ratio was four or more colleges after ten thousand persons. Against this, the ratio was of only one college in the four states of Assam, Bihar, Jharkhand and West Bengal. On the whole, states in the southern region fared well on this count, while quite the opposite was true of states in north-east and east India. **Among major states Himachal Pradesh shared second rank with Telangana.**

On the composite index of area and population ratios of universities and colleges among the major states, Haryana ranked number one, with index value of 70.1, and Jharkhand was at the bottom, with index value of 14.9. In other words, Haryana had the highest availability of universities and colleges in terms of area and population, while quality the opposite was true of Jharkhand. Himachal Pradesh was categorized among states with high availability along with Kerala, Tamil Nadu, Telangana, Haryana and Uttarakhand, all these states benefitting from private investment in the field of higher education in the post-privatization phase of the higher education in India.

Gross Enrolment Ratio (GER), popularly used indicator to measure the health of higher education at the state level, revealed that Tamil Nadu was at the top with GER value of 35.5 per cent and Chhattisgarh at the bottom, with GER value of only 12.4 per cent. Himachal Pradesh was placed fifth with GER value of 26.0 per cent among 21 major states of India. Male-female GER ratios differed widely among the major states of India. The small states and Union territories were better placed as compared to the major states of India. Within the major states, there were wide differentials on this count. In majority of major states, male GER was higher than that of females. Exceptions were five states of Jammu & Kashmir, Kerala, Punjab, Tamil Nadu and Uttarakhand, where female GER was higher than that of males. **In Himachal Pradesh male GER was marginally higher than that of females.**

The national average of teacher-student ratio was one teacher after 25 students; the major states differed widely on this count. Karnataka and Tamil Nadu were at the top with one teacher after 14 students. Against this, four states of Uttar Pradesh, Bihar, Rajasthan and Jharkhand were placed at the bottom with one teacher after 50 students. Himachal Pradesh shared third rank with Maharashtra and Chhattisgarh within the group of 21 major states with five students after one teacher.

A composite index prepared with the help of the three indices of GER, women enrolment, teacher-pupil ratio, is highly revealing. Among major states, Tamil Nadu ranked at the top with index value of 94.8 and Bihar at the bottom with index value of only 44.6. Himachal Pradesh ranked sixth among 21 major states, with index value of 74.8.

Himachal: Among Hill States

A comparison of Himachal Pradesh with other Indian hill states was an eye-opener and an interesting one. While in the university-population ratio Himachal Pradesh ranked third after Sikkim and Arunachal Pradesh, in college-population and college-area ratio it fared at the top among all the hill states. **In composite index, prepared on the basis of area and population served by universities and colleges, Himachal Pradesh was at the third position after Sikkim and Uttarakhand.**

On other parameters such as GER, women enrolment ratio, and teacher-pupil ratio, Himachal Pradesh held third, second, second position, respectively among the hill states. Its rank on the composite index prepared on the basis of GER, women enrolment and teacher-pupil ratio was third among the 10 hill states. Within hill states, Manipur was placed at the top and Arunachal Pradesh at the bottom, with huge difference in their index values. Manipur in GER and Sikkim in teacher-pupil ratio did exceedingly well among the hill states.

Higher Education in Himachal: Changing Geography

At the dawn of independence in 1947, higher education was almost non-existent in the state of Himachal Pradesh, which itself was a part of Punjab. Even the modern school education was confined to only a few hill stations patronized by the Britishers during the colonial rule. In rest of the areas traditional system of *Gurukuls* and *Pathshalas* was prevalent.

Territorial consolidation in 1966 and grant of full statehood in 1971 induced fresh blood and enthusiasm not only among the masses but also among the bureaucrats and politicians for higher attainments in the development of the state. School education always remained the top priority of the government in the beginning, higher education picked up soon to grow at a slow pace but higher education institutions were distributed randomly.

Growing at a slow pace in the next two decades between 1970 and 1990, higher education in Himachal Pradesh entered the phase of fast growth following the change in the economic policies at the national level. During 1991-2001, there was a spurt in the growth of higher education institutions which led to its reaching the peak during the next decade of 2001-2011. **Privatization, ruralization and vocationalization were the marked features of higher education in the state in the post-2001 phase.**

Generally termed as a paradigm shift in higher education, as many as 23 of 28 universities and 125 of total 279 colleges in the state were established in a single decade between 2001-2011. An overwhelming majority of these came in private sector, rural areas and in the field of technical education. The latest phase (2011-2016) was marked with reversal of trend in favour of government investment and general education courses. Though benefitting the peripheral and so-far neglected areas of the state, higher education in the state entered the phase of populism. Colleges were established without taking due consideration of infrastructure. The government opened several new colleges during this phase without their own buildings and adequate teaching staff. Quality of higher education was the biggest causality in the whole process.

In the early phase (1970s and 1980s), the higher education in the state was demand driven, there were wide inter-district and urban-rural disparities in the distribution of the higher education institutions. It entered supply driven phase after 2001 following the entry of the private sector. In this phase inter-district and urban-rural disparities in the distribution of higher education institutions declined considerably. In Himachal Pradesh, more than four-fifth of the total number of higher education institutions were located in the rural areas. **Availability of extensive and cheap land, required for establishing higher education institutions especially universities, in rural areas attracted the private investors to locate higher education institutions in the rural areas.**

Locational advantage especially in case of Kangra, Solan and Sirmaur districts played an important role to locate technical and professional colleges and universities in areas bordering Haryana, Uttarakhand, Uttar Pradesh, Panjab and Chandigarh union territory, so as to attract students as well as faculty from these states. Location of 28 universities and majority of these providing running technical and professional courses speaks of a realistically satisfying and rewarding situation in case of the hill state of Himachal Pradesh. Since they were mostly in private sector, where profit motive is the top-most objective behind entering the area of higher education by private sector; it is difficult to say with confidence that Himachalis are the main and sole beneficiaries of technical and professional higher education.

Dust free peaceful environment of Himachal Pradesh surely attracts the parents to send their sons and daughters to such institutions in the state. Nonetheless, it is also true that the size of middle class has been recently increasing in Himachal Pradesh and the middle class households always try to grab white collar jobs especially in the public sector. Hence, a part of the benefits coming due to rapid expansion in technical and professional higher education in Himachal Pradesh was accruing to Himachalis as well.

In the hill state of Himachal Pradesh, relief and transport network play an important role in the geographical location of higher education institutions. The analysis reveals that 800 metres and 1500 metres height are the two critical breaks in location of higher education institutions in the state. 125 or two-fifth of the total number of higher education institutions in the state were located below 800 metres contours height and another 104 or one-third between in between 800 and 1500 metres contour height. In all, three-fourth of the total number of higher educational institutions was located below 1500 metres height in the Outer and Central Himalayas. Secondly, accessibility of higher education institutions in rugged and hilly terrain conditions forced the concerned investors to locate colleges and universities on the major transport routes. Nearly, one-half (47.0%) of the colleges and universities in the state were located on national highways passing through the state and another more than one-fifth were located in the close proximity to the state highways. **Briefly three factors: (i) government policy, may it be privatization of higher education or aggressive role of the state government to open several new government colleges in the recent years for popularistic reasons, (ii) physiographic conditions especially relief, and (iii) transport network have played a crucial role in the making and remaking of the geography of higher education in the state of Himachal Pradesh.**

Structural Composition and Change

Of the two types of colleges offering general and vocational courses, colleges offering general education courses dominated the higher education scenario in Himachal Pradesh. In 2016, they made more than a half (51.3%) of the total number of colleges of the state. Among the districts, the shape of general education colleges ranged from a low of 34.5 per cent in Solan district to a high of cent per cent in Lahul and Spiti district. In other words, higher education was the least diversified in the latter district and the most diversified in the former one.

The maximum number (63) of such colleges was in Kangra and minimum (1) was in Lahul and Spiti. Roughly three-fifth of such colleges were located in the four districts of Kangra, Shimla, Sirmaur and Mandi. Against this, their combined population (of 18-23 age-group) made 55.6 per cent in total population of the state. Another more than one-third or about 37.0 per cent were located in the four districts of Bilaspur, Chamba, Solan, Kullu and Una. More than nine-tenth or 95.2 per cent of such colleges were, thus, distributed in nine districts, having, in combine, 92.4 per cent population of the state. Obviously, there was only a marginal mis-match between the population shares (age-group identified as higher education age-group) of districts and their respective shares in the total number of colleges of general education courses in the state.

The share of general education colleges in the total number of colleges in the respective districts made an interesting story. In Lahul and Spiti district, there was only one college and that too running general education courses. In other words, higher education in Lahul and Spiti was oriented entirely to the general education. In this thinly populated district, development of higher education was lopsided. Next to it was Chamba district, where more than four-fifth or 83.3 per cent of the higher education colleges was limited to the teaching of general courses. Bilaspur, Kullu, Sirmaur, Kangra and Una were other districts where the majority of colleges were teaching general courses. Kinnaur was yet another district in the state where one-half of the colleges imparted general education. The district has only two colleges, one imparting general-cum-technical education and another one imparting technical education. On the other side of the scale, Solan was the only district in the state where colleges of general education make only one-third or 34.5 per cent of the total number of colleges.

Broadly speaking, higher education was structurally least diversified in the four northern districts of Chamba, Lahul and Spiti, Kinnaur and Kullu, while the opposite was true of Solan, Shimla, Mandi and Sirmaur districts. Factors like locational advantage, physiographic setting and initial advantage played a crucial role in the diversification of structural composition of higher education in the colleges at the district level in the state.

In the beginning, the structural composition of higher education in Himachal Pradesh was highly dominated by institutions teaching general/traditional courses. It shifted towards technical education after

1991, coinciding with economic reforms policy at the national level. The surge in the demand for technical courses led to a spurt in the growth of technical and professional colleges. **In the last forty-five years, there came a remarkable change in the structural composition of the higher education in the state. There was a time when there was an overwhelming predominance of the institutions teaching General education courses, gradually such institutions were reduced to having simple majority. Rather, in 2011 institutions teaching vocational courses formed the majority in the total number of higher education institutions. Thus it's reversing the well-established trend.**

About two-third of the colleges teaching general/traditional courses were concentrated in one-third of the districts in the state. Mandi district had the largest number of such institutions. However, in the total number of higher education institutions of the district they made less than 40.0 per cent.

70.0 per cent of the total number of the colleges in the state imparting higher education, were located in rural areas. Here colleges teaching traditional/general courses were predominant. Notably, Himachal Pradesh is the least urbanized state where hardly one of each ten persons resides in urban areas of the state. From this angle, urban areas of the state shared nearly thirty per cent of such colleges, indicating a higher concentration of urban areas in total number of such colleges in the state.

Higher education in the state was still dominated by colleges teaching traditional/general courses. In Lahul and Spiti, Chamba, Bilaspur and Kullu districts, higher education was highly oriented to general or traditional courses. In another four districts (Kangra, Kinnaur, Sirmaur and Una), the share of such colleges was one-half or more of the total number of the colleges. Of late, more than one-third or 27.3 per cent of such colleges have started offering vocational and technical courses along with the traditional courses. Growing demand coupled with the offer of financial support from the University Grants Commission, New Delhi for opening of vocational and technical courses was responsible for such a noticeable change in the structural composition of higher education in the state. Such colleges were highly concentrated in a few districts of the state. Four districts of Kangra, Shimla, Sirmaur, and Mandi accounted for more than 56.6 per cent of such colleges. Moreover, such colleges showed a tendency to concentrate in the urban areas, since 20.9 per cent of them were located in the urban centres, against urban population making only about 10.0 per cent of the total population of the state.

There was no change in the number of technical education colleges between 1971 and 1991. Then another six such colleges/institutions came between 1991 and 2001. In other words, on an average, less than one such college/institution per year was added during the decade of 1991-2001. In 2001 when total number of such colleges was 94, they made only 8.5 per cent of the total number of colleges in the state. Evidently, there has been a slow progress in the area of technical education in the state till 2001. The next decade (2001-2011), however, saw immense growth of technical education in the state. As many as 80 new colleges of technical education were added to make the total number of such colleges 88 or 39.0 per cent of the total number of higher education colleges in the state.

A majority of technical colleges in the state were providing Bachelors and Masters Degree courses in the field of teachers' training. This was mainly because of a high demand for trained teachers to teach at the school level as well as to further train the teachers. A further inquiry reveals that overwhelming majority of such colleges to begin with were started as B.Ed. colleges, later on diversified to other technical courses including computer science applications, business administration, engineering and pharmaceutical sciences. 55 or 58 per cent of the total technical education colleges in the state provide B.Ed. and M.Ed. courses. Earlier, the aspirants for such courses used to migrate to neighbouring states of Jammu & Kashmir, Uttar Pradesh, Punjab and Haryana for such courses.

Inter-district distribution of technical higher education colleges was quite revealing. Two-fifth of such colleges was spread over the five districts of Mandi, Kangra, Solan, Shimla and Hamirpur. In Mandi district, which had the largest number of such colleges in the state, one-half of the total number of colleges in the district was running technical courses. On the other side of the scale, four districts (Bilaspur, Chamba, Kinnaur and Kullu), in combine, had only nine such colleges. There was no technical/professional education college in Lahul and Spiti district.

Another, twenty-two colleges in this category had been teaching engineering/pharmacy/management/computer courses. As these courses were considered to be job oriented, these attracted aspirants not only from within the state but also from the neighbouring states. Again, the highest number of such colleges was in Mandi, Hamirpur and Shimla districts. Established mainly after the change in the economic policies in mid-1991, a large number of such colleges in the state were in the private sector. The policy was modified again in 2001 to clear the path for the opening of new universities or to tie-up with existing ones in the private sector (foreign as well as Indian).

Another 95 or less than one-third of the total number of such colleges imparting technical education were running B.Ed. and M.Ed. courses. Such courses were greatly in demand and were concentrated in five districts of Mandi, Kangra, Shimla, Solan, and Hamirpur. In fact, Mandi is the only district in the state where more than half of the total number of colleges were running technical higher education courses. Two-fifth of technical colleges were not only recent in origin but also high in demand. Locationally, such colleges were highly concentrated in five districts of Mandi, Hamirpur, Solan, Shimla and Kangra in the state.

Professional education like the technical education is of recent origin in the state. The number of such colleges as it provides professional education was only six in 2001; it rose to 17 in 2011 and then reached 24 in 2016. Earlier in 1971, when Himachal Pradesh got statehood, there was only one college of this kind. Growing at a snail's pace between 1971 and 1981, it recorded high growth between 1991 and 2001, when the number grew by 300 per cent: from two to six. Between 2001 and 2011, the number of professional colleges jumped to almost three times to increase to about 40.0 per cent of the total number of colleges between 2011 and 2016. Against this, technical education colleges recorded an increase of eleven times during the decade of 2001-2011.

With privatization of higher education in 2001, technical education recorded unprecedented increase in the number of colleges teaching technical education courses. Number of such colleges rose from 8 in 2001 to 88 by 2011 and the share of such colleges in the total number of colleges of the state went to be 38.9 per cent from being just 8.5 per cent during the same period. Against this, the share of colleges teaching general courses fell down to 46.0 per cent from about 78.0 per cent during this period. However, 2001-2011 decade proved the peak period in the growth of technical higher education in the state, as there had been a sluggish growth of technical colleges between 2011 and 2016, indicating to melting down of privatization pot within a decade in the hill state of Himachal Pradesh.

Year 2011 marked the reversal of the trend again towards the public investment in the field of higher education in the state. There had been a spurt in the growth of general education colleges in the state. Of the 53 new colleges opened during 2011-2016, 41 were general education colleges with the investment made by the Government of Himachal Pradesh. Political populism driven by the desire to win the next state assembly elections, due in December 2017, brought smile on the face of people living in those tehsils or sub-tehsils which were without any government college of higher education till date. Norm of 25 km radius to have a new government college was adjusted and re-adjusted in such a manner as if there was no norm, at all. This resulted in giving an upper hand again to general education colleges in the overall structural composition of higher education in the state. **The essence of the story is that the government policy has always been a guiding force behind making or remaking of structural composition of the higher education in the state of Himachal Pradesh.**

Professional education was still in the incipient stage in the state of Himachal Pradesh. The share of colleges teaching such courses in the total number of colleges was less than one-tenth in the year 2016. There were only four districts of Bilaspur, Kangra, Shimla and Solan where the share of professional colleges in the total number of colleges was more than 10.0 per cent. **Notably, the professional higher education in the state is highly oriented towards nursing courses.**

In 2016, 24 professional colleges made only about 9.0 per cent of the number of total 279 colleges in the state. Against this, technical colleges made 34.0 per cent of the total number. Evidently, professional higher education in the state was not only progressing at a slower pace but was also far behind the technical education. Locationally, professional higher education colleges were mainly confined to the four districts of Kangra, Shimla, Mandi and Solan, having, in combine, about four-fifth of total number of such colleges in the state.

Thanks to the privatization boom, structural composition of higher education at the universities was high in favour of technical and professional education. Of the 28 universities in the state, 17 or three-fifth were teaching technical/professional courses. Nine or more than half of such universities were located in a single district of Solan, bordering Punjab, Haryana and Chandigarh Union Territory. Majority of technical and professional universities being in private hands, profit making was the top priority, it was difficult to say with confidence that Himachalis are the main beneficiaries of such a large number of technical universities in the state. Location of nine of the total 17 technical/professional universities of the state in a single district of Solan was a pointer in this direction. Selection of Solan district and location of these universities at places bordering Haryana, Punjab and Chandigarh (U.T.) speaks a lot. Nevertheless, there was no denying the fact that size of middle class in the state had grown in the recent decades. **The middle class households always try to grab white collared jobs especially those in the government sector. Hence, a part of the benefit must be accruing to Himachalis as well.**

Causal factors behind diversification in structure of higher education in the state differed across districts. For example, Solan and Sirmaur districts benefitted from the locational advantage, Shimla from the initial advantage combined with its status as the state capital headquarters, Hamirpur from getting the regional engineering college established under the central government scheme as early as in 1986 and Mandi district from its growing political clout in the recent decades.

Accessibility and Availability

Accessibility and availability of higher education in the state, measured with the help of a number of indicators, was low, widely differing in time and space but growing fast especially after 2011. In 2011, only about one-sixth of the total number of young persons in the 18-23 age-group were enrolled for higher education. Earlier in 1981, NER was only 0.5 per cent. **In other words, only one out of 200 young persons in the age-group of 18-23 was enrolled for higher education. The vocational education, in particular, remained quite low both in its availability and its accessibility till recently.** Even in 2001, NER of vocational education was as low as 0.68 per cent, picking up after 2001 to reach up to 5.53 per cent within a decade by 2011. In a way, the year 2001 acted as water mark in the history of NER in Himachal Pradesh for two main reasons: (i) shift in focus from general to vocational courses, and (ii) opening of higher education to the private sector.

Himachal Pradesh had benefitted a lot from private investment in higher education ever since the state opened the higher education to private sector, resulting in the opening of the new colleges and universities both in public and private sectors to register a quantum leap in NER between 1991 and 2001: from 1.08 per cent to 11.4 per cent. The NER grew further in the next decade between 2001 and 2011, to reach to 16.7 per cent by 2011.

However, different districts in the state responded differently to the privatization policy. Against the state average of 0.5 per cent in 1981, it ranged from a high of 1.8 per cent in Shimla district to negligible (only 0.04%) in Lahul and Spiti district. In one-half of the twelve districts in the state, namely Lahul and Spiti, Kinnaur, Chamba, Una, Bilaspur, Kullu and Sirmaur, NER ratio was either equivalent to or less than one-half of the state average. It was only in Solan and Shimla districts that NER ratio was higher than the state average. In fact, the NER ratio of Shimla district was responsible for keeping the state average on the higher side.

There are striking inter-district, urban-rural, male-female and social inequalities in higher education enrolment ratio even at low level of higher education development in the state. In 2011, NER ranged from a high of 23.6 per cent in Shimla district to a low of only 8.8 per cent in Chamba district, giving a range difference of about 15.0 per cent. Separately for vocational streams, inter-district inequalities were still sharp, ranging from a high of 10.3 per cent in Hamirpur district to only 1.4 per cent in Kinnaur district. Urban-rural inequalities in NER were equally marked both in general and vocational education. The NER of higher education for urban areas was nearly twice of rural areas. The former was 24.8 per cent against only 15.7 per cent of the latter. In vocational education, it was 10.7 per cent for urban areas and only 4.9 per cent for the rural areas. NER of Scheduled Castes and non-Scheduled population also differed. It was 14.1 per cent for the former and 18.0 per cent for the latter.

Interestingly, the general education inequalities in Himachal Pradesh go in favour of females. NER for females was 17.8 per cent against 15.6 per cent for the males. Even in rural areas, NER for females was higher than that of males. However, in the case of vocational education, the balance was in favour of males, the NER of vocational education for males was 5.4 per cent against 4.1 per cent for females in 2011. Even in the case of Scheduled Castes population, NER for female and male population in general education was almost the same. For the former, it was 14.6 per cent and for latter 14.8 per cent.

Higher education NER in the state was greatly influenced by the physiographic conditions. As one moves from the lower Himalayan zone to the middle and then to the higher and Trans-Himalayan zones, NER kept on declining. Lack of threshold population coupled with the paucity of financial resources, required to open higher education institutions in the state, seemed to be the plausible reason behind all this.

As is evident in differential index values, urban-rural disparity in NER declined in majority of districts. The maximum decline was recorded in Mandi district followed by Chamba district. Against this, Sirmaur district registered sharp increase, differential index value rising to 2.6 in 2011 from 1.6 in 2001. Another district, Kangra, recorded a marginal increase from 0.3 in 2001 to 0.4 in 2011. On the whole, five of the ten districts (excluding Lahul and Spiti and Kinnaur) had differential index value higher than the state average. **Vocational higher education, which is still at low level in Himachal Pradesh, recorded wide urban-rural differential in NER.** It is not a healthy trend.

As expected, NER of non-Scheduled population was higher than that of Scheduled (Castes plus Tribes) population in Himachal Pradesh. It was true of general and vocational education both. In 2011, NER of non-Scheduled and Scheduled population was 18.0 per cent and 14.0 per cent, respectively for general education courses. Earlier in 2001, the respective shares were 13.2 per cent and 6.8 per cent. Evidently, not only NER for both non-Scheduled and Scheduled population grew fast but also the gap between the two NER declined during 2001-2011. **The growth of NER in case of Scheduled population was faster than that of non-Scheduled population, helping in narrowing down gap between NER of non-Scheduled and Scheduled population. This makes not only a healthy trend from the angle of social inclusiveness but also speaks of the success of government policies in this context.**

The combined picture of accessibility in general and vocational education in the state reveals that there is a decline in the demand for higher education across districts, indicating a saturation stage in demand for higher education especially in districts, where private colleges and universities came quickly in the last ten to fifteen years.

Availability of higher education in the state recorded a spectacular increase during 1991-2016. The robust increase was registered between 2001 and 2011 when college-area ratio more than doubled, from less than two colleges/1000 km^2 to more than four colleges/1000 km^2, the private investment in higher education sector of the state playing the important role in this. **Private investment, which was based on the concept of demand-supply equation, not only increased the availability of colleges in area terms but also reduced inter-district gap on this count.** Interestingly, with the exception of Mandi district, all those districts performing well on this count made boundaries with neighbouring states of Punjab, Haryana and Uttar Pradesh, indicative of response to outside the state demand.

In 2016, when inter-district gap in college-area ratio was further reduced, state government policy of having at least one government degree college in all the state assembly constituencies is credited with reduction in inter-district inequalities in college-area ratio. **By 2016, there was one college available within a radius of 4.5 kms in the state. This distance was of more than 10 kms in 1991.**

Among districts, the biggest gainer was Kullu followed by Sirmaur, Shimla, Bilaspur and Kangra districts. The reverse was true of Kinnaur, Lahul and Spiti, Hamirpur, and Una districts, performing high or moderate during 2001-2011. It seems that a saturation level had been attained there. Against this, districts performing well during this period benefitted from the government policy of Himachal Pradesh of having at least one government college in all the state assembly constituencies. Backward and peripheral areas in all such districts benefitted from this policy decision.

The college-population ratio recorded a phenomenal increase in Himachal Pradesh between 1991 and 2016. Major change occurred during 2001-2011, when private investment in the field of higher education stepped up rapidly following a change in the higher education investment policy at the state level. **The inter-district disparities declined concomitantly with increase in college-population ratio.** Some of the districts such as Mandi, Sirmaur, Solan, Kangra and Hamirpur which had initially the low or moderate level of college-population ratio, recorded rapid increase in the post-2001 period. The opposite was true of districts such as Shimla, Una and Bilaspur, which had reached the saturation level.

A cross-examination of accessibility and availability of higher education in the state is highly revealing. In six districts of the state (Hamirpur, Una, Chamba, Kinnaur, Kullu and Sirmaur) availability and accessibility goes hand-in-hand. In other words, both are high or low in these districts. In another three districts of Bilaspur, Kangra, and Shimla notwithstanding the low availability, accessibility is high. **It means these districts could overcome the deficiency in availability by way of their external links.** Against this, Lahul and Spiti, Mandi and Solan districts present the case of low accessibility in spite of high availability of higher education institutions. This means that available higher institutions stood underutilized or supply was more than the demand for higher education in these districts. **This needs immediate attention of policy-makers for corrective measures, otherwise market forces will come in operation. In other words, higher education institutions failing to compete would be wiped out in due course of time.**

Finally, the analysis in the chapter made it evidently clear that may it be accessibility or availability of higher education in the state, the government policies of allowing private investment in higher education and the decision to open at least one government degree college in all the assembly constituencies in the state played a crucial role either in narrowing down or widening of the gaps in the availability or accessibility of higher education in the state.

Higher Education Quality

Three dimensions namely human resources, physical infrastructure and education attainments, which were used to measure the quality of higher education in the state, differed widely among districts as well as the universities.

There were wide inter-district disparities in the distribution of human resources for higher education. Only four districts of Shimla, Mandi, Kinnaur and Hamirpur were placed high on this count, the rest of the districts fared low to poor in this regard.

A variety of factors were responsible for inter-district disparities in physical infrastructure available for higher education in the state. Inter-district movement of students for higher education, share of technical and professional colleges in the total number of colleges in a district and the degree of private investment in higher education in a district played an important role among the factors involved in this regard.

In educational attainments, there was a clear cut distinction between the districts falling in those territories which were ruled by the native rulers and the British rulers in India during the pre-Independence period. Educational attainments were much higher in British rule areas in comparison to those remaining under princely rulers. However, tribal population dominated districts of Kinnaur and Lahul and Spiti were performing very well in educational attainments.

The migration of students in large number from the districts with large population of tribals namely those of districts of Chamba, Kinnaur and Lahul and Spiti to adjoining districts of Kangra, Shimla and Kullu, respectively was mainly responsible for creating a paradoxical situation. Such students leave behind huge higher education infrastructure to be used only by a few students, but their migration creates additional pressure on the available infrastructure in the colleges of the neighbouring districts. There was better higher education infrastructure available especially in Kinnaur and Lahul and Spiti districts, while quite the opposite was true of Shimla, Kangra and Kullu districts.

Political patronage helped some districts in the state to attain higher position in education infrastructure within a short span of one decade. Mandi district is a typical example of this kind. The district is a part of a parliamentary constituency represented till very recently by Mrs. Pratibha Singh, wife of the present Chief Minister, Shri Virbhadra Singh; and the assembly constituency of Thakur Kaul Singh, an influential cabinet minister in the present Congress Party Government in Himachal Pradesh also falls in the district. Due to this political influential patronage in a short span, huge private and public sector investment in the field of higher education has come up in the district.

In five of the 12 districts of the state, quality of infrastructure and

quality of educational attainments in higher education conform to each other. In other words, high or low level of educational attainments is closely associated with good quality or unsatisfactory level of physical and human resources availability. Another three districts could overcome deficiency in infrastructure to achieve high level of educational attainments due to their traditional links with educationally developed districts of neighbouring Punjab. Non-conformity between these two dimensions, high (well equipped) infrastructure but low attainment, in the case of Chamba, Kinnaur, Mandi and Sirmaur districts needs immediate attention of policy-makers and planners in the state. It represents an apt case of failure to convert opportunity into a boom.

The age and management of a university seems to have the strong association with share of professors or equivalents in the total teaching faculty at the university level in the state. In other words, older the university in age and managed by the public sector, the higher would the share of professors/equivalents in total teaching faculty would be. However, there was hardly any clear cut distinction between old and new universities on account of quality of human resources.

Universities in the state differed widely in quality of physical infrastructure. The three universities placed in high category of physical infrastructure quality were privately managed, recently established and running engineering-cum-technological courses. More than half of the universities of the state fall in the low category of physical infrastructure quality. Unfortunately, almost all the government managed universities/ institutes fall in the low category of physical infrastructure. High fee slabs charged by private sector universities/institutes make the affordability an important issue. The students who could afford were admitted to private universities. However, it also speaks of the flip-flop on the part of the Government of India, which was ignoring the need for investment in higher education in the name of privatization and competition.

Analysis

A number of hypotheses formulated at the beginning of the study were vindicated by the empirical analysis. Being a hill state, major parts of Himachal Pradesh were higher than 800 metres. In the southern part of the state, extending in south-west to south-east direction bordering Punjab-Haryana plains were the Siwalik Hills with altitude ranging between 450-650 metres. Then, there were gently sloping hills between 650 and 850 metres. Beyond that there were the lower and middle Himalayan zones having moderate slope and altitude ranging between 850 and 1500 metres. At last were higher Himalayas and Zanskar ranges having steep slope and altitude ranging between 1500 metres and 6500 metres; the longitudinal river valleys cut these high mountain ranges in between. Distribution of human settlements, economic activities and infrastructural facilities (physical and social) including higher education institutions followed these dictates of physical contours of the state.

The analysis reveals that 800 metres and 1500 metres height are the two critical breaks in location of higher education institutions in the state. 125 or two-fifth of the total higher education institutions in the state were located below 800 metres contour height and another 104 or one-third were in between 800 and 1500 metres contour height. In all, three-fourths of the total higher educational institutions were located below 1500 metres height in the Outer and Central Himalayas. Moreover, overwhelming majority of them was located in highly accessible areas bordering Punjab-Haryana plains in the districts of Solan, Kangra, Shimla, Una, and Hamirpur districts. More than half of such higher education institutions were under the private management.

In 2016, there were in total 28 universities/institutes and 279 colleges in the state teaching a variety of traditional and vocational courses. Among the universities, 17 were in private sector and eleven in the public sector. Of the eleven public sector universities/institutes, four were exclusively managed by the Himachal Pradesh Government, another three jointly with the Union Government and remaining five exclusively by the Union Government. All the 17 private sector universities and eight public sector universities/institutes were running vocational courses relating to engineering, technology, computer science, information technology, pharmacy and medical sciences. However, in case of colleges, majority of them were still running general/traditional courses. Nonetheless, all the 125 private colleges were running courses relating to engineering, electronics, technology, computer science, medical and paramedical and teacher's training.

Owing to undulating hill topography, accessibility is the most challenging task in Himachal Pradesh. To overcome this, higher education institutions in the state were located on or nearby important transport networks. Nearly, one-half (47.0%) of the colleges and universities in the state were located on national highways passing through the state and another more than one-fifth in close proximity of the state highways. In this way, seven of the ten higher education institutions in the state were located either on national or state highway.

Almost all the higher educational institutions in the state were struggling to get adequate land for running various activities. This was mainly because of undulating topography in this hill state. Hence, there has been a judicious use of available land. Those courses that required more land were not opened in the state. For this reason, there was not a single college/university in the state, which was running exclusively the courses related to sports.

Recommendations

During the last about three decades, higher education network in Himachal Pradesh experienced rapid growth and physical expansion. Himachal Pradesh was now in the category of major states having high level of availability of higher educational institutions both in terms of area and population. However, the quality of higher education in the state remained poor rather it deteriorated or worsened with the physical expansion of higher education. This could happen in spite of the fact that Government of Himachal Pradesh has adopted RUSA, a centrally sponsored programme to improve the quality, accessibility and availability of higher education. There was, in fact, an urgent need to focus on the improvement of quality instead of the physical expansion of higher education in the state.

Secondly, equally important was the need to improve not only the quality but also the quantity of human and physical infrastructure of higher education in different parts of the state especially in those districts, which have done well in education attainments in spite of low physical and human infrastructure of higher education. In this category were included the districts of Bilaspur, Una, Kangra, Hamirpur and Kullu, which were transferred to Himachal Pradesh after the linguistic reorganization of Punjab in 1966. Further, the new colleges opened by the Government of Himachal Pradesh after 2014 in backward and peripheral areas of different districts in the state were also highly deficient in infrastructural facilities. Also, they required infrastructure upgradation including that of the buildings to house the colleges properly.

Thirdly, there was wide gap in urban-rural distribution of colleges teaching vocational courses. This needs to be minimized through a policy intervention by the state government. Spread of vocational higher education to rural areas was in fact the need of the hour in the light of the fact that there was widespread unemployment of youths in the rural areas of the state.

Bibliography and References

Agarwal, P. (2006). Higher education in India: Need for change, *Indian Council for Research on International Economic Relations* (*ICRIER*) Working Paper No. 180. Retrieved from http://www.icrier.org/pdf/ICRIER_WP180_Higher_Education_in_India_pdf.

Agarwal, P. (2007). Higher education in India: Growth, concerns and change agenda. *Higher Education Quarterly*, *61*(2) May, 197-207.

Agarwal, P. (2009). *Indian higher education: Envisioning the future*. New Delhi: Sage Publication.

Agrawal, V. and Sharma, U.R. (2002). Privatization of higher education: Controversies and Suggestions. *University News, 40*(49), pp. 1-4.

Ahmed, J.U. (2016). Massification to marketization of higher education: Private university education in Bangladesh. *Higher Education for the Future, 3*(1), 76-92.

AICTE (1994). Report of the high power committee for mobilization of additional resources for technical education, All India Council for Technical Education, New Delhi.

Altbach, P.G. (1993). The dilemma of change in Indian higher education. *Higher Education Journal*, *26*(1), 3-20.

Altbach, P.G. (1999). Private higher education: Themes and variations in comparative perspective. *Prospects,* 3 September, *29*(3), 311-323.

Altbach, P.G. (2002). Knowledge and education as international commodities: The collapse of common good. *University News*, *40*(22), pp. 1-4.

Altbach, P.G. (2003). Asia: Trends and development in private higher education. *International Higher Education*, *29*, 10-11.

Altbach, P.G. (2005). The private higher education revolution: An introduction. In P.G. Altbach and D.C. Levy (Eds.), *Private higher education: A global revolution,* (pp. 1-13). Rotterdam, The Netherlands: Sense Publishers.

Altbach, P.G. (2009). One-third of the globe: The future of higher education in China and India. *Prospects, 39*:11-31.

Altbach, P.G. (2009). The Giant awake: Higher education systems in China and India. *Economic and Political Weekly, 44*(23), 39-51.

Altbach, P.G. and Chitnis, S. (1991). *Higher education reform in India*. New Delhi: Sage Publications.

Ambani, M., and Birla, K.M. (2000). *Report on a policy framework of reforms in higher education*, Prime Minister's Council on Trade and Industry, G.O.I. New Delhi: Department of Science and Technology. Retrieved from http://ispepune.org.in/PDF%20ISSUE/2003/JISPE403/2038DOCU-3.PDF.

Anand, C.L. (1999). Privatization of higher education in India: Rationale and perspective. *Dialogue: A quarterly journal of Astha Bharthi*, July-Sep., *1*(1).

Anand, S. (2014). Inter-state variations in public spending on higher education in india. *International Journal of Humanities and Social Science Invention*, *31*(9), 23-31.

Anandakrishnan, M. (2007). Higher education-II, critique of knowledge commission. *Economic and Political Weekly*, *42*(7), 557-560.

Angom, S. (2015). Private higher education in India: A study of two private universities. *Higher education for the Future*, *2*(1), 92-111.

Asif, M. and Searcy, C. (2014). A composite index for measuring performance in higher education institutions. *International Journal of Quality and Reliability Management*, *31*(9): 983-1001. Retrieved from https://doi.org/10.1108/IJQRM-02-2013-0023.

Balakrishnan, P. (2007). Higher education in India: Will 'six per cent' do it. *Economic and Political Weekly*, *42*(39), 3930-3934.

Ballal, H.S. (2009). *Chairman's speech at the FICCI higher education summit*, New Delhi: Federation of Indian Chamber of Commerce and Industry.

Balokhra, J.M. (1995). The wonderland Himachal Pradesh: An encyclopaedia on the state of Western Himalayas. New Delhi: H.G. Publications.

Basant and Sen (2010). Who participates in higher education in India? Rethinking the role of affirmative action. *Economic and Political Weekly*, *44*(39), 62-70.

Basil, H.V. (2017) *Higher education in India: Challenges of quality and accessibility in the context of inclusive growth* (June 21, 2017). Available at SSRN: https://ssrn.com/abstract=2990424.

Bhushan, S. (2004). Managing tertiary education for integrated knowledge economy. Private initiative in higher education. In K.B. Powers and K.L. Johar (Eds.), *Private initiatives in higher education* (pp. 268-275). Haryana: Sneh Prakashan.

Bhushan, S. (2005). Foreign universities in India: Market-driven new directions. *International Higher Education, 41*, 4-5.

Bhushan, S. (2008). Financial requirements in higher education during XI Plan period. In SukhdeoThorat (Eds.), *Higher education in India: Issues related to expansion, inclusiveness, quality and finance* (pp. 215-76). New Delhi: University Grants Commission.

Booth, W.C., Colomb, G.G., and Williams, J.M. (2008). *The craft of research (3rd ed.).* London: The University of Chicago Press.

Central Advisory Board of Education (2005). *Report of the CABE Committee on financing of higher and technical education*, New Delhi: NUEPA. Retrieved from http http://mhrd.gov.in/sites/upload_files/mhrd/files/document.

Chakrabarti, A. and Joglekar, R. (2006). Determinants of expenditure on education: an empirical analysis using state level data. *Economic and Political Weekly 41*(15), 1465-1472.

Chanana, K. (1993). Accessing higher education: The dilemma of schooling women, minorities, Scheduled Castes and Scheduled Tribes in contemporary India. *Higher Education*, *26*(1), 69-92.

Chanana, K. (2007). Globalisation, higher education and gender: Changing subject choices of Indian women students. *Economic and Political Weekly, 42*(7), 590-598.

Chathley, Y.P. (1995). Education, population and development: A regional perspective of north-west India. Chandigarh: CRRID.

Chattopadhyay, S. (2007). Exploring alternative sources of financing higher education in India. *Economic and Political Weekly, 42*(42), 4251-59.

Chaturvedi, S. and Gupta, P.V. (2009). Quality of higher education. *University News*, *47*(4), 5-15.

Chauhan, C.P.S. (2008). Higher education current status and future possibilities in Afghanistan, Bangladesh, Bhutan, India, Maldives, Nepal, Pakistan and Sri Lanka, *Analytical reports in International education*, *2*(1), 29-48.

Chitnis, S. (1972). Education for equality: Case of Scheduled Castes in higher education. *Economic and Political Weekly, 7*(33), 1675-1681.

Damme, D.V. (2001). Quality issues in the internationalisation of higher education. *Higher Education*, *41*(4), 415-441.

Daniel, C. Levy (2006). The unanticipated explosion: Private higher education's global surge. *Comparative Education Review*, *50*(2), 217-240.

Das, S.K. (2012). Self-financing scheme in post-graduate courses of government-sponsored college: A case study. *Excel International Journal of Multidisciplinary Management Studies, 2*(1).

Das, M.B., Mehta, S.K., Tas, E.O. and Zumbyte, L. (2015). *Scaling the heights: Social inclusion and sustainable development in Himachal Pradesh*. Washington: World Bank Group.

Dash (2011). Changing scenario in higher education in India. *The Indian Economic Review, 8*(15 Feb-15 May).

Daugherty, L., Miller, T., Dossani, R. and Clifford, M. (2013). *Building the links between funding and quality in higher education: India's challenge.* Retrieved from http://www.rand.org/content/dam/rand/pubs/research_reports/RR200/RR225/RAND_RR225.pdf.

De, A. and Endow, T. (2008). Public expenditure on education in India: Recent trends and outcomes, research consortium on educational outcomes and poverty, Working Paper No. 18. Retrieved from http://ceid.educ.cam.ac.uk/publications/WP18-ADfin.pdf.

De, U.K. (1999). Status of education in North East India: Some Reflections. In Lyndem, B. and De. U.K (Ed.), *Education in North East India: Experience and challenge* (pp. 5-21). New Delhi: Concept Publishing Company.

Deloitte (2012). Indian Higher education sector opportunities aplenty, growth unlimited. Retrieved from https://www2.deloitte.com/content/dam/Deloitte/in/Documents/IMO/in-imo-indian-higher_education_sector-noexp.pdf.

Deodhar, S.Y. (2002). Educational services: Issues for India in WTO negotiations, *Economic and Political Weekly*, *39*(19), 1791-1794.

Deshpande, S. and Zacharias, U. (2013). Beyond inclusion the practice of equal access in Indian higher education. New Delhi: Routledge.

Dhameja, N. and Gupta, R. (2010). Higher education in India: Its growth and private participation: Issues. *Indian Journal of Public Administration*, *56*(3), 519-536.

Express News Service (6 April, 2012). Only 20 private universities will be allowed in Himachal Pradesh, says CM Dhumal. Retrieved from http://archive.indianexpress.com/news/only-20-private-universities-will-be-allowed-in-himachal-pradesh-says-cm-dhumal/933233/

FICCI. (2009). *Making the Indian higher education system future ready*. Higher Education Summit. New Delhi: Ernst & Young.

FICCI (2012). *Higher education in India: Twelfth Five Year Plan (2012-2017) and beyond*. Higher Education Summit. New Delhi: Ernst & Young.

FICCI. (2014). *Higher Education in India: Moving towards global relevance and competitiveness*. Higher Education Summit. New Delhi: Ernst & Young.

FICCI (2016). *Future of jobs and its implications on Indian Higher Education*. New Delhi: Ernst & Young.

First Post online. (5 January, 2009). National mission on education through ICT approved. Retrieved from http://www.firstpost.com/business/biztech/national-mission-on-education-through-ict-approved-1869967.html.

Gautam, P.N. (1995). *Basic needs of the hill people: A study of social and administrative response in Himachal Pradesh*. New Delhi: Indus Publishing Company.

Ghosh, J. (2006). Case for caste-based quotas in higher education. *Economic and Political Weekly, 17*, 2428-2432.

Ghuman, B.S. (2014). Privatization and globlization of higher education in India. *In* S.L Sharma, B.S. Ghuman and S. Parkash (Eds.), *Higher education in India: The changing scenario* (pp. 35-49). Jaipur, India: Rawat Publications.

Gnanam, A., Bradbury D.B. and Stella, A. (2003). *Benchmarking quality in higher education: The Indo-UK perspective.* New Delhi: Sterling Publishers Private Limited.

Gopalan, P. (2013). *PPP paradox promise and perils of public-private partnership in education*. New Delhi: Sage Publications.

Gosai, M.R. (2004). Supreme court's interpretation of the judgment on private higher education: Freedom Fettered, *University News, 42*(12), 1-5.

Government of Himachal Pradesh (1998). *Ninth Five Year Plan*. Shimla: Planning Commission.

Government of Himachal Pradesh. (2007). *Himachal Pradesh state roads project environment screening report for 1675 km of feasibility study corridors.* Volume-1. Main Report. The Louis Berger Group, Inc: World Bank.

Government of Himachal Pradesh. (2012). *Draft 12th Five Year Plan 2012-17 and Annual Plan 2013-14*. Planning Department, Government of Himachal Pradesh, Shimla.

Government of Himachal Pradesh (2013). *Socio-economic indicators of Himachal Pradesh*. Shimla: Department of Economics and Statistics Himachal Pradesh. Retrieved from http://admis.hp.nic.in/himachal/economics/REPORTS/Socio2013_A1b.pdf.

Government of Himachal Pradesh (2013-14). *H.P. Private Educational Institutions Regulatory Commission, Annual Report*. Shimla: Majitha House Complex.

Government of Himachal Pradesh (2014). Government of Himachal Pradesh, Department Higher Education. No. EDN-A-Ka (1)-2/2012 Shimla-02.Retrieved from http://www.rajpatrahimachal.nic.in/openFile.aspx?id=17179&etype=Notice.

Government of India (2013). *ASHE: Annual status of higher education of states and UTs in India*. New Delhi: Ministry of Human Resource Development, p. 7.

Government of India (1950). *Report of the University Education Commission 1948-49*, Volume 1. New Delhi: Ministry of Education, Government of India.

Government of India. (2005) *Report of Central Advisory Board of Education Committee on Autonomy of Higher Education Institutions.* New Delhi: Ministry of Human Resource Development.

Government of India. (2005). *Himachal Pradesh Development Report*, published by Academic Foundation, New Delhi on behalf of Planning Commission, New Delhi, pp. 135-154.

Government of India. (2009). *National Knowledge Commission Report to the Nation 2006-09*, Retrieved from www.knowledgecommission.gov.in.

Government of India (2011). *Report of the Working Group on Higher Education for the XII Five Year Plan*. New Delhi: Ministry of Human Resource Development.

Government of India. (2012). *Statistics of higher and technical education 2008-2009*. New Delhi: Ministry of Human Resource Development, p. 1.

Government of India. (2016). *National policy on education 2016: Report of the Committee of the New Education Policy*. New Delhi: Ministry of Human Resource Development, pp. 121-122.

Government of India. (2017). *National Institutional Ranking Framework (NIRF): India rankings 2017*. New Delhi: Ministry of Human Resource Development.

Govinda, R. (2011). *Who goes to school? Exploring exclusion in Indian education*. New Delhi: Oxford University Press.

Gupta, A. (2008). Judicial interventions and private higher education in India. *In* A. Gupta, D.C. Levy, and K.B. Powar (Eds.), *Private higher education: Global trends and Indian perspectives,* (pp. 239-253). Delhi: Shipra Publications.

Gupta, D. and Gupta, N. (2012). Higher education in India: Structure, statistics and challenges. *Journal of Education and Practice*, *3*(2), 17-24.

Gupta, P. (2011). Status of Higher education India: An appraisal. *University News, 49*(37), 12-18.

Gupta, S.M. *et al.* (2005). Attitude of students towards privatization of higher education, *University News*, *43*(9), February-March, pp. 10-14.

Hatekar, N. (2009). Changing higher education scenario in India, *Economic and Political Weekly*, *44*(38), 22-24.

Helms, R.M. (2008). Transnational education in China: Key challenges, critical issues and strategies for success. London: Observatory on Borderless Higher Education.

Hill, S. and Chalaux, T. (2011). *Improving access and quality in the Indian education system*. OECD Economics departmental Working Papers, No. 885. France: OECD Publisher.

HP-PERC (2011-12). H.P. Private Educational Institutions Regulatory Commission. Shimla: Majitha House Complex.

Jeelani S. (2011). Innovation universities with world class standards. *University News, 49*(46), 1-5.

Jeelani, S. (2011). Faculty shortage in higher educational institutions. *University News, 49*(51), 1-3.

Jha, P. (2005). Withering commitments and weakening progress: State and education in the era of neoliberal reforms, *Economic and Political Weekly*, *40*(33), 3677-3684.

Joseph, T. (2004). Privatization and commercialization: The new paradigm in higher education, *University News*, *42*(7), 42-45.

Joseph, T. (2007). Commission versus commission in higher education. *Economic and Political Weekly*, *42*(50), 20-23.

Kamath, R., Mukherji, A. and Sandstrom, M. (2010). Accessing institutional finance: A demand side story for rural India. *Economic and Political Weekly*, *45*(37), 56-62.

Kapur, D. and Crowley, M. (2008). *Beyond the ABCs: Higher education and developing countries*. Working Paper Number 139. Washington, DC: Centre for Global Development.

Kapur, D. and Mehta, P.B. (2004). *Indian higher education reform: From half-baked socialism to half-baked capitalism*. CID Working Paper No. 108, Centre for International Development, Harvard University.

Kataria, S.K. (2011). Higher education in Rajasthan: Issues and impediments. *University News, 49*(21), 23-29.

Kaul, J.N. (1972). Development of Indian higher education. *Economic and Political Weekly, 7*(31/33), 1645-1652.

Kaul, J.N. (1974). *Higher education in India, 1951–1971: Two decades of planned drift.* Shimla: Indian Institute of Advanced Study.

Kharwar, P.S. (2010). Financing higher education: Problems and prospects, *University News, 48*(44), 14-18.

Kothari, C.R. (2004). *Research methodology methods and techniques.* New Delhi: New Age International (P) Ltd., Publishers.

Krishnamurthy, S. (2006). On backwardness and fair access to higher education: Result from NSS 55th Round Surveys 1999-2000. *Economic and Political Weekly 41*(50), 5173-82.

Kumar, R. (2004). Privatization of higher education and regulatory mechanism, *University News*, *42*(7), 98-101.

Kumar, S. (2014). Privatization of higher education in India: Hopes and despairs. *Social Change*, *44*(3): 451-458. London: Sage Publications.

Kumar, T. Ravi and Sharma, V. (2003). Downsizing higher education: An emergent crisis. *Economic and Political Weekly*, *38*(7), 603-607.

Kumar, V. (2016). Discrimination on campuses of higher learning. A perspective from below. *Economic and Political Weekly*, *6*(12-15).

Larocque, N. (2008). Comment on Intersectoral interfaces in higher education development: private and public in sync? by Daniel C. Levy. In J.U. Lin, and B. Pleskovic (Eds.), *Annual World Bank conference on development economics regional.* Higher Education and Development (pp. 133-139). Washington, DC.: The World Bank.

Levy, D.C. (2008). Access through private higher education: Global patterns and Indian illustrations, PROPHE Working Paper No. 11. Retrieved from http://www.prophe.org/cache/1018464_PROPHE-WP11.pdf.

Levy, D.C. (2008). Intersectoral Interfaces in higher education development: Private and public in sync? In J.Y. Lin and B. Pleskovic (Eds.), *Annual World Bank conference on development economics regional.* Higher Education and Development (pp. 101-123). Washington DC.: World Bank.

Levy, D.C. (2008). Private-public provision of higher education. In J.U. Lin, and B. Pleskovic (Eds.), *Higher education and development* (pp. 101-133). Washington, DC.: The World Bank.

Levy, Daniel C. (1999). When private higher education does not bring organizational diversity. In Philip G. Altbatch (Eds.), *Private prometheus: Private higher education and development in 21st century*. Boston: Boston College Centre for International Higher Education.

Live mint. (2015). 757 technical education courses shut down in 2015. Retrieved from http://www.livemint.com/.

Lohumi, M. (1996). *Development of tertiary education in Himachal*

Pradesh. Shimla: Highlanders Communications.

Mathews, E. (2010, November). Paucity of data on Indian higher education. *Economic and Political Weekly*, *45*(48), 17-18.

Mehta, H.R. (1929). *A History of the Growth and Development of Western education in the Punjab 1846-1884.* Punjab Government Record Office Monograph No. 5 published by Language Department, Punjab.

MHRD (2012). Consolidated Working group report of the department of higher education for XII Five Year Plan on higher education, technical education and private sector participation including PPP in higher education, 2012-17, New Delhi: Government of India.

Mishra, J.K., Abidi, N. and Sharma, R. (2008). *Indian higher education: Global challenges and local issues*. Working Paper Series. Noida: Jaypee Business School.

Mishra, R.P. (1989). *Research methodology in geography: a handbook.* New Delhi: Concept Publishing Company.

Modi, M. (2010). Higher education in Arunachal Pradesh: A proposition. *University News, 48*(17), 26.

Mohamedbhai, G. (2009). Higher education in Africa: Facing the challenges in the 21st century. *New frontiers in Education International Journal of Education*, *44*(2), 135-137.

Mohan, L. (2015, April 4). Government colleges in rural areas fail to draw students. *Tribune News Service*, Dharamshala. Retrieved from http://www.tribuneindia.com/news/himachal/community/govt-colleges-in-rural-areas-fail-to-draw-students/62933.html.

Moon, U. (2012).Women participation in higher education of India: The enrolment scenario. *International Journal of Education Economics and Development, 3*(1), 79-96.

Mukherjee, A.N. (2007). Public expenditure on education: A review of selected issues and evidence. Financing Human Development Working Paper 1, 2007. Retrieved from http://www.nipfp.org.in/media/medialibrary/2013/04/wp_2007_hd_51.pdf.

Muzammil, M. (2012). Governance and funding of higher education in England: Lesson for India. *University News*, *50*(6), 7-13.

Naik, J.P.G. (1975). *Equality, quality and quantity: the elusive triangle in Indian education.* New Delhi: Allied Publishers.

Nayak, D. (2014). Understanding the logic of neo-liberalism in education. *Economic and Political Weekly*, *49*(10), 10-13, March 29.

Nayyar, D. (2007). Globalization: What does it mean for higher education. *Economic and Political Weekly, 42*(50), 30-35.

Neema, S. (2012). *A case against public private partnerships in higher education in India*. Summer Research Internship Programme 2012. Centre for Civil Society.

NKC (National Knowledge Commission) (2006). *Report to the Nation 2006*. New Delhi: Government of India.

NSSO (2001). Employment and unemployment among social groups in India, 1999-2000. NSSO (55th Round) Report No. 469. MHRD, GOI.

OECD (Organisation for Economic Co-operation and Development) (1996). *The knowledge based economy*. Paris: OECD.

OECD (Organisation for Economic Co-operation and Development) (2004). *Education at a glance: OECD Indicators*. Paris: OECD.

OECD (Organisation for Economic Co-operation and Development) (2011). *Education at a glance 2011: OECD Indicators*. Paris: OECD.

Otieno, W. (2007). Private provision and its changing interface with public higher education: The Case of Kenya. *JHEA, 5*(2 and 3), 173-196.

Palshikar, S. (2010). Quality in higher education: Complex issues, superficial solutions. *Economic and Political Weekly*, *45*(20), 29-32.

Panda, H. (2012). Institutional changes in higher education and research in India. *Vision, 32*(1), 91-95.

Parekh, V. (2010). Towards an educated India: Improving gross enrolment ratio in higher education. New Delhi: *The Free Press Journal*.

Parhar, M. (2002). Access to higher education, *University News*, *40*(45), 5-9.

Parikh, G.D. (1967). Higher education in India. *Higher Education and Economic Development: Some Aspects of the Indian Scene*, pp. 11-24.

Parikh, P.P. and Sukhatme, S.P. (2004). Women engineers in India. *Economic and Political Weekly, 39*(2), 193-201.

Parmar, H.S. (1992). *Tribal development in Himachal Pradesh*. New Delhi: Mittal Publications.

Patel, P.J. (2003). Universities in western India: Problems and prospects. *Economic and Political Weekly*, *38*(46), 4841-4845.

Patel, S. (2004). Higher education at the crossroads. *Economic and Political Weekly*, *39*(21), 2151-2154.

Paul, S. (2009). Internationalisation of higher education: Strategic implications. *Economic and Political Weekly*, *44*(9), 36-41.

Peet, R. and Thrift, N. (1989). *New models in geography*. London: Academic Division of Unwin Hyman Ltd.

Planning Commission (2002). *Himachal Pradesh Development Report*. New Delhi: Government of India.

Planning Commission (2003). *Eighth Five Year Plan (2002-07)*. Volume 2, New Delhi: Government of India. Retrieved from http://

planningcommission.nic.in/plans/planrel/fiveyr/8th/vol2/8v2ch17.htm.

Planning Commission (2003). *Tenth Five Year Plan (2002-07).* New Delhi: Government of India.

Planning Department (2003). *An Overview of Planning.* Shimla: Himachal Pradesh Government.

Planning Department (2007). *Approach paper Eleventh Five Year Plan (2007-12) Himachal Pradesh.* Shimla: Government of Himachal Pradesh.

Planning Commission (2007). *Draft report of working group on higher education 11th Five Year Plan (2007-12)*, New Delhi: Government of India.

Planning Commission (2008). *Eleventh Five Year Plan (2007-12).* New Delhi: Government of India.

Planning Commission. (2011). *Faster, sustainable and more inclusive growth: An approach to the Twelfth Five Year Plan.* New Delhi: Planning Commission.

Planning Department. (2013*). Report of the committee to study development in hill states arising from management of forest lands with special focus on creation of infrastructure, livelihood and human development.* New Delhi: Government of India, p. 15.

Powar, K.B. (2002). WTO, GATS and higher education: An Indian Perspective, *University News, 40*(23), 5-13.

Powar, K.B. and Johar, K.L. (2004). Private higher education: An overview. In K.B. Powar and K.L. Johar (Eds.), *Private initiatives in higher education* (pp. 11-19). Haryana: Sneh Prakashan.

Prakash, V. (2007). Trends in growth and financing of higher education in India. *Economic and Political Weekly, 42*(31), 3249-3258.

Puri, K. (2015). *Policy discourse on higher education in India.* Chandigarh: Unistar Books Pvt. Ltd., p. 84.

Ramachandran, C.M. (1987). *Problems of higher education in India.* New Delhi: Mittal Publications.

Rana, K., Santra S., Mukherjee, A., Banerjee, T. and Kundu, M. (2005). Public-private interface in primary education: A case study in West Bengal. *Economic and Political Weekly, 40*(15), 1550-1555.

Rani, P.G. (2002). *Financing higher education in India in post-reform period: Focus on access and equity.* Occasional paper 31. New Delhi: NIEPA.

Rani, P.G. (2004). Economic reforms and financing higher education in India. *Indian Journal of Economics and Business, 3*, 79-102.

Rani, P.G. (2010). *Changing landscape of higher education in India: The case of engineering education in Tamil Nadu*. New Delhi: NIEPA.

Rao, S.K. and Singh, M. (2002). Self-financed courses in the universities and college. *University News*, *40*(43), 1-7.

Ravi, S. (2015) Impact of privatisation of education in Indian society. *Journal of Culture, Society and Development*, *6*(22-26).

Raza, M., Ahmad, A. and Nuna, S.C. (1990). *School education in India*. New Delhi: National Institute of Educational Planning and Administration.

Remesh, B.P. (2012). *Migration from North-East to urban centres: A study of Delhi region*. Noida: V.V. Giri National Labour Institute.

Rezende, M. (2010). The effects of accountability on higher education. *Economics of Education Review*, *29*, 842-856.

Roy, A., Kamaiah, B., and Rao, M.G. (2000). Educational expenditure of large states: A normative view. *Economic and Political Weekly*, *35*(17), 1465-1469.

Rudolph and Rudolph (1972). *Education and politics in India*. Delhi: Oxford University Press.

RUSA (2013). Rashtriya Uchchatar Shiksha Abhiyan. National higher education mission. MHRD. In association with the Tata Institute of Social Sciences, p. 2.

Saleem, S. (2003). Privatization of higher education. *University News*, *41*(28), 5-7.

Schukoske, J.E. (2004). Private higher education: a perspective from the United States. In K.B. Powar and Johar (Eds.), *Private initiatives in higher education* (pp. 69-75). Haryana: Sneh Prakashan.

Shafiqullah, S. (2011). Regional analysis of urban-rural differentials in literacy in Uttar Pradesh, India. *Journal of Geography and Regional Planning*, *4*(5), 287-296.

Shanghai Jiao Tong University Institute of Higher Education (SJTUIHE) (2008). Academic ranking of world universities, http://ed.sjtu.edu.cn/ranking.htm.

Sharma, H.N. (2004). Geographic perspectives on literacy and educational levels in North-East India. In Neelam Grover and K.N. Singh (Eds.), *Cultural geography forms and process* (pp. 374-391). New Delhi: Concept Publishing Company.

Sharma, K.K. and Sharma, J. (2012). Socio-economic transformation in India through higher education. *The Indian College Fōrum Journal*, *13*(1) Jan-March, 3-5.

Sharma, L.R. (1987). *The Economy of Himachal Pradesh: Growth and*

Structure (A Study in Development Performance. Delhi: Mittal Publications.

Shetty, P.K. *et al.* (2010). Research and higher education scenario in select Indian state universities: An analysis. *Indian Journal of Science and Technology*, *3*(3), 355-361.

Shukla, S. (2009, July 15). Gujarat scores low in higher education. *The Indian Express*, retrieved fromhttp://archive.indianexpress.com/news/gujarat-scores-low-in-higher education/489326/.

Shukla, S. (2009, July 15). Gujarat scores low in higher education. *The Indian Express*.Retrieved from http://indianexpress.com/article/cities/ahmedabad/gujarat-scores-low-in-higher-education/.

Singh, A. (1999). Educational imbalance in India transition from school to college. *Economic and Political Weekly*, *34*(26), 1675-1679.

Singh, M.G. (1994). *Himachal Pradesh: History, Culture and Economy*. Shimla: Minerva Book House.

Singh, R. (2005). Privatization of higher education in the era of globalization. *University News, 43*(34), August 22-28.

Singh, R.L. (1971). *India: A regional geography*. Varanasi: National Geographical Society of India, pp. 395-97.

Singh, T.C. (2002). Development of higher education in Manipur in post-independence era up to 2000 (Doctoral dissertation, Panjab University Chandigarh, Education Department, 2002).

Singh, V.V. (2008). *Regulatory management and reform in India*. Background Paper for OECD, p. 4. https://www.oecd.org/gov/regulatory-policy/44925979.pdf

Sinha, S. (2008). Identification of educationally backward districts. In UGC Report (Eds.), *Higher education in India – issues related to expansion, inclusiveness, quality and finance*, New Delhi: University Grants Commission.

Sundaram, K. (2006). On backwardness and fair access to higher education. *Economic and Political Weekly*, *41*(50), 5173-5182.

Swaminathan, P. (1992). Technical education and industrial development in Madras Presidency: illusions of a policy in the making. *Economic and Political Weekly*, July 25: 1611-1622.

Tavakol, M. (2007). *Higher education for development: special reference to the case of Iran*. Iran: Tehran University.

Teferra, D. and Altbach, P.G. (2004). African higher education: Challenges for the 21st Century. *Higher Education, 47*(1), 21-50.

Thakur, R.S. (1993). Development of education in Himachal Pradesh in the post-independence era up to 1991: policies, planning and implementation (Doctoral dissertation, Panjab University, 1993).

Tharakan, P.K.M. (1984). Socio-economic factors in educational development case of nineteenth century Travancore. *Economic and Political Weekly*, *19*(45), 1913-1928.

Thorat, S. (2008). Emerging issues in higher education approach and strategy of 11th Plan. In UGC Report (Eds.), *Higher Education in India – Issues Related to Expansion, Inclusiveness, Quality and Finance*, New Delhi: University Grants Commission.

Tilak, J.B.G. and Varghese, N.V. (1991). Financing higher education in India. *Higher Education*, *21*(1) 83-101.

Tilak, J.B.G. (1991). Privatization of Higher Education. *Prospects: Quarterly Review of Education* (UNESCO) *21*(2), 227-39.

Tilak, J.B.G. (1992). Student loans in financing higher education in India. *Higher Education, 23*(4), 389-404.

Tilak, J.B.G. (1993). Subsidies in higher education. *Economic and Political Weekly, 28*(24), June 12, 1259-60.

Tilak, J.B.G. (1999). Emerging trends and evolving public policies on privatization of higher education in India. In P.G. Altbach (Eds.), *Private prometheus: Private higher education and development in the 21st century,* (pp. 113-35). Westport: Greenwood Publishing.

Tilak, J.B.G. (2001). *Higher education and development in Kerala.* Working Paper No. 5, Kerala: Centre for Socio-economic and Environmental Studies.

Tilak, J.B.G. (2004). Absence of policy and perspective in higher education. (May 22) *Economic and Political Weekly*, *39*(21), 2159-64.

Tilak, J.B.G. (2004). Public subsidies in education in India. *Economic and Political Weekly*, *39*(4) (24-30), 343-59.

Tilak, J.B.G. (2005). Are we marching towards laissez-faireism in higher education development? National Institute of Educational Planning and Administration, India CICE Hiroshima University, *Journal of International Cooperation in Education*, *8*(1), 153-165.

Tilak, J.B.G. (2005). Students loans in financing higher education in India. *Higher Education*, *23*(4), 389-404.

Tilak, J.B.G. (2007). Knowledge Commission and Higher Education, *Economic and Political Weekly, 42*(8), 630-33.

Tilak, J.B.G. (2009). Private sector in higher education: A few stylized facts. *Social Change, 39*(1), 1-28.

Tilak, J.B.G. (2013). *Higher education in India in search of equality, quality and quantity*. New Delhi: Orient Black Swan Private Limited.

Tilak, J.B.G. (2014). Private higher education in India. *Economic and Political Weekly*, *49*(40), 32-38.

Tilak, J.B.G. (2016). *Public private partnership in education*. The Discussion Paper Series No. 3/2016. New Delhi: NUEPA.

Tiwari, A.K. (2000). *Infrastructure and economic development in Himachal Prdaesh.* New Delhi: Indus Publishing Company.

Tiwari, A.K. (2007). *Spatial dimension of socio-economic development: A Case Study of Himachal Pradesh.* New Delhi: Kanishka.

Trow, M.A. (2005). *Reflections on the transition from elite to mass to universal access: Forms and phases of higher education in modern societies since WWII.* Institute of Governmental Studies University of California, Berkeley: Institute of Governmental Studies. Retrieved from: http://escholarship.org/uc/item/96p3s213.

UGC. (1978). *Third all India educational survey: Higher education 1973-74*. New Delhi: Government of India.

UGC. (1993). *UGC funding of institutions of higher education*, Report of Justice Dr K. Punnayya Committee, 1992-93, University Grants Commission, New Delhi.

UGC. (2003). *Higher education in India: issues, concerns and new directions*. New Delhi: University Grants Commission.

UGC. (2007). Annual Report 2006-07. New Delhi: University Grants Commission.

UGC. (2008). Higher education in India: Issues related to expansion, inclusiveness, quality and finance. New Delhi: Government of India.

UGC. (2011). Higher education in India: Strategies and schemes during Eleventh Plan period (2007-12) for universities and colleges. New Delhi: Government of India.

UGC (2011). *Inclusive and qualitative expansion of higher education Twelfth Five-Year Plan*, 2012-17, University Grants Commission, New Delhi, p. 39.

UGC (2012). *Higher education in India,* New Delhi: University Grants Commission.

UGC (2016). *Annual Report 2015-16*. New Delhi: University Grants Commission.

UNESCO (1998). *Higher education in the twenty-first century vision and action*. World Conference on Higher Education, UNESCO, Paris 5–9 October, 1998.

UNESCO (1998). *World conference on higher education. Higher education in the twenty-first century vision and action*. Volume I. Paris: UNESCO, p. 58.

UNESCO (2011). Institute of Statistics database. Retrieved from http://uis.unesco.org/.

Upadhyay, S. (2007). Wastage in Indian higher education. *Economic and Political Weekly*, *42*(2), 161-168.

Varghese, N.V. (2013). Private higher education: The global surge and Indian concerns, *India Infrastructure Report 2012, Private sector in education*, London and New Delhi: Routledge Taylor and Francis Group (IDFC), pp. 145-156.

Varghese, N.V. (2014). *Massification of higher education in large system countries*. New Delhi: The Centre for Policy Research in Higher Education National University of Educational Planning and Administration, New Delhi and The British Council.

Varghese, N.V. (2015). *Challenges of massification of higher education in India*. Centre for Policy Research in Higher Education. New Delhi: National University of Educational Planning and Administration.

Wang, L. (2014). *The road to privatization of higher education in China: a new culture revolution?* New York: Springer.

Weisskope, T.M. (2004). Impact of reservation on admissions to higher education in India. *Economic and Political Weekly*, *39*(39), 4339-4348.

Wilkinson, R. and Yussof, I. (2005). Public and private provision of higher education in Malaysia: A Comparative Analysis. *Higher Education*, *50*(3), 361-386.

World Bank. (1986). *Financing education in developing countries: An exploration of policy options*. Washington DC: The World Bank.

World Bank. (1994). *Higher education: The lessons of experience*. Washington, DC.: World Bank.

World Bank. (2000). *Higher education in developing countries: Peril and promise*. Washington DC: The World Bank.

World Bank (2002). *Constructing knowledge societies: New challenges for tertiary education*. Washington, DC: World Bank.

World University Rankings. (2008). *The times higher education*. London, UK. http://www.timeshighereducation.co.uk.

Yogish, S.N. (2006). Education and economic development. *Indian Journal of Social Development*, *6*(2), 255-270.

Annexure-I (a)
General Education Courses

S. No.	*District*	*Tehsil*	*Loc.*	*Colleges*	*Management*	*Est. Year*	*Courses*
1	Mandi	Sundernagar	Urban	Government Sanskrit College, Sundernagar	Govt.	1923	Sanskrit
2	Una	Bangana	Rural	SD Adarsh Sanskrit College, Doghi	Govt.	1928	Sanskrit
3	Una	Una	Urban	SGSD Sanskrit College, Santokhgarh	Unaided	1928	Sanskrit
4	Solan	Solan	Urban	Govt. Skt. College, Solan	Govt.	1929	Sanskrit
5	Bilaspur	Bilaspur	Urban	Shri Shakti Sanskrit Degree College, Sri Naina Devi Ji	Unaided	1931	Sanskrit
6	Shimla	Theog	Rural	Govt. Skt College, Kiartoo	Govt.	1965	Sanskrit
7	Sirmaur	Nahan	Urban	Govt. Skt College, Nahan	Govt.	1965	Sanskrit
8	Shimla	Shimla	Urban	Nehru Govt. Skt College, Phagli	Govt.	1969	Sanskrit
9	Shimla	Chopal	Rural	Brijeshwari Sanskrit College Saranh, Chaupal	Unaided	1970	Sanskrit
10	Kangra	Nurpur	Rural	GC, Dehri	Govt.	1970	Arts, Sci., Comm. (UG)
11	Shimla	Theog	Rural	Shri Vashistha Vidyapeeth, Tungesh. PO Cheog	Aided	1971	Sanskrit
12	Kangra	Kangra	Rural	Trigart Sanskrit Mahavidyalaya, Shri Nandikeshwari Mandir	Aided	1972	Sanskrit
13	Kullu	Kullu	Rural	Shri Lal Devi Annapurna, Sanskrit College, Ramshila Lakkar Bazar	Unaided	1973	Sanskrit

(*Contd.*)

Annexure-I (a)
General Education Courses

(*Contd.*)

S. No.	District	Tehsil	Loc.	Colleges	Management	Est. Year	Courses
14	Shimla	Rohru	Rural	Himachal Adarsh Sanskrit College, Jangla	Unaided	1974	Sanskrit
15	Hamirpur	Barsar	Rural	Shri Vishwa Nath Sanskrit College, Chakmoh, Tehsil Barsar	Unaided	1975	Sanskrit
16	Solan	Solan	Rural	GGDSD College, Subathu	Unaided	1979	Arts and Commerce
17	Bilaspur	Ghumarwin	Rural	Shri Saraswati Sanskrit Degree College, Dangar	Unaided	1982	Sanskrit
18	Bilaspur	Bilaspur Sadar	Rural	Shri Ramanuj Sanskrit Mahavidyalaya, Panjgain	Local body	1985	Sanskrit
19	Shimla	Kotkhai	Rural	DAV Centenary College	Aided	1985	Arts and Commerce
20	Una	Amb	Rural	Swami Vivekanand College, Chintpurni	Unaided	1988	Arts and Commerce
21	Kangra	Thural	Rural	GC, Thural	Govt.	1988	Arts, Sci., Comm. (UG)
22	Chamba	Chamba	Urban	Sanatan Dharam Sanskrit College Near Degree College	Unaided	1989	Sanskrit
23	Kangra	Dehra	Rural	GC, Haripur	Govt.	1994	Arts and Commerce
24	Mandi	Karsog	Rural	GC, Karsog	Govt.	1994	Arts, Sci. Comm. (UG)
25	Chamba	Bhattiyat	Urban	GC, Chowari	Govt.	1994	Arts, Sci., Comm. (UG)
26	Mandi	Mandi	Rural	Guru Rimpoohe Padam Sembhav Degree College, Rewalsar	Unaided	1995	Arts and Commerce

(*Contd.*)

Annexure-I (a)

General Education Courses

(*Contd.*)

S. No.	*District*	*Tehsil*	*Loc.*	*Colleges*	*Management*	*Est. Year*	*Courses*
27	Kangra	Jaisinghpur	Rural	Swami V.G. Mahvidyalaya, P.O. Shivnagar	Unaided	1995	Arts and Commerce
28	Lahul and Spiti	Udaipur	Rural	GC, Kukumseri	Govt.	1995	Arts and Commerce
29	Kangra	Indora	Rural	GC, Indora	Govt.	1995	Arts, Sci., Comm. (UG)
30	Kangra	Baroh	Rural	Pt. Anant Ram S.D. College, Baroh	Unaided	1995	Arts, Sci., Comm. (UG)
31	Kangra	Baroh	Rural	GDC, Baroh	Govt.	1995	Arts (UG)
32	Kullu	Kullu	Urban	Shri Vyas Sanskrit College, Raghunathpur	Govt.	1995	Sanskrit
33	Una	Haroli	Rural	GC, Beetan	Govt.	1997	Arts and Commerce
34	Kullu	Banjar	Rural	GC, Banjar	Govt.	1999	Arts and Commerce
35	Kangra	Jawalamukhi	Rural	Jawalaji Degree College	Local body	1999	Arts, Sci., Comm. (UG)
36	Mandi	Mandi	Rural	GC, Bassa	Govt.	1999	Arts, Sci., Comm. (UG)
37	Bilaspur	Naina Devi Ji	Rural	Ruldu Ram Garg S.D. College	Unaided	2000	Arts and Commerce
38	Hamirpur	Bhoranj	Rural	Maharani Laxmi Bai Kanya Mahavidyalaya, Bhareri (Women college)	Unaided	2001	Arts (UG)
39	Kangra	Indora	Rural	FD Public Degree College, Mand Miani	Unaided	2002	Arts (UG)
40	Kangra	Nurpur	Urban	GC, Nurpur	Govt.	2002	Arts (UG)
41	Sirmour	Pachhad	Rural	Bhureshwar Mahadev Sanskrit Mahavidyalaya, Kawagdhar, P.O. Panwa	Local body	2002	Sanskrit

(*Contd.*)

Annexure-I (a)
General Education Courses

(*Contd.*)

S. No.	*District*	*Tehsil*	*Loc.*	*Colleges*	*Management*	*Est. Year*	*Courses*
42	Hamirpur	Bhoranj	Rural	GC, Bhoranj	Govt.	2002	Arts, Sci., Comm. (UG)
43	Shimla	Chopal	Rural	GC, Nerwa	Govt.	2002	Arts, Sci., Comm. (UG)
44	Kangra	Jaisinghpur	Rural	GC, Jaisinghpur	Govt.	2003	Arts (UG)
45	Solan	Nalagarh	Urban	Shri Sunaina Sanskrit Mahavidyalaya, Swarghat	Unaided	2003	Sanskrit
46	Una	Una	Rural	Lala Jagat Narayan Himotkarsh Kanya Mahavidyalaya, Kotla Khurd (WC)	Unaided	2004	Arts (UG)
47	Chamba	Bharmour	Rural	GC, Bharmour	Govt.	2005	Arts (UG)
48	Sirmaur	Pachhad	Rural	GC, Rajgarh	Govt.	2005	Arts (UG)
49	Chamba	Salooni	Rural	GC, Salooni	Govt.	2006	Arts (UG)
50	Chamba	Churah	Rural	GC, Tissa	Govt.	2006	Arts (UG)
51	Kangra	Shahpur	Rural	GC, Shahpur	Govt.	2006	Arts (UG)
52	Kangra	Nagrota	Rural	GC, Nagrota Bagwan	Govt.	2006	Arts (UG)
53	Kullu	Manali	Rural	GC, Haripur	Govt.	2006	Arts (UG)
54	Kullu	Anni	Rural	GC, Anni at Haripur	Govt.	2006	Arts (UG)
55	Mandi	Padhar	Rural	GC, Drang at Narla	Govt.	2006	Arts (UG)
56	Shimla	Sunni	Rural	GC, Sunni	Govt.	2006	Arts (UG)

(*Contd.*)

Annexure-I (a)

General Education Courses

(*Contd.*)

S. No.	*District*	*Tehsil*	*Loc.*	*Colleges*	*Management*	*Est. Year*	*Courses*
57	Sirmaur	Renuka	Rural	GC, Sangrah	Govt.	2006	Arts (UG)
58	Sirmaur	Shillai	Rural	GC, Shillai	Govt.	2006	Arts (UG)
59	Bilaspur	Gumarwin	Rural	GC, Jhanduta	Govt.	2007	Arts (UG)
60	Bilaspur	Bilaspur	Rural	GC, Jukhala	Govt.	2007	Arts (UG)
61	Chamba	Pangi	Rural	GC, Pangi	Govt.	2007	Arts (UG)
62	Kangra	Sullah	Rural	GC, Naura	Govt.	2007	Arts (UG)
63	Mandi	Dharampur	Rural	GC, Dharampur	Govt.	2007	Arts (UG)
64	Mandi	Thunag	Rural	GC Saraj at Lambathach	Govt.	2007	Arts (UG)
65	Una	Bangana	Rural	GC, Bangana	Govt.	2007	Arts (UG)
66	Sirmaur	Sangrah	Rural	GC, Haripur Dhar	Govt.	2011	Arts (UG)
67	Sirmaur	Nahan	Rural	Bhagwan Parshu Ram College of Arts, Khadal (Dadahu)	Unaided	2011	Arts (UG)
68	Kangra	Jawali	Rural	GDC, Nagroa Surian	Govt.	2014	Arts (UG)
69	Mandi	Lad Barol	Rural	GDC, Lad Barol	Govt.	2014	Arts (UG)
70	Shimla	Nankhari	Rural	GDC, Nankhari	Govt.	2014	Arts (UG)
71	Shimla	Kumarsain	Rural	GC, Kumarsain	Govt.	2014	Arts (UG)
72	Mandi	Mandi	Rural	GDC, Rewalsar	Govt.	2014	Arts (UG)

(*Contd.*)

Annexure-I (a)
General Education Courses

(Contd.)

S. No.	District	Tehsil	Loc.	Colleges	Management	Est. Year	Courses
73	Mandi	Sandhole	Rural	Aryabhatta Govt. Degree College	Govt.	2014	Arts (UG)
74	Kullu	Banjar	Rural	GC, Gadagusain	Govt.	2014	Arts (UG)
75	Kangra	Khudian	Rural	GDC, Khudian	Govt.	2014	Arts (UG)
76	Mandi	Nihri	Rural	GDC, Nihri	Govt.	2014	Arts (UG)
77	Mandi	Ghumarwin	Rural	GDC, Baldwara	Govt.	2014	Arts (UG)
78	Shimla	Junga	Rural	GDC, Chail-Koti	Govt.	2014	Arts (UG)
79	Sirmaur	Sarahan	Rural	GDC, Sarahan	Govt.	2014	Arts (UG)
80	Sirmaur	Paonta Sahib	Rural	GDC, Bharali (Anjbhoj)	Govt.	2014	Arts (UG)
81	Solan	Kunihar	Rural	GDC, Dharampur	Govt.	2014	Arts (UG)
82	Solan	Nalagarh	Rural	GDC, Diggal	Govt.	2014	Arts (UG)
83	Kangra	Kangra	Rural	GDC, Takipur	Govt.	2015	Arts (UG)
84	Kangra	Harchakia	Rural	GC, Lanj, Ranital	Govt.	2015	Arts (UG)
85	Kangra	Dehra	Rural	Baba Kanshi Ram GDC, Dadasiba	Govt.	2015	Arts (UG)
86	Mandi	Aut	Rural	GDC, Panarsa	Govt.	2015	Arts (UG)
87	Solan	Baddi	Rural	GDC, Barotiwala	Govt.	2015	Arts (UG)
88	Shimla	Shimla	Urban	Jawahar Lal Nehru Govt. Degree College of Fine Arts	Govt.	2015	Fine Arts (UG)

(Contd.)

Annexure-I (a)

General Education Courses

(*Contd.*)

S. No.	District	Tehsil	Loc.	Colleges	Management	Est. Year	Courses
89	Kangra	Palampur	Rural	GDC, Shivnagar	Govt.	2015	Arts (UG)
90	Solan	Kandaghat	Rural	GDC, Kandaghat	Govt.	2016	Arts (UG) & Comm.
91	Sirmaur	Shillai	Rural	GDC, Kafota	Govt.	2016	Arts (UG) & Comm.
92	Shimla	Tikkar	Rural	GDC, Tikker	Govt.	2016	Arts (UG) & Comm.
93	Shimla	Shimla	Rural	Govt. College, Dhami at 16 mile	Govt.	2016	Arts (UG) & Comm.
94	Bilaspur	Shri Naina Devi ji	Rural	GDC, Shri Naina Devi Ji	Govt.	2016	Arts (UG) & Comm.
95	Chamba	Sihunta	Rural	GDC, Sihunta	Govt.	2016	Arts (UG) & Comm.
96	Chamba	Chamba	Rural	GDC, Lylh Kothi	Govt.	2016	Arts (UG) & Comm.
97	Una	Bangana	Rural	GDC, Chowki Manyar	Govt.	2016	Arts (UG) & Comm.
98	Una	Una	Rural	GDC, Khad	Govt.	2016	Arts (UG) & Comm.
99	Kangra	Fatehpur	Rural	GDC, Rey	Govt.	2016	Arts (UG) & Comm.
100	Kangra	Rakkar	Rural	GDC, Rakkar	Govt.	2016	Arts (UG) & Comm.
101	Kangra	Jaswan	Rural	GDC, Jandaur	Govt.	2016	Arts (UG)
102	Hamirpur	Nadaun	Rural	GDC, Dhaneta	Govt.	2016	Arts (UG) & Comm.
103	Kullu	Sainj	Rural	GDC, Sainj	Govt.	2016	Arts (UG) & Comm.
104	Kullu	Nirmand	Rural	GDC, Nirmand	Govt.	2016	Arts (UG) & Comm.

(*Contd.*)

Annexure-I (b)

General Cum Technical Courses

S. No.	*District*	*Tehsil*	*Location*	*Colleges*	*Management*	*Est. Year*	*Courses*
1	Kangra	Palampur	Rural	KLB, DAV College for Girls, Palampur, Distt. Kangra	Unaided	1969	Arts, BBA, BCA, B.Ed (2005)
2	Kangra	Kangra	Urban	Mehar Chand Mahajan DAV College	Aided	1976	Arts, Sci, Comm., BCA
3	Shimla	Shimla	Urban	RKMV, Shimla (SDB College) WC	Govt.	1977	Arts, Sci., Comm., BCA
4	Kangra	Palampur	Rural	GGDSD College, Rajpur (Palampur) Distt. Kangra	Unaided	1984	Arts, Science and Commerce, BCA, BBA
5	Shimla	Jubbal	Rural	GC, Sarswati Nagar	Govt.	1986	Arts, Sci., Comm. (UG) and BCA
6	Shimla	Rohru	Rural	GC, Seema	Govt.	1988	Arts, Sci., Comm. (UG), BBA and BCA
7	Hamirpur	Sujanpur Tihra	Rural	GC, Sujanpur Tihra	Govt.	1989	Arts and Comm. (UG), BBA, BCA
8	Chamba	Dalhousie	Rural	B.T.C., DAV College, Banikhet	Unaided	1990	Arts, Sci., Comm, BBA, BCA
9	Kangra	Kangra	Rural	DDMP Degree College, P.O. Mandoli, Sugh Bhatoli, Distt. Kangra	Unaided	1992	Arts, Science and Commerce, B.Ed

(*Contd.*)

Annexure-I (b)

General Cum Technical Courses

(*Contd.*)

S. No.	District	Tehsil	Location	Colleges	Management	Est. Year	Courses
10	Sirmaur	Paonta Sahib	Urban	BKD Degree College for Women, Paonta Sahib	Unaided	1993	Arts and Commerce, B.Ed (1999)
11	Kinnaur	Kinnaur	Rural	GC, Reckong Peo	Govt.	1994	Arts, Sci., Comm. (UG) and B.C.A
12	Mandi	Joginder Nagar	Rural	GC, Joginder Nagar	Govt.	1994	Arts, Sci., Comm. (UG) M.A. Eco.
13	Bilaspur	Ghumarwin	Rural	Swami Vivekanand GC, Ghumarwin	Govt.	1994	Arts, Sci, Comm, (UG), BBA, BCA
14	Sirmaur	Paonta Sahib	Urban	GGS GC, Paonta Sahib	Govt.	1994	Arts, Sci., Comm. (UG) and B.C.A.
15	Solan	Arki	Rural	GC, Arki	Govt.	1994	Arts, Sci., Comm. (UG) and B.C.A.
16	Hamirpur	Nadaun	Rural	GC, Nadaun	Govt.	1995	Arts, Sci., Comm., BBA, BCA
17	Hamirpur	Nadaun	Rural	General Zorawar Singh Samarak Mahavidyalya, Dhaneta	Unaided	1995	Arts, Commerce, BCA
18	Shimla	Theog	Rural	GC, Theog	Govt.	1998	Arts, Sci., Comm., (UG) BCA
19	Hamirpur	Barsar	Urban	Din Dayal Upadhyaya Mahavidyalaya, Mehre, Barsar, Distt. Hamipur	Unaided	2003	Arts and Commerce, B.Ed (2007), BBA/BCA (2009)
20	Kangra	Baijnath	Rural	GC, Baijnath	Govt.	2006	Arts, BBA, BCA
21	Hamirpur	Nadaun	Rural	GC, Barsar	Govt.	2007	Arts, Sci. (UG) and BBA, BCA

Annexure-I (c)

Arts/Science/Commerce/Post Graduate/Technical Education (BBA/BCA/B.Ed)

S. No.	District	Tehsil	Location	Colleges	Management	Est. Year	Courses (UG & PG)
1	Chamba	Chamba	Rural	GC, Chamba	Govt.	1958	Arts, Sci., Comm, (UG), BBA, BCA, M.A. in Eco., English and History
2	Shimla	Rampur	Rural	GC, Rampur	Govt.	1959	Arts, Sci., Comm., (UG), M.A. in Eng., Political Sci., History, Hindi, M.Com (PG) and BCA
3	Solan	Solan	Urban	GC, Solan	Govt.	1959	Arts, Sci., Comm., (UG), M.A. in Eng., Eco. and BCA, BBA
4	Sirmaur	Nahan	Urban	GC, Nahan	Govt.	1963	Arts, Sci., Comm., (UG), M.A. in Eng., Political Sci., Eco., and BCA
5	Hamirpur	Hamirpur	Urban	GC, Hamirpur	Govt.	1965	Arts, Science, Comm., BCA Hon's, MA in Eng, Eco, Hindi and M.Com (PG)
6	Kullu	Kullu	Urban	GC, Kullu	Govt.	1967	Arts, Science, Comm., Tourism Management (UG), BCA, BBA, M.A. Eng. and Eco.
7	Una	Una	Urban	GC, Una	Govt.	1968	Arts, Sci., Comm., (UG), M.A in Eng., Political Sci., Eco., M.Com (PG) and BCA, BBA
8	Shimla	Shimla	Urban	GC, Sanjauli	Govt.	1969	Arts, Sci., Comm., BCA (UG) Eco. Geography, Physics, Chemistry, Zoo. Maths, History, Political Sci. and English Hon's course. (UG)
9	Una	Amb	Rural	GC, Amb	Govt.	1970	Arts, Sci. Comm. (U.G), M.A. English and Economics (PG), B.C.A. and B.B.A.

(*Contd.*)

Annexure-I (c)

Arts/Science/Commerce/Post Graduate/Technical Education (BBA/BCA/B.Ed)

(Contd.)

S. No.	District	Tehsil	Location	Colleges	Management	Est. Year	Courses (UG & PG)
10	Una	Una	Rural	SVSD College, Bhatoli, PO, Ajoli	Aided	1970	Arts, Science, Commerce, BBA, BCA, MA/ M.Sc. Maths, M.Com.
11	Una	Amb	Urban	GC, Daulatpur Chowk	Govt.	1972	Arts, Sci., Comm., (UG), MA in Eco, BCA, BBA
12	Kangra	Dehra	Rural	GC, Dhaliara	Govt.	1973	Arts, Sci., Comm (UG), BBA, BCA, MA Hindi, English
13	Solan	Nalagarh	Urban	GC, Nalagarh	Govt.	1973	Arts, Sci., Comm., (UG), MA in Eco., Political Sci., Eng., BCA
14	Mandi	Sundernagar	Urban	M.L.S.M. College	Aided	1976	Arts, Sci. Comm, MA, MSc, M.Com, BBA, BCA, BPE, B.Ed (1998), BP.Ed (2007)
15	Hamirpur	Hamirpur	Rural	BBN College	Unaided	1984	Arts, Science and Commerce, M.A. Hindi/ Sanskrit
16	Mandi	Sarkaghat	Rural	GC, Sarkaghat	Govt.	1985	Arts, Sci., Comm., (UG), MA in Eco., Political Sci., History, BCA and BBA
17	Kangra	Dharamshala	Rural	HPU Regional Centre	Govt.	1992	Graduate Course, LLB 3 Year (1999)
18	Kangra	Palampur	Rural	GC, Palampur	Govt.	1995	Arts, Sci., Comm., (UG), BP.Ed. BBA, BCA

Annexure-II (a)

Technical Education

S. No.	*District*	*Tehsil*	*Location*	*Colleges*	*Management*	*Est. Yr*	*Courses*
1	Bilaspur	Ghumarwin	Urban	Shiva College of Education, Abdhanighat (Panol), Near D.A.V. School, Ghumarwin	Unaided	2007	B.Ed
2	Bilaspur	Bilaspur	Rural	Gurukul Bharti College of Education, Vill. Benla Brahmna, PO Chandpur	Unaided	2011	B.Ed
3	Chamba	Chamba	Rural	Chamba Millenium Education College, Sarswati Nagar, Mugla P.O. Hardaspura	Aided	2007	B.Ed
4	Chamba	Bhattiyat	Rural	Priyadarshini College of Education, Vill. Kudnu Chowari	Unaided	2009	B.Ed
5	Hamirpur	Hamirpur	Rural	Nalanda College of Education, VPO Jhaniari, Hamirpur	Unaided	2000	B.Ed
6	Hamirpur	Hamirpur	Urban	Shanti Niketan College of Education, Hira Nagar	Unaided	2003	B.Ed
7	Hamirpur	Hamirpur	Urban	Hamirpur College of Education, Ram Nagar, Chaulla, Ramnagar	Unaided	2003	B.Ed
8	Hamirpur	Nadaun	Rural	Shri Satya Sai College of Education, Nadaun, Vill. Kohla	Unaided	2006	B.Ed
9	Hamirpur	Barsar	Rural	Raj Rajeshwari College of Education, Village Chorab (Mansui), P.O. Bhota	Unaided	2006	B.Ed
10	Hamirpur	Nadaun	Rural	Vijay Vallabh College of Education, V.P.O. Vela	Unaided	2007	B.Ed

(*Contd.*)

Annexure-II (a)
Technical Education

(*Contd.*)

S. No.	*District*	*Tehsil*	*Location*	*Colleges*	*Management*	*Est. Yr*	*Courses*
11	Kangra	Dharamshala	Urban	GCTE, Dharamshala	Govt.	1956	B.Ed
12	Kangra	Nurpur	Rural	Janak Raj Mahajan B.Ed. College, Gangath, Distt. Kangra	Unaided	2002	B.Ed
13	Kangra	Dehra	Rural	R.C. College of Education, Dhanot, Dehra Distt. Kangra	Unaided	2003	B.Ed
14	Kangra	Shahpur	Rural	Gian Jyoti Institute for Teachers Education Ichhi (Gaggal)	Unaided	2003	B.Ed
15	Kangra	Kangra	Rural	Sharan College VPO Ghurkari WC	Unaided	2004	B.Ed
16	Kangra	Jawali	Rural	Kanta College of Education, Chalwara, Tehsil Jawali	Unaided	2007	B.Ed
17	Kangra	Dehra	Rural	Thakur College of Education, Dhaliara, Tehsil Dehra	Unaided	2006	B.Ed
18	Kangra	Nurpur	Rural	A-One College of Education, Nerna Raja ka Bag, Teh. Nurpur	Unaided	2008	B.Ed
19	Kangra	Indora	Rural	Minerva College of Education, Village Changrara	Unaided	2008	B.Ed
20	Kangra	Dharamshala	Rural	Awasthi Memorial College of Education, Shamnagar	Unaided	2009	B.Ed
21	Kinnaur	Nichar	Rural	Him Institute of Education, Ponda, Tehsil Nichar	Unaided	2006	B.Ed

(*Contd.*)

Annexure-II (a)
Technical Education

(Contd.)

S. No.	*District*	*Tehsil*	*Location*	*Colleges*	*Management*	*Est. Yr*	*Courses*
22	Kullu	Kullu	Rural	Kullu College of Education, Vill. Bohgana, P.O. Garse	Unaided	2001	B.Ed
23	Mandi	Sundarnagar	Rural	Blooms College of Education, Kot, P.O. Chunahan	Unaided	2003	B.Ed
24	Mandi	Mandi	Rural	Jagriti Teacher Training College, Vill. Daodhar, Talyahar, Mandi	Unaided	2004	B.Ed
25	Mandi	Sundernagar	Rural	Himalyan College of Education, Poongh, Sundernagar	Unaided	2006	B.Ed
26	Mandi	Sundernagar	Rural	Gayatri College of Education, P.O. Kangoo, Tehsil Sundernagar, Mandi	Unaided	2006	B.Ed
27	Mandi	Karsog	Rural	Bhardwaj Shikshan Sansthan, V.P.O. Baral	Unaided	2006	B.Ed
28	Mandi	Sundernagar	Rural	Adarsh Public Educational College, Dehar Teh. Sunder Nagar, Distt. Mandi	Unaided	2007	B.Ed
29	Mandi	Sundernagar	Urban	Namdhari College of Education, V.P.O. Bhojpur, Sunder Nagar	Unaided	2007	B.Ed
30	Mandi	Sundernagar	Rural	Lord Buddha College of Education, Purana Bazar, Sunder Nagar, Distt. Mandi	Unaided	2007	B.Ed
31	Mandi	Mandi	Rural	Minerva Education Society, Baggi	Unaided	2007	B.Ed
32	Mandi	Mandi	Rural	Laljee College of Education, NH 21, Gutkar	Unaided	2007	B.Ed

(Contd.)

Annexure-II (a)
Technical Education

(*Contd.*)

S. No.	District	Tehsil	Location	Colleges	Management	Est. Yr	Courses
33	Mandi	Jogindernagar	Rural	Neelam College of Education, Village Jimjima, Manja, PO. Dul	Unaided	2010	B.Ed
34	Shimla	Shimla	Rural	Shanti Alya Institute of Education and Training, Vill. Rampur, Keonthal Distt. Shimla (Women College)	Unaided	2004	B.Ed
35	Shimla	Shimla	Urban	Laureate Institute of Education and Training Brance-peth Bharari	Unaided	2005	B.Ed
36	Shimla	Rampur Bushahr	Rural	Bushahr Institute of Education, Nogli, Teh. Rampur, Distt. Shimla	Unaided	2006	B.Ed
37	Shimla	Shimla	Rural	H.P. College of Education, Mauja Majeth, Totu (Shimla)	Unaided	2007	B.Ed
38	Shimla	Shimla	Urban	Modern Education College near Anand Marg School, Anandale	Unaided	2007	B.Ed
39	Shimla	Shimla	Urban	Shimla College of Education, Sheetal Kunj Estate Branch, PO Kamlanagar, Sanjauli	Unaided	2007	B.Ed
40	Sirmaur	Sirmaur	Rural	Himachal Pradesh College of Education, Kala Amb	Unaided	2003	B.Ed
41	Sirmaur	Rajgarh	Urban	Shiv Shakti College of Advanced Study in Education, Kheri Road, Rajgarh	Unaided	2006	B.Ed
42	Sirmaur	Paonta Sahib	Rural	Doon International College of Education, Rajban, Paonta Sahib	Unaided	2007	B.Ed

(*Contd.*)

Annexure-II (a)
Technical Education

(*Contd.*)

S. No.	*District*	*Tehsil*	*Location*	*Colleges*	*Management*	*Est. Yr*	*Courses*
43	Solan	Solan	Urban	SCERT	Govt.	1954	B.Ed
44	Solan	Nalagarh	Rural	Himachal College of Education Nalagarh at Kishanpura	Unaided	1999	B.Ed
45	Solan	Solan	Rural	Himachal Institute of Education, Bye Pass Road, Near Petrol Pump, Amar Building, Solan	Unaided	1999	B.Ed
46	Solan	Arki	Rural	Lakshay Institute of Education, Arki	Unaided	2008	B.Ed
47	Una	Una	Urban	DAV College, Daulatpur Chowk	Unaided	2003	B.Ed
48	Una	Amb	Rural	Jupitor College of Education	Unaided	2008	B.Ed
49	Mandi	Mandi	Rural	Krishma Educational Centre, Ner Chowk, Distt. Mandi	Unaided	2003	B.Ed, M.Ed (2006)
50	Shimla	Rampur Bushahr,	Rural	Servopalli Radhakrishnan Institute for Teachers Education, Nogli Near Rampur, Bushahr	Unaided	2006	B.Ed, M.Ed (2007)
51	Solan	Kasauli	Rural	Vaid Shanker Lal Memorial College of Education V.P.O. Chandi, Teh. Kasauli	Unaided	2006	B.Ed, M.Ed (2008)
52	Una	Amb	Rural	Shanti College of Education, Nakroh, Teh. Amb	Unaided	2007	B.Ed, M.Ed (2011)
53	Kangra	Nurpur	Rural	Tara College of Education	Unaided	2015	B.Ed
54	Mandi	Mandi Sadar	Rural	Sacred Heart Education Society, Gutkar	Unaided	2007	B.Ed
55	Shimla	Shimla	Rural	Sai Saraswati Institute for Teacher Education, Sangati	Unaided	2012	B.Ed

(*Contd.*)

Annexure-II (b)

Pharmacy/Engineering/MBA/MCA/BBA/BCA)

S. No.	*District*	*Tehsil*	*Loc.*	*Colleges*	*Management*	*Est. Year*	*Courses*
1	Shimla	Kotkhai	Rural	Atal Bihari Vajpayee Government Institute of Engineering and Technology, Pragatinagar	Govt.	2011	Computer Science and Engineering, Electronics and Communication Engineering
2	Hamirpur	Barsar	Rural	SRET College of Engineering and Technology, Vill. Bulha-tipper, Hamirpur	Unaided	2009	Electronic and Communication Eng., Computer Sci. Eng., Mechanical Engineering, Civil Eng., Pharmacy (2009)
3	Mandi	Sundernagar	Rural	SIRDA Institute of Engineering and Emerging Technologies for Women, Naulakha Troat, Sundernagar	Unaided	2009	Electronic and Communication Eng., Computer Sci. Eng., Mechanical Engineering, Civil Eng.
4	Bilaspur	Bilaspur	Rural	Shiva Institute of Engineering and Technology, Chandpur	Unaided	2009	Electronic and Communication Eng., Computer Sci. Eng., Mechanical Engineering, Civil Eng., Electrical and Electronic Eng., B. Pharmacy
5	Kangra	Shahpur	Rural	Himachal Institute of Engineering and Technology	Unaided	2010	Electronic and Communication Eng., Computer Sci. Eng., Mechanical Engineering, Civil Eng., Electrical Eng.

(*Contd.*)

Annexure-II (b)
Pharmacy/Engineering/MBA/MCA/BBA/BCA)

(*Contd.*)

S. No.	*District*	*Tehsil*	*Loc.*	*Colleges*	*Management*	*Est. Year*	*Courses*
6	Hamirpur	Barsar	Rural	MIT College of Engineering and Management, Village Ganoh Rajputana, P.O. Bani	Unaided	2009	Electronic and Communication Eng., Computer Sci. Eng., Mechanical Engineering, Civil Eng., Electrical Engineering, Hotel Management and LLB (2015)
7	Mandi	Chachyot	Rural	MG Institute of Engineering and Technology, Badhoo Village, Tehsil Chachyot	Unaided	2007	Electronic and Communication Eng., Electrical Eng., Computer Sci. Eng., Mechanical Engineering, Information and Technology
8	Mandi	Sundernagar	Rural	JN Government Engineering College, Sundernagar	Govt.	2006	Electronics and Communication Engineering, Civil Engineering, Mechanical Engineering, Textile Engineering
9	Sirmaur	Nahan	Rural	IITT College of Engineering, Kala Amb, Himachal Pradesh	Unaided	1997	Electronic and Communication Eng., Electrical Eng., Computer Sci. Eng., Mechanical Engineering, Information and Technology

(*Contd.*)

Annexure-II (b)

Pharmacy/Engineering/MBA/MCA/BBA/BCA)

(*Contd.*)

S. No.	District	Tehsil	Loc.	Colleges	Management	Est. Year	Courses
10	Solan	Solan	Rural	Green Hills Engineering College, Baholi, Gandhi Gram Nahan Road, Kumarhatti	Unaided	2003	Electronic and Communication Eng., Electrical Eng., Computer Sci. Eng., Mechanical Engineering, Information and Technology, Civil Eng.
11	Una	Una	Rural	KC Education and Social Welfare Society Group of Research and Professional Institute, VPO Pandoga Uparla, Tehsil & Dist. Una	Unaided	2009	Electronic and Communication Eng., Computer Sci. Eng., Mechanical Engineering, Civil Eng., MBA (2009), BBA/BCA (2010), Pharmacy (2010)
12	Shimla	Shimla	Rural	H.P Institute of Management Studies, Totu	Unaided	2008	MBA, MCA (2007), BBA/BCA (2011)
13	Sirmaur	Nahan	Rural	Himalayan Institute of Management, Sahhoura Road, Kala Amb	Unaided	2007	MCA, MBA, Pharmacy (2008), Engineering (2009)
14	Hamirpur	Nadaun	Rural	Himachal Institute of Pharmaceutical Education and Research, Nadaun	Unaided	2008	Pharmacy
15	Kangra	Dehra	Rural	Laureate Group of Institutes	Unaided	2007	Pharmacy, BBA/BCA (2008)
16	Kullu	Kullu	Rural	Vinayaka College of Pharmacy, Village Bahoguna, P.O. Garsa	Unaided	2008	Pharmacy

(*Contd.*)

Annexure-II (b)
Pharmacy/Engineering/MBA/MCA/BBA/BCA)

(*Contd.*)

S. No.	*District*	*Tehsil*	*Loc.*	*Colleges*	*Management*	*Est. Year*	*Courses*
17	Mandi	Sundernagar	Rural	Dreamz College of Pharmacy, Khilra, P.O. Mera Masit	Unaided	2007	Pharmacy
18	Shimla	Rohru	Rural	Govt. College of Pharmacy	Govt.	2005	Pharmacy
19	Solan	Nalagarh	Rural	Himachal Pharmacy College	Unaided	2015	Pharmacy
20	Shimla	Rampur	Rural	Govt. Engineering College, Kotla Jeori	Govt.	2015	Engineering and Technology
21	Kangra	Nagrota Bagwan	Rural	Rajiv Gandhi Govt. Engineering College	Govt.	2014	Engineering and Technology
22	Hamirpur	Barsar	Rural	Hamirpur Research Institute, Chakmoh	Unaided	1994	Reseach work

Annexure-II (c)

B.Ed/ M.Ed/BBA/BCA/Engineering/MBA

S. No.	*District*	*Tehsil*	*Loc.*	*Colleges*	*Management*	*Est. Yr.*	*Courses*
1	Kangra	Jawalamukhi	Rural	Baba Balak Nath College of Education and Management, Jawalaji	Unaided	2009	BBA/BCA
2	Shimla	Shimla	Urban	Bell's Institute of Management, Mehli	Unaided	2010	BBA/BCA (2008), MBA (2010), Engineering (2010)
3	Solan	Solan	Urban	Sai Institute of Higher Education, Shamti, Solan	Unaided	2005	BBA/BCA
4	Solan	Solan	Urban	Solan College of Business and Computer Education, Chambaghat, Solan	Unaided	2007	BBA/BCA
5	Una	Haroli	Rural	Dev Bhoomi Institute of Business Administration and Computer Application	Unaided	2010	BBA/BCA, Engineering (2010)
6	Una	Una	Rural	Indian Institute of Management Technology and Research, Basal	Unaided	2010	BBA/BCA
7	Kangra	Indora	Rural	Kshtriya College of Education, Kathgarh Road, Kursain, Nadaun	Unaided	2006	B.Ed, BBA/BCA (2008)
8	Mandi	Mandi	Rural	Vijay Memorial College of Education, Vill and P.O. Bhangrotu, Ner Chowk	Unaided	2006	B.Ed, BBA/BCA (2007)
9	Mandi	Mandi	Rural	Noble College of Education, NH-21, Vill. Seog, PO Pandoh	Unaided	2006	B.Ed, BBA/BCA (2010)

(Contd.)

Annexure-II (c)

B.Ed/ M.Ed/BBA/BCA/Engineering/MBA

(*Contd.*)

10	Solan	Arki	Rural	Ramanujam Royal College of Education, Vill. Mangal	Unaided	2006	B.Ed, BBA/BCA (2009)
11	Solan	Arki	Rural	Astha College of Education, Hatkot, Tehsil Arki, Kunihar	Unaided	2007	B.Ed, BBA/BCA (2007)
12	Solan	Solan	Rural	Venkateshwar Shiksha Samiti, Vill. Dhillon, PO Sultanpur	Unaided	2007	B.Ed, BBA/BCA (2009)
13	Una	Bangana	Rural	Shiksha Bharti B.Ed. College	Unaided	2002	B.Ed, BBA/BCA (2009)
14	Hamirpur	Bhoranj	Rural	Swami Vivekanand College of Education Tarkwari Education Tarkwari (Bhoranj)	Unaided	2000	B.Ed, BBA/BCA (2009), M.Ed (2007)
15	Hamirpur	Nadaun	Rural	Trisha College of Education, Thain, PO Jolsapper (Rangas)	Unaided	2002	B.Ed, M.Ed (2008), BBA/BCA (2009)
16	Kangra	Shahpur	Rural	Dronacharya College of Education, Rait	Unaided	2006	B.Ed, M.Ed (2013), BBA/BCA (2008)
17	Kangra	Nurpur	Rural	Mata Vaishno Devi College of Education, Vill. Thapkour, PO Bhadroya, Teh. Nurpur	Unaided	2005	B.Ed, M.Ed (2007), Engineering (2010)
18	Kullu	Kullu	Rural	Rameshwari Teachers Training Sarabai	Unaided	2002	B.Ed, BBA/BCA (2003), B.Ed

Annexure-III (a)

Professional Education

S. No.	District	Tehsil	Location	Colleges	Management	Est. Year	Courses
1	Shimla	Shimla	Urban	Indira Gandhi Medical College	Govt.	1966	MBBS, MD/MS, B.Sc. Medical Technology
2	Kangra	Paprola	Rural	Rajiv Gandhi Govt. P.G. Ayurvedic College, Paprola	Govt.	1978	BAMS (UG), MD/MS (PG)
3	Mandi	Sundernagar	Urban,	Himachal Dental College, Sundernagar	Unaided	1994	BDS, MDS
4	Shimla	Shimla	Urban	H.P Govt. Dental College and Hospital	Govt.	1994	BDS, MDS
5	Kangra	Kangra	Rural	Dr. Rajendra Prasad Medical College	Govt.	1996	MBBS, MD/MS, B.Sc. Medical Technology
6	Solan	Solan	Rural	MNDAV Dental College, Tatul, PO Oachghat, Distt. Solan	Unaided	1997	BDS, MDS
7	Mandi	Jogindernagar	Urban,	College of Ayurvedic Pharmaceutical Sciences, Jogindernagar, Mandi	Unaided	2010	B. Pharmacy
8	Solan	Solan	Rural	Solan Homeopathic Medical College and Hospital, Barog Bye-Pass, Kumarhatti	Unaided	2002	BHMS

Annexure-III (b)
Para-medical Professionals

S. No.	District	Tehsil	Location	Colleges	Management	Est. Yr	Courses
1	Sirmaur	Rajgarh	Rural	Akal College of Nursing, Baru Sahib, Sirmaur	Unaided	2008	Nursing
2	Kangra	Palampur	Rural	Netaji Subhash Nursing College, Behind Cinema Hall Building	Unaided	2009	Nursing
3	Shimla	Shimla	Urban	Shivalik Institute of Nursing, Chibber	Unaided	2009	Nursing
4	Bilaspur	Bilaspur	Rural	Kol Valley Institutes of Nursing, Vill. Nehar, P.O. Hamora (Sadar)	Unaided	2009	Nursing
5	Solan	Nalagarh	Rural	Lord Mahavira B.Sc. Nursing College, Ist Floor, PNB Building, Ropar Road, Nalagarh	Unaided	2009	Nursing
6	Solan	Solan	Rural	Murari Lal Memorial College of Nursing, Nagali, PO Oachghat	Unaided	2009	Nursing
7	Kangra	Nurpur	Rural	Kamakshi Nursing Institute, Bassa Wazira, Nurpur, Kangra	Unaided	2010	Nursing
8	Kangra	Dharamshala	Rural	Guru Dronacharya Nursing College, Tung, Narwana	Unaided	2010	Nursing
9	Shimla	Shimla	Urban	Sister Nivedita Govt. Nursing College, IGMC	Govt.	2010	Nursing
10	Shimla	Shimla	Urban	Shimla Nursing College, Anandale, Shimla	Unaided	2010	Nursing
11	Shimla	Shimla	Urban	Modern Nursing College, Anandale, Shimla	Unaided	2011	Nursing
12	Sirmaur	Nahan	Rural	Mata Padmavati Educational Society	Unaided	2011	Nursing
13	Kullu	Kullu	Rural	Chamunda Institute B.Sc. Nursing, Mohal, Kullu	Unaided	2012	Nursing
14	Kangra	Nurpur	Rural	Vidya Vati Memorial Institute of Nursing	Unaided	2013	Nursing
15	Bilaspur	Bilaspur Sadar	Rural	Yen Law College	Unaided	2013	Law
16	Mandi	Jogindernagar	Rural	Jai Durga Maa College of Nursing	Govt.	2014	Nursing

Annexure-IV

BBA/BCA/Technical (Engineering/MBA/Pharmacy)/Professional (Bio Sciences)

S. No.	District	Tehsil	Location	Colleges	Management	Est. Yr	Courses
1	Una	Amb	Rural	DDM College of Science and Technology, Gondpur, Una	Unaided	2008	BBA/BCA, Bio Sciences (2008), Pharmacy (2009)
B.Ed/M.Ed/Professional education/Technical Education							
1	Hamirpur	Nadaun	Rural	Dwarka Dass Memorial Sai College of Education, Vill. Kallar	Unaided	2003	B.Ed, LLB (2008)
2	Mandi	Mandi Sadar	Rural	Abhilashi College of Education, Ner Chowk	Unaided	2003	B.Ed, BBA/BCA (2003), Pharmacy (2006), Bio Sciences (2007), M.Ed (2007), MBA (2009), Engineering (2009), Nursing (2015)
3	Shimla	Shimla	Rural	Indian Institute of Education, Hari Devi Ghanahatti, District Shimla	Unaided	2002	B.Ed, BBA/BCA (2007), Bio Sci (2009), LLB (2009), M.Ed (2010)
Dental/Professional/Technical Education							
1	Sirmaur	Paonta Sahib	Rural	Himachal Institute of Dental Sciences, Paonta Sahib	Unaided	2003	BDS, MDS, Bio Sciences (2007), Pharmacy (2008), Engineering (2008), MCA (2007)
2	Solan	Nalagarh	Rural	Bhojia Dental College, Budh (Baddi)	Unaided	1999	BDS, MDS, Bio Sciences (2006), Nursing (2015)

(*Contd.*)

Annexure-IV

BBA/BCA/Technical (Engineering/MBA/Pharmacy)/Professional (Bio Sciences)

(*Contd.*)

S. No.	*District*	*Tehsil*	*Location*	*Colleges*	*Management*	*Est. Yr*	*Courses*
LLB/Technical							
1	Sirmaur	Nahan	Rural	Himachal College of Law, Kala Amb to be run by Mass Sarswati Educational Trust (Nissing), Karnal	Unaided	2003	LLB (3 Year course) BA LLB Hon's (5 year)
2	Sirmaur	Nahan	Urban	Mata Bala Sundari College of Legal Studies, Shimla Road	Unaided	2007	LLB (3 Year course) BA LLB (5 year)
3	Solan	Solan	Rural	L.R. Institute of Legal Studies, Jabli Kyar, Oachghat, Distt. Solan	Unaided	2004	BA LLB Hon's/MBA/ Pharmacy (2006), MCA/B. Ed (2007), BBA/BCA (2008), Engineering (2009)
4	Una	Haroli	Rural	HIMCAPES Co-operative School of Legal Studies, Badhera	Unaided	2006	LLB (3 Year) BA LLB (5 year)
Applied cum Life Sciences and Technical							
S. No	**District**	**Tehsil**	**Location**	**Colleges**	**Management**	**Est. Yr**	**Courses**
1	Solan	Solan	Urban	Shoolini Institute of Life Sciences and Business Management, Anand Campus	Unaided	2004	B.Sc. Hon's Biotech/ Microbiology, Botany, Chemistry

Annexure-V

Multi-Faculty: Arts/Commerce/Technical (BBA/BCA)/Professional

S. No.	*District*	*Tehsil*	*Location*	*Colleges*	*Management*	*Est. Yr*	*Courses*
1	Hamirpur	Hamirpur	Urban	Gautam Girls College, Hamirpur CWC	Unaided	1999	Arts and Commerce, BBA, BCA, Biotech. (2009)
Arts/Science/Commerce/PG/Technical/ (B.Ed, BBA, BCA)/Professional							
S. No	*District*	*Tehsil*	*Location*	*Colleges*	*Management*	*Est. Yr*	*Courses*
1	Bilaspur	Sadar	Urban	GC, Bilaspur	Govt.	1952	Arts, Sci., Comm., BCA, BBA, M.A (Eco.), MCom., B.Sc. Hon's and Biotech and BTA
2	Shimla	Shimla	Urban	GC, Chaura Maidan	Govt.	1984	Arts, Sci., Comm., BCA, BSc. Hon's, Microbiology and Biotech
3	Shimla	Shimla	Urban	St. Bede's College (WC)	Aided	1904	Arts, Sci., Comm., BBA, BCA, MA (Eng), M.Com., Bio Sciences (2009)
4	Kangra	Dharamshala	Urban	GC, Dharamshala	Govt.	1926	Arts, Sci., Comm., Physics Hon's, Chemistry and BBA, Biotech and MCA
5	Mandi	Mandi	Urban	GC, Mandi	Govt.	1948	Arts, Sci., Comm., Tourism Management (UG), Biotechnology, Eco, Political Sci., Eng., Hindi, Sanskrit. M.A./M.Sc. in Maths and M.Com., B.Ed (2005)

Annexure-VI

S. No.	*District*	*Tehsil*	*Location*	*Universities*	*Management*	*Est. Year*	*Courses*
1	Shimla	Shimla	Urban	H.P.U, Summer Hills, Shimla-171005	State Uni.	1970	Integrated
2	Sirmaur	Rajgarh	Rural	Eternal Universities at Baru Sahib	Unaided	2008	Integrated
3	Kangra	Indora	Rural	Arni University, Kathgarh	Unaided	2009	Integrated
4	Kangra	Dharamshala	Rural	Central University, Dharamshala	Cent. Uni.	2009	Integrated
5	Solan	Solan	Rural	Manav Bharti University, Vill. Lado, P.O. Sultanpur	Unaided	2009	Integrated
6	Una	Haroli	Rural	Indus International University at Una, V.P.O. Bathu	Unaided	2010	Integrated
7	Solan	Nalagarh	Rural	IEC University, Baddi, Distt. Solan, Kalluhanda Atal Educational Hub, Baddi	Unaided	2012	Integrated
8	Hamirpur	Nadaun	Rural	Career Point University, Hamirpur, VPO Tikker Bhoranj	Unaided	2012	Integrated
9	Solan	Nalagarh	Rural	Maharaja Agrasen University, Baddi, Solan, Kallu Jhanda, Atal Educational Hub, Baddi	Unaided	2013	Integrated
10	Kangra	Dehra	Rural	Rashtriya Sanskrit Sansthan, Garli	Deemed Uni.	1997	Sanskrit
11	Mandi	Chachiot	Rural	Abhilashi University	Unaided	2014	Integrated

Appendix-VII

S. No.	*District*	*Tehsil*	*Loc.*	*Universities*	*Management*	*Est. Year*	*Courses*
1	Hamirpur	Hamirpur	Urban	National Institute of Technology	INI	1986	Technical
2	Kangra	Palampur	Urban	Chaudhary Sarwan Kumar Himachal Pradesh Krishi Vishvavidyalaya	State Uni.	1978	Agriculture
3	Solan	Solan	Rural	Dr. Y.S. Parmar University of Horticulture and Forestry, Nauni	State Uni.	1985	Agriculture
4	Solan	Kandaghat	Rural	Jaypee University of Information Technclogy, Waknaghat	Unaided	2002	Technical
5	Solan	Nalagarh	Rural	Chitkara University at Kallu Jhanda	Unaided	2008	Engineering and Technology
6	Solan	Baddi	Rural	Baddi University of Emerging Sciences and Technology, Budh Makhanumajra	Unaided	2009	Technical
7	Solan	Solan	Rural	Shoolini University of Biotechnology and Management Sciences, Solan via Ochhghat	Unaided	2009	Biotechnology and Management Sciences
8	Kangra	Palampur	Urban	Sri Sai University, Palampur	Unaided	2010	Engineering and Technology

(*Contd.*)

Appendix-VII

(Contd.)

S. No.	District	Tehsil	Loc.	Universities	Management	Est. Year	Courses
9	Solan	Solan	Rural	Maharishi Markandeshwar University, Vill. Lado, PO Sultanpur via Kumarhatti	Unaided	2010	Engineering and Technology
10	Solan	Kandaghat	Rural	Bahra University, Waknaghat, Village Wakna Bisha, PO Kiarighat	Unaided	2010	Engineering and Technology
11	Hamirpur	Hamirpur	Rural	Himachal Pradesh Technical University, Gandhi Chowk	State Uni.	2010	Technical
12	Solan	Baddi	Rural	Institute of Chartered Financial Anaysis, Kallu Jhanda	Unaided	2011	Engineering and Technology
13	Shimla	Shimla	Rural	APG (Alakh Parkash Goyal) Shimla University, PO Panthaghati, Shimla	Unaided	2012	Engineering and Technology
14	Mandi	Mandi	Rural	Indian Institute of Technology	INI	2009	Integrated
15	Solan	Kasauli	Urban	Central Research Institute	Government	1905	B.Sc., M.Sc. M.Phil., Ph.D
16	Shimla	Shimla	Rural	Institute of Hotel Management Catering and Nutrition, Kufri	Government	1998	Hotel Management
17	Kangra	Kangra	Rural	National Institute of Fashion Technology	Government	2009	Design, Management and Technology

Index